landmarks
a process reader

second edition

edited by

roberta birks
university of british columbia

tomi eng

julie walchli
university of british columbia

PEARSON

Prentice
Hall

Toronto

National Library of Canada Cataloguing in Publication

Landmarks : a process reader/edited by Roberta Birks, Tomi Eng, Julie Walchli.

Includes bibliographical references and index.
ISBN 0-13-139870-9

1. College readers.   2. English language—Rhetoric.
I. Birks, Roberta   II. Eng, Tomi   III. Walchli, Julie

PE1417.L36 2003   808'.0427   C2003-902532-2

ISBN 0-13-139870-9

Vice President, Editorial Director: Michael J. Young
Acquisitions Editor: Marianne Minaker
Marketing Manager: Toivo Pajo
Developmental Editor: Paula Druzga
Production Editor: Avivah Wargon
Copy Editor: Susan Adlam
Production Coordinator: Patricia Ciardullo
Page Layout: Hermia Chung
Permissions Research: Paula Druzga
Art Director: Julia Hall
Interior Design: Gillian Tsintziras
Cover Design: Gillian Tsintziras
Cover Image: Colorstock/Getty Images

13 14 15 DPC 11 10 09

Printed and bound in Canada

CONTENTS

Chapter Four
Style: Pushing the Boundaries   204

Chapter Five
Delivery: Creating a Public Voice   274

Chapter Six
Identifying and Writing about Rhetorical Strategies   365

Chapter Seven
Writing Research Papers   377

ALTERNATIVE TABLE OF CONTENTS:
METHODS OF DEVELOPMENT AND RHETORICAL AIMS

Example and Illustration

Comparison and Contrast

ALTERNATIVE TABLE OF CONTENTS:
TOPICS AND ISSUES

PREFACE

landmark...*n* I : an object that marks a course or boundary or serves as a guide 2 : an event that marks a turning point 3 : a structure of unusual historical and, usually, aesthetic interest

—*Merriam-Webster Dictionary*

Introduction

Landmarks offers challenging essays written largely, but not exclusively, by Canadian writers. The text is student-centred in its approach. By taking students through the processes of invention, development, arrangement, style, and delivery, we adapt the model of classical rhetoric, making it relevant for writers today. We also provide chapters that focus on writing analyses and research papers; here, students have the opportunity to apply the strategies they have learned to specific academic writing situations across the disciplines.

The second edition of *Landmarks* builds on the goals of the first edition by incorporating feedback from students and instructors who have used the textbook. This new edition provides ten new essays whose authors range from past Canadian politicians to current journalists and academics. It also expands significantly on how to analyze texts by providing students with a step-by-step process for writing a rhetorical analysis. The chapter on writing research papers presents added details about evaluating and documenting electronic sources, as well as examples of documentation styles from a range of academic fields.

We hope that *Landmarks* will serve as a useful guide for all those engaged in exploring the process of writing.

Organization

The essays in *Landmarks* are organized around the steps in the writing process.

* Chapter 1, "Invention," offers students specific strategies for exploring ideas, questions, experiences, and information that they are interested in writing about.
* Chapter 2, "Development," explains the link between the process of cognition and ways of developing ideas in order to help writers communicate effectively.
* Chapter 3, "Arrangement," gives students models for arranging material in the introduction, body, and conclusion of their essays.
* Chapter 4, "Style," encourages students to push the boundaries of form in order to express themselves in new and memorable ways.
* Chapter 5, "Delivery," suggests ways for students to project a public voice.

- Chapter 6, "Identifying and Writing about Rhetorical Strategies," asks students to use their critical reading skills to produce an analytical essay.
- Chapter 7, "Writing Research Papers," provides students with a detailed guide to writing research papers. Both Chapters 6 and 7 present annotated sample essays.

Each essay is prefaced by a biographical note about the author and followed by Explorations, which provides questions that help students to explore their initial, personal reactions to the ideas in each essay.

The organization of the text will help students understand the decisions they must make in inventing, developing, and arranging ideas, considering style, and projecting their voices into the public forum. The final two chapters suggest ways in which students can apply these steps to two specific types of writing: rhetorical analyses and research papers.

Features

- Two alternative tables of contents: one classifies essays according to methods of development and rhetorical modes, and one classifies essays according to issues and topics.
- Essays—which range from formal academic research papers and journalistic articles to personal narratives—that span cultures, historical periods, and disciplines, and foreground the importance of communicating clearly in all rhetorical situations.
- Extensive examples and full-length sample essays in the last two chapters.
- Glosses of uncommon historical and cultural references that are indicated by a superscript circle.
- Questions at the end of each reading that encourage students to use their own experiences to explore the issues the writer raises.

Supplements

Landmarks is supplemented by a website (**www.pearsoned.ca/text/birks**) that offers annotated links to related topics and online writing resources, and provides course outlines developed by instructors who are currently using this textbook.

Acknowledgments

We are indebted to many people who helped at various stages of this project. Students, instructors, and reviewers offered valuable feedback on the first edition of *Landmarks*, which helped us make key editorial decisions for this edition. Our thanks to Carole Birks who provided research assistance and Kevin Stewart who offered insightful feedback on the manuscript. At Pearson Education Canada Marianne Minaker, Acquisitions Editor, Marta Tomins, Executive Developmental Editor, Paula Druzga, Developmental Editor, Avivah Wargon, Supervising Editor, and Susan Adlam, freelance copy editor, have all been efficient and enthusiastic guides. Special thanks to our families and friends whose support and encouragement have been indispensable.

CHAPTER ONE

Invention: Exploring the Landscapes of the Mind

Most writers write from a private place: a nation or a country in the mind, whose landscape and whose climate are made up of what has been seized and hoarded from the real world—en passant...

We are never still. If you live by the side of the road, as I do, you are very much awake to this fact (and, sometimes, awakened by it), since every time the shadows move it means that someone is passing. And my garden, my wall, my house, and the cat asleep on the roof will all become images fixed in someone's mind—part of their private hoardings, their collections—because they have come this way seeking passage.

I, too, pass. It is only natural: making my own collection, lifting my images from here and there—vistas, faces, gestures, accidents —carrying them forward with me, letting them rattle round my brain, my innards until they have settled themselves, either as landmarks or as residents. I am a travelling country of invention. A roadshow.

> *—Timothy Findley, "The Countries of Invention"*

In the above passage, Timothy Findley defines the writer as someone who is constantly engaged in invention, the process of gathering information and reshaping it. For this Canadian author, the act of writing begins in a private place: the imagination. As a student, you may find that writing from a private place is difficult. You may believe that you have nothing to say, or you may convince yourself that what you do have to say is dry and uncreative. Rather than paralyzing yourself with feelings of inadequacy or waiting in vain for divine inspiration to strike, you will want to take action—to create knowledge by exploring the landscapes of the mind.

This chapter introduces several strategies of invention, including freewriting, looping, clustering, brainstorming, and questioning. These strategies can be used at different times, in different places, for different reasons. But whether you are writing a journal entry, a letter, an in-class essay, a term paper, or a newspaper article, you will want to remain open-minded and flexible; indeed, there is no right or wrong way to approach invention.

Strategies for Invention

Freewriting

Peter Elbow's essay "Freewriting," on page 12, details freewriting techniques and benefits. This process will help you get started. Write without stopping for at least five minutes—without correcting spelling or grammatical errors, without crossing out mistakes. You will find that when you do not censor yourself, you will be able to generate ideas very quickly. As well as being able to write more, you will be able to write more honestly. While freewriting does not provide you with structure, it does allow you to uncover intense emotions and recall rich detail that may have been pushed back into the deepest realms of your experience.

The following is an example of the freewrite of a student who is discovering a topic for an argumentative essay she has been assigned:

> I feel stuck. is this the right room for an argument? I told you once. When getting help to work this infernal machine and set up a file named argument I had a shortlived argument about the spelling of the very word but have yet to verify with the red college dictionary whether I am wrong or right that sounds odd and many pairs are like that the vile man and wife which could never be turned around and so must be overturned altogether salt and pepper nickels and dimes, friends and acquaintences (there that one ought to go on the list the instructor suggested keeping of words one has trouble spelling; ence and ance present an ongoing dilemma) ahem enough. Back to persuasion. How can I persuade you that this is true or better or just or of more importance than what have you. What was I arguing about just recently? Action movies, i think and how I do not think that we? ought to support violence at all, even if it is packaged as entertainment or escapism or summer blockbuster adventure. I dont care how funny or sly or hip Pulp Fiction is or was because splattered brains cannot in my opinion elevate our society or teach children valuable moral lessons or sooth victims of violence; what I think this movie without I admit the benefit of knowing what its about beyond what people said regardless of my not having seen it, does do is further numb us to the more horrifying aspects contained

within it by packaging it as cool and therefore not only acceptable but (here I am at a loss for the word that means to be wanted oh) desirable and even necessary in a way because of the aura of hipness it and its followers exude "oh you havent seen it?" Well im telling you to go see it and im going to continue talking about it regardless of your not seeing it and not being interested in seeing it because frankly what you dont know about you cannot possibly have a valid opinion about. Yeah well I dont have to perform a murder to know its wrong and sickening but phew ive gotten off topic and off on a tangent.

Note that in the above freewrite—which was computer-generated—there are errors in spelling and grammar, and that the writer skips from one topic to the next, often abruptly. Rather than viewing your fragmented ideas as incoherent or pointless, you may want to view them as exploratory; for instance, they can help you discover your position regarding an argument or find a topic of discussion that interests you. Sometimes you may even surprise yourself with what you discover. Of course, you may feel a little inhibited at first; while some find that they can easily write for 10 minutes, others find that freewriting takes practice.

Looping
One freewrite can become the basis for the next one as you gradually narrow and focus your ideas through looping. Looping is a form of freewriting that focuses your attention on an established topic. After you have written freely on this topic, stop, find the idea that is most compelling, and then summarize this idea in a single sentence. This sentence will become the starting point for another "loop," or focused freewriting session. The above freewriting session resulted in the sentence "Violent movies are packaged and promoted as 'hip' to attract an audience, but the result is that violence itself then becomes acceptable," which was then used as the topic for another freewrite. With each loop, your idea will be further narrowed and you may eventually discover a limited topic or working thesis.

Clustering
Like freewriting and looping, clustering—otherwise known as mapping or diagramming—allows you to generate a number of ideas in a short period of time. The diagram below was produced by a student who was asked to write on the topic "speaking in class." When given a topic, begin by jotting down key words or asking questions, as she does. These key words and phrases will generate more ideas, which you will cluster together around the original word or phrase; you will quickly be able to see connections between thoughts. This strategy emphasizes spontaneous, nonlinear thinking, and is useful to those who benefit from visual aids: you can actually *see* the connections you are making as you move from one idea to another.

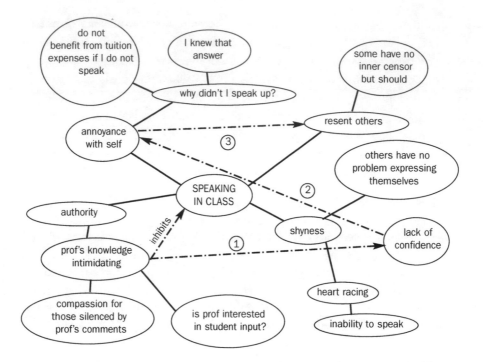

Once you have a map that shows connections between ideas, you can try to formulate a topic. This student began with a simple, general idea: "Speaking in class is difficult for many reasons." However, once she surveyed her clusters, she realized that the relationship between herself, her professor, and the other students in the class—indicated by the arrows in the map above—suggested a more complex and intriguing topic: "A professor's authoritative attitude may inhibit communication in a college or university classroom." She discovered this narrow topic when she began to see that her difficulty in speaking in class, which she had thought stemmed from a problem within herself (shyness), was in fact caused by the professor's "teacher-centred" pedagogy—an intimidating way of teaching that caused her to lose confidence in her own abilities (see arrow 1). This lack of confidence led to a verbal paralysis, which subsequently led to annoyance with herself for not speaking up (see arrow 2), and resentment towards others who spoke too much (see arrow 3).

Brainstorming

When you brainstorm, you make a list of all the thoughts you have on a subject. Again, your goal is to allow your ideas to flow as freely as possible. Later, you may want to organize these ideas in an outline. Once a brainstorm has been generated, you can narrow your focus by selecting from among the ideas, determining which are appropriate for the type of essay you want to develop. The following is an example of a brainstorming session on the topic of campus safety:

rumours of attacks

little light at night

dark shadows

keep shrubbery trimmed back

need regularly spaced emergency telephones

outdoors

in office buildings

near classrooms

"Safewalk" program needs more promo

buddy programs needed in night classes

nighttime buses to parking lots

library nooks and crannies—easy to get lost

emergency phones in library too

offer free courses in self defense—AMS?

weather conditions; easy to slip on ice, snow

wheelchair, crutch access in bad weather

speed bumps too low

restrict traffic on campus

Brainstorming is especially useful if you think best in a group situation. In a group, you can bounce ideas off those around you, and you may become more aware of differing points of view. In effect, this method of invention becomes less of an individual exploration and more of a social act.

Questioning

Questioning is the strategy that journalists often use to gather information from the public. When writing articles for a magazine or newspaper, a journalist will ask the following six questions: Who? What? When? Where? Why? and How? These questions can be applied to any given writing situation. Highly systematic, they can also help you sequence ideas in a logical order. For instance, the following questions may lead to a well-structured response to the topic of campus safety:

What safety hazards exist?

Where are the greatest safety hazards on campus?

When is campus most unsafe?

Why have safety problems not been addressed?

How can campus safety be improved?

Who is responsible for student safety?

Overview

After applying the above strategies to your own writing projects, you may gather information, but you still may find yourself struggling—struggling with ideas, struggling with language, struggling with words on the page. Some of the authors in this chapter reflect on the basics of the writing "self" by considering the relationship between language and personal experience, and language and the public sphere; others seek to understand their identities or even to create new identities through their words. All of the readings, however, highlight the trauma and the triumphs involved in exploring the landscapes of the mind.

Joan Didion was born in 1934 in Sacramento, California. She has worked as both a columnist and an editor, including as a features editor at Vogue *from 1956 to 1963. Didion has published four novels, but she is best known for her four essay collections,* Slouching Towards Bethlehem, The White Album, Salvador, *and* Miami. *She has most recently published* Political Fictions *(2001), a collection of essays for the* New York Review of Books. *The collection, for which Didion won a Polk award for book-length journalism, focuses on her observations of presidential elections.*

Why I Write

Joan Didion

Of course I stole the title for this talk, from George Orwell. One reason I stole it *1* was that I like the sound of the words: *Why I Write.* There you have three short unambiguous words that share a sound, and the sound they share is this:

I

I

I

In many ways writing is the act of saying *I,* of imposing oneself upon other *2* people, of saying *listen to me, see it my way, change your mind.* It's an aggressive, even a hostile act. You can disguise its aggressiveness all you want with veils of subordinate clauses and qualifiers and tentative subjunctives, with ellipses and evasions—with the whole manner of intimating rather than claiming, of alluding rather than stating—but there's no getting around the fact that setting words on paper is the tactic of a secret bully, an invasion, an imposition of the writer's sensibility on the reader's most private space.

I stole the title not only because the words sounded right but because they *3* seemed to sum up, in a no-nonsense way, all I have to tell you. Like many writers I have only this one "subject," this one "area": the act of writing. I can bring you no reports from any other front. I may have other interests: I am "interested," for example, in marine biology, but I don't flatter myself that you would come out to hear me talk about it. I am not a scholar. I am not in the least an intellectual, which is not to say that when I hear the word "intellectual" I reach for my gun, but only to say that I do not think in abstracts. During the years when I was an undergraduate at Berkeley I tried, with a kind of hopeless late-adolescent energy, to buy some temporary visa into the world of ideas, to forge for myself a mind that could deal with the abstract.

In short I tried to think. I failed. My attention veered inexorably back to the *4* specific, to the tangible, to what was generally considered, by everyone I knew then and for that matter have known since, the peripheral. I would try to contemplate the Hegelian dialectic and would find myself concentrating instead on a flowering pear tree outside my window and the particular way the petals fell on my floor. I would try to read linguistic theory and would find myself wondering instead if the lights were on in the bevatron up the hill. When I say that I was wondering if the lights were on in the bevatron you might immediately suspect, if you deal in ideas at all, that I was registering the bevatron as a political symbol, thinking in shorthand about the military-industrial complex and its role in the university community, but you would be wrong. I was only wondering if the lights were on in the bevatron, and how they looked. A physical fact.

5   I had trouble graduating from Berkeley, not because of this inability to deal with ideas—I was majoring in English, and I could locate the house-and-garden imagery in "The Portrait of a Lady" as well as the next person, "imagery" being by definition the kind of specific that got my attention—but simply because I had neglected to take a course in Milton. For reasons which now sound baroque I needed a degree by the end of that summer, and the English department finally agreed, if I would come down from Sacramento every Friday and talk about the cosmology of "Paradise Lost," to certify me proficient in Milton. I did this. Some Fridays I took the Greyhound bus, other Fridays I caught the Southern Pacific's City of San Francisco on the last leg of its transcontinental trip. I can no longer tell you whether Milton put the sun or the earth at the center of the universe in "Paradise Lost," the central question of at least one century and a topic about which I wrote 10,000 words that summer, but I can still recall the exact rancidity of the butter in the City of San Francisco's dining car, and the way the tinted windows on the Greyhound bus cast the oil refineries around Carquinez Straits into a grayed and obscurely sinister light. In short my attention was always on the periphery, on what I could see and taste and touch, on the butter, and the Greyhound bus. During those years I was traveling on what I knew to be a very shaky passport, forged papers: I knew that I was no legitimate resident in any world of ideas. I knew I couldn't think. All I knew then was what I couldn't do. All I knew then was what I wasn't, and it took me some years to discover what I was.

6   Which was a writer.

7   By which I mean not a "good" writer or a "bad" writer but simply a writer, a person whose most absorbed and passionate hours are spent arranging words on pieces of paper. Had my credentials been in order I would never have become a writer. Had I been blessed with even limited access to my own mind there would have been no reason to write. I write entirely to find out what I'm thinking, what I'm looking at, what I see and what it means. What I want and what I fear. Why did the oil refineries around Carquinez Straits seem sinister to me in the summer of 1956? Why have the night lights in the bevatron burned in my mind for twenty years? *What is going on in these pictures in my mind?*

8   When I talk about pictures in my mind I am talking, quite specifically, about images that shimmer around the edges. There used to be an illustration in every elementary psychology book showing a cat drawn by a patient in varying stages of schizophrenia. This cat had a shimmer around it. You could see the molecular

structure breaking down at the very edges of the cat: the cat became the background and the background the cat, everything interacting, exchanging ions. People on hallucinogens describe the same perception of objects. I'm not a schizophrenic, nor do I take hallucinogens, but certain images do shimmer for me. Look hard enough, and you can't miss the shimmer. It's there. You can't think too much about these pictures that shimmer. You just lie low and let them develop. You stay quiet. You don't talk to many people and you keep your nervous system from shorting out and you try to locate the cat in the shimmer, the grammar in the picture.

Just as I meant "shimmer" literally I mean "grammar" literally. Grammar is a *9* piano I play by ear, since I seem to have been out of school the year the rules were mentioned. All I know about grammar is its infinite power. To shift the structure of a sentence alters the meaning of that sentence, as definitely and inflexibly as the position of a camera alters the meaning of the object photographed. Many people know about camera angles now, but not so many know about sentences. The arrangement of words matters, and the arrangement you want can be found in the picture in your mind. The picture dictates the arrangement. The picture dictates whether this will be a sentence with or without clauses, a sentence that ends hard or a dying-fall sentence, long or short, active or passive. The picture tells you how to arrange the words and the arrangement of the words tells you, or tells me, what's going on in the picture. *Nota bene:*

> It tells you. *10*
> You don't tell it. *11*

Let me show you what I mean by pictures in the mind. I began "Play It As It *12* Lays" just as I have begun each of my novels, with no notion of "character" or "plot" or even "incident." I had only two pictures in my mind, more about which later, and a technical intention, which was to write a novel so elliptical and fast that it would be over before you noticed it, a novel so fast that it would scarcely exist on the page at all. About the pictures: the first was of white space. Empty space. This was clearly the picture that dictated the narrative intention of the book—a book in which anything that happened would happen off the page, a "white" book to which the reader would have to bring his or her own bad dreams—and yet this picture told me no "story," suggested no situation. The second picture did. This second picture was of something actually witnessed. A young woman with long hair and a short white halter dress walks through the casino at the Riviera in Las Vegas at one in the morning. She crosses the casino alone and picks up a house telephone. I watch her because I have heard her paged, and recognize her name: she is a minor actress I see around Los Angeles from time to time, in places like Jax and once in a gynecologist's office in the Beverly Hills Clinic, but have never met. I know nothing about her. Who is paging her? Why is she here to be paged? How exactly did she come to this? It was precisely this moment in Las Vegas that made "Play It As It Lays" begin to tell itself to me, but the moment appears in the novel only obliquely, in a chapter which begins:

13   "Maria made a list of things she would never do. She would never: walk through the Sands or Caesar's alone after midnight. She would never: ball at a party, do S-M unless she wanted to, borrow furs from Abe Lipsey, deal. She would never: carry a Yorkshire in Beverly Hills."

14   That is the beginning of the chapter and that is also the end of the chapter, which may suggest what I meant by "white space."

15   I recall having a number of pictures in my mind when I began the novel I just finished, "A Book of Common Prayer." As a matter of fact one of these pictures was of that bevatron I mentioned, although I would be hard put to tell you a story in which nuclear energy figured. Another was a newspaper photograph of a hijacked 707 burning on the desert in the Middle East. Another was the night view from a room in which I once spent a week with paratyphoid, a hotel room on the Colombian coast. My husband and I seemed to be on the Colombian coast representing the United States of America at a film festival (I recall invoking the name "Jack Valenti"° a lot, as if its reiteration could make me well), and it was a bad place to have fever, not only because my indisposition offended our hosts but because every night in this hotel the generator failed. The lights went out. The elevator stopped. My husband would go to the event of the evening and make excuses for me and I would stay alone in this hotel room, in the dark. I remember standing at the window trying to call Bogotá (the telephone seemed to work on the same principle as the generator) and watching the night wind come up and wondering what I was doing eleven degrees off the equator with a fever of 103. The view from that window definitely figures in "A Book of Common Prayer," as does the burning 707, and yet none of these pictures told me the story I needed.

16   The picture that did, the picture that shimmered and made these other images coalesce, was the Panama airport at 6 a.m. I was in this airport only once, on a plane to Bogotá that stopped for an hour to refuel, but the way it looked that morning remained superimposed on everything I saw until the day I finished "A Book of Common Prayer." I lived in that airport for several years. I can still feel the hot air when I step off the plane, can see the heat already rising off the tarmac at 6 a.m. I can feel my skirt damp and wrinkled on my legs. I can feel the asphalt stick to my sandals. I remember the big tail of a Pan American plane floating motionless down at the end of the tarmac. I remember the sound of a slot machine in the waiting room. I could tell you that I remember a particular woman in the airport, an American woman, a *norteamericana*, a thin *norteamericana* about 40 who wore a big square emerald in lieu of a wedding ring, but there was no such woman there.

17   I put this woman in the airport later. I made this woman up, just as I later made up a country to put the airport in, and a family to run the country. This woman in the airport is neither catching a plane nor meeting one. She is ordering tea in the airport coffee shop. In fact she is not simply "ordering" tea but insisting that the water be boiled, in front of her, for twenty minutes. Why is this woman in

this airport? Why is she going nowhere, where has she been? Where did she get that big emerald? What derangement, or disassociation, makes her believe that her will to see the water boiled can possibly prevail?

"She had been going to one airport or another for four months, one could see it, looking at the visas on her passport. All those airports where Charlotte Douglas's passport had been stamped would have looked alike. Sometimes the sign on the tower would say 'Bienvenidos' and sometimes the sign on the tower would say 'Bienvenue,' some places were wet and hot and others dry and hot, but at each of these airports the pastel concrete walls would rust and stain and the swamp off the runway would be littered with the fuselages of cannibalized Fairchild F-227's and the water would need boiling.   *18*

"I knew why Charlotte went to the airport even if Victor did not.   *19*

"I knew about airports."   *20*

These lines appear about halfway through "A Book of Common Prayer," but I wrote them during the second week I worked on the book, long before I had any idea where Charlotte Douglas had been or why she went to airports. Until I wrote these lines I had no character called "Victor" in mind: the necessity for mentioning a name, and the name "Victor," occurred to me as I wrote the sentence. *I knew why Charlotte went to the airport* sounded incomplete. *I knew why Charlotte went to the airport even if Victor did not* carried a little more narrative drive. Most important of all, until I wrote these lines I did not know who "I" was, who was telling the story. I had intended until that moment that the "I" be no more than the voice of the author, a 19th-century omniscient narrator. But there it was: *21*

"I knew why Charlotte went to the airport even if Victor did not.   *22*

"I knew about airports."   *23*

This "I" was the voice of no author in my house. This "I" was someone who not only knew why Charlotte went to the airport but also knew someone called "Victor." Who was Victor? Who was this narrator? Why was this narrator telling me this story? Let me tell you one thing about why writers write: had I known the answer to any of these questions I would never have needed to write a novel. ◆   *24*

1976

Glossary

Jack Valenti: (b. 1926) president of the Motion Picture Association of America.

Explorations

- Why do you write? Is it for the same reason as the author, who says, "I write entirely to find out what I'm thinking, what I'm looking at, what I see and what it means"?

- Do you agree or disagree with Didion's concept of writing as "an invasion…[of] the reader's most private space"?

- Do you have difficulties writing in an academic situation? If so, why?

Peter Elbow was born in 1935 in New York City. He began his university education with the goal of becoming a professor of literature but found that his own writing was not strong enough to complete his graduate work. After taking time away from school to teach, he decided to return to graduate studies where, through reflection on his own challenges with writing, he became interested in writing and the writing process. Now a member of the Department of English at the University of Massachusetts at Amherst, he is a consultant to many university and college writing programs throughout the United States, and the author of several books on writing and composition, including Writing without Teachers, Writing with Power, *and* Embracing Contraries.

Freewriting

Peter Elbow

1   Freewriting is the easiest way to get words on paper and the best all-around practice in writing that I know. To do a freewriting exercise, simply force yourself to write without stopping for ten minutes. Sometimes you will produce good writing, but that's not the goal. Sometimes you will produce garbage, but that's not the goal either. You may stay on one topic, you may flip repeatedly from one to another: it doesn't matter. Sometimes you will produce a good record of your stream of consciousness, but often you can't keep up. Speed is not the goal, though sometimes the process revs you up. If you can't think of anything to write, write about how that feels or repeat over and over "I have nothing to write" or "Nonsense" or "No." If you get stuck in the middle of a sentence or thought, just repeat the last word or phrase till something comes along. The only point is to keep writing.

2   Or rather, that's the first point. For there are lots of goals of freewriting, but they are best served if, while you are doing it, you accept this single, simple, mechanical goal of simply not stopping. When you produce an exciting piece of writing, it doesn't mean you did it better than the time before when you wrote one sentence over and over for ten minutes. Both times you freewrote perfectly. The goal of freewriting is in the process, not the product.

3   Here is an example of freewriting—this one done in a group led by an experienced writer but not a writing teacher:

> The second class of no teacher and I'm finding it hard to see how anything will come of it without someone who *knows* something being here. I really mean who knows *something* about writing. I know a little about writing, even that speed writing cramps the muscles just inside the thenar curve and I know the grip on my pen is too tight. I know what

sounds right when I write right or when someone else writes right. But, is that right just because I hear it right or someone else's right writing listens right. If no one who knows what is right is here to right what we write rightly to our own ears, how will we know who's right really?

The sound of "-ite" and "-ight" and "r's" rolling around is pleasant or sibilant I believe is the right word to describe writing by rule rightly for right writers to hear or rule on. Does sibilant have to have "s's" hissing or are "r's" running rapidly reasonably rationale for sibilance without "s's". My cramp is gaining on me even though I remember my father writing my mother all "f's" in a letter from Frankfurt in the days when "f's" had other meaning than what my youngest son at eight called the "King of Swears."

"Dear Effie," he wrote from Frankfurt. "Four foolish fellows followed me from fearful..." I can't go on with it. To follow my original thought, "It doesn't sound right." And with the cramp now slowing me down and running off the paper, I'm hoping our non-leader tells us to stop. She did.

Russell Hoxsie, M.D.

The Benefits of Freewriting

Freewriting makes writing easier by helping you with the root psychological or existential difficulty in writing: finding words in your head and putting them down on a blank piece of paper. So much writing time and energy is spent *not* writing: wondering, worrying, crossing out, having second, third, and fourth thoughts. And it's easy to get stopped even in the middle of a piece. (This is why Hemingway made a rule for himself never to end one sheet and start a new one except in the middle of a sentence.) Frequent freewriting exercises help you learn simply to *get on with it* and not be held back by worries about whether these words are good words or the right words.   4

Thus, freewriting is the best way to learn—in practice, not just in theory —to separate the producing process from the revising process. Freewriting exercises are push-ups in withholding judgment as you produce so that afterwards you can judge better.   5

Freewriting for ten minutes is a good way to warm up when you sit down to write something. You won't waste so much time getting started when you turn to your real writing task and you won't have to struggle so hard to find words. Writing almost always goes better when you are already started: now you'll be able to start off already started.   6

Freewriting helps you learn to write when you don't feel like writing. It is practice in setting deadlines for yourself, taking charge of yourself, and learning   7 gradually how to get that special energy that sometimes comes when you work fast under pressure.

8   Freewriting teaches you to write without thinking about writing. We can usually speak without thinking about speech—without thinking about how to form words in the mouth and pronounce them and the rules of syntax we unconsciously obey—and as a result we can give undivided attention to what we say. Not so writing. Or at least most people are considerably distracted from their meaning by considerations of spelling, grammar, rules, errors. Most people experience an awkward and sometimes paralyzing *translating* process in writing: "Let's see, how shall I say this?" Freewriting helps you learn to *just say* it. Regular freewriting helps make the writing process *transparent*.

9   Freewriting is a useful outlet. We have lots in our heads that makes it hard to think straight and write clearly: we are mad at someone, sad about something, depressed about everything. Perhaps even inconveniently happy. "How can I think about this report when I'm so in love?" Freewriting is a quick outlet for these feelings so they don't get so much in your way when you are trying to write about something else. Sometimes your mind is marvelously clear after ten minutes of telling someone on paper everything you need to tell him. (In fact, if your feelings often keep you from functioning well in other areas of your life frequent freewriting can help: not only by providing a good arena for those feelings, but also by helping you understand them better and see them in perspective by seeing them on paper.)

10   Freewriting helps you to think of topics to write about. Just keep writing, follow threads where they lead and you will get to ideas, experiences, feelings, or people that are just asking to be written about.

11   Finally, and perhaps most important, freewriting improves your writing. It doesn't always produce powerful writing itself, but it leads to powerful writing. The process by which it does so is a mysterious underground one. When people talk about the Zen of this or that I think they are referring to the peculiar increase in power and insight that comes from focusing your energy while at the same time putting aside your conscious controlling self. Freewriting gives practice in this special mode of focusing-but-not-trying; it helps you stand out of the way and let words be chosen by the sequence of the words themselves or the thought, not by the conscious self. In this way freewriting gradually puts a deeper resonance or voice into your writing.

12   But freewriting also brings a surface coherence to your writing and it does so immediately. You cannot write *really* incoherently if you write quickly. You may violate the rules of correctness, you may make mistakes in reasoning, you may write foolishness, you may change directions before you have said anything significant. That is, you may produce something like "Me and her we went down and saw the folks but wait that reminds me of the thing I was thinking about yester oh dam what am I really trying to say." But you won't produce syntactic

chaos: language that is so jumbled that when you read it over you are frightened there is something the matter with you.

However, you wouldn't be frightened if you looked more closely at how you actually produced that verbal soup. If you had movies of yourself you would see yourself starting four or five times and throwing each start away and thereby getting more and more jumbled in your mind; finally starting; stopping part way through the sentence to wonder if you are on the wrong track and thereby losing your syntactic thread. You would see yourself start writing again on a slightly different piece of syntax from the one you started with, then notice something really wrong and fix it and lose the thread again; so when you finally conclude your sentence, you are actually writing the conclusion of a different sentence from the ones you had been writing. Thus, the resulting sentence—whether incorrect or just impossibly awkward—is really fragments of three different syntactic impulses or sentences-in-the-head tied together with baling wire. When you write quickly, however, as in freewriting, your syntactic units hang together. Even if you change your mind in mid-sentence, as above, you produce a clear break. You don't try to plaster over two or three syntactic units as one, as you so often do in painstaking writing. Freewriting produces syntactic coherence and verbal energy which gradually transfer to your more careful writing. 13

What to Do with Freewriting

If you can view freewriting as an exercise to help you to grow in the long run rather than give you good writing in the short run, then you can use some of the good pieces that freewriting sometimes produces. But if you slip into freewriting for the sake of producing good pieces of writing, then you put a kind of short-run utilitarian pressure on the process and hinder yourself from getting all the other benefits. 14

I suspect there is some added benefit if you read freewriting over after you have written it (better yet out loud) and if you let someone else read it. I think it may help you integrate better into your conscious controlling mind the energies that are available to your innards. But don't get criticism or comment of any sort. 15

If reading over your freewriting or giving it to someone else gets in the way of future freewriting, as it may well do, then it's better just to throw it away or stash it somewhere unread. Reading it over may make you too self-conscious or make you feel "YEEEcchh, what garbage this is," or "Oh, dear, there must be something the matter with me to be so obsessed." This may start you censoring yourself as you engage in more freewriting. Don't read over your freewriting unless you can do so in a spirit of benign self-welcoming. I used to be fascinated with my freewriting and save them and read them periodically. Now I just throw them away. 16

A Hunch about Resistance

I remember agonizing over a particular section of something I hoped I would be able to publish. It seemed forever that I struggled and still couldn't get my 17 thought right. I was knotted and incoherent. Finally I broke through into fluency. What a relief. For two days I hadn't been able to say what I wanted; then I could say it. But when I read the whole thing over a day or two later I noticed that the passage was particularly dead. It was limp, it was like a firehose after someone turns off the water.

18   This illustrates a kind of a myth I have come to believe without quite knowing how to integrate it into the rest of my beliefs about writing. To write is to overcome a certain resistance: you are trying to wrestle a steer to the ground, to wrestle a snake into a bottle, to overcome a demon that sits in your head. To succeed in writing or making sense is to overpower that steer, that snake, that demon.

19   But if, in your struggles to write, you actually break its back, you are in trouble. Yes, now you have power over it, you can say what you need to say, but in transforming that resistant force into a limp noodle, somehow you turn your words into limp noodles, too. Somehow the force that is fighting you is also the force that gives life to your words. You must overpower that steer or snake or demon. But not kill it.

20   This myth explains why some people who write fluently and perhaps even clearly—they say just what they mean in adequate, errorless words—are really hopelessly boring to read. There is no resistance in their words; you cannot feel any force-being-overcome, any orneriness. No surprises. The language is too abjectly obedient. When writing is really good, on the other hand, the words themselves lend some of their own energy to the writer. The writer is controlling words which he can't turn his back on without danger of being scratched or bitten.

21   This explains why it is sometimes easier for a blocked and incoherent writer to break into powerful language than for someone who is fluent and verbal and can always write just what he wants. Picture the two of them: one has uneven, scrunched handwriting with pointy angles, the other has round, soft, even handwriting. When I make these two people freewrite, the incoherent scrunched one is often catapulted immediately into vivid, forceful language. The soft handwriting, on the other hand, just continues to yield what it has always yielded: language that is clear and perfectly obedient to the intentions of the writer, but lifeless. It will take this obedient writer much longer to get power. It will take the scrunched writer longer to get control.

22   The reason the scrunched writer is so incoherent and hates writing is that he is ruled by the steer, the snake, the demon. He is unable to take charge as he writes and make all those tiny decisions you must make second by second as you write. When I force him to do a freewriting exercise—or he forces himself to do one—he finally gets words on the page but of course he is still not completely in charge. He is not instantly transformed into someone who can make all the micro-decisions needed for writing. He gets words down on the page, but a lot of

the decisions are still being made by the words themselves. Thus he has frequent bursts of power in his writing but little control.

The rounded fluent writer on the other hand is so good at making the quick *23* decisions involved in writing—at steering, at being in charge—that even though he writes fast without stopping, his writing still lacks the vitality that comes from exploiting the resistant force.

The goal of freewriting, then, is not absolutely limpid fluency. If you are a *24* blocked writer, freewriting will help you overcome resistance and move you gradually in the direction of more fluency and control (though your path will probably involve lots of writing where you feel totally out of control). But if you are a very controlled writer who can write anything you want, but without power—if you have killed the demon—freewriting will gradually bring it back to life. Forcing yourself to write regularly without stopping for ten minutes will put more *resistance* back into your language. The clay will fight you a bit in your hands as you try to work it into a bowl, but that bowl will end up more alive and powerful. ◆

1975

Explorations

- How do you usually approach a writing assignment? What is the first thing you do?

- Does the process of invention excite you? Scare you? Frustrate you? What might account for your reactions?

- How do you usually feel about your relationship to the audience you are writing for? How do you usually feel about yourself as a writer while you are writing? What kind of impact do you think these feelings have on the work you produce?

Eva Hoffman was born in Cracow, Poland, in 1945 and immigrated to Canada at the age of 13; she is now a resident of the United States. She has been a professor of literature at a number of universities including Columbia University, the University of Minnesota, and Tufts University, and she edited the New York Times Book Review *from 1979 until 1990. She is best known for her autobiography* Lost in Translation: A Life in a New Language *(1989), winner of the Jean Stein Award for Non-Fiction. Her first fictional work,* The Secret: A Fable for Our Time, *was published in 2001.*

Life in a New Language

Eva Hoffman

1   By the time we've reached Vancouver, there are very few people left on the train. My mother has dressed my sister and me in our best outfits—identical navy blue dresses with sailor collars and gray coats handmade of good gabardine. My parents' faces reflect anticipation and anxiety. "Get off the train on the right foot," my mother tells us. "For luck in the new life."

2   I look out of the train window with a heavy heart. Where have I been brought to? As the train approaches the station, I see what is indeed a bit of nowhere. It's a drizzly day, and the platform is nearly empty. Everything is the colour of slate. From this bleakness, two figures approach us—a nondescript middle-aged man and woman—and after making sure that we are the right people, the arrivals from the other side of the world, they hug us; but I don't feel much warmth in their half-embarrassed embrace. "You should kneel down and kiss the ground," the man tells my parents. "You're lucky to be here." My parents' faces fill with a kind of naïve hope. Perhaps everything will be well after all. They need signs, portents, at this hour.

3   Then we all get into an enormous car—yes, this is America—and drive into the city that is to be our home.

4   The Rosenbergs' house is a matter of utter bafflement to me. This one-storey structure surrounded by a large garden surely doesn't belong in a city—but neither can it be imagined in the country. The garden itself is of such pruned and trimmed neatness that I'm half afraid to walk in it. Its lawn is improbably smooth and velvety (Ah, the time and worry spent on the shaving of these lawns! But I will only learn of that later), and the rows of marigolds, the circles of geraniums seem almost artificial in their perfect symmetries, in their subordination to orderliness.

5   Still, I much prefer sitting out here in the sun to being inside. The house is larger than any apartment I have seen in Poland, with enormous "picture" win-

dows, a separate room for every member of the family and soft pastel-coloured rugs covering all the floors. These are all features that, I know, are intended to signify good taste and wealth—but there's an incongruity between the message I'm supposed to get and my secret perceptions of these surroundings. To me, these interiors seem oddly flat, devoid of imagination, ingenuous. The spaces are so plain, low-ceilinged, obvious; there are no curves, niches, odd angles, nooks, or crannies—nothing that gathers a house into itself, giving it a sense of privacy, or of depth—of interiority. There's no solid wood here, no accretion either of age or dust. There is only the open sincerity of the simple spaces, open right out to the street. (No peering out the window here, to catch glimpses of exchanges on the street; the picture windows are designed to give everyone full view of everyone else, to declare there's no mystery, nothing to hide. Not true, of course, but that's the statement.) There is also the disingenuousness of the furniture, all of it whitish with gold trimming. The whole thing is too revealing of an aspiration to good taste, but the unintended effect is thin and insubstantial—as if it was planned and put up just yesterday, and could just as well be dismantled tomorrow. The only rooms that really impress me are the bathroom and the kitchen—both of them so shiny, polished, and full of unfamiliar, fabulously functional appliances that they remind me of interiors which we occasionally glimpsed in French or American movies, and which, in our bedraggled Poland, we couldn't distinguish from fantasy. "Do you think people really live like this?" we would ask after one of these films, neglecting all the drama of the plot for the interest of these incidental features. Here is something worth describing to my friends in Cracow, down to such mind-boggling details as a shaggy rug in the bathroom and toilet paper that comes in different colours.

For the few days we stay at the Rosenbergs', we are relegated to the basement, 6 where there's an extra apartment usually rented out to lodgers. My father looks up to Mr. Rosenberg with the respect, even a touch of awe due to someone who is a certified millionaire. Mr. Rosenberg is a big man in the small Duddy Kravitz° community of Polish Jews, most of whom came to Canada shortly after the war, and most of whom have made good in junk peddling and real estate—but none as good as he. Mr. Rosenberg, who is now almost seventy, had the combined chutzpah and good luck to ride on Vancouver's real-estate boom—and now he's the richest of them all. This hardly makes him the most popular, but it automatically makes him the wisest. People from the community come to him for business advice, which he dispenses, in Yiddish, as if it were precious currency given away for free only through his grandiose generosity.

In the uncompromising vehemence of adolescence and injured pride, I begin 7 to see Mr. Rosenberg not as our benefactor but as a Dickensian° figure of personal tyranny, and my feeling toward him quickly rises to something that can only be called hate. He has made stinginess into principle; I feel it as a nonhuman hardness, a conversion of flesh and feeling into stone. His face never lights up with humour or affection or wit. But then, he takes himself very seriously; to him too his wealth is the proof of his righteousness. In accordance with his principles, he demands money for our train tickets from Montreal as soon as we arrive. I never forgive him. We've brought gifts we thought handsome, but in addition, my father gives him all the dollars he accumulated in Poland—something that would start us off in Canada, we thought, but is now all gone. We'll have to scratch out our living somehow, starting from zero: my father begins to pinch the flesh of his arms nervously.

8   Mrs. Rosenberg, a worn-faced, nearly inarticulate, diffident woman, would probably show us more generosity were she not so intimidated by her husband. As it is, she and her daughter, Diane, feed us white bread with sliced cheese and bologna for lunch, and laugh at our incredulity at the mushy textures, the plastic wrapping, the presliced convenience of the various items. Privately, we comment that this is not real food: it has no taste, it smells of plastic. The two women also give us clothing they can no longer use. I can't imagine a state of affairs in which one would want to discard the delicate, transparent bathrobes and the angora sweaters they pass on to us, but luscious though these items seem—beyond anything I ever hoped to own—the show of gratitude required from me on receiving them sours the pleasure of new ownership. "Say thank you," my mother prompts me in preparation for receiving a batch of clothing. "People like to be appreciated." I coo and murmur ingratiatingly; I'm beginning to master the trick of saying thank you with just the right turn of the head, just the right balance between modesty and obsequiousness. In the next few years, this is a skill I'll have to use often. But in my heart I feel no real gratitude at being the recipient of so much mercy.

9   On about the third night at the Rosenbergs' house, I have a nightmare in which I'm drowning in the ocean while my mother and father swim farther and farther away from me. I know, in this dream, what it is to be cast adrift in incomprehensible space; I know what it is to lose one's mooring. I wake up in the middle of a prolonged scream. The fear is stronger than anything I've ever known. My parents wake up and hush me up quickly; they don't want the Rosenbergs to hear this disturbing sound. I try to calm myself and go back to sleep, but I feel as though I've stepped through a door into a dark place. Psychoanalysts talk about "mutative insights," through which the patient gains an entirely new perspective and discards some part of a cherished neurosis. The primal scream of my birth into the New World is a mutative insight of a negative kind—and I know that I can never lose the knowledge it brings me. The black, bituminous terror of the dream solders itself to the chemical base of my being—and from then on, fragments of the fear lodge themselves in my consciousness, thorns and pinpricks of anxiety, loose electricity floating in a psyche that has been forcibly pried from its structures. Eventually, I become accustomed to it; I know that it comes, and that it also goes; but when it hits with full force, in its pure form, I call it the Big Fear.

After about a week of lodging us in his house, Mr. Rosenberg decides that he   *10*
has done enough for us, and, using some acquired American wisdom, explains
that it isn't good for us to be dependent on his charity; there is of course no question of kindness. There is no question, either, of Mrs. Rosenberg intervening on
our behalf, as she might like to do. We have no place to go, no way to pay for a
meal. And so we begin.

"Shut up, shuddup," the children around us are shouting, and it's the first word   *11*
in English that I understand from its dramatic context. My sister and I stand in
the schoolyard clutching each other, while kids all around us are running about,
pummelling each other, and screaming like whirling dervishes. Both the boys and
the girls look sharp and aggressive to me—the girls all have bright lipstick on,
their hair sticks up and out like witches' fury, and their skirts are held up and
out by stiff, wiry crinolines. I can't imagine wanting to talk their harsh-sounding
language.

We've been brought to this school by Mr. Rosenberg, who, two days after our   *12*
arrival, tells us he'll take us to classes that are provided by the government to
teach English to newcomers. This morning, in the rinky-dink wooden barracks
where the classes are held, we've acquired new names. All it takes is a brief conference between Mr. Rosenberg and the teacher, a kindly looking woman who
tries to give us reassuring glances, but who has seen too many people come and
go to get sentimental about a name. Mine—"Ewa"—is easy to change into its
near equivalent in English, "Eva." My sister's name—"Alina"—poses more of a
problem, but after a moment's thought, Mr. Rosenberg and the teacher decide
that "Elaine" is close enough. My sister and I hang our heads wordlessly under
this careless baptism. The teacher then introduces us to the class, mispronounc-
ing our last name—"Wydra"—in a way we've never heard before. We make our
way to a bench at the back of the room; nothing much has happened, except a
small, seismic mental shift. The twist in our names takes them a tiny distance
from us—but it's a gap into which the infinite hobgoblin of abstraction enters.
Our Polish names didn't refer to us; they were as surely us as our eyes or hands.
These new appellations, which we ourselves can't pronounce, are not us. They
are identification tags, disembodied signs pointing to objects that happen to be
my sister and myself. We walk to our seats into a roomful of unknown faces, with
names that make us strangers to ourselves.

When the school day is over, the teacher hands us a file card on which she has   *13*
written, "I'm a newcomer. I'm lost. I live at 1785 Granville Street. Will you
kindly show me how to get there? Thank you." We wander the streets for several
hours, zigzagging back and forth through seemingly identical suburban avenues,
showing this deaf-mute sign to the few people we see, until we eventually recognize the Rosenbergs' house. We're greeted by our quietly hysterical mother and
Mrs. Rosenberg, who, in a ritual she has probably learned from television, puts
out two glasses of milk on her red Formica counter. The milk, homogenized, and

too cold from the fridge, bears little resemblance to the liquid we used to drink called by the same name.

14 Every day I learn new words, new expressions. I pick them up from school exercises, from conversations, from the books I take out of Vancouver's well-lit, cheerful public library. There are some turns of phrase to which I develop strange allergies. "You're welcome," for example, strikes me as a gaucherie, and I can hardly bring myself to say it—I suppose because it implies that there's something to be thanked for, which in Polish would be impolite. The very places where language is at its most conventional, where it should be most taken for granted, are the places where I feel the prick of artifice.

15   Then there are words to which I take an equally irrational liking, for their sound, or just because I'm pleased to have deduced their meaning. Mainly they're words I learn from books, like "enigmatic" or "insolent"—words that have only a literary value, that exist only as signs on the page.

16   But mostly, the problem is that the signifier° has become severed from the signified.° The words I learn now don't stand for things in the same unquestioned way they did in my native tongue. "River" in Polish was a vital sound, energized with the essence of riverhood, of my rivers, of my being immersed in rivers. "River" in English is cold—a word without an aura. It has no accumulated associations for me, and it does not give off the radiating haze of connotation. It does not evoke.

17   The process, alas, works in reverse as well. When I see a river now, it is not shaped, assimilated by the word that accommodates it to the psyche—a word that makes a body of water a river rather than an uncontained element. The river before me remains a thing, absolutely other, absolutely unbending to the grasp of my mind.

18   When my friend Penny tells me that she's envious, or happy, or disappointed, I try laboriously to translate not from English to Polish but from the word back to its source, to the feeling from which it springs. Already, in that moment of strain, spontaneity of response is lost. And anyway, the translation doesn't work. I don't know how Penny feels when she talks about envy. The word hangs in a Platonic stratosphere, a vague prototype of all envy, so large, so all-encompassing that it might crush me—as might disappointment or happiness.

19   I am becoming a living avatar of structuralist wisdom; I cannot help knowing that words are just themselves. But it's a terrible knowledge, without any of the consolations that wisdom usually brings. It does not mean that I'm free to play with words at my wont; anyway, words in their naked state are surely among the least satisfactory play objects. No, this radical disjoining between word and thing is a desiccating alchemy, draining the world not only of significance but of its colours, striations, nuances—its very existence. It is the loss of a living connection.

The worst losses come at night. As I lie down in a strange bed in a strange   *20*
house—my mother is a sort of housekeeper here, to the aging Jewish man who
has taken us in in return for her services—I wait for that spontaneous flow of
inner language which used to be my nighttime talk with myself, my way of
informing the ego where the id had been. Nothing comes. Polish, in a short time,
has atrophied, shrivelled from sheer uselessness. Its words don't apply to my new
experiences; they're not coeval with any of the objects, or faces, or the very air I
breathe in the daytime. In English, words have not penetrated to those layers of
my psyche from which a private conversation could proceed. This interval before
sleep used to be the time when my mind became both receptive and alert, when
images and words rose up to consciousness, reiterating what had happened during the day, adding the day's experiences to those already stored there, spinning
out the thread of my personal story.

Now, this picture-and-word show is gone; the thread has been snapped. I have   *21*
no interior language, and without it, interior images—those images through
which we assimilate the external world, through which we take it in, love it,
make it our own—become blurred too. My mother and I met a Canadian family
who live down the block today. They were working in their garden and engaged
us in a conversation of the "Nice weather we're having, isn't it?" variety, which
culminated in their inviting us into their house. They sat stiffly on their couch,
smiled in the long pauses between the conversation, and seemed at a loss for what
to ask. Now my mind gropes for some description of them, but nothing fits.
They're a different species from anyone I've met in Poland, and Polish words slip
off of them without sticking. English words don't hook on to anything. I try,
deliberately, to come up with a few. Are these people pleasant or dull? Kindly or
silly? The words float in an uncertain space. They come up from a part of my
brain in which labels may be manufactured but which has no connection to my
instincts, quick reactions, knowledge. Even the simplest adjectives sow confusion
in my mind; English kindliness has a whole system of morality behind it, a system that makes "kindness" an entirely positive virtue. Polish kindness has the
tiniest element of irony. Besides, I'm beginning to feel the tug of prohibition, in
English, against uncharitable words. In Polish, you can call someone an idiot
without particularly harsh feelings and with the zest of a strong judgment. Yes, in
Polish these people might tend toward "silly" and "dull"—but I force myself
toward "kindly" and "pleasant." The cultural unconscious is beginning to exercise its subliminal influence.

The verbal blur covers these people's faces, their gestures with a sort of fog.   *22*
I can't translate them into my mind's eye. The small event, instead of being
added to the mosaic of consciousness and memory, falls through some black
hole, and I fall with it. What has happened to me in this new world? I don't
know. I don't see what I've seen, don't comprehend what's in front of me. I'm
not filled with language anymore, and I have only a memory of fullness to

anguish me with the knowledge that, in this dark and empty state, I don't really exist. ...

◆ ◆ ◆

23   For my birthday, Penny gives me a diary, complete with a little lock and key to keep what I write from the eyes of all intruders. It is that little lock—the visible symbol of the privacy in which the diary is meant to exist—that creates my dilemma. If I am indeed to write something entirely for myself, in what language do I write? Several times, I open the diary and close it again. I can't decide. Writing in Polish at this point would be a little like resorting to Latin or ancient Greek—an eccentric thing to do in a diary, in which you're supposed to set down your most immediate experiences and unpremeditated thoughts in the most unmediated language. Polish is becoming a dead language, the language of the untranslatable past. But writing for nobody's eyes in English? That's like doing a school exercise, or performing in front of yourself, a slightly perverse act of self-voyeurism.

24   Because I have to choose something, I finally choose English. If I'm to write about the present, I have to write in the language of the present, even if it's not the language of the self. As a result, the diary becomes surely one of the more impersonal exercises of that sort produced by an adolescent girl. These are no sentimental effusions of rejected love, eruptions of familial anger, or consoling broodings about death. English is not the language of such emotions. Instead, I set down my reflections on the ugliness of wrestling; on the elegance of Mozart, and how Dostoyevsky° puts me in mind of El Greco.° I write down Thoughts. I Write.

25   There is a certain pathos to this naïve snobbery, for the diary is an earnest attempt to create a part of my persona that I imagine I would have grown into in Polish. In the solitude of this most private act, I write, in my public language, in order to update what might have been my other self. The diary is about me and not about me at all. But on one level, it allows me to make the first jump. I learn English through writing and, in turn, writing gives me a written self. Refracted through the double distance of English and writing, this self—my English self—becomes oddly objective; more than anything, it perceives. It exists more easily in the abstract sphere of thoughts and observations than in the world. For a while, this impersonal self, this cultural negative capability, becomes the truest thing about me. When I write, I have a real existence that is proper to the activity of writing—an existence that takes place midway between me and the sphere of artifice, art, pure language. This language is beginning to invent another me. However, I discover something odd. It seems that when I write (or, for that matter, think) in English, I am unable to use the word "I." I do not go as far as the schizophrenic "she"—but I am driven, as by a compulsion, to the double, the Siamese-twin "you." ◆

1989

Glossary

Duddy Kravitz: main character in Mordecai Richler's 1959 "coming of age" novel, *The Apprenticeship of Duddy Kravitz*.

Dickensian: a term, adapted from the last name of English novelist Charles Dickens (1812–1876), which is frequently used to describe either a distinctly cruel or suffering, comic or repugnant, character or setting of the sort found throughout Dickens's fictional oeuvre.

signifier and **signified**: two basic components of Swiss linguist Ferdinand de Saussure's (1857–1913) theory of the linguistic sign, as developed in his posthumously published *Course in General Linguistics* (1916); the signifier, whether an audible utterance of speech or a visible mark of writing, is the object of perception that is before us; the signified is the signifier's absent referent or meaning, the abstract concept or imperceptible psychic reality evoked by a given sound-image.

Fyodor Dostoyevsky: (1821–1881) Russian novelist, journalist, and short-story writer known for his dark psychological studies of human relationships. Among his most famous works are *Notes from the Underground* (1864) and *Crime and Punishment* (1866).

El Greco: (1541–1614) Greek-born painter and portraitist known for his large religious scenes and elongated human figures, mournful souls who would be at home in any of Dostoyevsky's novels. Most of his best-known works adorn church ceilings and walls in Spain, including the celebrated *Burial of the Conde de Orgaz* (1586–1588).

Explorations

- Have you ever had to learn a new language? Were your experiences learning this language pleasant, or do you remember feeling lost and frustrated?

- Does the language you use in private differ from the language you use in public? If so, how and why?

- Do you feel that writing helps to give you an identity? Does it allow you to invent different selves?

Susan Saltrick is an independent consultant for the Teaching, Learning, and Technology Group, a non-profit corporation. She often speaks and writes about connections among education, technology, and publishing, and how they affect our lives and our world. She received her B.A. from Princeton University and has completed graduate work at Columbia University's Teachers College and New York University's Interactive Telecommunications Program.

A Campus of Our Own: Thoughts of a Reluctant Conservative

Susan Saltrick

1   Having attained my 39th birthday, I've been observing more frequently the signs of impending middle age. Besides the usual cosmetic distress, I realize I'm now being labeled as one of the conservatives of the new media scene. I find myself agreeing a lot with the Neil Postmans° and the Sven Birkertses° of the world who urge us all, when asked about technology, to just say no. If I don't watch myself, I'll soon be voting Republican....

2   All this is a somewhat disconcerting state to find myself in—after spending 12 years as a new media director for a major book publisher where I was, by executive fiat, the brave scout out on the wild frontier, clearing the trail so the rest of the folks back East could settle down and homestead.

3   I used to be a real new media cheerleader. My talks of only a few years ago were upbeat panegyrics to the scintillating adventures that awaited us all in the digital future, if we could only navigate the tricky water that surrounded us today. Given that I was in higher education publishing, I used to talk a lot about technology's potential for transforming the educational process—for exploiting new modes of learning, for expanding to new types of students.

4   And, you know, I pretty much believed it. And, you know, I pretty much still do. But what I find myself thinking about these days is a question Steve Gilbert° poses when considering any technological change: "What is it," he asks, "that we cherish and don't want to lose?" In other words, what are the things we need to watch out for—the things we risk sacrificing if we are too readily seduced by technology's siren song?

5   Two recent works have provoked some thoughts in this area. The first of these, *The City of Bits*, by William Mitchell, the dean of architecture at MIT, is an exploration of how our notion of space—and the structures we humans have created to order that space—are being transformed by our increasing involvement with, or better put, our envelopment in, cyberspace.

The second is Eli Noam's recent article in *Science* magazine, "Electronics and 6
the Future of the University." Noam notes that universities flourished because
they were the centralized repositories for information—and that scholars and students gathered there because that was where they found the raw materials they
needed to do their work. But now that information is distributed and available
all over the Net, he asks, what becomes of the physical university?

Both Mitchell and Noam are concerned how the Infobahn is changing our 7
notion of community from a spatially defined entity to a virtually connected
body—and both address the notion of the virtual communities that are developing out on the Web. But, for me, at least, the Net is so damned evanescent. We
may bookmark our favorite sites, but we never really retrace our steps. With each
Web journey, we inscribe a new path, spinning a digital lace as unique and con-
voluted as our genetic code. Click by click, we spiral down, seeking those elusive
gems of content, while all around us the landscape is in constant flux—links
forming and dissolving like a seething primordial soup. We never quite know
where we're going, and God only knows where we'll end up—Accidental
Tourists° all in this floating world, this web.

So let's be careful when we use that term: community. Doesn't it imply some sort 8
of common code of behavior or attitude or association? Can something so mutable,
so ephemeral, count? If we gain admittance to it through a mere mouse click, can
something so easily won, so temporary, truly impart a sense of belonging? If we
can belong to as many communities as time and carpal tunnel strength permit,
what then of loyalty? Can it be so diffuse? Is community then a less binding concept in this less bounded world?

How we define community is critical, because the notion of community is at 9
the heart of any speculation about the university in the 21st century. Of course,
the university is not one community, but many. But for simplicity's sake, let's
focus on two groups within academe—the faculty and the students—and see how
their roles, their behaviors, and their sense of belonging have been and will be
affected by technology's advance.

I need first to acknowledge that my thinking is, not surprisingly, the result of 10
my experience. I was fortunate to have an exceptional undergraduate experience
at a beautiful residential college with a very low student-to-teacher ratio, with
world-class faculty, and a diverse and stimulating student body. I would wish that
educational setting for everyone, but with tuition at my college now exceeding
$18,000,° that's clearly not going to happen. As a student, I received financial
aid, but the national grants that made it possible for me to attend aren't around
anymore. But this is an old, sad story for another time and another forum.

So keep my bias in mind; perhaps it will explain some of my nostalgia. Or per- 11
haps it will just make it easier for you to call me a snob. But let's look now at the
faculty and their use of technology.

12   College faculty make up one of the most plugged-in professions in their use of technology for research—and one of the most retrograde in their use of technology for teaching. This seeming paradox has a lot to do with simple human behavior. If a tool makes it easier to perform a frequent task, it will be adopted. If, however, the tool requires a new type of behavior, or doesn't conform well with the existing modus operandi, then you can build it, but they probably won't come. For many faculty, the Internet has become a basic way of life because it meshes well with their work patterns. It mirrors nicely their image of themselves.

13   Communication with one's peers is integral to any line of work. And for many workers outside academia, their office location and the colleagues housed therein define their professional communities. Academics, though, have always embraced the idea of a geographically dispersed community of scholars. In the Middle Ages, universities—and the Church—functioned as true multinational institutions, at a time when most people never traveled more than 20 miles from the hovel in which they were born. Today, though, academics are likely to affiliate along disciplinary lines. A chemistry professor in Ann Arbor is likely to have more interaction with a chemistry professor in Palo Alto than with her counterpart in Germanic Languages in the building 50 yards away.

14   When the Net functions as a scholarly connectivity tool, it is just continuing the tradition of information-sharing that has always linked faculty who share a common disciplinary focus. So as a means of facilitating academic collaboration and resource sharing, the Net's a no-brainer.

15   But what of the professor's other hat—the teaching enterprise? There the Net offers no neat analogue to the usual work patterns because classroom instruction, unlike scholarly research, has traditionally been a highly autonomous, largely decentralized activity. No wonder, then, that until very recently the percentage of courses utilizing the Internet—or any new media at all—hovered in the single digits.

16   Finally, though, the winds of change appear to be blowing. On quite a few campuses today, computer access is a given, and the network is almost ubiquitous. But we're still just at the beginning. The epistemological transformations, the ones that change not just the way one teaches but *what* one teaches, are still few and far between. The big changes are still going to take a long time—and a fair amount of pain—to achieve.

17   My conservatism is founded on some very practical—and one could say short-sighted—concerns. Number one, who's going to pay for all this stuff? In *The City of Bits*, Mitchell tells of sitting in his Cambridge office instructing students from six different universities across the globe via two-way teleconferencing. With all due respect to him and the great institution he represents, we don't all have the same craft to navigate the information ocean. It's one thing to sit at MIT in front of one's high-end workstation complete with video camera, hooked to a super-

high-speed network with monster bandwidth—but that's not quite the reality for the rest of us. At a community college I visited last spring, the faculty were no longer able to make long-distance calls because the school couldn't afford it. While enrollments keep going up at this school, the state and local governments keep decreasing the funding. How long will it be before they have what MIT has today?

I'm sure we'd all love to sit in on that MIT teleconferenced course, sharing *18* ideas with Mitchell's great mind and with students all across the world: it sounds extraordinary. And I'm afraid it's just that—anything but ordinary. The notion of increased access to higher education is an unarguably worthwhile societal goal. Unfortunately, in marked contrast with Mitchell's class, a lot of what passes for distance education today seems a pretty poor substitute for an admittedly less-than-ideal large-classroom lecture delivered live. That's because a lot of distance education is just asynchronous transposition of that same ol' large-classroom lecture—but now you get to watch it on TV. And as we all know from watching our home videos, video tends to flatten reality. Any mediated experience has to be at one remove from the real thing. And a flattened version of the average large-audience lecture is a rather dismal thing to contemplate.

But despite all this gloom, there's some cause for optimism. E-mail might just *19* be the flying wedge. It could ultimately have the biggest impact on instruction of all the new technologies. It may not be as sexy as a two-way teleconference with Hong Kong, but e-mail changes behavior. With e-mail, students who didn't talk before, now do—and faculty find they're working longer hours to keep up with them. Steve Gilbert tells me of numerous conversations in which his correspondents say they started with e-mail and ended up rethinking what teaching is and how they could do it better.

On the train from Washington, DC, to New York this fall, I had the opportunity *20* to overhear the conversation of two students—the woman a college sophomore and the young man a high school senior. Their conversation centered on how she had chosen her school and on the criteria he was using to determine his college next year. She's studying international relations and had chosen her school because of its proximity to the nation's capital. Her major gripe was that she was a residential student on a largely commuter campus, and that made for some pretty lonely weekends.

He had just returned from a visit to Georgetown°—which was high on his list *21* because of the beauty of the campus. And as a kid from Queens who had spent the last four years in a very small town in Delaware, he was eager to return to an urban location. As a prospective business major, he felt a city location would provide him more internship opportunities.

What's so unusual about this conversation? Absolutely nothing, and that's the *22* whole point. Every one of their stated pros and cons was based on a reaction to the physical environment, be it access to certain urban resources or the attributes of a particular style of architecture—their criteria were all material. Where the students were, or wanted to be, mattered. It was all about place. Their conversation just demonstrated what we all know—that college is more than academics (a topic notably absent from the students' discussion).

23   College for many of us is a process of socialization, a rite of passage, which requires its own material culture—its real things—whether this means football games, fraternity row, the quad in front of Old Main, or any of the myriad other places on campus where students connect with one another, including those places their parents don't want to think about. In the *Science* article, Noam states, "The strength of the future physical university lies less in pure information and more in college as community."

24   The student body is, of course, a community, one largely defined today by a connection with a physical place—a campus. I think many students will still want to experience this kind of community. What's less clear is how the colleges of today are going to be able to offer that kind of experience. Soaring costs coupled with drastic budget reductions don't offer a lot of hope. Undoubtedly, other kinds of educational experiences are going to be available—and other kinds of educational institutions will arise to deliver them.

25   Perhaps higher education in the future will resemble the proverbial onion: at the core, the traditional type of real-time, face-to-face instruction, surrounded by rings of other educational experiences. Some instruction will be imported onto the campus from long-distance professors, while other types of instruction will be exported from the campus to long-distance students. I'd hope that college life in the future will be more like work life right now—a rich mixture of real-time and asynchronous interaction with peers, advisors, and external information sources.

26   When we think about the future, the trap we keep falling into is to see technology as a replacement for experience rather than an enhancement of capability. The old ways don't always get supplanted, they just get crowded as more and newer options come into play. Technology permits more, makes more possible, but it doesn't obliterate what went before.

27   There's a lot of black or white thinking out there. Computer logic may be binary, but our rational processes don't have to be. We're not hurtling towards a digital apocalypse (at least not faster than towards any other), but that doesn't mean we should unquestioningly adopt any technology, heedless of the consequences, simply because everyone seems to be doing it. Technology will change us—it will change us fundamentally—but that doesn't mean we can't influence its course. And let's remember, we can always just turn the damned things off.

28   We hear a lot these days about the social implications of technology—ironically much of it is going on between the covers of the good old-fashioned book. The argument seems to have polarized many commentators. On the one hand, we

have the high priests of the digital culture, who see all things as reducible to data. In their eyes, the human enterprise is just another bunch of bits in the cosmic data stream. On the other side, the neo-Luddites practice their own form of reductionism, fearing that silicon will eradicate all that is carbon. Can't we instead pursue some middle course? I don't accept the notion that the only difference between a computer-mediated exchange and a lover's kiss is bandwidth—nor do I fear that I will become a mere appendage on the ubiquitous Web.

Technology enables us to do more work. We can connect with more people; *29* we can learn from more sources; we can cast our nets farther. The irony is that—thanks to my computer, thanks to the Net—I now have more face-to-face encounters, more meetings, more travel, more experiences in the real world. I still have to, want to, and need to get out there and talk to people. Between my three e-mail accounts, my two voice mailboxes, and the fax machine—not to mention the plain old phone and mail—I spend most of my day dealing with representations of reality (isn't that what text and images are?). Because of this, and because I no longer work in an office, I find I need to get out for a walk once a day just to connect with tangible things, with flesh-and-blood humans, even if my primary contact with them occurs across the counter of the nearest coffee bar.

Just look at the crowded airways, the boom in business travel, the explosion of *30* conferences. We all still board those planes and drive those cars to travel hours in order to meet with our colleagues. Theoretically, at least, we could do it all by phone. We could receive print-outs of the talks and just read them. We could watch it on TV. But we don't. We like it live.

Why? Because we all know the good stuff at a conference happens during the *31* coffee breaks. Because we all know we don't really know someone until we've eaten with them. Because we all know the camera doesn't always follow the ball carrier. Because we know that even the world's best programmer can't anticipate all the possibilities that real life throws at us every second of the day.

We used to say computers would be pretty good if only they could talk—then *32* they did. Then we said, well, if only they had pictures—and now they've got those in spades. Touch may be more difficult—but there's a pretty good simulacrum of that already in the labs. But something will always be missing, because while they are wonderful amplifiers of the human potential, computers can never be replacements for the human experience. Someone else said it, but my yoga classes confirm it: "There's no prahna° in a computer," no *qi*,° no life-force. And all the bandwidth in the world won't ever change that.

In our rush to embrace the wonders that technology can provide, let's never *33* confuse its images, its sounds, its symbols, with what's real. Perhaps all this talk of reality seems patently obvious, yet with the new media hype we are sometimes unable to distinguish the real from the *trompe l'oeil*° of the screen. We need to be aware of the danger of complacency, and be ever alert for opportunities to celebrate the real. Our lives are ever more built upon mediated experience, but in our increasing immersion in the digital sea, let's not forget that at bottom, it's just zeros and ones.

34   And just in case we do forget, there's Virginia Woolf° to remind us in *A Room of One's Own*:

> What is meant by "reality"? It would seem to be something very erratic, very undependable—now to be found in a dusty road, now in a scrap of newspaper in the street, now in a daffodil in the sun. It lights up a group in a room and stamps some casual saying. It overwhelms one walking home beneath the stars and makes the silent world more real than the world of speech—and then there it is again in an omnibus in the uproar of Picadilly. Sometimes, too, it seems to dwell in shapes too far away for us to discern what their nature is. But whatever it touches, it fixes and makes permanent. That is what remains over when the skin of the day has been cast into the hedge; that is what is left of past time and of our loves and hates.

35   The happiest day of my life was April 14, 1995. My husband and our two preschoolers were in Rome. I was watching, awestruck, as the kids used the Forum as a sort of archeological playground—clambering about the columns that Julius Caesar and Pompey and Claudius and Titus and all the rest had walked through conducting the affairs of the world a couple millennia ago. What made that day so extraordinary? I can't quite put it into words, but it was all about history, it was all about place, it was all about being there. It could not have happened in a Virtual Reality park in Las Vegas. It was real.

36   I recognize that that's a privileged story, the personal equivalent of teleteaching at MIT, but the second happiest time of my life is just about every day—when the kids come home and they run into my office. I turn from the computer and see them there, beaming and bright, and wondrously, miraculously, real.

37   And I'm reminded once again that what really counts is the ineluctable—the mystery, the reality of life. It's what remains over from the skin of the day—it's what we cherish and don't want to lose. It's what belongs to the realm of the sensuous—it's walking home beneath the stars—it's those things we can't program or code. These are the things that will save us. ◆

1996

Glossary

Neil Postman: an American critic and educator. His interests include media and learning, illustrated in many of his 17 books, including *Amusing Ourselves to Death* (1985), *Technopoly: The Surrender of Culture to Technology* (1992), and *The End of Education* (1995). Postman, along with **Sven Birkerts**, has resisted technological dependence.

Steve Gilbert: president and founder of the Teaching, Learning, and Technology (TLT) Group.

The Accidental Tourist: a novel by Anne Tyler, made into a movie starring William Hurt, Kathleen Turner, and Geena Davis.

$18,000: approximately $28 000 Canadian in 1998.

Georgetown University: university founded in 1789, the same year the U.S. Constitution took effect. Georgetown University is the United States' oldest Catholic and Jesuit university.

prahna: universal life force; a synonym of *qi*.

qi: represents the body's energy in Chinese medicine.

trompe l'oeil: French for "optical illusion."

Virginia Woolf: (1882–1941) essayist, critic, short-story writer, diarist, biographer, and novelist. She is best known for her novel *To the Lighthouse* (1927).

Explorations

- Have you used technology in the classroom? If so, what kind of impact did this technology have on your learning process?

- Would you consider taking a distance education course? What do you believe are the pros and cons of being a student in a physical classroom and being a student in a virtual classroom?

- Do you believe that genuine communities are possible in cyberspace?

Audrey Thomas was born in Birmingham, New York, in 1935, moved to Vancouver, B.C., and later earned an M.A. at the University of British Columbia. Thomas is best known as a writer of experimental fiction; she has published novels, novellas, and five collections of short stories, and has won numerous awards for her writing, including the Ethel Wilson Fiction Prize for both Coming Down from Wa *(1995) and* Wild Blue Yonder *(1991). Thomas taught creative writing at both the University of Victoria and the University of British Columbia and was writer-in-residence at Concordia and Simon Fraser Universities. Thomas now lives on Galiano Island, British Columbia.*

Basmati Rice: An Essay about Words

Audrey Thomas

1   My study is on the second floor of our house and faces East. I like that and I get up early to write, perhaps not simply because I enjoy the sunrise (especially in winter, when all has been so black, and then gradually light, like hope, returns) but out of some atavistic hope that my thoughts, too, will rise with the sun and illumine the blank pages in front of me.

2   We live in a corner house and my study is right above a busy street. People whom I cannot see often pass beneath my window and throw up snatches of conversation before moving out of earshot. And I hear footsteps, light, heavy, singly or in groups, and the sound of buggy wheels or grocery carts. Now, I can see the sidewalk on the other side of the street, see people hurrying along or dawdling, the young woman from the St. James Daycare a block away, out for a walk with her little charges who all seem to march (or skip or run) to a different drummer, a father with his baby tucked inside his ski jacket, a blind man, a woman with her arms full of grocery bags. I cannot hear their footsteps nor anything they might be saying and sometimes a wonderful thing happens where someone will pass beneath my window, and say something while someone is walking by on the other side of the street, and so I get the wonderful absurdity of seeing the old lady in the red coat who lives at the Senior Citizen Lodge at 16th and Macdonald (I know because she asked me to take her picture, waving her hand-made Union Jack, the day the Queen came down 16th Avenue) going by on one side and hearing a gruff teenage male voice saying, "so I said to him nobody talks like that to me and…." The movie I watch has the wrong soundtrack!

3   I am interested in such absurdities, in the word *absurd* itself, from the Latin for inharmonious, foolish. L. *ab*, from, *surdus*, deaf, inaudible, harsh (used metaphorically here, deaf to reason, hence irrational). I am interested in the fact that I

spend a lot of my days at a desk, or table, and that the desk or table needs always to face a window. This is not just so I will have something to look at when "illumination" comes slowly (or not at all) but because, in what is essentially an inside occupation (and a very lonely one at that, I can't even stand to have a radio on when I'm working) I am able to feel even a little bit connected with the outside. I often see myself like a diver in one of those old-fashioned diving bells, both in and apart from everything in the universe around me. There is a little piece of brown paper taped to the window frame. I got it from a bread wrapper several years ago when I was spending a winter in Montreal. It says

PAIN

FRAIS DU JOUR

in blue letters and underneath

BREAD

BAKED FRESH DAILY

Some days, if I'm wrestling with a piece or a passage that seems especially difficult I fold the paper so that it reads:

PAIN

BAKED FRESH DAILY

and for some perverse reason that cheers me up. That the French word for bread and the English word for misery of one kind or another *look* alike is another of those absurdities that interest me. There is no real connection, as there is, say, with the English *blessed* and the French *blesser*, to wound—it's just chance. But my mind, when in a certain state of heightened awareness (which I might point out, can just as easily be brought on by laughter as by tears), makes that kind of connection easily.

Here's another. It was early November when I began thinking about this essay, and the tree outside my window was almost bare of leaves. The weather was turning cold and a cold rain was falling. "Autumn leaves" I wrote on my pad, "autumn leaves." Over and over. And then suddenly "WINTER enters." Again, no real linguistic connection, but writing the phrase over and over gave me a new way of looking at the leaves. 4

I love words. I love the way they suddenly surprise you; I love the way *everyone*, high or low, uses them to paint pictures—that is to say metaphorically. In the past week a phrase, not new, but surely not much in vogue of recent years, has been said in my hearing, or I've read it in the paper, no less than five times: so and so is "between a rock and a hard place." Once in a line-up at the main post office downtown, once spoken by a friend, and in three different newspaper articles. Where does this phrase come from? I can't find it in Bartlett's, at least not under "rock," or "place," or "hard." Why is it suddenly being said? It is certainly a most poetic (and uncomfortable) image. I wouldn't want to be there, nor would you. Somebody says, of somebody else, "I've got him eating out of my hand," probably unaware of the root of the word "manipulate." When I was a child I 5 heard constant warnings about kids who were "too big for their britches" or "too big for their boots" and we were all, without exception, potential big-eared little pitchers. And yet it seemed to me that all the adults I knew—parents, relatives, teachers, corrected me if I played around with words myself—or with grammar or sentence structure. It was as though all the metaphorical language in the world had already been invented and I wasn't there on the day that it happened. Once I started reading poetry I realized that poets seemed to have a certain freedom that ordinary, hard-working decent folks didn't (or didn't allow themselves to) have. They invented and re-invented language all the time. (Prose that got too metaphorical was considered suspect unless it were in the Sunday Sermon or spoken by Roosevelt° or Churchill.°) That was when I decided I would become a poet, and probably why. My poems were terrible—a lot of them were very "Christian" in a romantic way, full of Crusaders, lepers, infidels, and angels—and some of them, I regret to say, won prizes. But I do remember the day we were asked to write limericks (Grade 4? Grade 5?) and I came up with this in about five minutes:

> There was once a fellow named Farrell
> Whose life was in terrible peril
> He fell in with some rogues
> Who stole all but his brogues
> And had to slink home in a barrel.

(I don't know where I got "brogues" from or how I knew what it meant; it certainly wasn't a word used in our family.)

6   I wrote dozens of limericks after that first one. I knew it wasn't Real Poetry but I also suspected the other stuff, the stuff my teachers and my mother and various judges liked, wasn't Real Poetry either. Nevertheless, for all my desire to write poetry, what I was always better at was prose. Who knows why one writer works better in one genre than another? What I'd really like to be is "ambidextrous," like Michael Ondaatje or Margaret Atwood, but I'm not. It's always prose for me. (Why do most of us see poetry as "higher"? Because it seems more of a distillate of the creative unconscious than prose? Perfume as opposed to cologne? I once had a poet in a graduate prose class in Montreal. He needed one more course to get his degree and had chosen mine. We were all working on stories and one night he said to me, in much despair, "I've never written 'he said' and 'she said' before." Of course he wasn't a *narrative* poet: not for him *Beowulf*° or *The Idylls of the King*,° or, closer to home, *The Titanic*,° or *Brébeuf and His Brethren*.°) I still sometimes have the awful feeling that I failed because I failed to write poetry, even while I know that prose can be just as exciting or dense, "packed," innovative as any poem. It probably has something to do with the fact that we write our notes, our memos, our letters, in prose, we speak in prose to one another, even

when we speak metaphorically: "Lay off me, will you?", "I'm really blue today," "What's for dinner, honey?", "You're driving me up the wall."

Sometimes a sentence or a phrase gives me the idea for an entire story (once, 7 even, for the very last line of a novel I didn't write for another three years, when I overheard a man in a pay phone say to whomever was on the other end: "Get rid of it." That's all I heard him say and then he hung up). This summer my daughter and I were in Greece. We witnessed a very bizarre incident involving a young English boy, an octopus, and a man in a panama hat. I knew that that in itself could provide the central image for a new story but then, a few days later, I heard a French woman on another beach say "La méduse; il faut prener garde,"° and suddenly, because of this incident with the octopus, I saw not the jelly fish to which she had been referring but the great snaky tentacles of an octopus and *then* I saw that what I really wanted to write about was all that sexuality that was there on the beach, in that heat, under the intense blue sky: the bare-breasted European woman, the young Greek men showing off to their girlfriends and who-ever else would watch. All the bodies. The story is seen through the eyes of a 12-year-old English boy, very properly brought up, for whom the octopus becomes the symbol of everything most feared and most desired, "the nightmare spread out upon the rock." Later on, on quite a different island, a Greek man said two things that have become incorporated into the octopus story. He said, when we were listening to some very sad Greek music, "There are no happy men in Greece, only happy childrens." He also asked, "you like this ice-land?" and since the temperature was over 80° we stared at him. He meant "island" but it took us a while to figure that out. Now, in my story, the young boy hears words and phrases he doesn't completely understand ("la méduse; il faut prener garde" "you like this ice-land?") and this just adds to his general sense of unease.

Another recent story was inspired by a newspaper clipping about a man who 8 had been charged with common assault for massaging the feet of strange women. I began to do some foot research and discovered something I must have learned in my university zoology course, that the number of bones in the human foot is the same as the number of letters in the alphabet. And so the story begins: "There are twenty-six bones in the foot; that is the alphabet of the foot" and goes on to tell a story which is a complete fabrication except for the fact that both men (the "real" man and the man in my story) get arrested, charged and fined.

Another story, which is the title story of the collection I'm presently working 9 on, came as a message written on a mirror in the George Dawson Inn in Dawson Creek. The message was not intended for me but showed up on the mirror in the bathroom after my daughter had taken a very hot shower. It said, "Good-bye Harold, Good Luck" and whoever had written it must have counted on the fact that Harold would take a shower. (And the maid had obviously not gone over the mirror with *Windex*.) We had a lot of fun trying to figure out who Harold was and whether the message was written in anger or love. In the story, "they" (a mother who is contemplating a divorce and her child) do meet up with Harold, but of course he doesn't know that they have seen the message (and they're not absolutely sure he has).

10   I cut things out of newspapers, often really horrible things and I'm never sure why.

MURDERER SET WIFE ADRIFT ON RAFT

TIGER BITES TRAINER TO DEATH
(Horrified Wife Looks On)

DOLPHINS NUDGE BOY'S BODY TO SHORE

That last one really haunts me, not just the image, but that word "nudge." The dolphins with their blunt "noses," gently nudging the dead boy towards the shore. That one will probably end up in a story.

PLAN YOUR PLOT

(this one was in the gardening column of the *Province*) and one from the *Vancouver Courier* recently prompted a note to a friend.

POUND WARNS PETS

I cut it out, and wrote underneath, "You're an old bitch gone in the teeth."

11   And so it goes. And so it goes. And so it goes on and on. I read Rev. Skeat, I read Bartlett's, I read Fowler's *Modern English Usage*, given to me by an ex-boyfriend who wrote, as a greeting, the definition of *oxymoron*, which just about summed up our relationship! I have the *Shorter Oxford Dictionary* but long to have the real one, all those volumes as full of goodies as good Christmas puddings. I have the Bible, the *Book of Common Prayer*, Shakespeare and *Partridge's Origins*. I have Collins' phrase books in several languages ("that man is following me everywhere"). I have maps and rocks and shells and bits of coral from various places to which I have travelled. I scan the personal columns, the names of the ships in port. And I have my eyes and ears.

12   I am a dilettante (related to the Italian for "delight"). I never learn any language properly but love to dabble in them. I have studied, at one time or another, Latin, Anglo-Saxon, Middle English, Old Norse, French, Italian and, most recently Greek. I spent a winter in Athens a few years ago and saw, every day, little green vans scurrying around the city with ΜΕΤΑΦΟΡΗ posted on a card in the front windshield. "Metaphors." When I enquired I discovered that these vans are for hire and they *transfer* goods from one section of the city to another. Now I long to write an essay called "A Metaphor is not a Truck."

13   Last year I took two terms of sign language at night school. I was amused by the fact that in ASL (American Sign Language) the sign for "woman" has to do with the tying of bonnet strings and the sign for man with the tipping of a hat. These are charming archaisms, like "horsepower" in English. (I am also interested in mirrors, mirror images, going into and through mirrors, so signing, which one does to someone facing you, is fascinating—and very difficult. I often came home

with an aching hand.) I would like to take more sign language; I would like to become, as an African man once said to me, about English, "absolutely fluid in that language."

Words words words. Sometimes it all gets on top of me and I feel like the mon- *14* ster made out of words in *The Faerie Queene*.° I can't leave them alone; I am obsessed. I move through the city watching for signs with letters missing ("Beef live with onions" advertises a cheap café near Granville and Broadway, "ELF SERVE" says a gas station out on Hastings) and I am always on the lookout for messages within words: can you see the harm in pharmacy, the dent in accident, the over in lover? In short, I play.

There is a phenomenon, most commonly observed in photography but also *15* talked about by people who make stained glass. It is called "halation" and it refers to the spreading of light beyond its proper boundary. (With stained glass it happens when two colours are next to one another.) I think words can do that too, or perhaps I should say that I would like to think that there is no "proper boundary" for words. Let them spill over from one language to another, let them leap out at us like kittens at play. "Wit," said Mark Van Doren,° "is the only wall between us and the dark." If a writer, if an artist of *any* sort, stops approaching his materials with wit, with laughter, then he is lost. The other day I was making a curry and listening to some old Beatles' songs on the radio. John or Paul was yelling, "Can't Buy Me Love" and I was thinking about Basmati rice. Suddenly I realized "Basmati rice" had the same number of syllables as "Can't Buy Me Love," so every time John or Paul or whoever got to the chorus I yelled out "Basmati Rice!" and did a little soft shoe shuffle while I stirred the curry sauce. (Everybody had a good time.) ◆

1984

Glossary

Franklin Delano Roosevelt: (1882–1945) thirty-second president of the United States (1933–1945). Roosevelt brought in the New Deal during his first term in office in order to alleviate some of the economic distress caused by the Depression; during an unprecedented third term in office he oversaw the U.S. entry into World War II.

Sir Winston Churchill: (1874–1965) statesman, politician, and author. Churchill was prime minister of England during World War II; he was awarded the Nobel Prize in Literature in 1953.

Beowulf: an Old English (Anglo-Saxon) epic of 3200 lines of alliterative verse dating from the early eighth century that is the earliest extant written composition of such length in the English language.

Idylls of the King: a 10-book series of poems based on the legend of King Arthur written by Alfred, Lord Tennyson between 1859 and 1885.

The Titanic: a long 1935 poem by Canadian writer E.J. Pratt based on the sinking of the famous *White Star* liner in the Atlantic Ocean on April 14, 1912.

Brébeuf and His Brethren: another epic poem by Pratt that garnered a Governor General's Award in 1940.

"La méduse; il faut prener garde": translates loosely as "The jellyfish; one must be careful."

The Faerie Queene: a religious and political allegorical poem of six books composed by British poet Edmund Spenser between 1590 and 1596; it draws heavily on the conventions of chivalric romance, the King Arthur legend, and the historical context of the reign of Queen Elizabeth I.

Mark Van Doren: (1894–1970) American poet, critic, and novelist who taught at Columbia University in New York from 1920 to 1959; known for his critical biographies of Henry David Thoreau, John Dryden, William Shakespeare, and Nathaniel Hawthorne. His *Collected Poems* (1939) won a Pulitzer Prize.

Explorations

- Do you notice any patterns in the kinds of abstract nouns you use? If so, what are they?

- With the benefit of hindsight, would you choose the same words again? Why or why not?

Trinh T. Minh-ha was born in 1952 in Vietnam. An academic, writer, and documentary filmmaker, Trinh makes her home in San Francisco, where she teaches women's studies at the University of California at Berkeley and cinema at San Francisco State University. She originally trained in music as a composer and received an M.F.A. and Ph.D. from the University of Illinois. Her books include Woman, Native, Other; When the Moon Waxes Red; *and* Framer Framed, *which collects the scripts of three of her films:* Reassemblage; Naked Spaces: Living Is Round; *and* Surname Viet Given Name Nam. *She is the recipient of several awards and grants, including the AFI National Independent Filmmaker Maya Deren Award.*

From "Commitment from the Mirror-Writing Box"

Trinh T. Minh-ha

Clear expression, often equated with *correct* expression, has long been the criterion set forth in treatises on *rhetoric*, whose aim was to order discourse so as to *persuade*. The language of Taoism° and Zen,° for example, which is perfectly accessible but rife with paradox does not qualify as "clear" (paradox is "illogical" and "nonsensical" to many Westerners), for its intent lies outside the realm of persuasion. The same holds true for vernacular speech, which is not acquired through institutions—schools, churches, professions, etc.—and therefore not repressed by either grammatical rules, technical terms, or key words. Clarity as a purely rhetorical attribute serves the purpose of a classical feature in language, namely, its instrumentality. To write is to communicate, express, witness, impose, instruct, redeem, or save—at any rate to *mean* and to send out *an unambiguous message*. Writing thus reduced to a mere vehicle of thought may be *used* to orient toward a goal or to sustain an act, but it does not constitute an act in itself. This is how the division between the writer/the intellectual and the activists/the masses becomes possible. To use the language well, says the voice of literacy, cherish its classic form. Do not choose the offbeat at the cost of clarity. Obscurity is an imposition on the reader. True, but beware when you cross railroad tracks for one train may hide another train. Clarity is a means of subjection, a quality both of official, taught language and of correct writing, two old mates of power: together they flow, together they flower, vertically, to impose an order. Let us not forget that writers who advocate the instrumentality of language are often those who cannot or choose not to see the suchness of things— a language as language—and therefore, continue to preach conformity to the norms of well-behaved writing: principles of composition, style, genre, correction,

1

and improvement. To write "clearly," one must incessantly prune, eliminate, forbid, purge, purify; in other words, practice what may be called an "ablution of language" (Roland Barthes).°

2   "Writing for me," says Toni Cade Bambara,° "is still an act of language first and foremost."[1] Before being the noble messenger and the loyal message of her/his people, the writer is a wo/man "whose most absorbed and passionate hours are spent arranging words on pieces of paper" (Joan Didion).[2] S/He does not express her/his thoughts, passion, or imagination in sentences but *thinks sentences*: she is a sentence-thinker (i.e., "not altogether a thinker and not altogether a sentence parser" [Barthes])[3] who radically questions the world through the questioning of a how-to-write. Drawing attention to the very nature of writing, acknowledging its constraints and artificiality do not, however, necessarily imply laying emphasis on craftsmanship as a criterion for "good" (literary) writing. To substitute a work-value for a use-value is simply to shift from the norms of the clearly written (correct behavior) to those of the well written (patient apprenticeship). The image of the writer as a crafts wo/man who spends regular hours of solitary effort cutting, polishing, and setting her/his form "exactly as a jeweller extracts art from his material"[4] has too often been set forth as the sole determining value. Good writing is thus differentiated from bad writing through a building up of skill and vocabulary and a perfecting of techniques. Since genius cannot be acquired, sophisticated means, skills, and knowledge are dangled before one's eyes as *the* steps to take, *the* ladder to climb if one wishes to come any closer to the top of this monument known as Literature. Invoke the Name. Follow the norms. Of. The Well Written. The master-servant's creed carries on: *you must learn* through patience and discipline. And what counts most is what it costs in *labor* to engender a work, hence the parallel often abusively drawn between the act of writing and the birth process.

> The poet is in labor [Denise Levertov° wrote]. She has been told that it will not hurt but it has hurt so much that pain and struggle seem, just now, the only reality....she hears the doctor saying, "Those are the shoulders you are feeling now"—and she knows the head is out then, and the child is pushing and sliding out of her, insistent, a poem.[5]

3   In her *Journal*, Katherine Mansfield° acknowledged:

> What is it that makes the moment of delivery so difficult for me?...*Work*. Shall I be able to express one day my love of work—my desire to be a better writer—my longing to take greater pains....Oh, to be a *writer*, a real writer given up to it and to it alone!...My deepest desire is to be a writer, to have "a body of work" done...[6]

The reflections offered throughout this *Journal* insist on the painstaking 4 aspects of writing and on moments where Mansfield despaired, overwhelmed by fear of *failing*, of not *working* regularly enough, in other words, of not meeting the (Good) Writer's requirements. Labor and craft have become so cherished as values in writing that it suffices to read any interview, any account of a writer's life, any statement about the creative process to recognize how highly prized they remain. Invited to speak for a course on "How the Writer Writes," Flannery O'Connor° observes:

> there is no such thing as THE writer....
> But there is a widespread curiosity about writers and how they work....
> [People] are interested in being a writer, not in writing....And they seem
> to feel that this can be accomplished by learning certain things about
> working habits....[7]

To write well, in this framework of mind, is to arrange the signs of literary con- 5 ventions so as to reach an optimum form to "express" a reality—such as, for example, the self (hence the concept of art as self-expression), which is often taken for something given, as solid, as referable as an object that lies deeply hidden under my layers of artificialities, waiting patiently to be uncovered and proven. Yet I-the-writer do not express (a) reality more than (a) reality impresses itself on me. Expresses me. The function of the craftswo/man-writer is, therefore, "not so much to create work as to supply a literature which can be seen from afar" (Barthes). The display of craftsmanship, when assumed clear-sightedly however, is a self-confessed, sometimes self-reflexive, form of art for art's sake that holds pragmatic bourgeois activity up to ridicule and, at best, invalidates it. By laying bare the codes of literary labor, it unequivocally acknowledges the writer's contradictory stand—her being condemned to do "good work" in choosing to "write well" and to produce Literature. *She writes*, finally not to express, nor so much to materialize an idea or a feeling, as *to possess and dispossess herself of the power of writing*. Bliss. ◆

1989

Endnotes

1. Toni Cade Bambara, "Commitment...," *Sturdy Black Bridges*, p. 236.

2. Joan Didion, "Why I Write," *The Writer on Her Work*, p. 20.

3. Roland Barthes, *The Pleasure of the Text*, tr. R. Miller (New York: Hill & Wang, 1975), p. 51.

4. Roland Barthes, *Writing Degree Zero*, tr. A. Lavers & C. Smith (New York: Hill & Wang, 1967), p. 63.

5. *Woman as Writer*, ed. J.L. Webber and J. Grumman (Boston: Houghton Mifflin, 1978), p. 85.

6. Ibid., pp. 15–16.

7. Ibid., p. 98 ("The Nature and Aim of Fiction").

Glossary

Taoism: a Chinese philosophical and religious system based on the writings of Lao Tzu and Chuang Tzu which is opposed to the ritualistic and moralistic social order of Confucianism.

Zen: an aspect of Buddhist philosophy introduced from China to Japan in the late 12th and early 13th centuries, it emphasizes meditation and physical work as a means to enlightenment.

Roland Barthes: (1915–1980) French literary critic and semiotician who asserted that language is a system of signs that reflects the society and times in which it is used.

Toni Cade Bambara: (b. 1939) African-American short-story writer and novelist whose works include *Gorilla, My Love* (1972), *The Sea Birds Are Still Alive* (1977), *The Salt Eaters* (1980), and *If Blessing Comes* (1987).

Denise Levertov: (b. 1923) American poet and essayist.

Katherine Mansfield: (1888–1923) New Zealand-born short-story writer known for her slice-of-life technique.

(Mary) Flannery O'Connor: (1925–1964) American short-story writer and novelist known for her vivid descriptions of the southern United States, her keen ear for dialect, and her irreverent humour.

Explorations

*   Do you feel that clear, direct language is the key to writing well? Why or why not?

*   Have you ever struggled between writing clearly and correctly, and expressing your ideas and feelings? If so, how did you resolve your struggle?

William Zinsser was born in New York in 1922 and received a B.A. from Princeton in 1944. He was an editor, critic, and editorial writer with the New York Herald Tribune *for 13 years. In 1959 he became a freelance writer, writing regularly for magazines such as* The New Yorker, The Atlantic Monthly, *and* Life *magazine. Today he is a journalist, writing teacher, and essayist. "Simplicity," published in* On Writing Well, *foregrounds Zinsser's concern with approaching writing, particularly revision, as a process.*

Simplicity

William Zinsser

Clutter is the disease of American writing. We are a society strangling in unnecessary words, circular constructions, pompous frills and meaningless jargon. 1

Who can understand the clotted language of everyday American commerce: the memo, the corporation report, the business letter, the notice from the bank explaining its latest "simplified" statement? What member of an insurance or medical plan can decipher the brochure explaining his costs and benefits? What father or mother can put together a child's toy from the instructions on the box? Our national tendency is to inflate and thereby sound important. The airline pilot who announces that he is presently anticipating experiencing considerable precipitation wouldn't think of saying it may rain. The sentence is too simple—there must be something wrong with it. 2

But the secret of good writing is to strip every sentence to its cleanest components. Every word that serves no function, every long word that could be a short word, every adverb that carries the same meaning that's already in the verb, every passive construction that leaves the reader unsure of who is doing what—these are the thousand and one adulterants that weaken the strength of a sentence. And they usually occur in proportion to education and rank. 3

During the 1960s the president of my university wrote a letter to mollify the alumni after a spell of campus unrest. "You are probably aware," he began, "that we have been experiencing very considerable potentially explosive expressions of dissatisfaction on issues only partially related." He meant the students had been hassling them about different things. I was far more upset by the president's English than by the students' potentially explosive expressions of dissatisfaction. I would have preferred the presidential approach taken by Franklin D. Roosevelt° when he tried to convert into English his own government's memos, such as this blackout order of 1942: 4

> Such preparations shall be made as will completely obscure all Federal buildings and non-Federal buildings occupied by the Federal government

during an air raid for any period of time from visibility by reason of internal or external illumination.

5   "Tell them," Roosevelt said, "that in buildings where they have to keep the work going to put something across the windows."

6   Simplify, simplify. Thoreau° said it, as we are so often reminded, and no American writer more consistently practiced what he preached. Open *Walden* to any page and you will find a man saying in a plain and orderly way what is on his mind:

> I went to the woods because I wished to live deliberately, to front only the essential facts of life, and see if I could not learn what it had to teach, and not, when I came to die, discover that I had not lived.

7   How can the rest of us achieve such enviable freedom from clutter? The answer is to clear our heads of clutter. Clear thinking becomes clear writing; one can't exist without the other. It's impossible for a muddy thinker to write good English. You may get away with it for a paragraph or two, but soon the reader will be lost, and there's no sin so grave, for the reader will not easily be lured back.

8   Who is this elusive creature, the reader? The reader is someone with an attention span of about 30 seconds—a person assailed by other forces competing for attention. At one time these forces weren't so numerous: newspapers, radio, spouse, home, children. Today they also include a "home entertainment centre" (TV, VCR, tapes, CDs), e-mail, the Internet, the cellular phone, the fax machine, a fitness program, a pool, a lawn, and that most potent of competitors, sleep. The person snoozing in a chair with a magazine or a book is a person who was being given too much unnecessary trouble by the writer.

9   It won't do to say that the reader is too dumb or too lazy to keep pace with the train of thought. If the reader is lost, it's usually because the writer hasn't been careful enough. That carelessness can take any number of forms. Perhaps a sentence is so excessively cluttered that the reader, hacking through the verbiage, simply doesn't know what it means. Perhaps a sentence has been so shoddily constructed that the reader could read it in several ways. Perhaps the writer has switched pronouns in midsentence, or has switched tenses, so the reader loses track of who is talking or when the action took place. Perhaps Sentence B is not a logical sequence to Sentence A—the writer, in whose head the connection is clear, hasn't bothered to provide the missing link. Perhaps the writer has used an important word incorrectly by not taking the trouble to look it up. The writer may think "sanguine" and "sanguinary" mean the same thing, but the difference is a bloody big one. The reader can only infer (speaking of big differences) what the writer is trying to imply.

5 --   10

is too dumb or too lazy to keep pace with the ~~writer's~~ train

of thought. My sympathies are ~~entirely~~ with him. ~~He's not~~

~~so dumb.~~ If the reader is lost, it is generally because the

writer ~~of the article~~ has not been careful enough to keep

him on the ~~proper~~ path.

This carelessness can take any number of ~~different~~ forms.   11

Perhaps a sentence is so excessively ~~long and~~ cluttered that

the reader, hacking his way through ~~all~~ the verbiage, simply

doesn't know what it ~~the writer~~ means. Perhaps a sentence has

been so shoddily constructed that the reader could read it in

any of several ~~two or three different~~ ways. ~~He thinks he knows what~~

~~the writer is trying to say, but he's not sure.~~ Perhaps the

writer has switched pronouns in mid-sentence, or ~~perhaps he~~

has switched tenses, so the reader loses track of who is

talking ~~to whom~~ or ~~exactly~~ when the action took place. Per-

haps Sentence B is not a logical sequel to Sentence A--the

writer, in whose head the connection is ~~perfectly~~ clear, has

not bothered to provide ~~given enough thought to providing~~ the missing link. Per-

haps the writer has used an important word incorrectly by not

taking the trouble to look it up ~~and make sure.~~ He may think

that "sanguine" and "sanguinary" mean the same thing, but

~~I can assure you that~~ the difference is a bloody big one ~~to the~~

~~reader.~~ The reader ~~He~~ can only ~~try to~~ infer ~~what~~ (speaking of big differ-

ences) what the writer is trying to imply.

Faced with these ~~such a variety of~~ obstacles, the reader   12

is at first a remarkably tenacious bird. He ~~tends to~~ blames

6 --

himself. He obviously missed something, ~~he thinks~~ and he goes back over the mystifying sentence, or over the whole paragraph, piecing it out like an ancient rune, making guesses and moving on. But he won't do this for long.) ~~He will soon run out of patience.~~ (The writer is making him work too hard~~, harder than he should have to work~~ (and the reader will look for ~~a writer~~ one who is better at his craft.

13 (The writer must therefore constantly ask himself: What am I trying to say? ~~in this sentence?~~ (Surprisingly often, he doesn't know.) ~~And~~ Then he must look at what he has just written and ask: Have I said it? Is it clear to someone encountering ~~who is coming upon~~ the subject for the first time? If it's not, ~~clear,~~ it is because some fuzz has worked its way into the machinery. The clear writer is a person ~~who is~~ clear-headed enough to see this stuff for what it is: fuzz.

14 (I don't mean ~~to suggest~~ that some people are born clear-headed and are therefore natural writers, whereas others ~~other people~~ are naturally fuzzy and will ~~therefore~~ never write well. Thinking clearly is a ~~an entirely~~ conscious act that the writer must force ~~keep forcing~~ upon himself, just as if he were embarking ~~starting out~~ on any other ~~kind of~~ project that requires ~~calls for~~ logic: adding up a laundry list or doing an algebra problem ~~or playing chess~~. Good writing doesn't ~~just~~ come naturally, though most people obviously think it does ~~it's as easy as walking~~. The professional

Two pages of the final manuscript of this chapter from the First Edition of On *Writing Well.* Although they look like a first draft, they had already been rewritten and retyped—like almost every other page—four or five times. With each rewrite I try to make what I have written tighter, stronger and more precise, eliminating every element that is not doing useful work. Then I go over it once more, reading it aloud, and am always amazed at how much clutter can still be cut. (In a later edition of this book I eliminated the sexist pronoun "he" to denote "the writer" and "the reader.")

Faced with such obstacles, readers are at first tenacious. They blame them- 15
selves—they obviously missed something, and they go back over the mystifying
sentence, or over the whole paragraph, piecing it out like an ancient rune, making guesses and moving on. But they won't do that for long. The writer is making them work too hard, and they will look for one who is better at the craft.

Writers must therefore constantly ask: What am I trying to say? Surprisingly 16
often they don't know. Then they must look at what they have written and ask:
Have I said it? Is it clear to someone encountering the subject for the first time?
If it's not, some fuzz has worked its way into the machinery. The clear writer is
someone clearheaded enough to see this stuff for what it is: fuzz.

I don't mean that some people are born clearheaded and are therefore natural 17
writers, whereas others are naturally fuzzy and will never write well. Thinking
clearly is a conscious act that writers must force upon themselves, as if they were
working on any other project that requires logic: making a shopping list or doing
an algebra problem. Good writing doesn't come naturally, though most people
seem to think it does. Professional writers are constantly bearded by strangers
who say they'd like to "try a little writing sometime"—meaning when they retire
from their real profession, like insurance or real estate, which is hard. Or they say,
"I could write a book about that." I doubt it.

Writing is hard work. A clear sentence is no accident. Very few sentences 18
come out right the first time, or even the third time. Remember this in moments
of despair. If you find that writing is hard, it's because it *is* hard. ◆

1976; last revised 1998

Glossary

Franklin Delano Roosevelt: (1882–1945) thirty-second president of the United
States (1933–1945). Roosevelt brought in the New Deal during his first term in
office in order to alleviate some of the economic distress caused by the
Depression; during an unprecedented third term in office he oversaw the U.S.
entry into World War II.

Henry David Thoreau: (1817–1862) American essayist, naturalist, and poet whose
two-year experiment living by himself in a log cabin near Walden Pond,
Massachusetts, became the basis for his most celebrated work, *Walden*.

Explorations

- Is writing hard work for you? Why or why not?

- Has an instructor ever criticized you for using unnecessary words and awkward phrasings? If so, what steps did you take to control such "clutter"?

- Is "clutter" necessarily bad? Can you think of an occasion where using plain,
  simple language is inappropriate or undesirable?

CHAPTER TWO

Development: Bridging the Gap Between Writer and Audience

After using strategies of invention to generate ideas, your mind will seek ways to sort through detail, choosing material that is most relevant. The Greek philosopher Aristotle believed that when selecting ideas to develop your subject, you could consult a list of *topoi*, or topics. *Topoi*, meaning "places," "regions," or "haunts," serve as metaphors for the thought processes that the mind naturally engages in: the mind works to find meaning, to describe, to categorize, to find similarities and differences, and to understand how and why things work. You can visit these places in your mind in order to make sense of ideas and information; you can use them as guides or landmarks, as grounding for copious or chaotic thoughts.

Today, we call these *topoi* "modes of discourse" or "methods of development." We seem to have lost sight, however, of the connection between the process of cognition and the methods of development we employ to describe an event, tell a story, support an idea, or prove a point. We tend to use particular methods of development because our instructor has asked us to rather than remembering the crucial link between thinking and writing. Indeed, too often we see the methods of development—description, narration, process analysis, definition, example and illustration, comparison and contrast, classification and division, cause and effect—as entities that are separate from the process we have gone through to make sense of our ideas.

By appreciating the link between thinking and writing, between the ideas in our minds and the ideas on the page, you can more easily see how methods of development can help readers understand your thought processes. This chapter will examine these methods of development, thus providing you with the tools to bridge the gap between your mind and your audience's.

Methods of Development

Description

When you want to convey to your audience your dominant impression of a person, place, or thing—what you see, smell, taste, hear, or touch—you use description. For example, Heather Menzies, in her essay "When Roots Grow Back into the Earth," uses description to show us what her hands look like after she has been working in soil: "My hands are stiff with cold, and puffed up like pink sausages…. My fingertips burn as they slip from under the unyielding stone." Menzies' description enables her reader to understand the hardship of digging in the soil. As writers, you can articulate abstractions by using vivid sensory details.

A decision you will have to make is whether you want to provide your reader with an objective or a subjective description of your subject. An objective description uses denotative language to record, in words, a photograph-like image, whereas a subjective description relies more heavily on connotative language to create a unique impression of what the writer feels, as Menzies has done in her description of her hands. Compare Menzies' subjective description to an objective description of hands: my hands are stiff and swollen with cold; my fingertips hurt as they try to move a large stone. The decision you make about how much objective and how much subjective description to use will depend on what you want to communicate to your audience. If you want to convey the facts, you will use objective description; if you want to convey emotion, you will use subjective description. Sometimes, you may want to use both.

Narration

When you want to tell your audience about an event that has taken place over time, you use narration, visiting the place in your mind that records events in a sequence. In "The Suit," Norman Doidge refers to this place as "the valley of memory." He visits this valley to express how he felt when he tried on a suit that had belonged to his father, who died when the author was a child:

> I put it on and was immediately amazed by the length of the sleeves, which were almost perfect—just a quarter of an inch too long on the palm. I fingered the edges, my fingers filled with yearning. Years of being unable to sense his bulk, his corporeal worth, faded. I am his size in the shoulders, I thought.

By using narration, you can take your readers back in time to feel what you felt, see what you saw: you can make them experience something important that has happened to you. Not surprisingly, then, description is often used in creating a narrative. In the example above, the concrete, sensory details of the suit help the reader to share Doidge's moment of connection with his father.

The events in a narrative are usually presented in the order in which they actually happened, but writing a story involves more than simply telling your audience about everything you did and saw: you must create meaning by emphasizing the important events. For instance, Doidge does not tell the audience about taking off the clothes he was wearing and putting on the jacket and pants of his father's suit. Instead, he skips those mundane details and jumps right to the important part: how he felt when he had the suit on.

As writers, you have the power to slow down and speed up time so that you can put emphasis on the important details. Flashbacks, time stretches, and time summaries are methods you can use to control time. A flashback is inserted at a moment in the narrative where you think your audience needs background information to understand the significance of the event or the person involved. A time stretch is used to slow down time: you focus on one moment, describing it in detail to give it emphasis. In contrast, a time summary allows you to make generalizations about a long period of time in only one or two sentences, so that the chronology of your narrative will remain clear. Doidge uses all three of these devices in "The Suit."

Process Analysis

When you want to explain how to make an object, complete a task, or explore how a process works, you will want to list the steps in the process and analyze them. While narration and process analysis are both usually arranged chronologically, the main difference is that while a narration is used to reveal the significance of a sequence of events, a process analysis is usually written to investigate or explain a series of steps so that your audience can see their value and follow them easily.

In "The Maker's Eye: Revising Your Own Manuscript," Donald Murray gives writers tips on the steps they should go through to revise their writing. He does not tell his audience about an experience he had revising a piece of his writing; rather, he explains in a general way the principles and process and shows why revision is a valuable part of writing. One of the challenges of process analysis is to do more than take your readers through a series of steps. Like Murray, you must reveal the significance of the process.

Definition

Definition involves more than just looking up a word in the dictionary. When you want to set limits or boundaries on a topic or term in order to explain its meaning to your audience, you are using definition. You can place it into the class to which it belongs and then list its distinctive features, or, if you want to define a single word or concept, you might choose to trace its etymology, or semantic history, in order to understand its current usage.

In "The Remastered Race," Brian Alexander draws attention to the word "eugenics." He warns us that the word is like a "hand grenade from history," and then goes on to argue that rather than being a relic from the past, eugenics is part of our present and future development. Defining this key term allows Alexander to explore the ways in which genetic engineering is evolving, and examine the ethical questions being raised in the biotechnology debate. Definition can be used in a limited way, as Alexander uses it, or it can be expanded to develop an entire essay, which is called extended definition.

Example and Illustration

You may feel that your audience will understand your ideas more easily if you provide them with hypothetical examples or specific details; your audience cannot make sense of your ideas if you provide them with only generalizations. Basil Johnston, in "One Generation from Extinction," supports his contention that non-Native writers write Native stories badly by providing specific examples: "Is it any wonder then that the stories in *Indian Legends of Canada* by E. E. Clark or in *Manabozho* by T. B. Leekley are so bland and devoid of sense. Had the authors known the stories in their 'Indian' sense and flavour, perhaps they might have infused their versions with more wit and substance." While Johnston's examples do not provide irrefutable proof, they do provide evidence that non-Native writers, in these instances, have misrepresented Native culture. Johnston allows his audience to judge the evidence rather than asking them to blindly accept his claim.

Comparison and Contrast

Often this method of development is useful to examine the similarities and differences between two or more objects, concepts, or experiences in order to convey your ideas. In "The Spirit Weeps," for example, Stephen Hume compares the decimation of the First Nations people with acts of brutality committed by Roman conquerors. You should keep in mind that comparisons and contrasts work best when similarities and differences are made explicit. For example, Hume notes that while the Romans ordered every tenth person to be executed, "not one out of every ten, but nine out of every ten people of the Micmac and Maliseet nations died or were killed—a number which makes Caligula seem moderate by comparison." If Hume had simply stated that the destruction of these two First Nations in Canada was similar to or different from what happened in Roman times, his comparison would be less effective.

A special kind of comparison is an analogy, a startling comparison designed to advance an idea. Annie Dillard uses an analogy between weasels and humans in "Living like Weasels" in order to convince her audience that people should passionately strive to fulfill their destinies, no matter what this may involve. Analogies are a useful tool to help you make your ideas memorable.

Classification and Division

If you are considering the questions "How is it structured?" and "What are its components?" you may find yourself creating categories. You may organize multiple items with similar features into one inclusive category, a process referred to as classification, or you may take a single class and divide it into smaller parts, a process referred to as division. For instance, in "Hooked on Trek," Dawn Hanna divides fans of the television show *Star Trek* into three categories: "Trek junkies," "Trekkers," and "Trekkies," but they all belong to the class of *Star Trek* fans. Although creating categories and breaking ideas into parts can sometimes be restrictive, this approach can help your audience comprehend information one piece at a time.

Cause and Effect

You may find you need to answer the questions "Why?" and "So what?" If so, use the method of development that examines the reasons for or consequences of a process, experience, or issue. For example, Dawn Hanna is interested not just in understanding the different kinds of *Star Trek* fans, but in exploring why the show is so popular. She claims that one of the reasons for, or causes of, the show's popularity is that "Most of the time, it is an intelligent TV show." While Hanna explores multiple causes for a single effect—*Star Trek*'s popularity—there are other ways to use this method of development. You may develop a single cause, examine multiple effects, or show a chain of cause/effect relationships. As you can see, cause and effect allows you to communicate complex and important relationships to your audience.

Development for Different Purposes

Now that you are aware of the ways you select particular methods of development to communicate your ideas, consider the ways these methods can be used for different purposes: to express, to inform, or to persuade. For example, you may use narration to express your feelings, as Menzies does when she reminisces about a place that she loves; you may use narration to present information, as Andrew Nikiforuk does when he presents the history of bacteria in order to explain the role that humans play in the creation of epidemics and plague; or you may use narration to sway your audience, as Marni Jackson does when she uses her own experience with children playing with guns and dolls to advocate "the moral value of 'bad' toys." You can use one method of development throughout an essay or combine several to attain your purpose.

However, when used to persuade, methods of development take on more complex functions. While in expressive writing you want to help your readers share your experiences, and in exposition you want to explain a concept or process, in persuasion your principal purpose is to change your readers' minds, to make them see your point of view, or to move them to take action on behalf of your cause. Methods of development can help you to achieve persuasive purposes by allowing you to appeal to readers through what Aristotle calls "*logos*," "*pathos*," and "*ethos*."

Logical Appeal

Logos is an appeal to logic, or reason. When we argue, we want to appear to be rational thinkers, and we can use the methods of development to achieve this. For example, in "Letter from Birmingham Jail," Martin Luther King, Jr. begins his essay by narrating Birmingham's racist treatment of African-Americans in order to explain why the civil rights movement, which he led, was engaging in non-violent protest. By reasoning with his audience, he is able to show the validity of his cause.

Writing that employs reason is often referred to as argument; most persuasive essays are grounded in reason and supplemented by the other appeals. When reasoning, your mind works in two ways. You may begin with a general claim, support it with evidence, and then reach a conclusion: this is called deduction. You may also explore specific evidence, and then draw a conclusion from it: this is called induction. Deduction and induction are ways to take your audience through your thought processes so that you can convince them to agree with your opinions. Often, writers use both patterns of reasoning to appeal to logic, as King does.

Emotional Appeal

Whereas *logos* makes your audience respond at an intellectual level, *pathos* makes your audience respond at an emotional level. Because many issues that writers care deeply about involve feelings, not just thoughts, *pathos* can help you to persuade your audience. For example, while King uses reason throughout his essay, he also uses vivid images, concrete examples, and connotative language to make his audience feel the suffering caused by the inhumane treatment of African-Americans.

Ethical Appeal

Finally, writers may attempt to convince their audience by showing themselves to be people of good sense, good will, and moral integrity; classical rhetoricians called this *ethos*. The strategies you will use to build up your character are numerous and include the material you choose to develop your ideas and the stylistic choices you make. In King's essay, for example, he shows that he has experienced racism first hand: he is knowledgeable about his subject. His humble and eloquent tone and his concern for his audience establish his good will. In addition, King communicates his moral integrity by foregrounding his position as a clergyman who is fighting for a just cause. You should keep in mind that appeals to reason, emotion, and character can also be achieved through patterns of arrangement and through stylistic devices. For instance, a problem-solution arrangement can be used to appeal to logic, and figurative language can be used to appeal to readers' emotions. Please see Chapters 3 and 4 for a further discussion of arrangement and style.

Overview

The essays in this chapter provide some particularly good illustrations of methods of development, but remember that all of the essays throughout *Landmarks* employ these modes. In this chapter, you will witness how the writers use particular methods of development to convey their ideas to their audiences, whether their purpose is to express, inform, or persuade. By considering the thought processes that your mind naturally engages in and the ways you can articulate those ideas on the page, you will find it easier to bridge the gap between yourself and your audience, to begin to experience the thrill of saying what you think.

Brian Alexander is a contributing editor for the magazine Wired, *for which he writes articles on genetic and technological research. He has also written about health and medicine for several publications, including* Esquire *and* The New York Times Magazine.

The Remastered Race

Brian Alexander

You'll hear the debate on *Crossfire* or *NewsHour* or perhaps *The 700 Club.* 1
There'll be coverage in your newspaper, probably accompanied by thundering editorials—ripe with clichés like "slippery slope" and "brave new world." It will sound, in fact, a lot like last year's dustup over stem cells and cloning. But this summer's biotech grudge match will be over designer babies.

Two new books are framing the debate. In *Our Posthuman Future*, heavyweight 2
social and political theorist Francis Fukuyama warns of "class war" and the eventual obliteration of what it means to be human—all as a direct consequence of genetic fiddling. It comes out April 10. The very next day, Gregory Stock's *Redesigning Humans* will hit stores. Stock, director of the UCLA School of Medicine's Program on Medicine, Technology, and Society, celebrates the promise of genetic engineering: longer lifespans, better health, smarter kids.

In the ensuing made-for-TV matchups, expect Fukuyama's followers to toss a 3
hand grenade from history—eugenics. Look for Stock and his supporters to cry foul and bat the word away as a relic from the Third Reich.

Do not get caught up in the rhetoric. The fact is, eugenics is here. Brought to 4
you by high technology and the free market, it looks nothing like a Nazi newsreel. The question isn't "Should we have eugenics?" but rather, "How far should we go?"

This is not an academic question. The technology to create wholesale alter- 5
ations in the genome, and to take charge of human evolution, is already in development.

Take the notion of an artificial chromosome. Chromos, a Vancouver-based 6
biotech firm, is growing artificial chromosomes inside cells the way the Japanese grow pearls in oysters. Chromos farms them, seeding cells with a DNA structure called a centromere. Then its scientists use a machine called a flow cytometer to separate natural chromosomes from artificial ones at a rate of up to 2 million an hour.

Just like natural chromosomes, these artificial ones are made of chromatin, 7
ropes of DNA molecules and proteins. But there's a difference. Natural chromosomes are like a CD issued by a record company. They come prerecorded with genes that tell cells what to do. The artificial chromosomes flowing out of the cytometers at Chromos are blank, ready for anything from the Melvins to Mozart, meaning that Chromos can burn onto them whatever genes it wants.

8   The company says it's not interested in making genetically modified people; it wants to alter animal cells used in the manufacture of drugs. New protein-based pharmaceuticals are often made by stewing cells in big vats. The cells produce the desired drug. Chromos can pack those cells with more copies of the gene that makes the drug, so the cells will produce double or triple their natural amount. Or if you're a person with, say, sickle-cell anemia, artificial chromosomes might be recorded with correct copies of the malfunctioning gene and placed in blood-making cells. When the CD is played, your platelets wouldn't be skinny and cockeyed, but round and fat.

9   "We could modify cells with our chromosomes and have them reside in a dish, a liver, or a muscle and express a therapeutic protein," CEO and president Alistair Duncan says. "That would be very cool."

10   Indeed, but as cool as that would be, the impact of these near-term applications would make barely a ripple compared with what Stock has in mind: an age of genetically enhanced people. Chromos steers clear of such talk, but, Stock asks, why stop at modifying cells in a vat? Why not engineer disease-free life from the get-go?

11   Rob and Suzy Ashley couldn't care less about how artificial chromosomes may change the future. But they're supremely grateful for the reproductive technologies available today. When Rob, a NASA engineer, and Suzy, a former teacher, were first married and settling into life in Florida, they never suspected that their union could produce a tragic genetic combination. Unknowingly, both are carriers of Gaucher's disease, and in the roll of the dice that is reproduction, they passed it to their first child, Jared.

12   Gaucher's disease is a gene-based disorder in which a critical enzyme, controlling the disposal of old blood cells, malfunctions. Some types of Gaucher's can be treated by replacing the enzyme. Jared's could not. The Ashleys' pediatrician first noticed that something was wrong at Jared's six-month checkup. The child's eyes did not quite move with his head. Rob and Suzy had thought that the trait was a cute affectation; they were shocked to hear that he had roughly one year to live. It would be a torturous year. Jared suffered daily throat spasms that left him gasping and coughing, forcing the Ashleys to perform mouth-to-mouth resuscitation two or three times a day to keep him alive.

13   Then, in December 1997, just two months after Jared's diagnosis, Suzy discovered she was pregnant. "'Give me a gun,' that's how I felt," Suzy says. "It was horrible. I was a nervous wreck. I cried and cried over Jared's crib. I could only pray for Jared. I did not have the strength to pray for another baby."

14   Suzy decided to undergo a common prenatal test called chorionic villus sampling. Like amniocentesis, CVS can tell a woman whether the fetus she carries has certain genetic diseases. If the test is positive for any of them, parents are faced with a difficult decision.

15   Such a choice has been available for centuries. The history of eugenics traces at least as far back as the ancient Greco-Roman world, when deformed or weak new-

borns were often killed. Prenatal testing allows a decision to be made as early as 10 weeks after conception. Most women who test positive for diseases like Down's syndrome opt to abort: up to 86 percent, according to one Boston-area study.

In the end, Suzy and Rob did not have to choose. The CVS was negative, and 16
Quentin was born healthy. Jared died almost exactly a year after his diagnosis. The ability of CVS to prevent such tragedies is why society on the whole approves of prenatal testing, why even people like the Ashleys—both devout Catholics—are willing to consider abortion.

Today, the Ashleys are thinking that they may want another child and have 17
looked into a new screening technology called PGD—pre-implantation genetic diagnosis. This is a test that goes beyond CVS and amnio, looking at embryos before they become fetuses. Here's how it works: A couple undergoes in vitro fertilization to make an embryo in a dish. When the embryo has divided into eight cells, one is removed. The DNA in that cell is then analyzed for known disease-causing genetic mutations. Only embryos that are disease-free are implanted in the uterus.

The Catholic church condemns PGD on the same right-to-life grounds as it 18
condemns abortion, but to Suzy Ashley, at least, there is a big difference between not implanting an eight-cell embryo and aborting a growing fetus. Technology has pushed the eugenic moment almost to the point of conception.

To learn about PGD, the Ashleys called on Mark Hughes at Wayne State 19
University in Detroit, who runs one of the world's top PGD labs. One of only a handful of PGD experts, he screens for single-gene disorders like Gaucher's, cystic fibrosis, and Tay-Sachs disease. Another PGD pioneer, Santiago Munne of New Jersey's Saint Barnabas Center for Reproductive Medicine, focuses on chromosomal abnormalities like Down's syndrome. And then there's Yuri Verlinsky, at Chicago's Reproductive Genetics Institute, whose use of PGD to detect early-onset Alzheimer's disease was featured in a February issue of the *Journal of the American Medical Association*.

Munne, Verlinsky, and Hughes—the three tenors of PGD—account for most 20
of the testing on earth. So far, about 1,000 babies worldwide have been born healthy after receiving the PGD stamp of approval, and the numbers are growing exponentially.

The increase is driven in part by the ability of PGD to ferret out many diseases, 21
even disease propensity. Hughes has screened embryos for BRCA1, one of the so-called breast cancer genes, and for the cancer-suppressing p53 gene.

Furthermore, PGD can be used to make a baby with certain sought-after traits. 22
Increasingly, says Hughes, parents are seeking to match their child's tissue types with that of a sibling embryo, conceived for this very purpose. Some children suffer from diseases that can be treated by transfusing umbilical cord blood from a tissue-matched newborn. This practice gained notoriety in 2000 with the birth of Adam Nash..., but Hughes—who consulted with the Nashes—has been doing

it since at least 1995. One of his first cases involved a little girl named Lisa who suffered from SCIDs, the "boy in the bubble" immune disorder. Before taking her on, Hughes sought consultations with ethicists and review boards. Finally, Lisa's impatient father burst into his office. He was fuming. "Our daughter is dying! Give us a break. What's the matter with us loving a new member of our family who can also save the life of our daughter? How could that be bad?" Hughes knew at that moment he had to help. Now he handles two or three such cases per week.

23   While ethicists now generally agree that tissue-matching within families is an acceptable use of the technology, there's less consensus on the issue of using PGD to select for sex. Fukuyama opposes gender selection as dehumanizing. Stock thinks it's a nonissue, arguing that most parents don't care about the sex of their babies and that those who do are better off being able to choose the sex they want.

24   The schism widens further when the discussion turns to the subject of "enhancement"—the use of technology to actually improve the genome instead of merely curing a genetic disease. Stock is in favor, Fukuyama adamantly opposed. This is the crux of the debate: Should eugenics move beyond where it stands right now? Should we take ever-more exquisite control over our evolutionary destinies? The problem is that, while all sides agree enhancement is very close, no one can agree on what qualifies as an enhancement.

25   Theodore Friedmann works out of a small office next to his lab at UC San Diego. When it comes to the implications of genetic manipulation, he has a reputation as one of the most thoughtful scientists in the field: He holds an ethics chair at UCSD and serves on the government's Recombinant DNA Advisory Committee; in addition, he works with the World Anti-Doping Agency, an investigative bureau established by the International Olympic Committee.

26   In 1972, Friedmann coauthored a seminal paper in the journal *Science* that proposed the then-radical idea of inserting new genes into people as a way to treat disease. Friedmann was one of the first to worry that gene therapy could be misused. In that paper, he specifically cited enhancement—"the improvement of human intelligence or other traits"—as a danger.

27   Today, Friedmann worries less: "It's now *not* clear to me that there are these taboos against all kinds of enhancement." In 1972, he says, any kind of enhancement just somehow sounded wrong. But, Friedmann continues, "I don't believe that any longer. Enhancement isn't off the table... eugenics is a very different kettle of fish from what it was 100 years ago."

28   Enhancement is inevitable, he argues, because it is impossible to distinguish it from medicine: "There is no sharp division between disease and nondisease traits." For example, one of many ongoing gene therapy trials is aimed at overcoming a mutation that prevents the proper processing of cholesterol. People with this defect tend to suffer from heart attacks in their thirties. A question that Friedmann and others have asked is, what happens if the therapy works so well

it reduces a patient's "bad" cholesterol from beyond 100, which is about normal, to, say, 65? Is this enhancement? Could somebody who did not have the mutation but simply wanted to eat rib-eye steaks and still avoid cardiovascular disease undergo the treatment? Is this enhancement? Or is it preventive medicine?

Fukuyama doesn't buy this line of reasoning. Government, he says, makes such 29 distinctions every day. Take Ritalin. It's illegal when used as a study aid but not when prescribed to treat attention deficit disorder. "We need a regulatory system to permit therapeutic uses and go slow on the enhancement ones," he says.

And, he continues, we need regulation, because enhancement is just plain wrong. 30 Fukuyama believes that it betrays human nature, destroying something he calls essence or factor X. Start mucking around with our genes, and we'll lose whatever it is that makes us human. Leon Kass, the chair of the White House's Council on Bioethics, seconds Fukuyama (who also sits on the council), calling the argument "the wisdom of repugnance." Kass' commission, which meets almost every month, is expected to issue its first official findings this summer. The report will address human cloning. For now, Kass, Fukuyama, and their allies have the president's ear.

But there are other voices struggling to be heard. A small but growing faction 31 argues that enhancement is the most human of all instincts. Ted Peters, a theologian at the Pacific Lutheran Theological Seminary, thinks it is our job. He calls human beings "created cocreators." God made us, he reasons, but the rest is up to us. "We humans are responsible for making the world a better place, and technology is one means whereby we can do it.... My approach is a free-market eugenics."

Both Friedmann and Peters see potential dangers, but Peters rejects appeals to 32 the divine plan, saying, "I know of no theological reason why anyone would say that God has deemed DNA sacred."

Stock, an enhancement radical, argues that we have been tinkering with our 33 own evolution for a long time now. "Every intervention we make that allows a person with diabetes to have a larger family, or to have a family at all instead of dying young, has a big impact," he says. Enhancement technology is no different, except that it would work better and faster. So why not get under the hood of the genome, Stock argues, and fix it—even soup it up—and not just for every new generation, but for all time?

Stock is proposing a type of genetic engineering in which the changes we make 34 to our DNA are passed on to our kids, and our kids' kids, and so on down the line. But such meddling is so morally fraught that, before any gene therapy trial is approved, the federal government demands assurances that such changes will not occur. The medical consensus is dead set against creating heritable genetic alterations. Genetic experiments affecting somatic (body) cells are OK, but those that affect sperm or eggs—germ cells—are not. Yet here Stock is, advocating germline engineering.

He has been cheerleading for the practice for about five years and has always 35 been a lonely voice. Not only are there practical considerations, such as how to conduct a safety test of a technology that might not play out for generations, there is the ethical question: Should we be making medical choices for people who have not yet even been conceived?

36   To Stock, germline engineering is no more morally confounding than PGD. "We are making choices about the genetic constitutions of our children right now," he says, "and we are doing it in more and more sophisticated ways. Soon these will include actual genetic manipulations."

37   Recently, Stock has gotten a lot less lonely. A number of scientists are now willing to talk openly about the idea of gene therapy on embryos or fetuses. As they see it, therapy on embryos could be more effective than postnatal therapy. Gene therapy at that early, embryonic stage would almost certainly create germline changes.

38   Perhaps the most promising germline engineering technology is Chromos' artificial chromosomes. Not only can they carry huge genetic payloads, they can be wired with on-off switches to permit parents, or even the genetically engineered children themselves, to activate the genes they carry, thus solving the moral dilemma of imposing parental will on the unborn.

39   Such on-off switches already exist and are routinely deployed in lab animals like rabbits and monkeys. Of course, introducing an extra chromosome could prove dicey. After all, a spare chromosome in humans causes Down's syndrome, though scientists theorize that it's the genes on the extra chromosome that actually produce the defects. Chromos bred a mouse, Lucy, with an artificial chromosome. She passed it to her pups and they, like Lucy, were normal.

40   It's easy to imagine the possibilities for making genetically modified people, whether with artificial chromosomes or some other technology. A double helping of genes that boost memory, intelligence, longevity, or strength could be on the menu soon. That might seem scary to us. But will it seem scary to our kids?

41   Could it be that in 20 years artificial chromosomes become the tool that turns us into Ted Peters' "cocreators"? That's what Stock thinks. For him, there's no slippery slope. Instead, he says, we've been on a "slippery sidewalk" for thousands of years, not uncontrollably sliding toward a genetic dystopia but doing what we've always done, whether it's called eugenics or some less-loaded term. "The whole argument against enhancement denies the reality. It's what we want. We want to be healthier. We want to be stronger. We want to be smarter. We want to live longer. It's obvious." ◆

2002

Explorations

- What does the term "eugenics" mean to you? How have attitudes towards eugenics changed over the last 100 years? How do you think attitudes will change in the next 20 years?

- Alexander raises the following ethical question: "Should we be making medical choices for people who have not yet even been conceived?" Discuss your thoughts about this question.

Annie Dillard, born in 1945, grew up in Pittsburgh and earned an M.A. in English from Hollins College in Virginia. She has published nine books, including both poetry and a novel, but is best known as an essayist; she won a Pulitzer Prize for general non-fiction for her first collection of essays, Pilgrim at Tinker Creek. *She is currently an adjunct professor of English and a writer-in-residence at Wesleyan University in Connecticut.*

Living like Weasels

Annie Dillard

A weasel is wild. Who knows what he thinks? He sleeps in his underground den, his tail draped over his nose. Sometimes he lives in his den for two days without leaving. Outside, he stalks rabbits, mice, muskrats, and birds, killing more bodies than he can eat warm, and often dragging the carcasses home. Obedient to instinct, he bites his prey at the neck, either splitting the jugular vein at the throat or crunching the brain at the base of the skull, and he does not let go. One naturalist refused to kill a weasel who was socketed into his hand deeply as a rattlesnake. The man could in no way pry the tiny weasel off, and he had to walk half a mile to water, the weasel dangling from his palm, and soak him off like a stubborn label.

And once, says Ernest Thompson Seton°—once, a man shot an eagle out of the sky. He examined the eagle and found the dry skull of a weasel fixed by the jaws to his throat. The supposition is that the eagle had pounced on the weasel and the weasel swiveled and bit as instinct taught him, tooth to neck, and nearly won. I would like to have seen that eagle from the air a few weeks or months before he was shot: was the whole weasel still attached to his feathered throat, a fur pendant? Or did the eagle eat what he could reach, gutting the living weasel with his talons before his breast, bending his beak, cleaning the beautiful airborne bones?

I have been reading about weasels because I saw one last week. I startled a weasel who startled me, and we exchanged a long glance.

Twenty minutes from my house, through the woods by the quarry and across the highway, is Hollins Pond, a remarkable piece of shallowness, where I like to go at sunset and sit on a tree trunk. Hollins Pond is also called Murray's Pond; it covers two acres of bottomland near Tinker Creek with six inches of water and six thousand lily pads. In winter, brown-and-white steers stand in the middle of it, merely dampening their hooves; from the distant shore they look like miracle itself, complete with miracle's nonchalance. Now, in summer, the steers are gone. The water lilies have blossomed and spread to a green horizontal plane that is

terra firma to plodding blackbirds, and tremulous ceiling to black leeches, cray-
fish, and carp.

5   This is, mind you, suburbia. It is a five-minute walk in three directions to rows
of houses, though none is visible here. There's a 55 mph highway at one end of
the pond, and a nesting pair of wood ducks at the other. Under every bush is a
muskrat hole or a beer can. The far end is an alternating series of fields and
woods, fields and woods, threaded everywhere with motorcycle tracks—in whose
bare clay wild turtles lay eggs.

6   So. I had crossed the highway, stepped over two low barbed-wire fences, and
traced the motorcycle path in all gratitude through the wild rose and poison ivy
of the pond's shoreline up into high grassy fields. Then I cut down through the
woods to the mossy fallen tree where I sit. This tree is excellent. It makes a dry,
upholstered bench at the upper, marshy end of the pond, a plush jetty raised from
the thorny shore between a shallow blue body of water and a deep blue body of
sky.

7   The sun had just set. I was relaxed on the tree trunk, ensconced in the lap of
lichen, watching the lily pads at my feet tremble and part dreamily over the
thrusting path of a carp. A yellow bird appeared to my right and flew behind me.
It caught my eye; I swiveled around—and the next instant, inexplicably, I was
looking down at a weasel, who was looking up at me.

8   Weasel! I'd never seen one wild before. He was ten inches long, thin as a curve,
a muscled ribbon, brown as fruitwood, soft-furred, alert. His face was fierce, small
and pointed as a lizard's; he would have made a good arrowhead. There was just
a dot of chin, maybe two brown hairs' worth, and then the pure white fur began
that spread down his underside. He had two black eyes I didn't see, any more
than you see a window.

9   The weasel was stunned into stillness as he was emerging from beneath an
enormous shaggy wild rose bush four feet away. I was stunned into stillness
twisted backward on the tree trunk. Our eyes locked, and someone threw away
the key.

10   Our look was as if two lovers, or deadly enemies, met unexpectedly on an over-
grown path when each had been thinking of something else: a clearing blow to
the gut. It was also a bright blow to the brain, or a sudden beating of brains, with
all the charge and intimate grate of rubbed balloons. It emptied our lungs. It
felled the forest, moved the fields, and drained the pond; the world dismantled
and tumbled into that black hole of eyes. If you and I looked at each other that
way, our skulls would split and drop to our shoulders. But we don't. We keep our
skulls. So.

11   He disappeared. This was only last week, and already I don't remember what
shattered the enchantment. I think I blinked, I think I retrieved my brain from
the weasel's brain, and tried to memorize what I was seeing, and the weasel felt

the yank of separation, the careening splash-down into real life and the urgent current of instinct. He vanished under the wild rose. I waited motionless, my mind suddenly full of data and my spirit with pleadings, but he didn't return.

Please do not tell me about "approach-avoidance conflicts." I tell you I've been   *12* in that weasel's brain for sixty seconds, and he was in mine. Brains are private places, muttering through unique and secret tapes—but the weasel and I both plugged into another tape simultaneously, for a sweet and shocking time. Can I help it if it was a blank?

What goes on in his brain the rest of the time? What does a weasel think   *13* about? He won't say. His journal is tracks in clay, a spray of feathers, mouse blood and bone: uncollected, unconnected, loose-leaf, and blown.

I would like to learn, or remember, how to live. I come to Hollins Pond not so   *14* much to learn how to live as, frankly, to forget about it. That is, I don't think I can learn from a wild animal how to live in particular—shall I suck warm blood, hold my tail high, walk with my footprints precisely over the prints of my hands?—but I might learn something of mindlessness, something of the purity of living in the physical senses and the dignity of living without bias or motive. The weasel lives in necessity and we live in choice, hating necessity and dying at the last ignobly in its talons. I would like to live as I should, as the weasel lives as he should. And I suspect that for me the way is like the weasel's: open to time and death painlessly, noticing everything, remembering nothing, choosing the given with a fierce and pointed will.

I missed my chance. I should have gone for the throat. I should have lunged for   *15* that streak of white under the weasel's chin and held on, held on through mud and into the wild rose, held on for a dearer life. We could live under the wild rose wild as weasels, mute and uncomprehending. I could very calmly go wild. I could live two days in the den, curled, leaning on mouse fur, sniffing bird bones, blinking, licking, breathing musk, my hair tangled in the roots of grasses. Down is a good place to go, where the mind is single. Down is out, out of your ever-loving mind and back to your careless senses. I remember muteness as a pro-longed and giddy fast, where every moment is a feast of utterance received. Time and events are merely poured, unremarked, and ingested directly, like blood pulsed into my gut through a jugular vein. Could two live that way? Could two live under the wild rose, and explore by the pond, so that the smooth mind of each is as everywhere present to the other, and as received and as unchallenged, as falling snow?

We could, you know. We can live any way we want. People take vows of   *16* poverty, chastity, and obedience—even of silence—by choice. The thing is to stalk your calling in a certain skilled and supple way, to locate the most tender and live spot and plug into that pulse. This is yielding, not fighting. A weasel doesn't "attack" anything; a weasel lives as he's meant to, yielding at every moment to the perfect freedom of single necessity.

17   I think it would be well, and proper, and obedient, and pure, to grasp your one necessity and not let it go, to dangle from it limp wherever it takes you. Then even death, where you're going no matter how you live, cannot you part. Seize it and let it seize you up aloft even, till your eyes burn out and drop; let your musky flesh fall off in shreds, and let your very bones unhinge and scatter, loosened over fields, over fields and woods, lightly, thoughtless, from any height at all, from as high as eagles. ◆

1982

Glossary

Ernest Thompson Seton: (1860–1946) English-born American naturalist well-known for his book of stories and paintings, *Wild Animals I Have Known* (1898).

Explorations

* Have you ever encountered a person whom you immediately envied or admired? If so, how did you react? Did he/she inspire you to change the way you live?

* Do you have any role models? What effects do role models such as TV celebrities and sports stars have on the public?

Norman Doidge, born in 1954, is a poet, medical doctor, psychiatrist, and psychoanalyst who is head of long-term psychotherapy for the University of Toronto Psychotherapy Program. He is also a member of the Research Faculty, Center for Psychoanalytic Training and Research at Columbia University in New York. He has presented his own psychiatric research at the White House and around the world. Dr. Doidge has won four National Magazine Awards, including the President's Medal for the best non-fiction article published in Canada, for his conversation with the Nobel Prize winner Saul Bellow. In the past, he has edited Books in Canada: The Canadian Review of Books. *He writes frequently for the* National Post, *and his work has appeared in* Time *magazine,* Reader's Digest, Saturday Night, *and the* Weekly Standard *and has been translated into French, German, Spanish, and Hebrew. "The Suit" won a CBC Radio/*Saturday Night *Literary Award for Best Personal Essay and a National Magazine Award.*

The Suit

Norman Doidge

This is a true story about a suit. The suit has lived in my Uncle Henry's closet for thirty-three years. It is my dead father's suit.

Though never on display, its exact whereabouts is never in doubt. Whenever weather changes, or soldiers are imagined, it is always his brother's suit that comes first to Uncle Henry's mind. It has to do with refusing to give up. The suit has been there since my father went to get an elevator, waited for the door to open, and stepped into an elevator shaft that turned out to be empty and fell to the bottom. He lay there unconscious for a day until he was discovered. His head was smashed and his brain stem injured. My father, a Holocaust survivor, died in Toronto two days later at the age of thirty-three. Uncle Henry was visiting from New York at the time, looking into setting up a furniture business with my father. I was seventeen months then, my brother two months. Now, in my thirties myself, I think of the empty suit.

Perhaps I saw the awe-inspiring but silent suit on its hanger six or seven times. I can't remember my father wearing it, and I don't think I can remember my father. But I remember the suit.

Where there are no readily retrievable memories, substitutes must suffice. I knew him as one knows the numbness of the phantom limb which out of nowhere speaks out to say "I am here, but I am missing"; I had the indelible knowledge that a number was tattooed on his arm° but didn't know the number; I knew stories of him telling stories to survive and his life-giving gift of the gab; heard others hum the songs he was always singing; I remember standing as a child of four or five with my mother and brother, staring at his tombstone, and I knew

that the name on the stone was not his real name, Leon Greenspan, but the alias
that he used to escape and that he became saddled with after the war. And yes, I
knew of his suit.

5   But Henry had lots of solid memories of him, and the suit was just the beginning. "There are no brothers now like there were then," Henry said in his thick
Polish accent, which was either lilting or severe, his eyebrows quivering as he
turned to the closet every third or fourth of my almost yearly visits to New York.
In Toronto, I heard only stories of him after the war, his brief happy years after
the Holocaust. Such stories were always told in the strained voices of adults looking at a child who has lost his parent.

6   Arriving in Ontario from Europe, a wandering polyglot who had become
accustomed in concentration camps to physical labour, Leon took the first job he
was offered, as a lumberjack in the north. With his earnings he soon made his
way to Toronto. He was a "greener," emerging from a line of immigrants, when my
mother met him and soon fell in love. When she herself died in her mid-forties,
I had nowhere near mined her memory of him.

7   But in New York there was Uncle Henry who knew him during the war and
before. Hence many trips. Always the discussion turned to the suit. "I would not
trade this suit for anything of any kind, and I would not trade this suit for my
life," said Henry each time he pulled it out. And he meant it.

8   First Henry had two brothers, then only one, then only a suit. When the Nazis
invaded Poland, my father attempted to smuggle his ten-year-old brother, Arthur,
out of the city of Cracow, and then out of the country, by paying a Polish woman
to hide Arthur until he got him Hungarian papers and a passport. For more
money, she turned the Jewish child over to the Gestapo. They murdered him.
Such baggage Leon carried with him when he was arrested in 1939 and sent to
Heinrich Himmler Prison in Lublin, because he had the same last name,
Greenspan, as the man who had assassinated Ernst vom Rath, a German embassy
worker, in Paris. Snippets of the story of the two surviving brothers, and my
father's experiences in the Plaszów° camp, then Auschwitz° from the middle of
1942 to 1944, emerged. Then Mauthausen° and Gusen° and Melk.° Uncle
Henry asked him, "How did you survive in Auschwitz for two years, when people frequently didn't last there for two weeks?" "Luck, and people liked me," said
Leon. Stories that could be told were buried in stories that could not be. Then
the unspeakable stories came out, in spurts of agonizing pain, in these visits to
New York. Every third or fourth time Henry would go to the closet where the
suit was.

9   Stories of disappearance, and stories of escape. Sitting quietly at the table on
each visit was Grandma Golda, her sad, beautiful face finely lined and swirled,
stamped with the fingerprint of her fate. Occasionally she would have a flashback
to the camps, and the family would remind her that this was New York, 1980. At
the age of sixteen Grandma Golda travelled alone from Poland to Italy to buy

corals for the family business, reciting Dante's *Divine Comedy°* in Italian on the train. As she recounted the story, she would begin singing the Italian and her face would light up, as though the musical verses were enough of a cue to transport her back to the adventures of her youth.

In her mid-fifties, Golda, her youngest son already murdered and her husband's whereabouts unknown, was forced onto another train and when she got off she found herself standing face to face with Dr. Josef Mengele° in Auschwitz. In that fateful moment she was able to overcome vain hopes, and ascertain what the Nazis really had planned for those in the line to the left which was filled with the old, the grey, and the weak. She reasoned that, no matter what Mengele told her, she would go into the line to the right where the younger Jews were being directed. Despite his instructions, she moved quietly to the right. In this way she escaped the crematoria the first time. She quickly reckoned that further survival would require that she convey the impression of eternal youth. Her Italian came in handy when she realized that one of the camp's doctors, an Italian (also a Jewish prisoner), had access in the infirmary to purple cleaning crystals with which she concocted a black hairdye that she used herself, shared with inmates, or exchanged for food. Grandma Golda died at the age of ninety-six, with a full head of white hair.

In Austria, towards the end of the war, my father chanced upon and seized his ex-commandant who was in disguise, trying to escape at the train station. The man, who had killed thousands of Jews, offered him money not to turn him in. "But your father said that won't be necessary and he forced the man's head onto the track and broke his neck with his foot like that." Henry slammed down his foot. Silence. The suit.

Today when I was visiting, Uncle Henry was proud because he had recently lost twenty pounds. But all topics still led to my father. "Your father became heavy." I thought of the dashing pictures of him several years after the liberation. "Oh yes, he put on a lot of weight in the year after he married your mother," said Henry as he turned to the back of the room, "a lot of weight."

I followed, under the usual spell. He pulled out the suit and held it out like a newborn baby. "He always went to the finest tailor." "Exactly how tall was he?" I asked, with respect to the suit. "Your height, about," said Henry.

An idea was forming in my head which seemed, after all these years of awe and fear, not sacrilegious. It seemed just the thing to do. With the possible exception of his broken watch and his tefillin, I had, at that point in my conscious memory, never touched an article of my father's, let alone his clothing. The broken watch seemed outside of time, the tefillin a binding to another world. Each time I had touched them they had seemed to disappear into a hole in the valley of memory. But somehow the suit that had enveloped him seemed different: it was a menacing presence. Until today. The uncanny sense that Uncle Henry had been showing me something forbidden to me faded. Here was a man's brother, showing his

10

11

12

13

14

nephew who couldn't remember his father, his father's rather expensive, rather unworn suit. He was conducting the ceremony quite beautifully, linking me to my rightful inheritance, sewing together generations torn asunder.

15   "Should I try it on?"

16   The question that for years I would have thought obscene came out loud and clear. "Why not?" said Henry. "Have you... ever..." I began. "Of course," he said as he unbuttoned it and slipped it off the hanger, "many times."

17   I put it on and was immediately amazed by the length of the sleeves, which were almost perfect—just a quarter of an inch too long on the palm. I fingered the edges, my fingers filled with yearning. Years of being unable to sense his bulk, his corporeal worth, faded. I am his size in the shoulders, I thought. Therefore, he is my father. QED. And the familiar girth. I too bloat up like this if I don't watch myself. Another proof for the existence. I am his son. I *am* a Greenspan. Surely, given the chance, he would have lost the weight, had the suit taken in. My God he must have been a forty-four, no, six, no, eight! In deep dark brown. My colour. Did we have the same colouring? I had always assumed he was fair, like my brother. I was tugged by a force to the mirror to see myself in the dazzling suit, hoping that Henry would not for a moment think this avarice, that I wanted the suit for myself, but would realize, as one who loved the suit, that this was beyond a great privilege. It was a necessary rite, even a responsibility.

18   And as I began thinking that this could last forever, me locked in the suit, as I began to look towards the corner in the closet, and thought of drawing its sleeves sleepily off my arms, I half heard Uncle Henry say, "I had to have that suit cleaned three times." But I was not listening until he said, "Your father died in that suit."

19   It seemed all over. Now I was dazed. Marked for death. Henry in the background talking about how the bloodstains wouldn't come out at first washing, while I was realizing my worst fear about the cracked face of his watch, my eyes racing from the broken two buttons on the sleeve to the collar near where his limp head had lain, Leon, me, someone in this suit at the bottom of the elevator shaft groaning over Tisha B'av,° July 29, 1955, until he was found, comatose... but by now I was dizzy—what had I joined? for forever? having so recklessly put my hands through the holes of the sleeves! Strangling in the grip of the perfect fit my heart pounded. "His heart was very strong," said Henry. "His brain was dead but his heart wouldn't die for two days." O God, I thought, Henry was terrifying the life out of me! Why? I had only wanted a moment to make up for a lifetime without the weight of his hand on my shoulder. (In an age that belittles its patrimony, trust the fatherless to seek out and cherish the weight of a man.)

20   But as I looked up, I did not see in Henry's eyes the ambush I had feared, so much as I realized, as my heart began to slow, that this peculiar, uncanny ceremony conveyed weight. Henry seemed off in the corner of the room mumbling, but actually he was, as he was typically, about three inches from my dissociated

face. Henry was saying something that would seem ghoulish, but which was, if one knew what he knew, an attempt at reassurance; giving himself through me a speech which said that my father's heart lasted, long after his brain had died. With tears in his eyes he was saying, "For several whole days, though his brain had been destroyed, his heart refused to die." Torn from the man we both loved, torn after all those losses, something in us could last. It had to do with not giving up. I saw all this written on his tormented avuncular face. I lowered my head, and wept. This too was a story of survival. This was not a story of lightness, absence, or that which cannot be. This was a story about a suit. ◆

1994

Glossary

a number was tattooed on his arm: refers to the identification number tattooed on the inside forearm of every prisoner in Nazi concentration camps.

Plaszów, Auschwitz, Mauthausen, Gusen, and Melk: the names of Nazi death camps in Eastern Europe. Plaszów and Auschwitz were located in Poland; Mauthausen, Gusen, and Melk were in Austria.

Dante's *Divine Comedy*: the Italian poet Dante Alighieri's (1265–1321) masterpiece, completed the year of his death, telling the story of the poet's epic journey through hell, purgatory, and on to paradise.

Dr. Josef Mengele: (1911–1979) the Nazi doctor at Auschwitz, known as the Angel of Death, who oversaw the operation of the gas chambers and conducted medical experiments on many of the camp's prisoners.

Tisha B'av: in Judaism, a traditional day of mourning.

Explorations

- Do you know any Holocaust survivors, war veterans, or victims of political persecution? If so, what do you know about their stories of struggle, disappearance, and/or escape?

- How can you understand what soldiers and civilians went through during wartime if you have not experienced war yourself? Is it possible? Why or why not?

Dawn Hanna was born in 1959 in California and holds both Canadian and American citizenship. She earned a B.A. in film studies at the University of British Columbia in 1983, and is currently a recreation editor for The Vancouver Sun. *Hanna also writes for several magazines on a freelance basis, and has written two hiking guidebooks titled* Best Hikes and Walks in Southwestern British Columbia *(1997) and* Easy Hikes and Walks in Southwestern British Columbia *(2002).*

Hooked on Trek

Dawn Hanna

1   First, let me confess I am a *Star Trek* junkie. My heart beats just a little faster when I hear William Shatner intone the *Star Trek* mantra: "Space. The final frontier..."

2   I get a little giddy every time my favorite episode—*Mirror, Mirror*, where a transportation malfunction sends Kirk, Sulu, Uhura and Scotty into a savage mirror universe—comes on. I will even admit to keeping Saturday nights sacrosanctly clear, so I can watch all three *Star Trek* shows back to back (*Star Trek* at 5 p.m., *Star Trek: Deep Space Nine* at 6, and *Star Trek: The Next Generation* at 7.)

3   It all started with the original series. The year was 1968 and I was living with my dad and my brother in Laguna Beach, Calif. That would have made me nine precocious years of age.

4   Not only did I watch all the shows. I wrote scripts for *Star Trek*, usually with a role in which I could star. Inevitably, I was Captain Kirk's daughter. Inevitably, I got myself into some intergalactic trouble—you know, kidnapped by Klingons or forced to wed some pagan alien—and Captain (Dad) Kirk, along with the other 400 crew members of the USS Enterprise, would have to rescue me. I also designed costumes I would wear. The outfits were very mod, very mini, very '60s and, oh, yes, they had matching go-go boots.

5   Later in my teen years, my devotion to all things Trek began to exhibit the first signs of serious addiction. Every day at 3 p.m. one of the local channels showed re-runs of the Enterprise crew boldly going where they had all gone before. I raced home from school every day. I kept a list of each show's title—*Spock's Brain, Dagger of the Mind, The Doomsday Machine*—and how many times I'd seen it. I developed a crush on Pavel. You might know him better as Mr. Chekhov. I don't know, maybe it was the accent ("Meester Spock, the sensors are picking up a wery, wery big planet directly ahead)". During my university days, I went cold turkey. I stopped watching *Star Trek*. Mostly because I didn't own a TV. For years, I stayed away from the re-runs.

6   I did, however, play Lieut. Uhura in a University of B.C. Film Society production. (We overcame the ethnic differences by making our Uhura Swedish

instead of Swahili.) Gene Roddenberry, who created the actual series, saw the short film. He liked it. In fact, in a letter, he singled out my performance as *Trek*-calibre.

When *Star Trek: The Next Generation* started up in 1987, I couldn't bring myself to watch. It would have felt too much like betrayal to the old crew. 7

Then, a couple of years ago, I dated a man who got me hooked again. This time 8 to the 24th-century version. Without going into too much detail, let's just say I got it bad this time. Not that I started writing scripts or designing costumes or— heaven, forbid—attending *Star Trek* conventions. But I knew I was in trouble when *Star Trek* entered my dreams. I am somewhat embarrassed to admit it—but that is the first step: admitting that I have a problem—but... I had an erotic dream about Lieut. Worf. (All I remember now is that he growled at me. What happened after that remains in my *Star Trek* memories.)

Compared to other folks, however, my *Star Trek* affliction is nothing. The 9 equivalent of a minor rash to an all-consuming cancer. With *Star Trek* I have decided, there are three kinds of devotees: *Trek* junkies, like myself, are those who have a minor addiction to the series and their characters. Usually, this is a guilty pleasure, one not made public except to close friends and family. We don't own *Trek* paraphernalia—T shirts, coffee mugs, collector plates.

Those are the Trekkers. These folks might write letters to their favorite actors. 10 Or stand in line for a couple of hours to collect an autograph. They have a *Star Trek* library. They buy tricorders and phasers and communicators. They know almost everything you ever wanted to know about all the *Star Trek* characters, and the actors who portray those characters. But these folks can still talk about *Star Trek* as a television show and they still are able to distinguish this universe from the *Trek* universe.

Then there are the hard core Trekkies—the ones who get all the media atten- 11 tion, the ones most folks think of when they think of *Star Trek*. The ones who speak Klingon at *Trek* cocktail parties, who have the technical manuals for the *Trek* ships. The people who are truly living in another space-time continuum.

What, you are asking yourself, what is it that *Star Trek* does to relatively nor- 12 mal human beings? What is it that transforms nice, intelligent, capable people into cult-like devotees of a television show?

I cannot hope to answer for all of *Star Trek*dom. I can only offer my own the- 13 ories. First, I will offer no apologies for my infatuation with the original series. I was a child when I first saw it—that should be explanation enough. Still, I do remember it as a show which dealt with the big questions and topical issues of the time: whether it was Mr. Spock dealing with a Vulcan-bashing crew member or Capt. Kirk coping with his savage-animal self. Or Dr. McCoy facing the prospect of life with a terminal disease.

As an adult, I find the original *Star Trek* hokey but lovable, like a favorite 14 uncle who still tries to fool his adult niece with the pulling-a-quarter-out-of-the-ear joke. But *Star Trek: The Next Generation* (or *TNG*, as it's known in *Trek* jargon) really does have its merits.

15   Most of the time, it is an intelligent TV show. I know that's usually an oxymoron, but which other TV series sets itself to questioning the nature of time and space, discussing quantum fluctuations or making you confront your worst fears about yourself?

16   Which other major TV character reads Homeric hymns in the original Greek, quotes passages from Shakespeare and plays Mozart flute concertos? Captain Jean-Luc Picard does. And where else can you see Stephen Hawking,° Albert Einstein° and Sir Isaac Newton° play poker? On the Enterprise.

17   Sure, not all *TNG* episodes are worthy. My least favorite is the oddly-titled *Justice*, when the Enterprise visits the planet of the intergalactic bimbos, peopled by nubile blonds who wear tiny bits of Kleenex over their naughty bits. But at least there was a certain equality: both men and women were bimbos.

18   Nonetheless, at its best, some *TNG* episodes make me think. Whether it's about the concept of an infinite number of possible realities at any given time. Or the possibility that time is not simply linear. Or what it is that determines a living being—intelligence? reproductive capability? organic matter?

19   There is also the allure of a civilization which has overcome unsolvable problems such as war, poverty and discrimination. And, okay, I covet the holodeck, the replicators and the fully functional (nudge, nudge, wink, wink) Lt. Commander Data.

20   But more than anything else, what makes *Star Trek* so appealing is that it's a society of universal acceptance. Everyone belongs. It's the cosmic equivalent of one big happy family. You're an ugly alien? So what, you still belong to the family. You're a long way from home? Doesn't matter, because as Picard says in one episode: "No one is alone on the Enterprise." You're a dysfunctional misfit? Hey, welcome on board the good ship NCC-1701D.

21   The other thing about *Star Trek: TNG* is that it is more than science fiction. It's the equivalent of modern mythology. And it performs the same functions as myths always have—as guidelines, as metaphors, as clues to the potential of human life.

22   According to the late mythologist and philosopher Joseph Campbell, myths are the stories of our search for truth, for meaning, for significance. They are stories about life experience; stories about the wisdom of life. In *The Power of Myth*, Campbell describes the four functions of myth: "The first is the mystical function—realizing what a wonder the universe is, and what a wonder you are and experiencing awe before this mystery. Myth opens the world to the dimension of mystery.

23   "The second is a cosmological dimension, the dimension with which science is concerned—showing you what the shape of the universe is.

24   "The third function is the sociological one—supporting and validating a certain social order—the laws of life as it should be in the good society. The fourth

function of myth is the pedagogical function, of how to live a human lifetime under any circumstances. Myths can teach you that."

Star Trek: TNG fulfills all the criteria. It takes us into the mystery of the uni-   25
verse (even if it is mostly the realm of the imagination) and gives us contact with many of its phenomena—muons and quasars, neutrinos and neurotransmitters.

It serves as a blueprint of an idealistic future society (remember, tolerance and   26
understanding for all). And it serves as an example of how to live life. ("Seize the moment," Picard tells his imaginary daughter in one episode. "Make now always the most precious time.")

This does not mean one can find the answers to the universe in *Star Trek*. It is,   27
after all, a TV show, not a set of holy scriptures. But at its best *Star Trek* is a lit-erature of the spirit, as Campbell called mythology. And as with other forms of fiction, it has stories to relate, perspectives to share, ideas to ponder.

"Myths and dreams come from the same place," Campbell once said. "They   28
come from realizations of some kind that have then to find expression in sym-bolic form. And the only myth that is going to be worth thinking about in the immediate future is one that is talking about the planet... When you see the earth from the moon, you don't see any divisions there of nations or states. This might be the symbol for the new mythology to come."

Sounds an awful lot like *Star Trek*. ◆   29

                                                                                1994

Glossary

Stephen Hawking: (b. 1942) English theoretical physicist and author of *A Brief History of Time* whose theories of exploding black holes and space-time dimen-sions draw on relativity theory and quantum mechanics.

Albert Einstein: (1876–1955) German-born, Swiss-educated American physicist best known for his 1905 theory of relativity.

Sir Isaac Newton: (1642–1727) English mathematician and philosopher. Newton first developed the laws of gravity.

Explorations

- Do you know anyone who is hooked on *Star Trek*? What category does he/she fall under: Trek junkie, Trekker, or Trekkie?

- Are you a regular viewer of a particular television show or series? If so, why? What is so appealing about the storylines and/or the characters?

Stephen Hume was born in 1947 in the United Kingdom. An award-winning writer and journalist, he has published six books of poetry, essays, and natural history. His books include Ghost Camps, *winner of a 1989 Alberta Writer's Guild Literary Award, and* Bush Telegraph: Discovering the Pacific Province, *winner of a B.C. 2000 book award. He currently resides in Vancouver, where he is a columnist and senior writer for* The Vancouver Sun.

The Spirit Weeps

Stephen Hume

1   In anticipation of the high international profile Canada would achieve during the 1988 Winter Olympics in Calgary, organizing officials planned a dazzling constellation of parallel events intended to showcase the richness and diversity of our national culture. Writers, poets, musicians and painters were to celebrate the Greek ideal of mind and body with demonstrations of their creative prowess to match the physical performances of athletes. As part of this program, Alberta's Glenbow Institute, backed by the major corporate sponsorship of an oil industry giant, Shell Canada Limited, began preparations for what was to be the most complex and complete display of the art of Canadian aboriginal peoples in world history.

2   For five years before the Olympic Games began, a committee of six distinguished scholars, each bringing specialized knowledge from one of the six cultural regions of aboriginal Canada, began planning the exhibition. The Glenbow is itself a world-class museum and archive, particularly with reference to the culture and ethnology of Plains Indians. But it was clear from the beginning that the scope and magnitude of the exhibition planned could not be mounted with the resources of the Glenbow alone. Starting with the commitment of $600,000 in seed money from the Olympic Organizing Committee and $1,100,000 from Shell, the curatorial scholars began taking inventory of where Canadian aboriginal artifacts might be located outside Canada and subsequently borrowed for exhibition before national and international audiences. By the time they were finished, the committee had scoured more than one hundred and fifty museums and private collections across twenty foreign countries and arranged the display of more than six hundred artifacts.

3   The show was staged in two segments. The first took place at the Glenbow itself, preceding and coinciding with the Olympic Games; the second, in association with the new National Museum of Civilization, was mounted three months later in Ottawa, using the former premises of Canada's national art gallery for the eastern venue.

4   The Spirit Sings proved a curator's tour de force. The committee had mounted a show of stunning power and intensity. All the displays resonated with aesthetic

genius and a deep sense of spiritual place. Yet this exhibition of the artistic traditions of Canada's first people, so wonderful in the hermetic context of ethnological display, was also an act of national hypocrisy so shocking as to border on the
obscene. It triggered deep anger and hurt among the very people it purported to
celebrate and raised profound questions regarding the integrity of Canada's social
and intellectual conscience.

Art cannot be detached from the social and historical matrix in which it orig-   5
inates, however much museum curators might desire to do so in the interests of
neat classification and compartmentalized analysis, and however much the state
might seize upon it as an opportunity for shameless propagandizing and outright
lying. And that was the great irony of The Spirit Sings. Mounted in celebration
of our first peoples, it used their art to tell the world a fundamental lie about our
national concern for their rights and well-being. The exhibits displayed in The
Spirit Sings and the powerful controversy surrounding them were testimony not
only to the richness and diversity of native culture but also to the rapacious and
destructive force of European settlement in North America and the continued
brutality of Canadian institutions toward native social and political aspirations.

If much of the early destruction of aboriginal culture was caused by people who   6
were not Canadians but the worst of European adventurers—the ancestors of
those who now piously seek to deprive remote and impoverished native communities of their economic base in hunting and trapping—Canadians later had the
opportunity to chart a different course. The Spirit Sings exhibited damning evidence of our choice not to do so.

While the relics displayed were the beautiful works of sensitive and intelligent   7
artists, they also represented the debris that we robbed from the rubble of cultures
whose traditions we first demolished, then sought to extinguish.

Indiscriminate bombardments of Indian villages by naval flotillas, massacres of   8
women and children by punitive fur traders, tolerance of the ravages of disease
and economic impoverishment, denial of universal access in the law, selective
official segregation, the corporal punishment of children for speaking their own
language in federal schools, the legal banning of ritual, ceremony and religion,
denial of the vote—these are phenomena not of some barbarous Dark Age but of
recent Canadian history.

It was significant that while the officials and curators were congratulating   9
themselves on the commercial success and aesthetic quality of their show,
Georges Erasmus of the Assembly of First Nations was warning Canadians that a
new generation of young native "warriors" may be contemplating armed violence
instead of talk, having learned that negotiation in good faith with Canada's political institutions appears to be a failure. Indeed, as Alberta officials basked in the
Olympic limelight, the Sioux nation was announcing the appointment of its first
formal war chief since Sitting Bull crossed the Medicine Line not far from
Calgary, carrying the scalps of Custer's Seventh Cavalry.° The Sioux had called

back the fifty-nine-year-old great grandson of Chief Standing Bull. Now head of a multi-million-dollar engineering firm, he was to be charged with responsibility for recovering the Black Hills, a sacred spiritual centre for the Sioux nation which was never surrendered by treaty.

10   In Alberta, while The Spirit Sings talked about the importance of art, no less than a dozen outstanding aboriginal claims awaited some kind of formal adjudication in the courts. Some of them, like the question of title to the lands of the dispossessed—and now conveniently dispersed—Papaschase band, are matters of historic and legal curiosity. The Papaschase lands, now occupied by the University of Alberta and most of the south side of Edmonton, may have been surrendered to land speculators under manipulated, defective and highly questionable procedures. But with no survivors of the band, who might legally reopen the issue? Other aboriginal claims are more immediate, from those among the Peigan of southern Alberta who object that the Oldman River dam constructed by the provincial government destroys their ancestral spiritual centres, to the Lubicons of the north who simply want a settlement after half a century of administrative dithering, legalistic equivocating and political indecision by federal and provincial authorities.

11   The tiny and isolated Lubicon band, 20 per cent of which had just tested positive for tuberculosis—a disease long banished from the general population—went so far as to attempt political action, demonstrating outside the Glenbow in Calgary and seeking public support for a boycott of The Spirit Sings during the Olympics. The 350 Lubicons were joined in protest by the Mohawks, who went to court in an unsuccessful attempt to block the showing of a sacred ceremonial mask, public display of which amounted to a religious desecration. As the simple, rural Lubicons made their small public protest outside the Glenbow, the racist and abusive remarks of Calgarians entering the exhibition shocked even the worldly correspondent from the *Chicago Tribune*, assigned to cover the show and no stranger to racism. The attitude of the public toward the Indians, of course, marred the Olympic spirit in a far more fundamental way than the Lubicons' protest had. It also revealed the true nature of The Spirit Sings exhibition: not so much a celebration of native culture as self-congratulatory propaganda regarding the importance of such peoples to the Canadian state.

12   In this context, passing through the opening gallery at The Spirit Sings and gazing upon the thirty or so pathetic little artifacts that represented Canada's extinguished Beothuk nation in Newfoundland, what manner of person could not feel appalled and shamed that the memory of an exterminated nation should be so evoked in the service of our national pride? What perverted manner of pride could be taken from this? It was as though the Berlin Olympics had put on a display of Jewish religious objects to celebrate the diversity, pluralism and tolerance of Nazi culture.

Staring at the tiny pair of baby's moccasins or, near them, the little effigy taken   *13*
from the grave of a four-year-old child, I could think only of the story of
Demasduwit. She had given birth only two days earlier when she was seized by
fur trader John Peyton's party in 1819. Peyton was ostensibly charged with establishing contact with the Beothuks on behalf of the government, although the
choice of such a man for any mission of diplomacy reveals the cynicism of the
authorities. On one occasion, Royal Navy Lieutenant George Pulling complained to his British superiors about the barbarous way in which Peyton had
used one of his steel traps to beat out the brains of a wounded, helpless Indian.
This was the man with whom Demasduwit's husband pleaded fruitlessly for his
wife's return. When he struggled to free her, he was killed before her eyes like a
troublesome cur. Demasduwit's baby was abandoned in the snow to die. The
mother was taken off to be civilized. A month later, in an act of unusual generosity, her corpse was returned to her dwindling people in a coffin—a gesture
intended, no doubt, to emphasize her captor's civilized concern with appearances. Ten years later, the last of her people had died in captivity and the
Beothuk nation was extinct.

Demasduwit had not even the dignity of a quiet grave. In 1827, in the inter-   *14*
ests of preserving for posterity something of the vanished Beothuk culture,
William Cormack robbed the grave of the woman, her husband and the little
baby, taking two skulls and the collection of burial offerings. To witness the murdered woman's modest possessions—for murder it most certainly was—displayed
in honour of a sports event and Canadian self-aggrandizement, is to sense the
trivialization of a tragedy of enormous proportions.

Elaborate apologies have been written regarding the fate of the Beothuk in   *15*
Canadian history, dismissing as mere legend the popular accounts of bounties
paid for ears and eighteenth century hunting expeditions by European settlers.
The Pulling manuscript notes that settlers referred to Beothuk males as "Cock"
Indians, as though they were a kind of game animal, and quotes Richard
Richmond regarding an expedition in the winter of 1790 in search of Beothuk
and in which "we set out with a determination to kill every one we came across
both big and small." When the opportunity arose, Richmond admitted, they
could not bring themselves to shoot down the defenceless Indians but, although
none were killed, two women and a child were made captive.

Newfoundland historian Frederick Rowe, while acknowledging atrocities   *16*
against Indians by the white newcomers, calls for even-handedness in examining
the Beothuk's extermination. He manages to suggest that the Indians brought
about their own destruction by provoking settlers with the raids and pilfering of
a desperate and starving population. Furthermore, he implies that assigning
responsibility for the extinction to the white settlers amounts to a slur against the
descendants of Newfoundland's brave pioneers. The book *Historic Newfoundland
and Labrador*, published by the provincial government, disposes of Demasduwit's

cruel fate as a captive with the bland observation that she and her relative Shanawdithit "both lived among the settlers in various communities," offering no further details. In many cases, the demise of the Beothuk is blamed upon incursions by warlike Micmac, Naskapi and Montagnais neighbours from the mainland. Denial, prevarication and casting of blame upon the victims are typical of the consistent Canadian refusal to take ownership of the ugly parts of our past, although this approach fails to address the simple fact that the Beothuk were a coastal people when the European settlers arrived, then suddenly fled to a bitter and inhospitable interior that remains largely uninhabited even today. It was there, as far from the settlers as they could get, that they finally perished in poverty, starvation and disease.

17   The magnificent artefacts of the Beothuk's neighbours in the Maritime provinces, also displayed by The Spirit Sings, are equally poignant in forcing our attention to the brutality of European conquest and occupation. Think of their creators' fate this way: when the most bloodthirsty Roman despots set out to terrorize dissident elements, they would order a decimation in which every tenth person was executed. Between 1600 and 1700, not one out of every ten, but nine out of every ten people of the Micmac and Maliseet nations died or were killed— a number which makes Caligula° seem moderate by comparison. And this was not by accident. The Micmac were subject to a bounty placed on their scalps by the governor of the English settlement at Halifax. When they proved too elusive for the European hunters, Mohawk mercenaries were employed to help clear the land for settlement. After the crafts of the Micmac and Maliseet, one might admire the lovely decoration of deerskin dresses by Huron women. The Huron population declined by 65 per cent, from twenty-five thousand to nine thousand people, in little over a decade. A similar rate of decline in contemporary Canada would see the disappearance of every person living outside Quebec. The Huron's major mistake was in becoming an ally of the French, who lost to the English. By the time the winners were finished, the Huron were in diaspora, some fleeing as far as the present state of Oklahoma. This pattern is characteristic of the Canadian experience. It is estimated by some scholars that the total native population of the Canadian landmass might have been as high as one million people at the time of first European contact. At the turn of the century, it had declined to about one hundred thousand. This is a cultural destruction that approaches genocidal proportions.

18   The Spirit Sings exhibition dealt with these unpleasant realities in an oblique and less than forthright way. It was, after all, an ethnological display rather than an expression of historical context. On reflection, it is clear, the show was actually intended to tell the world and ourselves what a generous and tolerant country we live in; how quick we are to recognize and honour the way in which the culture of native peoples has enriched our broader society. In fact, the social, ethical, political, spiritual and philosophical values of native culture have been

almost universally rejected by the dominant society. On the other hand, native culture has certainly enriched museums, even if we consistently exclude it from contributing to the mainstream. And many of the museums that have been enriched are not even Canadian. Douglas Cole, an historian at Simon Fraser University in Vancouver, exhaustively documents the patterns of theft and acquisition in his important book *Captured Heritage*. An estimated three hundred thousand artefacts from the Northwest Pacific coastal cultures are now held by international collections—this is looting on the scale of the Visigoths.°

The cataloguing and administration of such collections have made fine careers   *19* for curators, who by some extraordinary ethical gymnastics find easy praise for the value of native art while remaining strangely ineffectual regarding the social value of the human beings who produced it. But instead of debating the collective responsibility of the collectors, we might consider instead the social context of a selection of wonderful Assiniboine drawings, kindly loaned by their European owner to The Spirit Sings organizers for display in Canada.

The Assiniboines, numbering about twelve hundred lodges and among the   *20* great traders of the Plains tribes, ranged across the central Canadian prairies. In 1833, the winter counts of the Teton Sioux, Kiowa and Blackfoot record unusual numbers of shooting stars, generally considered a harbinger of some natural catastrophe. Major Alexander Culbertson at Fort McKenzie confirms the sightings. The native people did not have long to wait. By 1837, horrified European travellers were reporting the whole prairie region littered with the rotting corpses of men, women and children, abandoned equipment, straying horse herds and the encampments that brought a new term to Plains Indian language—the Ghost Camp, where the lodges are occupied only by the dead.

The pestilence and infection of smallpox reduced the Assiniboines to four   *21* hundred lodges. They had gone in one season from being the most powerful nation on the Great Plains to a pitiful, ragged remnant, begging for food. They had been, in the reports of appalled observers, virtually exterminated. While the cycle of plagues which ravaged the Plains cultures in 1837 and again in 1864, 1868 and 1883 could hardly be attributed to federal policy, they did offer a convenient clearing of the landscape for unencumbered settlement by the huge influx of farmers that was deliberate policy in Ottawa.

Shortly thereafter, the strategic elimination of the Plains Indians' primary food   *22* source occurred. In 1875, the Baker Company of Fort Benton, Montana, shipped seventy-five thousand buffalo hides to the east. Most of them had been taken from the hunting grounds of Canada's Blackfoot, Blood, Peigan and Sarcee tribal groups, the carcasses left to rot in the summer sun, the bones later collected and shipped for fertilizer production. Four years later, dated precisely by North-West Mounted Police dispatch, the buffalo were gone forever from the southern Alberta grasslands and Canadian society marched its native people into the concentration camp.

23   Today, we call them Indian reserves, sharing our love of the euphemism with the South Africans, who call them homelands, but let us not deceive ourselves about their original function. The rationalization for reserves, of course, was that they were created to save the few aboriginals who managed to survive the dismantling of their economy and the wrecking of their political structure, social organization, religion and family units. Indian reserves were invented by bureaucrats to control the movements of free-ranging people and to concentrate them in one place and bring them under the power of the dominant society. We may wrap ourselves in the comforting belief that reserves were an act of state generosity, seeking to save native nations from oblivion. The cold eye of political science sees that Indian reserves could not have been better designed for the specific purpose of destroying Plains Indian culture, which was predicated upon movement and freedom, so that the land might be carved up by newcomers who could get more productive use out of it by farming. As the topsoil of Palliser's Triangle, the arid region of southeastern Alberta and southwestern Saskatchewan, blows away on the dry winds of drought, demanding more and more dams and irrigation districts, with the attendant hazards of salinization—not to mention the overall tax burden—the definitions of what constitutes productivity require a new evaluation.

24   The most intense element of The Spirit Sings was its remarkable and moving celebration of the deep and complex spiritual nature of Indian life. In this, too, the exhibition brings shame upon us. Consider all those missionaries, acting in the name of a compassionate Christ, whose objective was the displacement of all the spiritual beliefs the exhibition purports to celebrate.

25   To this day the church, in its various manifestations, has difficulty bringing itself to acknowledge its role as an agent of cultural destruction. Yet, with all the best of intentions, missionaries representing the two mainstreams of Christian religion waged an active campaign to displace traditional religious belief and value systems among native peoples. At a time when aboriginal societies faced enormous upheaval and change, their societies threatened by the growing military, economic and commercial pressure from the European invaders, the missionaries set about sucking out the glue which held native communities together. By devaluing the moral force of traditional spiritual leaders and co-opting the belief and value systems of native peoples, the church served as an active agent in fomenting confusion and increasing vulnerability—always there with compassion, of course, to help pick up the pieces and shape them into a Christian and, essentially, European framework.

26   Evocative examples of the disruptive influence of Christian missionaries can be found almost everywhere. The Inuit settlement of Igloolik, high in Canada's Central Arctic, provides one good example. It was the site of a shameless war for souls which raged between Anglicans and Roman Catholics, as though the numbers of converted were pieces to be captured in a chess game. Fifty years later, a visitor from outside could still witness the scars of sectarian division in a com-

munity that had been homogeneous and secure. The Tsartlip Indian Reserve of Vancouver Island is another example. One of its elders told me that the people who eventually became its residents had the early distinction of having been formally converted by visiting priests to Roman Catholicism, Anglicanism and Methodism—all in the same year.

The state certainly concurred with this approach, seeing the church as a power-   27 ful instrument of assimilation. Missionaries like William Duncan, who established a mission to the Tsimshian at Metlakatla, off the coast of what is now the Alaska Panhandle, saw traditional native rites as an obstacle to Christian conversion and lobbied for their prohibition. Duncan was particularly offended by the ancient puberty rites that accompanied potlatch ceremonials. By 1885, with the whole-hearted backing of the various churches, Canada's parliament had passed legislation which prohibited the practice of native religious and spiritual ceremonies.

The Canadian state took suppression of native ceremonies seriously indeed. In   28 1922, following a traditional potlatch at Alert Bay, a prosperous Kwakiutl community located just off the northeast coast of Vancouver Island, a large number of men and women (the Indians say forty-five, the official records say twenty-nine) were arrested for the offenses of making speeches, singing, dancing, arranging and distributing gifts. The police action followed complaints from federal Indian agent William Halliday, who, in a gross conflict of interest, conveniently doubled as magistrate for the trial. The arresting officer, an RCMP sergeant, took the role of prosecutor. In this perversion of justice, twenty of the men and women arrested were sentenced to prison terms of two and three months. Fines were levied in the form of their ancestral ceremonial regalia, which was seized by the federal government. Halliday reported more than four hundred and fifty items filling three hundred cubic feet of space. Some, according to Cole, he sold off to a foreign collector for $291, the rest went to the curators at the National Museum in Ottawa, the forerunner of the same Museum of Civilization which hosted The Spirit Sings.

These officials salved their conscience in the matter by assigning arbitrary   29 commercial values to the items and sending cheques to the Indian agent for distribution. Cole points out in *Capture Heritage* that some Indians claim never to have received a penny's compensation for the priceless material—one item was believed by the Indians themselves to have a value of 18,250 Hudson's Bay Company blankets. Just at the retail value of quality blankets today, it would be worth more than $4 million. Ultimately, part of the stolen property was returned after sixty-six years and a legal battle, but much of it has been lost to the owners and, in any event, as Cole points out, "The charges and convictions, the surrenders and imprisonments, were a severe blow even to so resilient a culture as that of the Kwakiutl.... But the forced cessation of the public potlatch, the feasts, and the dances was a more severe blow."

This essential contempt by the collectors of artefacts for the validity of tradi-   30 tional cultural values which the material items represent continues today. At the Calgary segment of The Spirit Sings, the curators insisted on displaying sacred objects in bald defiance of the wishes of those who consider them sacred. Sacred objects, it seems, are merely property, and in Canadian society ownership is nine-tenths of the law. Would the Pope and the Archbishop of Canterbury feel this way about the sacraments and holy relics of their faith, one wonders. At the Ottawa segment of the exhibition, at least, the authorities reportedly decided not to include the false face mask of the Mohawk nation, public display of which the Indians had fruitlessly sought to block by court action. One wonders, however, whether this decision had more to do with the proximity of angry Iroquois to Ottawa than with real understanding or compassion for the ethical issue.

31   At the Glenbow exhibit in Calgary, which is surrounded by the Blood, Peigan, Sarcee, Blackfoot and Stoney reserves, cards were provided for observers to record their feelings.

32   "Sometimes our spirit has wept," wrote one viewer. "Sadness for my people who lost so much of their spirit when their ceremonial objects were laid down or taken away"—an interesting irony considered in the context of the consistent robbing of native cultural items in order that museums might provide evidence of the "preservation" of native culture. This juxtaposition of the aboriginal view and the official view says much about Canadian values. It confirms what has long been clear, that we actually prefer our native culture in museums. We certainly do not prefer it running the Department of Indian Affairs or the Department of Fisheries. Nor do we prefer native culture announcing the news on national television or determining its own political destiny.

33   "Where are the natives whose heritage this is?" asked another observer in Calgary. "Couldn't you find ANY to guide us through THEIR history ... the spirits must be crying." This, too, draws attention to the wretched lie at the heart of The Spirit Sings. We prefer native culture that we may put on display when it conveniences us, called out for ceremonies that make us appear magnanimous— whether the creators of the artefacts like it or not.

34   "Why get upset, it's all in the past," one young white observer said to me after hearing my feelings about the show. "We didn't do it, somebody else did. Don't expect me to feel guilty for my great grandfather." This view I did not find surprising. It is the constant bleat of Canadian society with respect to native peoples. It was somebody else's fault. It is somebody else's responsibility. This familiar refrain lies at the very heart of Northern Alberta's Lubicon band dispute, still festering at the time of writing after fifty years of political buck-passing and evasion of moral responsibility by the federal and provincial governments.

35   "It's all in the past."

36   Tell that to the people of Peerless Lake, where on March 10, 1986, six young people died after drinking methyl hydrate—children erasing their futures with reproducing fluid.

Tell it to Richard Cardinal, the Cree teenager who hanged himself in despair *37*
after being shunted through twenty-eight foster homes and institutions in his
brief seventeen years of life.

Tell it to Donald Marshall, imprisoned for eleven years for a crime he did not *38*
commit because of a justice system that made more assumptions about his racial
origins than the evidence.

Tell it to the relatives of Helen Betty Osborne in The Pas, Manitoba. She was *39*
abducted, raped, stabbed fifty times with a screwdriver and left dying in the snow
by four white teenagers. For sixteen years, the murderers were sheltered from the
law by their community. Testimony at the trial made it clear that the identities
of Helen's abductors were no secret in The Pas—but, then, the victim was only
an Indian.

Try telling the Lubicons that the injustice is all in the past, they who struggle *40*
today to defend their tiny cultural enclave against the encroachments of the very
same oil industry that so sanctimoniously sponsored The Spirit Sings exhibition
in honour of native culture.

All of this adds up to the old Canadian story. Native culture is nice, but not if *41*
it gets in our way. Native culture is important, but not in terms of the people in
whom it resides, only in the artefacts—the *things* we can collect and display in
museum cases.

In the context of what The Spirit Sings claimed to say about the importance *42*
and value of native culture, Canadians need to ask some pointed questions of
ourselves and our governing authorities. We need to ask why, in a province as
wealthy as Alberta, we permit continuation of the conditions which lead to a
death rate among Indian infants that is more than twice what it is for the general population? Why, in a country prepared to spend millions of dollars telling the
world how much we value native culture, we tolerate conditions in which native
people are four times as likely as the rest of us to die before reaching their life
expectancy? Why is it acceptable that aboriginal Canadians are three times as
likely to die by violence?

We need to ask how we can accept the conditions under which native people *43*
are ten times as likely to be diagnosed as alcoholics? Why it was possible, for
nearly a decade, for the suicide rate for native people in northern Saskatchewan
to remain fifteen times greater than the national average? What landscape of sorrow and despair do such people inhabit?

Why do 75 per cent of native students in the Northwest Territories abandon *44*
school between Grade 7 and Grade 12? Is this a failure to be blamed on the victims, or is the failure in the structure of a system which can neither visualize nor
address their needs? How can it be that only 2 per cent of the Canadian population provides 10 per cent of the prison inmates—perhaps because the unemployment rate for native people consistently runs about 800 per cent higher than that
deemed acceptable for mainstream society?

45   Whatever we put on display in the glass cases, the numbers betray the lie. These statistics provide the reality behind the self-serving falsehoods of exhibitions like The Spirit Sings. They reveal far more about the hypocrisy of the dominant culture than they do about the propensities of aboriginal people. They tell us that far from honouring native culture, Canadian society dismisses it in all its living forms.

46   Made invisible by our denial of the worth of their own cultural values, excluded from real economic participation in the dominant culture, squeezed into ghettos at the least productive margins of society, cheated of their promised patrimony, cheated of an equal opportunity at life itself and fully cognizant of our hypocrisy, aboriginal people are far from the honoured participants in Canadian society that exhibitions like The Spirit Sings would have the world believe. They remain deeply estranged from the social and political process of this nation. How long before, as Georges Erasmus warns, the sorrow and despair becomes rage and vengeance?

47   The tragedy, unfortunately, is not all in the past. It is all in the present. It is not somebody else's responsibility. It is Canadians' responsibility. If The Spirit Sings served one purpose, it was to remind thinking Canadians that the pathetic remnants of the Beothuk should be on display all right. They should be on display in a national shrine of shame and humility. The very first act of every prime minister should be to kneel before them and pray to the God that we invoke in our national anthem—both for national forgiveness and that Canada itself may never suffer what was suffered by the Beothuk, the Micmac, the Huron, the Assiniboine. ◆

1989

Glossary

Custer's Seventh Cavalry: reference to June 25, 1876, when General George Custer led his cavalry into battle at Little Bighorn against the Sioux, not knowing how large their numbers were. Every member of the Seventh Cavalry was killed.

Caligula: emperor of Rome (37–41) who succeeded his adoptive father, Tiberius. After a severe illness, he displayed the ruthlessness, extravagance, and megalomania that led to his assassination.

Visigoths: a barbaric tribe of western Goths who invaded the Roman Empire in the fourth century A.D. and settled in France and Spain, establishing a monarchy that lasted until the early eighth century.

Explorations

- Did Hume's essay change the way you view the role of a museum? If so, describe how your perspective changed.

- Hume speaks about the hypocrisy behind exhibitions such as The Spirit Sings. Do you think that the way Canadians honour Native art and culture is different from the way we treat First Nations people themselves? Explain your answer.

- According to Hume, a prevailing attitude amongst Canadians is "Why get upset, it's all in the past." Give specific examples of how past history has caused conflict between current Native and non-Native communities.

Marni Jackson was born in 1947 and lives in Toronto. She has written for film and theatre, and has contributed articles to such periodicals as Saturday Night, Rolling Stone, This Magazine, *and* Toronto Life, *winning two National Magazine Awards for Humour. Jackson also spent two years as co-host of TV Ontario's book show "Imprint." In 1992 she published her first book,* The Mother Zone: Love, Sex and Laundry in the Modern Family, *and she published* Pain: The Fifth Vital Sign *in 2002.*

Gals and Dolls:
The Moral Value of "Bad" Toys

Marni Jackson

In the days before I actually had a child, child-rearing was a clearcut proposition: 1 simply Raise Them Right. Minimal TV, no hooker-type dolls or plastic Uzis, and a constant flow of high-fibre ideas from the morally evolved parent to the vulnerable, blank-slate child. I felt sorry for parents who didn't have the gumption to stick to this plan. Then I had a son, and the rest is—well, not so much history as culture.

Not since the days of Spock° have we had so much parental advice in the air— 2 how to raise kids, how to ruin them, how to "juggle work and family." This is why it's so refreshing to read someone like Alice Miller, the psychoanalyst-turned-writer whose books explore the childhood roots of violence and creativity. She doesn't have a theory about raising kids. In fact, she argues that *any* system of moral values imposed on children is potentially damaging, because too often the rules are there to serve the emotional needs of the parents, not the children. In the name of morality, we try to keep the unruly passions of children—not to mention memories of our own childhood—safe, tidy, and under control. Most pedagogy, good or bad, sends a hidden message to the child: "Your desires and feelings are not good enough. Feel this, think that, instead." If children require so much correction, then deep down—so they reason—they must be bad. Sooner or later the child who only hears this message learns to assemble an other-pleasing, false self around a core of inexplicable shame.

This doesn't mean that Miller thinks children ought to fingerpaint with their 3 food and otherwise disport themselves as gods. Post-Spockian permissiveness is just another form of pedagogy, really. But the experience of her own patients convinced her that it was the ones who were raised rigidly, with an overabundance of "good values," who were most likely to grow into benumbed adults, lost to themselves and predisposed to violence. The violence erupts in response to long-stifled childhood anger, which began as a perfectly human response to a voice that said "Don't be who you are, be good." The moral here—if we dare draw one—is that excessive handwringing about the values we are giving our kids may be as much about peer vanity as anything else. Values are not external; they are intrinsic to the sort of relationship we have with our children, arising out of the ordinary, humdrum way a family works and plays. The boy or girl who receives fair treatment, as opposed to "moral" correction, quickly develops an exquisite sense of justice—one that is more likely to shame the parent, rather than the other way round. (I'm moralizing here, of course.) Even young children bring a surprising amount of savvy and shit-detection to the moral bargaining table. To assume otherwise is to inflate our roles as parents into the architects and owners of our children's souls.

4   Now, Miller was talking about some fairly rigid, loveless households—Hitler's° and Goebbels's,° for instance. She wasn't necessarily addressing the problem of whether or not to buy your son a Nintendo, or to give your niece a Wet 'n' Wild Barbie. Nevertheless, I detect a lot of dubious pedagogy in our much-cogitated attitudes towards "good" and "bad" toys.

5   I know what happened with toy guns in our household. I went from a serene pre-child conviction that guns would never cross our threshold to the ridiculous but amiable compromise my seven-year-old son and I have reached. Childish logic is impeccable. If you give him an innocent green water pistol for the bath-tub, then why not the hideous toy M-16 in the backyard? If he can brandish a popsicle stick, why not a space laser? So he now owns a bow and arrow and a non-combat rawhide whip (history? art?), but he knows I have a "thing" about realis-tic guns, so he doesn't ask for them. He watches plenty of TV (right, too much), but after flat-out indoctrination on my part—moral interference in the name of what I can or cannot stand to overhear—he now flips past the more violent kids' shows, of his own volition. Of course, our definitions of "violent" are continually being refined. But he's kind by nature, and always has been. I try not to improve on that too much.

6   There was a time, not so long ago, that Barbie dolls were considered the worst sort of sex-stereotype propaganda. Barbie, with her foot permanently arched in the shape of a high heel, her long, scissoring legs, her high, hard, de-nippled breasts. It's true she's unswervingly represented as a career gadfly, a weak-chinned Caucasian princess and a fashion flibbertigibbet—11 1/2 inches of beige plastic that has been accused of encouraging eating disorders, mindless consumerism and low self-esteem in little girls. Small wonder that to the Birkenstock generation,° Barbie was bad.

7   But little girls are not pushovers. They know what they like and they like Barbie. Now 31 years old (but ever ageless and firm of chin), Barbie has tri-umphed over pedagogy, to the tune of over $500-million annually. Last year was the biggest year for Barbie sales in history. Some 98 per cent of Canadian girls aged four to ten have a Barbie—or four—in their bedrooms. Like Coca-Cola, she has insinuated her hourglass, bottle-shaped self into 67 countries

around the world. None of this will surprise parents with daughters, but it was news to me.

I went into several department stores to get a blast of Barbie, a feel for Barbie, and there she was—row upon row of her and her almost identical pals, including li'l sister Skipper, brown-skinned Christie, freckle-faced sporty Midge, Hispanic Nia, red-haired vixen Ashley. Her countless outfits run the gamut from the tiny tubes of her pantyhose to wild salsa dresses, purses that turn into skirts and skirts that turn into hair bows. Her eminently loseable accessories include teacups, toe paint, Ferraris, guitars and running shoes.   8

After twenty years of feminism, you may ask, why don't little boys play with Barbies? What *is* it about girls and dolls, anyway? Boys play with He-men and Ninja turtle figures but the marriage between girls and their Barbies seems more enduring. Girls' sense of pink and blueness also seems more acute, more precocious, although I base this only on the fact that I bought my son some plain but *purplish* boots last year. They didn't bother him until he came home from school one day and announced he couldn't wear them because they were "girls' boots." Who had decreed this? "The girls in my room."   9

Are girls more proprietorial about identifiable girl things because they've already detected an imbalance in the adult world, between boy toys (tanks and guns) and female fun? Or is it something simpler—that at a certain age, children want some kind of sex identity. Just because adults have bequeathed them a culture that offers only testosterone-poisoned orange He-men and anorexic beige Barbies, must we insist on snuffing out any sign of gender?   10

An eight-year-old girl in the neighbourhood lugged over her five Barbies, in two pink vehicles, for my inspection. While twirling and braiding the long blonde tresses on one of them, she explained that although she doesn't want to *be* Barbie, she really likes to play with her. "We make up stories that are like real life and then we make the Barbies act them out," she said with admirable succinctness. "Her body isn't very realistic," she admits, pointing the ballistic bosom of one towards me. "In fact, the only realistic thing about it is her ears." If she were designing them, she would go for more variation. "Like, it would be neat to have a tattooed Barbie, or one with a bigger head. Her head is too small for her body." And Ken's definitely in a rut. "I wouldn't mind a bald Ken, for example."   11

The sad truth is, Barbie has left the bland, rug-haired Ken behind in a spangled cloud of dust. Ken sales only amount to 35 percent of their combined total—and in fact, his shelf presence suggests more like a ratio of ten Barbies to one Ken. Ken is looking more and more like a rented gigolo, or the guy who takes Barbie's outfits to the cleaners and back. His accessories are laughable (a slice of pizza, a kite, a basketball) and his weekend outfits are a bore (blue pin-striped smock and navy pants). The only thing you can do with him, apart from suicidal dives off the couch, is change his hair colour from a terrible fecal-mustard colour to an obviously touched-up brown. While Barbie has a choice of five stylish wedding   12 gowns, Ken's lone wedding tuxedo is deplorable, a nylon unitard with an ill-fitting white jacket and a shiny bow tie. His loafers are interchangeable little boats. No wonder Barbie seems to prefer the company of her on-the-go girlfriends.

13   When I saw Ken strapped stiffly into the passenger seat of Barbie's huge new pink RV trailer, with plates that say "Barbie," I felt a stab of compassion for him. As I was gazing at this harsh spectacle, a couple wandered down the aisle. "Oh there's Ken," said the woman. "We were always so mean to Ken with our Barbies, we used to do terrible things to him. I don't know why." Laughing, they moved down the aisle to inspect a Baby Uh-Oh ("Give her a drink and uh-oh!…time to change her diaper!").

14   However retrograde she appears to be, I sense Barbie is a survivor. Her maddeningly firm little bosom and fashion-victim personality, her fickle careers are all voodoo tricks to ward off parental approval. If we had given Barbie a social conscience and sensible shoes, she might have moldered away at the bottom of the toy bin. As it is, girls play with their uneducational Barbies as they always have, playing out the "mean babysitter" scenario, madly acting away, with no parent-pleasing values to inhibit their stories. Therapists may envy the Barbie blankness—she too can create a private, privileged space where any and every feeling is permitted. May Barbie be "bad" as long as she reigns, for it is her lack of redeeming social value that helps keep her true to the child's sense of play, instead of the parents' worst fears. ◆

1991

Glossary

Dr. Spock: Benjamin Spock (1903–1998), American pediatrician whose books on child-rearing influenced generations of parents.

Hitler: Adolf Hitler (1889–1945), Austrian-born demagogue who, as Führer, or leader, of the National Socialist Party, became chancellor of Germany in 1933; Hitler was the architect of Germany's "Final Solution," a plan which led to the mass extermination of millions of people, mostly Jews, in death camps across eastern Europe during World War II.

Goebbels: Josef Goebbels (1897–1945), propaganda minister for the Nazi Party under Hitler.

the Birkenstock generation: a reference to the hippie counter-culture of the 1960s; many who participated in the social movement wore the famously comfortable Birkenstock sandals.

Explorations

- What toys do you think are most popular amongst children these days? Is there still a distinction between boys' and girls' toys?

- What kind of toys did you play with as a child? Which ones did you like the least? Which ones did you like the best?

- Did your parents ever ban "bad" toys? If so, what were their reasons for doing so? What was your reaction?

- Looking back, do you think that your parents had good reason to worry about certain toys and their effects on your moral development?

Basil H. Johnston was born on the Parry Island Reserve in 1929. A member of the Department of Ethnology at the Royal Ontario Museum, he is a highly respected writer, educator, and historian of Ojibway language and culture. His books include Ojibway Heritage, How the Birds Got Their Colours, Moose Meat and Wild Rice, *and* Indian School Days. *Johnston's contributions and accomplishments have been rewarded several times: in 1967 he received the Centennial Medal for his work on behalf of the Native community; he won the Samuel J. Fels Literary Award in 1976 for his essay "Zhowmin and Mandamin"; in April of 1989 he received the Order of Ontario for his contributions to society in Ontario; and on June 8, 1994, the University of Toronto awarded him an honorary doctoral degree.*

One Generation from Extinction

Basil H. Johnston

1 Within the past few years Gregor Keeshig, Henry Johnston, Resime Akiwenzie, Norman McLeod, and Belva Pitwaniquot died. They all spoke their tribal language, Anishinaubae° (Ojibwa). When these elders passed away, so did a portion of the tribal language come to an end as a tree disintegrates by degrees and in stages until it is no more; and, though infants were born to replenish the loss of life, not any one of them will learn the language of their grandfathers or grandmothers to keep it alive and to pass it on to their descendants. Thus language dies.

2 In some communities there are no more Gregor Keeshigs, Henry Johnstons, Resime Akiwenzies, Norman McLeods, Belva Pitwaniquots; those remaining have no more affinity to their ancestral language than they do to Swahili or Sanskrit; in other communities the languages may not survive beyond a generation. Some tribal languages are at the edge of extinction, not expected to survive for more than a few years. There remain but three aboriginal languages out of the original fifty-three found in Canada that may survive several more generations.

3 There is cause to lament but it is the native peoples who have the most cause to lament the passing of their languages. They lose not only the ability to express the simplest of daily sentiments and needs but they can no longer understand the ideas, concepts, insights, attitudes, rituals, ceremonies, institutions brought into being by their ancestors; and, having lost the power to understand, cannot sustain, enrich, or pass on their heritage. No longer will they think Indian or feel Indian. And though they may wear "Indian" jewellery and take part in pow-wows, they can never capture that kinship with and reverence for the sun and the moon, the sky and the water, or feel the lifebeat of Mother Earth or sense the change in her moods; no longer are the wolf, the bear and the caribou elder brothers but beasts, resources to be killed and sold. They will have lost their iden-

tity which no amount of reading can ever restore. Only language and literature can restore the "Indianness."

Now if Canadians of West European or other origin have less cause than   4
"Indians" to lament the passing of tribal languages and cultures it is because they may not realize that there is more to tribal languages than "ugh" or "how" or "kimu sabi." At most and at best Euro-Canadians might have read or heard about Raven and Nanabush and Thunderbirds and other "tricksters"; some may have even studied "Culture Myths," "Hero Tales," "Transformation Tales," or "Nature Myths and Beast Fables," but these accounts were never regarded as bearing any more sense than "Little Red Riding Hood" or "The Three Little Pigs." Neither language nor literature were ever considered in their natural kinship, which is the only way in which language ought to be considered were its range, depth, force and beauty to be appreciated.

Perhaps our Canadian compatriots of West European origin have more cause   5
to lament the passing of an Indian language than they realize or care to admit. Scholars mourn that there is no one who can speak the Huron° language and thus assist scholars in their pursuit of further knowledge about the tribe; scholars mourn that had the Beothuk° language survived, so much more would be known about the Beothuk peoples. In mourning the extinction of the language, scholars are implicitly declaring that the knowledge derived from a study of snowshoes, shards, arrowheads, old pipes, shrunken heads and old bones, hunting, fishing, transportation, food preparation, ornamentation and sometimes ritual is limited. And so it is; material culture can yield only so much.

Language is crucial. If scholars are to increase their knowledge and if they are   6
to add depth and width to their studies, they must study a native language and literature. It is not enough to know linguistics or to know a few words or even some phrases or to have access to the Jesuit *Relations*, Chippewa *Exercises*, Ojibwa *Texts*, or a *Dictionary of the Otchipwe Language*. Without a knowledge of the language scholars can never take for granted the accuracy of an interpretation or translation of a passage, let alone a single word; nor can they presume that their articles, tracts, treatises, essays bear the kind of accuracy that scholarship and integrity demand. They would continue to labour under the impression that the word "manitou" means spirit and that it has no other meaning. Superstitious nonsense, according to the white man. They do not know that the word bears other meanings even more fundamental than "spirit," such as, and/or pertaining to the deities; of a substance, character, nature, essence, quiddity beyond comprehension and therefore beyond explanation, a mystery; supernatural; potency, potential. What a difference such knowledge might have made in the studies conducted by Ruth Landes or Thomas B. Leekley, and others on the Anishinaubae tribe. Perhaps, instead of regarding "Indians" as superstitious for positing "spirits" in trees or in other inanimate or insensate objects, they might have credited them with insight for having perceived a vital substance or essence

that imparted life, form, growth, healing, and strength in all things, beings, and places. They might have understood that the expression "manitouwan" meant that an object possessed or was infused with an element or a feature that was beyond human ken; they might have understood that "w'manitouwih" meant that he or she was endowed with extraordinary talents, and that it did not mean that he or she was a spirit.

7   Language is essential. If scholars and writers are to know how "Indians" perceive and regard certain ideas they must study an "Indian" language. When an "Anishinaubae" says that someone is telling the truth, he says "w'daeb-awae." But the expression is not just a mere confirmation of a speaker's veracity. It is at the same time a philosophical proposition that, in saying, a speaker casts his words and his voice only as far as his vocabulary and his perception will enable him. In so doing the tribe was denying that there was absolute truth; that the best a speaker could achieve and a listener expect was the highest degree of accuracy. Somehow that one expression "w'daeb-awae" set the limits of a single statement as well as setting limits on all speech.

8   There was a special regard almost akin to reverence for speech and for the truth. Perhaps it was because words bear the tone of the speaker and may therefore be regarded as belonging to that person; perhaps it is because words have but a fleeting momentary existence in sound and are gone except in memory; perhaps it is because words have not ceased to exist but survive in echo and continue on in infinity; perhaps it is because words are medicine that can heal or injure; perhaps it is because words possess an element of the manitou that enabled them to conjure images and ideas out of nothing, and are the means by which the autissokanuk (muses) inspired men and women. It was not for nothing that the older generation did not solicit the autissokanuk to assist in the genesis of stories or in the composition of chants in seasons other than winter.

9   To instil respect for language the old counselled youth, "Don't talk too much" (Kegon zaum-doongaen), for they saw a kinship between language and truth. The expression is not without its facetious aspect but in its broader application it was intended to convey to youth other notions implicit in the expression "Don't talk too much," for the injunction also meant "Don't talk too often...Don't talk too long...Don't talk about those matters that you know nothing about." Were a person to restrict his discourse, and measure his speech, and govern his talk by what he knew, he would earn the trust and respect of his (her) listeners. Of that man or woman they would say "w'daeb-awae." Better still, people would want to hear the speaker again and by so doing bestow upon the speaker the opportunity to speak, for ultimately it is the people who confer the right of speech by their audience.

10   Language was a precious heritage; literature was no less precious. So precious did the tribe regard language and speech that it held those who abused language and speech and truth in contempt and ridicule and withheld from them their trust

and confidence. To the tribe the man or woman who rambled on and on, or who let his tongue range over every subject or warp the truth was said to talk in circles in a manner no different from that of a mongrel who, not knowing the source of alarm, barks in circles (w'geewi-animoh). Ever since words and sounds were reduced to written symbols and have been stripped of their mystery and magic, the regard and reverence for them have diminished in tribal life.

As rich and full of meaning as may be individual words and expressions, they   *11* embody only a small portion of the entire stock and potential of tribal knowledge, wisdom, and intellectual attainment; the greater part is deposited in myths, legends, stories, and in the lyrics of chants that make up the tribe's literature. Therein will be found the essence and the substance of tribal ideas, concepts, insights, attitudes, values, beliefs, theories, notions, sentiments, and accounts of their institutions and rituals and ceremonies. Without language scholars, writers, and teachers will have no access to the depth and width of tribal knowledge and understanding, but must continue to labour as they have done these many years under the impression that "Indian" stories are nothing more than fairy tales or folklore, fit only for juvenile minds. For scholars and academics Nanabush, Raven, Glooscap, Weesaukeechauk and other mythological figures will ever remain "tricksters," culture heroes, deities whose misadventures were dreamed into being only for the amusement of children. Primitive and pagan and illiterate to boot, "Indians" could not possibly address or articulate abstract ideas or themes; neither their minds nor their languages could possibly express any idea more complex than taboos, superstitions and bodily needs.

But were ethnologists, anthropologists, linguists, teachers of native children   *12* and writers of native literature—yes, even archaeologists—to learn a native language, perhaps they might learn that Nanabush and Raven are not simply "tricksters" but the caricatured representations of human nature and character in their many facets; perhaps they might give thought to the meaning and sense to be found in Weessaukeetchauk [*sic*], The Bitter Soul. There is no other way except through language for scholars to learn or to validate their studies, their theories, their theses about the values, ideals or institutions or any other aspect of tribal life; there is no other way by which knowledge of native life can find increase. Not good enough is it to say in hushed tones after a reverential description of a totem pole or the lacing of a snowshoe, "My, weren't they clever."

Just consider the fate of "Indian" stories written by those who knew nothing of   *13* the language and never did hear any of the stories in their entirety or in their original version but derived everything that they knew of their subject from second, third and even fourth diluted sources. Is it any wonder then that the stories in *Indian Legends of Canada* by E. E. Clark or in *Manabozho* by T. B. Leekley are so bland and devoid of sense. Had the authors known the stories in their "Indian" sense and flavour, perhaps they might have infused their versions with more wit and substance. Had the authors known that the creation story as the

Anishinaubae understood it to mean was intended to represent in the most dramatic way possible the process of individual development from the smallest portion of talent to be retrieved from the depths of one's being and then given growth by breath of life. Thus a man and a woman are to develop themselves, create their own worlds, and shape their being and give meaning to life. Had the authors known this meaning of the Creation Story, perhaps they might have written their accounts in terms more in keeping with the sense and thrust of the story. But not knowing the language nor having heard the story in its original text or state, the authors could not, despite their intentions, impart to their accounts the due weight and perspective the story deserved. The stories were demeaned.

14 With language dead and literature demeaned, "Indian" institutions are beyond understanding and restoration. Let us turn back the calendar two and a half centuries, to that period when the "Indian" languages were spoken in every home, when native literature inspired thought and when native "Indian" institutions governed native "Indian" life. It was then that a native institution caught the imagination of the newcomers to this continent. The men and women who founded a new nation to be known as the United States of America took as their model for their constitution and government the principles of government and administration embodied in The Great Tree of Peace of the Five Nations Confederacy.° The institution of The Great Tree of Peace was not then too primitive nor too alien for study or emulation to the founders of the United States. In more recent years even the architects of the United Nations regarded the "Indian" institution of The Great Tree of Peace not as a primitive organization beneath their dignity and intellect, but rather as an institution of merit. There exist still "Indian" institutions that may well serve and benefit this society and this nation, not as dramatically as did The Great Tree of Peace the United States of America, but bestow some good as yet undreamed or unimagined. Just how much good such institutions may confer upon this or some future generation will not be known unless the "Indian" languages survive.

15   And what is it that has undermined the vitality of some of the "Indian" languages and deprived this generation and this society of the promise and the benefit of the wisdom and the knowledge embodied in tribal literature?

16   In the case of the Beothuk and their language, the means used were simple and direct: it was the blade, the bludgeon, and the bullet that were plied in the destruction of the Beothuk in their sleep, at their table, and in their quiet passage from home to place of work, until the tribe was no more. The speakers were annihilated; no more was the Beothuk language spoken; whatever their wisdom or whatever their institutions, the whole of the Beothuk heritage was destroyed.

17   In other instances, instead of bullets, bludgeons, and bayonets, other means were used to put an end to the speaking of an "Indian" language. A kick with a

police riding boot administered by a 175-pound man upon the person of an eight-year-old boy for uttering the language of a savage left its pain for days and its bruise upon the spirit for life. A boy once kicked was not likely to risk a second or a third. A slap in the face or a punch to the back of the head delivered even by a small man upon the person of a small boy left its sting and a humiliation not soon forgotten. And if a boot or a fist were not administered, then a lash or a yardstick was plied until the "Indian" language was beaten out. To boot and fist and lash was added ridicule. Both speaker and his language were assailed. "What's the use of that language? It isn't polite to speak another language in the presence of other people. Learn English! That's the only way you're going to get ahead. How can you learn two languages at the same time? No wonder kids can't learn anything else. It's a primitive language; hasn't the vocabulary to express abstract ideas, poor. Say 'ugh.' Say something in your language!…How can you get your tongue around those sounds?" On and on the comments were made, disparaging, until in too many the language was shamed into silence and disuse.

And how may the federal government assist in the restoration of the native lan- 18
guages to their former vigour and vitality and enable them to fulfil their promise?

The Government of Canada must finance the establishment of either provin- 19
cial or regional language institutes to be affiliated with a museum or a university
or a provincial native educational organization. The function of the "institute,"
to be headed by a native person who speaks, reads, and writes a native language,
will be to foster research into language and to encourage the publication of lexi-
cons, dictionaries, grammars, courses, guides, outlines, myths, stories, legends,
genealogies, histories, religion, rituals, ceremonies, chants, prayers, and general
articles; to tape stories, myths, legends, grammars, teaching guides and outlines
and to build a collection of written and oral literature and to make same accessible to scholars, teachers and native institutions; and to duplicate and distribute
written and oral literature to the native communities and learning institutions.
The native languages deserve to be enshrined in this country's heritage as much
as do snowshoes, shards, and arrowheads. Nay! More.

But unless the writings, the essays, stories, plays, the papers of scholars, aca- 20
demics, lexicographers, grammarians, etymologists, playwrights, poets, novelists,
composers, philosophers are published and distributed, they can never nurture
growth in language and literature. Taking into account the market represented
by each tribe, no commercial publisher would risk publication of an "Indian"
book. Hence, only the federal government has the means to sponsor publication
of an "Indian text," either through a commercial publisher or through the
Queen's Printer. The publication of an "Indian" book may not be a commercially
profitable enterprise, but it would add to the nation's intellectual and literary
heritage. ♦

1990

Glossary

Anishinaubae: (or Anishinabe) a traditional name for the Chippewa or Ojibwa tribes indigenous to what is now north-central Minnesota and southern Manitoba.

Huron: a confederacy of five Iroquoian-speaking aboriginal tribes who occupied the area around Georgian Bay, Ontario, during the first half of the 17th century; the name was given to them by the French, with whom they traded furs.

Beothuk: the now-extinct first peoples (Beothuk means "the people" or "true people") of Newfoundland.

Five Nations Confederacy: a term that designates a union of five indigenous tribes (Seneca, Cayuga, Oneida, Onondaga, and Mohawk) inhabiting what is now the northern part of New York state, and whose population numbered between 10 000 and 15 000 at the time of European contact.

Explorations

- Have you read literature by Native writers? If so, in what context?

- Have you ever read an "Indian" story that was written by a non-aboriginal? Did it articulate abstract ideas and themes that gave insight into Native life, or did it appear to be a simple legend or folktale?

- Do you think that learning the language and reading the literature of another culture is crucial to understanding it?

Martin Luther King, Jr. was born in Atlanta, Georgia, in 1929. A Baptist preacher, he also held a doctorate in philosophy from Boston University. His organization of the year-long Montgomery, Alabama, bus boycott by African-Americans in 1956 gained him national prominence, and quickly made him the leader of the burgeoning civil rights movement in the United States. His "I Have a Dream" speech at the 1963 march on Washington invoked the moral conscience of the American nation and remains a classic instance of the impassioned use of rhetoric. In 1964, Time *magazine chose King as its Man of the Year, the first African-American so honoured; later the same year he was awarded the Nobel Peace Prize. On April 4, 1968, King was assassinated in Memphis, Tennessee.*

Letter from Birmingham Jail in Response to Public Statement by Eight Alabama Clergymen

Martin Luther King, Jr.

[Public Statement by Eight Alabama Clergymen:]
April 12, 1963

We the undersigned clergymen are among those who, in January, issued "An Appeal for Law and Order and Common Sense," in dealing with racial problems in Alabama. We expressed understanding that honest convictions in racial matters could properly be pursued in the courts, but urged that decisions of those courts should in the meantime be peacefully obeyed. 1

Since that time there had been some evidence of increased forbearance and a willingness to face facts. Responsible citizens have undertaken to work on various problems which cause racial friction and unrest. In Birmingham, recent public events have given indication that we all have opportunity for a new constructive and realistic approach to racial problems. 2

However, we are now confronted by a series of demonstrations by some of our Negro citizens, directed and led in part by outsiders. We recognize the natural impatience of people who feel that their hopes are slow in being realized. But we are convinced that these demonstrations are unwise and untimely. 3

We agree rather with certain local Negro leadership which has called for honest and open negotiations of racial issues in our area. And we believe this kind of facing of issues can best be accomplished by citizens of our own metropolitan area, white and Negro, meeting with their knowledge and experience of the local situation. All of us need to face that responsibility and find proper channels for its accomplishment. 4

5   Just as we formerly pointed out that "hatred and violence have no sanction in our religious and political traditions," we also point out that such actions as incite to hatred and violence, however technically peaceful those actions may be, have not contributed to the resolution of our local problems. We do not believe that these days of new hope are days when extreme measures are justified in Birmingham.

6   We commend the community as a whole, and the local news media and law enforcement officials in particular, on the calm manner in which these demonstrations have been handled. We urge the public to continue to show restraint should the demonstrations continue, and the law enforcement officials to remain calm and continue to protect our city from violence.

7   We further strongly urge our own Negro community to withdraw support from these demonstrations, and to unite locally in working peacefully for a better Birmingham. When rights are consistently denied, a cause should be pressed in the courts and in negotiations among local leaders, and not in the streets. We appeal to both our white and Negro citizenry to observe the principles of law and order and common sense.

Signed by:

C.C.J. Carpenter, D.D., LL.D., *Bishop of Alabama*

Joseph A. Durick, D.D., *Auxiliary Bishop, Diocese of Mobile, Birmingham*

Rabbi Milton L. Grafman, *Temple Emanu-El, Birmingham, Alabama*

Bishop Paul Hardin, *Bishop of the Alabama-West Florida Conference of the Methodist Church*

Bishop Nolan B. Harmon, *Bishop of the North Alabama Conference of the Methodist Church*

George M. Murray, D.D., LL.D., *Bishop Coadjutor, Episcopal Diocese of Alabama*

Edward V. Ramage, *Moderator, Synod of the Alabama Presbyterian Church in the United States*

Earl Stallings, *Pastor, First Baptist Church, Birmingham, Alabama*

[King's Response to the Clergymen's Public Statement:]
April 16, 1963
My Dear Fellow Clergymen:

1   While confined here in the Birmingham City Jail, I came across your recent statement calling my present activities "unwise and untimely." Seldom do I pause to answer criticism of my work and ideas. If I sought to answer all the criticisms that cross my desk, my secretaries would have little time for anything other than such correspondence in the course of the day, and I would have no time for constructive work. But since I feel that you are men of genuine good will and that your criticisms are sincerely set forth, I want to try to answer your statements in what I hope will be patient and reasonable terms.

2   I think I should indicate why I am here in Birmingham, since you have been influenced by the view which argues against "outsiders coming in." I have the

honor of serving as president of the Southern Christian Leadership Conference, an organization operating in every southern state, with headquarters in Atlanta, Georgia. We have some eighty-five affiliated organizations across the South, and one of them is the Alabama Christian Movement for Human Rights. Frequently we share staff, educational and financial resources with our affiliates. Several months ago the affiliate here in Birmingham asked us to be on call to engage in a nonviolent direct-action program if such were deemed necessary. We readily consented, and when the hour came we lived up to our promise. So I, along with several members of my staff, am here because I was invited here. I am here because I have organizational ties here.

But more basically, I am in Birmingham because injustice is here. Just as the 3
prophets of the eighth century B.C. left their villages and carried their "thus saith the Lord" far beyond the boundaries of their home towns, and just as the Apostle Paul left his village of Tarsus and carried the gospel of Jesus Christ to the far corners of the Greco-Roman world, so am I compelled to carry the gospel of freedom beyond my own home town. Like Paul, I must constantly respond to the Macedonian° call for aid.

Moreover, I am cognizant of the interrelatedness of all communities and states. 4
I cannot sit idly by in Atlanta and not be concerned about what happens in Birmingham. Injustice anywhere is a threat to justice everywhere. We are caught in an inescapable network of mutuality, tied in a single garment of destiny. Whatever affects one directly, affects all indirectly. Never again can we afford to live with the narrow, provincial "outside agitator" idea. Anyone who lives inside the United States can never be considered an outsider anywhere within its bounds.

You deplore the demonstrations taking place in Birmingham. But your statement, I am sorry to say, fails to express a similar concern for the conditions that 5
brought about the demonstrations. I am sure that none of you would want to rest content with the superficial kind of social analysis that deals merely with effects and does not grapple with underlying causes. It is unfortunate that demonstrations are taking place in Birmingham, but it is even more unfortunate that the city's white power structure left the Negro community with no alternative.

In any nonviolent campaign there are four basic steps: collection of the facts 6
to determine whether injustices exist; negotiation; self-purification; and direct action. We have gone through all these steps in Birmingham. There can be no gainsaying the fact that racial injustice engulfs this community. Birmingham is probably the most thoroughly segregated city in the United States. Its ugly record of brutality is widely known. Negroes have experienced grossly unjust treatment in the courts. There have been more unsolved bombings of Negro homes and churches in Birmingham than in any other city in the nation. These are the hard, brutal facts of the case. On the basis of these conditions, Negro leaders sought to negotiate with the city fathers. But the latter consistently refused to engage in good-faith negotiation.

7   Then, last September, came the opportunity to talk with leaders of Birmingham's economic community. In the course of the negotiations, certain promises were made by the merchants—for example, to remove the stores' humiliating racial signs. On the basis of these promises, the Reverend Fred Shuttlesworth and the leaders of the Alabama Christian Movement for Human Rights agreed to a moratorium on all demonstrations. As the weeks and months went by, we realized that we were the victims of a broken promise. A few signs, briefly removed, returned; the others remained.

8   As in so many past experiences, our hopes had been blasted, and the shadow of deep disappointment settled upon us. We had no alternative except to prepare for direct action, whereby we would present our very bodies as a means of laying our case before the conscience of the local and the national community. Mindful of the difficulties involved, we decided to undertake a process of self-purification. We began a series of workshops on nonviolence, and we repeatedly asked ourselves: "Are you able to accept blows without retaliating?" "Are you able to endure the ordeal of jail?" We decided to schedule our direct-action program for the Easter season, realizing that except for Christmas, this is the main shopping period of the year. Knowing that a strong economic-withdrawal program would be the by-product of direct action, we felt that this would be the best time to bring pressure to bear on the merchants for the needed change.

9   Then it occurred to us that Birmingham's mayoral election was coming up in March, and we speedily decided to postpone action until after election day. When we discovered that the Commissioner of Public Safety, Eugene "Bull" Connor,° had piled up enough votes to be in the run-off, we decided again to postpone action until the day after the run-off so that the demonstrations could not be used to cloud the issues. Like many others, we waited to see Mr. Connor defeated, and to this end we endured postponement after postponement. Having aided in this community need, we felt that our direct-action program could be delayed no longer.

10   You may well ask: "Why direct action? Why sit-ins, marches and so forth? Isn't negotiation a better path?" You are quite right in calling for negotiation. Indeed, this is the very purpose of direct action. Nonviolent direct action seeks to create such a crisis and foster such a tension that a community which has constantly refused to negotiate is forced to confront the issue. It seeks so to dramatize the issue that it can no longer be ignored. My citing the creation of tension as part of the work of the nonviolent-resister may sound rather shocking. But I must confess that I am not afraid of the word "tension." I have earnestly opposed violent tension, but there is a type of constructive, nonviolent tension which is necessary for growth. Just as Socrates felt that it was necessary to create a tension in the mind so that individuals could rise from the bondage of myths and half-truths to the unfettered realms of creative analysis and objective appraisal, so must we see the need for nonviolent gadflies to create the kind of tension in society that

will help men rise from the dark depths of prejudice and racism to the majestic heights of understanding and brotherhood.

The purpose of our direct-action program is to create a situation so crisis-   11
packed that it will inevitably open the door to negotiation. I therefore concur with you in your call for negotiation. Too long has our beloved Southland been bogged down in a tragic effort to live in monologue rather than dialogue.

One of the basic points in your statement is that the action that I and my asso-   12
ciates have taken in Birmingham is untimely. Some have asked: "Why didn't you give the new city administration time to act?" The only answer that I can give to this query is that the new Birmingham administration must be prodded about as much as the outgoing one, before it will act. We are sadly mistaken if we feel that the election of Albert Boutwell as mayor will bring the millennium to Birmingham. While Mr. Boutwell is a much more gentle person than Mr. Connor, they are both segregationists, dedicated to maintenance of the status quo. I have hope that Mr. Boutwell will be reasonable enough to see the futility of massive resistance to desegregation. But he will not see this without pressure from devotees of civil rights. My friends, I must say to you that we have not made a single gain in civil rights without determined legal and nonviolent pressure. Lamentably, it is an historical fact that privileged groups seldom give up their privileges voluntarily. Individuals may see the moral light and voluntarily give up their unjust posture; but, as Reinhold Niebuhr has reminded us, groups tend to be more immoral than individuals.

We know through painful experience that freedom is never voluntarily given   13
by the oppressor; it must be demanded by the oppressed. Frankly, I have yet to engage in a direct-action campaign that was "well timed" in the view of those who have not suffered unduly from the disease of segregation. For years now I have heard the word "Wait!" It rings in the ear of every Negro with piercing familiarity. This "Wait" has almost always meant "Never." We must come to see, with one of our distinguished jurists, that "justice too long delayed is justice denied."

We have waited for more than 340 years for our constitutional and God-given   14
rights. The nations of Asia and Africa are moving with jetlike speed toward gaining political independence, but we still creep at horse-and-buggy pace toward gaining a cup of coffee at a lunch counter. Perhaps it is easy for those who have never felt the stinging darts of segregation to say, "Wait." But when you have seen vicious mobs lynch your mothers and fathers at will and drown your sisters and brothers at whim; when you have seen hate-filled policemen curse, kick and even kill your black brothers and sisters; when you see the vast majority of your twenty million Negro brothers smothering in an airtight cage of poverty in the midst of an affluent society; when you suddenly find your tongue twisted and your speech stammering as you seek to explain to your six-year-old daughter why she can't go to the public amusement park that has just been advertised on television, and see tears welling up in her eyes when she is told that Funtown is closed to colored

children, and see ominous clouds of inferiority beginning to form in her little mental sky, and see her beginning to distort her personality by developing an unconscious bitterness toward white people; when you have to concoct an answer for a five-year-old son who is asking: "Daddy, why do white people treat colored people so mean?"; when you take a cross-country drive and find it necessary to sleep night after night in the uncomfortable corners of your automobile because no motel will accept you; when you are humiliated day in and day out by nagging signs reading "white" and "colored"; when your first name becomes "nigger," your middle name becomes "boy" (however old you are) and your last name becomes "John," and your wife and mother are never given the respected title "Mrs."; when you are harried by day and haunted by night by the fact that you are a Negro, living constantly at tiptoe stance, never quite knowing what to expect next, and are plagued with inner fears and outer resentments; when you are forever fighting a degenerating sense of "nobodiness"—then you will understand why we find it difficult to wait. There comes a time when a cup of endurance runs over, and men are no longer willing to be plunged into the abyss of despair. I hope, sirs, you can understand our legitimate and unavoidable impatience.

15   You express a great deal of anxiety over our willingness to break laws. This is certainly a legitimate concern. Since we so diligently urge people to obey the Supreme Court's decision of 1954 outlawing segregation in the public schools, at first glance it may seem rather paradoxical for us consciously to break laws. One may well ask: "How can you advocate breaking some laws and obeying others?" The answer lies in the fact that there are two types of laws: just and unjust. I would be the first to advocate obeying just laws. One has not only a legal but a moral responsibility to obey just laws. Conversely, one has a moral responsibility to disobey unjust laws. I would agree with St. Augustine° that "an unjust law is no law at all."

16   Now, what is the difference between the two? How does one determine whether a law is just or unjust? A just law is a man-made code that squares with the moral law or the law of God. An unjust law is a code that is out of harmony with the moral law. To put it in the terms of St. Thomas Aquinas°: An unjust law is a human law that is not rooted in eternal law and natural law. Any law that uplifts human personality is just. Any law that degrades human personality is unjust. All segregation statutes are unjust because segregation distorts the soul and damages the personality. It gives the segregator a false sense of superiority and the segregated a false sense of inferiority. Segregation, to use the terminology of the Jewish philosopher Martin Buber, substitutes an "I-it" relationship for an "I-thou" relationship and ends up relegating persons to the status of things. Hence segregation is not only politically, economically and sociologically unsound, it is morally wrong and sinful. Paul Tillich° has said that sin is separation. Is not segregation an existential expression of man's tragic separation, his awful estrangement, his terrible sinfulness? Thus it is that I can urge men to obey

the 1954 decision of the Supreme Court, for it is morally right; and I can urge them to disobey segregation ordinances, for they are morally wrong.

Let us consider a more concrete example of just and unjust laws. An unjust law   *17* is a code that a numerical or power group compels a minority group to obey but does not make binding on itself. This is *difference* made legal. By the same token, a just law is a code that a majority compels a minority to follow and that it is willing to follow itself. This is *sameness* made legal.

Let me give another explanation. A law is unjust if it is inflicted on a minority   *18* that, as a result of being denied the right to vote, had no part in enacting or devising the law. Who can say that the legislature of Alabama which set up that state's segregation laws was democratically elected? Throughout Alabama all sorts of devious methods are used to prevent Negroes from becoming registered voters, and there are some counties in which, even though Negroes constitute a majority of the population, not a single Negro is registered. Can any law enacted under such circumstances be considered democratically structured?

Sometimes a law is just on its face and unjust in its application. For instance,   *19* I have been arrested on a charge of parading without a permit. Now, there is nothing wrong in having an ordinance which requires a permit for a parade. But such an ordinance becomes unjust when it is used to maintain segregation and to deny citizens the First Amendment privilege of peaceful assembly and protest.

I hope you are able to see the distinction I am trying to point out. In no sense   *20* do I advocate evading or defying the law, as would the rabid segregationist. That would lead to anarchy. One who breaks an unjust law must do so openly, lovingly, and with a willingness to accept the penalty. I submit that an individual who breaks a law that conscience tells him is unjust, and who willingly accepts the penalty of imprisonment in order to arouse the conscience of the community over its injustice, is in reality expressing the highest respect for law.

Of course, there is nothing new about this kind of civil disobedience. It was   *21* evidenced sublimely in the refusal of Shadrach,° Meshach° and Abednego° to obey the laws of Nebuchadnezzar,° on the ground that a higher moral law was at stake. It was practiced superbly by the early Christians, who were willing to face hungry lions and the excruciating pain of chopping blocks rather than submit to certain unjust laws of the Roman Empire. To a degree, academic freedom is a reality today because Socrates practiced civil disobedience. In our own nation, the Boston Tea Party represented a massive act of civil disobedience.

We should never forget that everything Adolf Hitler did in Germany was   *22* "legal" and everything the Hungarian freedom fighters° did in Hungary was "illegal." It was "illegal" to aid and comfort a Jew in Hitler's Germany. Even so, I am sure that, had I lived in Germany at the time, I would have aided and comforted my Jewish brothers. If today I lived in a Communist country where certain principles dear to the Christian faith are suppressed, I would openly advocate disobeying that country's antireligious laws.

23   I must make two honest confessions to you, my Christian and Jewish brothers. First, I must confess that over the past few years I have been gravely disappointed with the white moderate. I have almost reached the regrettable conclusion that the Negro's great stumbling block in his stride toward freedom is not the White Citizen's Counciler or the Ku Klux Klanner, but the white moderate, who is more devoted to "order" than to justice; who prefers a negative peace which is the absence of tension to a positive peace which is the presence of justice; who constantly says: "I agree with you in the goal you seek, but I cannot agree with your methods of direct action"; who paternalistically believes he can set the timetable for another man's freedom; who lives by a mythical concept of time and who constantly advises the Negro to wait for a "more convenient season." Shallow understanding from people of good will is more frustrating than absolute misunderstanding from people of ill will. Lukewarm acceptance is much more bewildering than outright rejection.

24   I had hoped that the white moderate would understand that law and order exist for the purpose of establishing justice and that when they fail in this purpose they become the dangerously structured dams that block the flow of social progress. I had hoped that the white moderate would understand that the present tension in the South is a necessary phase of the transition from an obnoxious negative peace, in which the Negro passively accepted his unjust plight, to a substantive and positive peace, in which all men will respect the dignity and worth of human personality. Actually, we who engage in nonviolent direct action are not the creators of tension. We merely bring to the surface the hidden tension that is already alive. We bring it out in the open, where it can be seen and dealt with. Like a boil that can never be cured so long as it is covered up but must be opened with all its ugliness to the natural medicines of air and light, injustice must be exposed, with all the tension its exposure creates, to the light of human conscience and the air of national opinion before it can be cured.

25   In your statement you assert that our actions, even though peaceful, must be condemned because they precipitate violence. But is this a logical assertion? Isn't this like condemning a robbed man because his possession of money precipitated the evil act of robbery? Isn't this like condemning Socrates because his unswerving commitment to truth and his philosophical inquiries precipitated the act by the misguided populace in which they made him drink hemlock? Isn't this like condemning Jesus because his unique God-consciousness and never-ceasing devotion to God's will precipitated the evil act of crucifixion? We must come to see that, as the federal courts have consistently affirmed, it is wrong to urge an individual to cease his efforts to gain his basic constitutional rights because the quest may precipitate violence. Society must protect the robbed and punish the robber.

26   I had also hoped that the white moderate would reject the myth concerning time in relation to the struggle for freedom. I have just received a letter from a

white brother in Texas. He writes: "All Christians know that the colored people will receive equal rights eventually, but it is possible that you are in too great a religious hurry. It has taken Christianity almost two thousand years to accomplish what it has. The teachings of Christ take time to come to earth." Such an attitude stems from a tragic misconception of time, from the strangely rational notion that there is something in the very flow of time that will inevitably cure all ills. Actually, time itself is neutral; it can be used either destructively or constructively. More and more I feel that the people of ill will have used time much more effectively than have the people of good will. We will have to repent in this generation not merely for the hateful words and actions of the bad people but for the appalling silence of the good people. Human progress never rolls in on wheels of inevitability; it comes through the tireless efforts of men willing to be coworkers with God, and without this hard work, time itself becomes an ally of the forces of social stagnation. We must use time creatively, in the knowledge that the time is always ripe to do right. Now is the time to make real the promise of democracy and transform our pending national elegy into a creative psalm of brotherhood. Now is the time to lift our national policy from the quicksand of racial injustice to the solid rock of human dignity.

You speak of our activity in Birmingham as extreme. At first I was rather disappointed that fellow clergymen would see my nonviolent efforts as those of an extremist. I began thinking about the fact that I stand in the middle of two opposing forces in the Negro community. One is a force of complacency, made up in part of Negroes who, as a result of long years of oppression, are so drained of self-respect and a sense of "somebodiness" that they have adjusted to segregation; and in part of a few middle-class Negroes who, because of a degree of academic and economic security and because in some ways they profit by segregation, have become insensitive to the problems of the masses. The other force is one of bitterness and hatred, and it comes perilously close to advocating violence. It is expressed in the various black nationalist groups that are springing up across the nation, the largest and best-known being Elijah Muhammad's Muslim movement. Nourished by the Negro's frustration over the continued existence of racial discrimination, this movement is made up of people who have lost faith in America, who have absolutely repudiated Christianity, and who have concluded that the white man is an incorrigible "devil." 27

I have tried to stand between these two forces, saying that we need emulate neither the "do-nothingism" of the complacent nor the hatred and despair of the black nationalist. For there is the more excellent way of love and nonviolent protest. I am grateful to God that, through the influence of the Negro church, the way of nonviolence became an integral part of our struggle. 28

If this philosophy had not emerged, by now many streets of the South would, I am convinced, be flowing with blood. And I am further convinced that if our white brothers dismiss as "rabble-rousers" and "outside agitators" those of us who 29 employ nonviolent direct action, and if they refuse to support our nonviolent efforts, millions of the Negroes will, out of frustration and despair, seek solace and security in black-nationalist ideologies—a development that would inevitably lead to a frightening racial nightmare.

30   Oppressed people cannot remain oppressed forever. The yearning for freedom eventually manifests itself, and that is what has happened to the American Negro. Something within has reminded him of his birthright of freedom, and something without has reminded him that it can be gained. Consciously or unconsciously, he has been caught up by the *Zeitgeist*,° and with his black brothers of Africa and his brown and yellow brothers of Asia, South America and the Caribbean, the United States Negro is moving with a sense of great urgency toward the promised land of racial justice. If one recognizes this vital urge that has engulfed the Negro community, one should readily understand why public demonstrations are taking place. The Negro has many pent-up resentments and latent frustrations, and he must release them. So let him march; let him make prayer pilgrimages to the city hall; let him go on freedom rides—and try to understand why he must do so. If his repressed emotions are not released in nonviolent ways, they will seek expression through violence; this is not a threat but a fact of history. So I have not said to my people: "Get rid of your discontent." Rather, I have tried to say that this normal and healthy discontent can be channeled into the creative outlet of nonviolent direct action. And now this approach is being termed extremist.

31   But though I was initially disappointed at being categorized as an extremist, as I continued to think about the matter I gradually gained a measure of satisfaction from the label. Was not Jesus an extremist for love: "Love your enemies, bless them that curse you, do good to them that hate you, and pray for them which despitefully use you, and persecute you." Was not Amos° an extremist for justice: "Let justice roll down like waters and righteousness like an ever-flowing stream." Was not Paul° an extremist for the Christian gospel: "I bear in my body the marks of the Lord Jesus." Was not Martin Luther° an extremist: "Here I stand; I cannot do otherwise, so help me God." And John Bunyan°: "I will stay in jail to the end of my days before I make a butchery of my conscience." And Abraham Lincoln°: "This nation cannot survive half slave and half free." And Thomas Jefferson°: "We hold these truths to be self-evident, that all men are created equal...." So the question is not whether we will be extremists, but what kind of extremists we will be. Will we be extremists for hate or for love? Will we be extremists for the preservation of injustice or for the extension of justice? In that dramatic scene on Calvary's hill three men were crucified. We must never forget that all three were crucified for the same crime—the crime of extremism. Two were extremists for immorality, and thus fell below their environment. The other, Jesus Christ, was an extremist for love, truth and goodness, and thereby rose above his environment. Perhaps the South, the nation and the world are in dire need of creative extremists.

I had hoped that the white moderate would see this need. Perhaps I was too *32* optimistic; perhaps I expected too much. I suppose I should have realized that few members of the oppressor race can understand the deep groans and passionate yearnings of the oppressed race, and still fewer have the vision to see that injustice must be rooted out by strong, persistent and determined action. I am thankful, however, that some of our white brothers in the South have grasped the meaning of this social revolution and committed themselves to it. They are still all too few in quantity, but they are big in quality. Some—such as Ralph McGill, Lillian Smith, Harry Golden, James McBride Dabbs, Ann Braden and Sarah Patton Boyle—have written about our struggle in eloquent and prophetic terms. Others have marched with us down nameless streets of the South. They have languished in filthy, roach-infested jails, suffering the abuse and brutality of policemen who view them as "dirty nigger-lovers." Unlike so many of their moderate brothers and sisters, they have recognized the urgency of the moment and sensed the need for powerful "action" antidotes to combat the disease of segregation.

Let me take note of my other major disappointment. I have been so greatly dis- *33* appointed with the white church and its leadership. Of course, there are some notable exceptions. I am not unmindful of the fact that each of you has taken some significant stands on this issue. I commend you, Reverend Stallings, for your Christian stand on this past Sunday, in welcoming Negroes to your worship service on a nonsegregated basis. I commend the Catholic leaders of this state for integrating Spring Hill College several years ago.

But despite these notable exceptions, I must honestly reiterate that I have *34* been disappointed with the church. I do not say this as one of those negative critics who can always find something wrong with the church. I say this as a minister of the gospel, who loves the church; who was nurtured in its bosom; who has been sustained by its spiritual blessings and who will remain true to it as long as the cord of life shall lengthen.

When I was suddenly catapulted into the leadership of the bus protest in *35* Montgomery, Alabama, a few years ago, I felt we would be supported by the white church. I felt that the white ministers, priests and rabbis of the South would be among our strongest allies. Instead, some have been outright opponents, refusing to understand the freedom movement and misrepresenting its leaders; all too many others have been more cautious than courageous and have remained silent behind the anesthetizing security of stained-glass windows.

In spite of my shattered dreams, I came to Birmingham with the hope that the *36* white religious leadership of this community would see the justice of our cause and, with deep moral concern, would serve as the channel through which our just grievances could reach the power structure. I had hoped that each of you would understand. But again I have been disappointed.

I have heard numerous southern religious leaders admonish their worshippers *37* to comply with a desegregation decision because it is the law, but I have longed to hear white ministers declare: "Follow this decree because integration is morally right and because the Negro is your brother." In the midst of blatant injustices inflicted upon the Negro, I have watched white churchmen stand on the sideline and mouth pious irrelevancies and sanctimonious trivialities. In the midst of a mighty struggle to rid our nation of racial and economic injustice, I have heard many ministers say: "Those are social issues, with which the gospel has no real concern." And I have watched many churches commit themselves to a completely otherworldly religion which makes a strange, un-Biblical distinction between body and soul, between the sacred and the secular.

38   I have traveled the length and breadth of Alabama, Mississippi and all the other southern states. On sweltering summer days and crisp autumn mornings I have looked at the South's beautiful churches with their lofty spires pointing heavenward. I have beheld the impressive outlines of her massive religious-education buildings. Over and over I have found myself asking: "What kind of people worship here? Who is their God? Where were their voices when the lips of Governor Barnett dripped with words of inter-position and nullification? Where were they when Governor Wallace gave a clarion call for defiance and hatred? Where were their voices of support when bruised and weary Negro men and women decided to rise from the dark dungeons of complacency to the bright hills of creative protest?"

39   Yes, these questions are still in my mind. In deep disappointment I have wept over the laxity of the church. But be assured that my tears have been tears of love. There can be no deep disappointment where there is not deep love. Yes, I love the church. How could I do otherwise? I am in the rather unique position of being the son, the grandson, and the great-grandson of preachers. Yes, I see the church as the body of Christ. But, oh! How we have blemished and scarred that body through social neglect and through fear of being nonconformists.

40   There was a time when the church was very powerful—in the time when the early Christians rejoiced at being deemed worthy to suffer for what they believed. In those days the church was not merely a thermometer that recorded the ideas and principles of popular opinion; it was a thermostat that transformed the mores of society. Whenever the early Christians entered a town, the people in power became disturbed and immediately sought to convict the Christians for being "disturbers of the peace" and "outside agitators." But the Christians pressed on, in the conviction that they were "a colony of heaven," called to obey God rather than man. Small in number, they were big in commitment. They were too God-intoxicated to be "astronomically intimidated." By their effort and example they brought an end to such ancient evils as infanticide and gladiatorial contests.

41   Things are different now. So often the contemporary church is a weak, ineffectual voice with an uncertain sound. So often it is an archdefender of the status quo. Far from being disturbed by the presence of the church, the power structure of the average community is consoled by the church's silent—and often even vocal—sanction of things as they are.

But the judgment of God is upon the church as never before. If today's church *42*
does not recapture the sacrificial spirit of the early church, it will lose its authenticity, forfeit the loyalty of millions, and be dismissed as an irrelevant social club
with no meaning for the twentieth century. Every day I meet young people whose
disappointment with the church has turned into outright disgust.

Perhaps I have once again been too optimistic. Is organized religion too inex- *43*
tricably bound to the status quo to save our nation and the world? Perhaps I must
turn my faith to the inner spiritual church, the church within the church, as the
true *ekklesia*° and the hope of the world. But again I am thankful to God that
some noble souls from the ranks of organized religion have broken loose from the
paralyzing chains of conformity and joined us as active partners in the struggle
for freedom. They have left their secure congregations and walked the streets of
Albany, Georgia, with us. They have gone down the highways of the South on
tortuous rides for freedom. Yes, they have gone to jail with us. Some have been
dismissed from their churches, have lost the support of their bishops and fellow
ministers. But they have acted in the faith that right defeated is stronger than
evil triumphant. Their witness has been the spiritual salt that has preserved the
true meaning of the gospel in these troubled times. They have carved a tunnel of
hope through the dark mountain of disappointment.

I hope the church as a whole will meet the challenge of this decisive hour. *44*
But even if the church does not come to the aid of justice, I have no despair
about the future. I have no fear about the outcome of our struggle in
Birmingham, even if our motives are at present misunderstood. We will reach
the goal of freedom in Birmingham and all over the nation, because the goal of
America is freedom. Abused and scorned though we may be, our destiny is tied
up with America's destiny. Before the pilgrims landed at Plymouth, we were
here. Before the pen of Jefferson etched the majestic words of the Declaration
of Independence across the pages of history, we were here. For more than two
centuries our forebears labored in this country without wages; they made cotton
king; they built the homes of their masters while suffering gross injustice and
shameful humiliation—and yet out of a bottomless vitality they continued to
thrive and develop. If the inexpressible cruelties of slavery could not stop us, the
opposition we now face will surely fail. We will win our freedom because the
sacred heritage of our nation and the eternal will of God are embodied in our
echoing demands.

Before closing I feel impelled to mention one other point in your statement *45*
that has troubled me profoundly. You warmly commended the Birmingham
police force for keeping "order" and "preventing violence." I doubt that you
would have so warmly commended the police force if you had seen its dogs sinking their teeth into unarmed, nonviolent Negroes. I doubt that you would so
quickly commend the policemen if you were to observe their ugly and inhumane
treatment of Negroes here in the city jail; if you were to watch them push and

curse old Negro women and young Negro girls; if you were to see them slap and kick old Negro men and young boys; if you were to observe them, as they did on two occasions, refuse to give us food because we wanted to sing our grace together. I cannot join you in your praise of the Birmingham police department.

46 It is true that police have exercised a degree of discipline in handling the demonstrators. In this sense they have conducted themselves rather "nonviolently" in public. But for what purpose? To preserve the evil system of segregation. Over the past few years I have consistently preached that nonviolence demands that the means we use must be as pure as the ends we seek. I have tried to make clear that it is wrong to use immoral means to attain moral ends. But now I must affirm that it is just as wrong, or perhaps even more so, to use moral means to preserve immoral ends. Perhaps Mr. Connor and his policemen have been rather nonviolent in public, as was Chief Pritchett in Albany, Georgia, but they have used the moral means of nonviolence to maintain the immoral end of racial injustice. As T. S. Eliot° has said: "The last temptation is the greatest treason: To do the right deed for the wrong reason."

47 I wish you had commended the Negro sit-inners and demonstrators of Birmingham for their sublime courage, their willingness to suffer and their amazing discipline in the midst of great provocation. One day the South will recognize its real heroes. They will be the James Merediths,° with the noble sense of purpose that enables them to face jeering and hostile mobs, and with the agonizing loneliness that characterizes the life of the pioneer. They will be old, oppressed, battered Negro women, symbolized in a seventy-two-year-old woman in Montgomery, Alabama, who rose up with a sense of dignity and with her people decided not to ride segregated buses, and who responded with ungrammatical profundity to one who inquired about her weariness: "My feets is tired, but my soul is at rest." They will be the young high school and college students, the young ministers of the gospel and a host of their elders, courageously and nonviolently sitting in at lunch counters and willingly going to jail for conscience' sake. One day the South will know that when these disinherited children of God sat down at lunch counters, they were in reality standing up for what is best in the American dream and for the most sacred values in our Judaeo-Christian heritage, thereby bringing our nation back to those great wells of democracy which were dug deep by the founding fathers in their formulation of the Constitution and the Declaration of Independence.

48 Never before have I written so long a letter. I'm afraid it is much too long to take your precious time. I can assure you that it would have been much shorter if I had been writing from a comfortable desk, but what else can one do when he is alone in a narrow jail cell, other than write long letters, think long thoughts and pray long prayers?

49 If I have said anything in this letter that overstates the truth and indicates an unreasonable impatience, I beg you to forgive me. If I have said anything that

understates the truth and indicates my having a patience that allows me to settle for anything less than brotherhood, I beg God to forgive me.

I hope this letter finds you strong in faith. I also hope that circumstances will   50
soon make it possible for me to meet each of you, not as an integrationist or a
civil-rights leader but as a fellow clergyman and a Christian brother. Let us all
hope that the dark clouds of racial prejudice will soon pass away and the deep fog
of misunderstanding will be lifted from our fear-drenched communities, and in
some not too distant tomorrow the radiant stars of love and brotherhood will
shine over our great nation with all their scintillating beauty.

Yours for the cause of Peace and Brotherhood
Martin Luther King, Jr. ◆

1963

Glossary

Macedonia: a region north of Greece, thought by the classical Greeks to be "barbarian." St. Paul visited Macedonia and founded two churches after dreaming he had been beckoned there, and, though he alludes in 2 Corinthians 7:5 to the problems he encountered there, he praises the Macedonians for being generous in spite of their poverty.

Eugene "Bull" Connor: (1897–1973) Birmingham's Commissioner of Public Safety, Connor was a segregationist who unleashed the city's resources against the civil rights demonstrators.

St. Augustine: (354–430 AD) early Christian father and philosopher known for his *Confessions* (397–401), a spiritual autobiography, and for the 22-volume treatise *The City of God* (413–426).

St. Thomas Aquinas: (1225–1274) Italian scholastic theologian and philosopher known for his two *Summae*, or accounts of human knowledge.

Paul Tillich: (1886–1965) German-born American theologian and philosopher who fled the Nazis and who used existential philosophy to interpret Christian doctrine; his major work is *Systematic Theology*.

Shadrach, Meshach, Abednego, Nebuchadnezzar: Nebuchadnezzar, king of Assyria, figures prominently in the Old Testament, particularly the book of Daniel, where he dispatches the Hebrews Shadrach, Meshach, and Abednego into a fiery furnace because they refuse to worship a graven image instead of God; the three do not burn, however, and Nebuchadnezzar is forced to admit the power of their God.

Hungarian freedom fighters: leaders of a popular uprising against the ruling Stalinist regime in Hungary in 1956; the uprising was brutally suppressed by the Soviet army.

Zeitgeist: spirit of the times.

Amos: third book of minor prophets in the Old Testament; Amos foretold of the destruction of Israel in five visions.

Paul: passionate apostle and missionary of Christianity, Paul was the author of the Epistles in the New Testament.

Martin Luther: (1483–1546) German religious reformer who posted his critique of the Roman Catholic Church, *The Ninety-Five Theses*, on the door of a church in Wittenberg in 1517; this action is generally regarded as the starting point of the Protestant Reformation.

John Bunyan: (1628–1688) English writer and preacher, Bunyan is the author of *Pilgrim's Progress*.

Abraham Lincoln: (1809–1865) 16th president of the U.S. (1861–1865). Lincoln governed the country during the American Civil War until his assassination in 1865; Lincoln signed the Emancipation Proclamation freeing the slaves in January 1863.

Thomas Jefferson: (1743–1826) third president of the United States (1801–1809) and author of the Declaration of Independence (1776).

ekklesia: the Greek word for the early Christian church.

T.S. Eliot: (1888–1965) American-born English poet, critic, and playwright whose *The Waste Land* (1926) is considered a landmark in modern poetry.

James Meredith: the first black student enrolled at the University of Mississippi.

Explorations

- Can you think of contemporary examples of civil disobedience? How did government authorities react to these situations?

- Do you think that non-violent protest is effective in fighting oppression? Why or why not?

- Do you think that King is a credible speaker, despite the fact that he is writing from jail? Why or why not?

Heather Menzies, born in 1949, is an adjunct research professor in Canadian studies at Carleton University. She has taught at many Canadian universities, including McGill, Simon Fraser, and the University of Victoria. Menzies has written a number of books, including the best-seller Whose Brave New World?: The Information Highway and the New Economy *(1996). In addition to teaching and writing, Menzies is a social activist and a producer.*

When Roots Grow Back into the Earth

Heather Menzies

I've always been skeptical about loving the whole planet Earth. For me, you can love it best when you love a particular place, and even then, you can't do it in a moment, but only as you know that place and are involved in it over a long period of time. So I dateline this essay very specifically: 1st. Concession, Locheil Township, Glengarry County, Ontario. Spring 1994.

I've read that the women who used to live here went off by themselves when it   1
was their bleeding time. In sacred menstrual huts, they sat on the ground, on beds of moss. They rested, meditated, and visited with each other while their blood seeped out of their bodies and into the living earth.[1]

I think of this as I walk between the trees I helped to plant as a girl. Every   2
spring, beginning when I was eight, we planted trees here, in the thin, hard soils of eastern Ontario, on a run-down little farm my parents had bought in the 1950s, in lieu of a summer cottage. Armed with shovels and buckets, we tramped the land where it slopes up from the river, digging hopeful seedlings into the inhospitable ground.

I worked the ground with my bare hands: scratching among gravel and stones,   3
finding the edge of rocks and prying them out, then foraging around for handfuls of precious soil, sweet black humus with which to cover the roots of the ten-inch nursery trees. The idea was to re-forest the land, which probably should never have been cleared in the first place. The soil had become too poor for farming. "Barren," they called it in the soil-testing lab; leached and eroded from having been used too hard, then left open, and exposed to the elements. The 200-acre farm had been abandoned like so many others around here after the Second World War, when mechanization imposed its implacable choice: get bigger or get out.

The trees came through a government reforestation program. Red pine, white   4
pine, and spruce, they arrived in bundles of twenty-five packed in peat moss in slapped-together wooden boxes made of spruce lath. Once, the year we planted 13,000 and my mother carried a solution of soda and water in a screw-cap bottle to keep herself from throwing up, there were ten boxes, each five feet long and

three feet deep. When the last tree had been taken out and planted, my brother and I made forts with the empty boxes, our hands too tough to catch the splinters.

5   It's my hands in the ground I remember the most: eight-year-old, nine-year-old, ten-year-old hands. And the ground perpetually cold, with frost still glinting amongst the stones. I'd bang away with my shovel, trying to find a way in for the trees, and hitting rock after rock under last year's withered weeds. The reverberations jarred my head, and I threw the shovel aside.

6   On one side of me, I sensed my older brother and sister moving steadily ahead. On the other side, my mother kept an eye on my little brother while working her own row of trees. She worked doggedly, stooping but never once getting down on her hands and knees—a girls' school product even there. My father was, as usual, way on ahead, never stopping, never even slowing down. But I knew he'd double back, then help me catch up. He had a shiny, round-mouthed shovel, which he sharpened regularly so it would cut fast and neat.

7   My hands are stiff with cold, and puffed up pink like sausages. I know this, but I don't really notice as I work in a universe reduced to impenetrable earth riddled with stones and rough-edged gravel. I've pulled or shovelled aside a scruffy brown patch of last year's twitch grass, along with the collapsed seedhead of a burdock plant. The burr barbs are lodged in the skin between my fingers. My fingers are caked in half-dried mud as I rake through the ground, seeking passage for the tree roots. The stones here are a mix of shale and granite, the tag end of the Precambrian Shield° littered like bones beneath the surface. I find the edge of the stone I'm up against, and yank to pull it out. Nothing happens. I scratch for a fingerhold deeper underneath, feel the dirt drive farther beneath my nails, the nails separating a little from the skin. Still I push, past gravel and frost crystals hard as diamonds. I get a grip and brace myself, knees apart, on the thawing ground. I pull hard, shoulder and stomach muscles straining. My fingertips burn as they slip from under the unyielding stone. Tears run down my face. The rock's too big. I'll have to dig another hole. Warm salt water drops onto the backs of my hands, moistening where the dirt has dried. My head throbs as I dig again, kneel again, and struggle with the stones.

8   I plunge my hands into the bucket. Sweet release. The water's cold, yet seems warmer than the ground. And the wetness soothes my fingers. I pull out a tree. A seedling with its spritely main shoot, its tentative side branches, and its prodigious roots.

9   I hold the tree by the stem, my swollen fingers tingling. I tuck the root filaments carefully into the hole. I curl them around so they all fit in, and push the tips down into the fertile hole. I do this with every tree, an extra boost so they're sure to take root here, and survive. The root tendrils lie there like a hank of my own fly-away tangled hair, kept in place only by my twelve-year-old hand. Still holding, I pile the precious black soil in on top of them. Crumbs of still-fecund living earth for them to cling to, draw nourishment from.

10   Take, eat. This is my body....°

I scoop a handful of muddy water out of my pail, pour it off the tips of my   *11*
fingers, and watch it seep into the ground, down among the root hairs.

I rake the last bits of dirt into the hole, then plunk the patches of turf back   *12*
on top, and press them in place with my hands. One tree planted. One out of
thousands and thousands and thousands. And now they blanket the slope, a
skein of green in infinite tones and variations, with the wind sighing through
them, lightly or heavily, depending on the weather.

Now their trunks are thicker than my body. Their roots are gnarled fingers   *13*
worrying the edges of the few still-protruding rocks. Whether it's new soil building
up or the rocks themselves subsiding, I don't know. But now only the boulders are
visible.

The biggest boulder we pulled out of the fields, a fisted hunk of pink-tinged   *14*
granite, is now a sort of family monument. It's parked along the path between the
hayfields in the lowlands close to the river and the higher ground where we
planted the trees. My father hired a stone mason to write on the rock, beginning
with the phrase: "They cared for this land." He listed all our names, and our birth
dates. Then, at the head of the list, he put the name of Duncan "the Night"
Macmillan. Some research I'd done in the archives established that he was the
first to clear this land. And that's how my father counted things.

The man was nicknamed "the Night" because he was such a fine, hard-working   *15*
Presbyterian that he worked at night if there was a moon to see by. He cared that
much for his family: children of emigrant Scots seeking a better life in the New
World. I can imagine him out there day and night, hectoring his workhorses as
they strained to pull out the deep, resisting tree roots. I can imagine his relentless
labour, and the faith that kept him at it. Until he'd broken the land to the plough
and the discipline of crops.

It never occurred to me while planting those trees every spring that it was his   *16*
diligence I was covering up for. Nor did I consider the compulsion to be productive as anything but admirable. He was hard-working. So were we, pushing ourselves from early morning 'til nearly dark those cool, sometimes cold and wet,
spring weekends. I have no memory of what we did after we returned, exhausted,
to the farmhouse and the stew Mum simmered at the back of the woodstove. We
were weekend pioneers, with little time for contemplation.

When my father died, we buried his ashes at the memorial rock, and I visit it   *17*
often when I'm walking these woods. The rock is overshadowed now by the trees.
A thick branch of a spruce droops down and brushes the top. Lichen and moss
creep microscopically across its surface, obscuring my father's chosen words.

I gaze at the bough of spruce, its deep dark green turning black in the shadows   *18*
beyond. I see the buds where new growth will emerge, fragile as seedlings, in the
spring. I see where old needles are sloughing themselves off, cascading across the
rock and settling on the ground. I understand these trees, know them as minutely
as I know the flesh of my son named after my father and now twelve years old
himself.

19   It's strange I came to love these trees, after all I went through helping to plant, then tend them through their first years of life. Every spring we walked the still rock-strewn land where we'd dug in the seedlings, trying to find them under the collapsed remains of last year's overwhelming weeds. Spotting a toothbrush bristle of green, I'd pull the grasses apart and frisk the tiny branches free of entangling debris. It sometimes took days to find all the buried ones, and not all of them in time.

20   Then it was the snow itself which posed a threat. The red pines got it the worst, with their bushier boughs and thicker needles. The snow took them down, and by spring, they'd be bent right over, twisted sideways and unable to right themselves. It became our chore as children to scout out these cripples and set them straight, using broken branches from dead elm trees, or hawthorns and other scrub bushes that had infiltrated the long-abandoned fields. It wasn't hard work. In fact, I remember actually enjoying it. At some point too, I crossed over, and continued doing it on my own. For them. For us. I'd encountered the word "pantheism" by then, and I was a pantheist; though still a church-going one.

21   It was pleasant solitary work, and I used to alternately talk to the trees and sing to them: hymns in the early days, then Beatles' tunes about love, love, love.

22 There's been a little rain, and now the sun is coming out. I walk toward it, up the path through the woods, in the direction we moved with our buckets and shovels over thirty years ago. A mellow, honey-thick glow slants through the trees and onto the path, which is spongy with moss and fallen pine needles. The sun comes through the branches of an overhanging pine, and I stop to contemplate a water droplet hanging, like a diamond, at the tip of one of its needles. I duck in under the branches knowing it's drier there, and sit on a mound of moss-covered ground.

23   I think of my mother, busy as ever and still battling headaches. I think of my older brother, my younger brother, and my older sister: one's a lawyer, one's a doctor, one's a telecommunications manager. Then there's me, busily writing to meet the next deadline, to have another book in print. A drop of water descends from a branch above me, and lands on the back of my hand. It occurs to me that the whole bunch of us could be out there clearcutting at Clayoquot.° It's that much in our blood, the diligence and hard-working spirit; what Nietzsche° called the endless becoming, with no horizon but the perpetual invention of new objectives: the next tree to cut, the next one to plant, the next cause to write about.

24   The drop of water slides down my hand where I rest it against the ground. But I think it's not the will and the diligence themselves that are so bad. It's their monopoly within us: our hearts, minds, bodies, and souls all dedicated to the dynamo of doing, without respite. No time for rest and contemplation. No time for rooting and taking root. No time for remembrance and reciprocity.

25   I watch the drop of water, now warmed by my skin, roll steadily down my hand, and slip away into the earth. I feel the moss soft beneath me, feel its moisture seep into my jeans. Around me, shadows drift up like root hairs seeking passage. A

breeze whiffles the upper branches, light as surf bubbles caressing a shore. I sit on the moss, enveloped by these trees I helped grow into this ground over so many years. They're in my blood now. I feel them.

> When I take the time
> to remember myself as part of them,
> and remember them
> as part of me. ◆

1994

Endnote

1. The information about Native women's menstrual rites comes from Anne Cameron's *Daughters of Copper Woman* (Press Gang, 1981) and from Beth Richard's article, "Blood of the Moon," in *Herizons* (Vol. 7, No. 4).

Glossary

the Precambrian Shield: a vast geological expanse of rock dating from 3.8 billion years ago that stretches across the north of Canada from Labrador to the Yukon and that contains rich mineral deposits and prehistoric fossils.

Take, eat. This is my body...: words spoken during the Christian Holy Communion ceremony, in which bread and wine are ingested to commemorate the body and blood of Christ.

Clayoquot Sound: an area comprising 260 000 hectares (1004 square miles) of Crown-owned land that is the largest intact ancient temperate rainforest on Vancouver Island. The Nuu-chah-nulth First Nations have considered the region sacred for thousands of years. In the summer of 1993 the Kennedy Lake bridge, which provides access to the forest, was the site of a blockade by more than 800 people protesting plans by Macmillan Bloedel to log the area.

Nietzsche: Friedrich Nietzsche (1844–1900), German philosopher, classical scholar, and poet who rejected Christian doctrine, rationalist philosophy, and systemic thought in his investigations into human will and the "irrational"; his theories influenced the artistic movement of expressionism, and his concept of the "super-man" would later be exploited in Nazi attempts to purify the Aryan race.

Explorations

- Do you have a place where you have planted your "roots"? If not, what has prevented you from doing so?

- If you do feel firmly rooted in a particular place, why do you feel this way? Why is this place so meaningful?

- Do you ever find yourself in a state of "endless becoming, with no horizon but the perpetual invention of new objectives"? If so, how do you react? Do you stop, take a rest, and contemplate your situation, or do you keep on moving?

Donald M. Murray was born in 1924 in Boston, Massachusetts, and lives in Durham, New Hampshire. He is currently professor emeritus of English at the University of New Hampshire. He worked for many years as a journalist at the Boston Globe, *where in 1954 he won a Pulitzer Prize for editorial writing. He has also served as an editor at* Time *magazine, published a book for children,* The World of Sound Recording, *and authored a number of novels, poetry collections, and books on the art of writing and teaching writing.*

The Maker's Eye: Revising Your Own Manuscript

Donald M. Murray

1   When students complete a first draft, they consider the job of writing done—and their teachers too often agree. When professional writers complete a first draft, they usually feel that they are at the start of the writing process. When a draft is completed, the job of writing can begin.

2   That difference in attitude is the difference between amateur and professional, inexperience and experience, journeyman and craftsman. Peter F. Drucker, the prolific business writer, calls his first draft "the zero draft"—after that he can start counting. Most writers share the feeling that the first draft, and all of those which follow, are opportunities to discover what they have to say and how best they can say it.

3   To produce a progression of drafts, each of which says more and says it more clearly, the writer has to develop a special kind of reading skill. In school we are taught to decode what appears on the page as finished writing. Writers, however, face a different category of possibility and responsibility when they read their own drafts. To them the words on the page are never finished. Each can be changed and rearranged, can set off a chain reaction of confusion or clarified meaning. This is a different kind of reading which is possibly more difficult and certainly more exciting.

4   Writers must learn to be their own best enemy. They must accept the criticism of others and be suspicious of it; they must accept the praise of others and be even more suspicious of it. Writers cannot depend on others. They must detach themselves from their own pages so that they can apply both their caring and their craft to their own work.

5   Such detachment is not easy. Science fiction writer Ray Bradbury supposedly puts each manuscript away for a year to the day and then rereads it as a stranger. Not many writers have the discipline or the time to do this. We must read when our judgment may be at its worst, when we are close to the euphoric moment of creation.

Then the writer, counsels novelist Nancy Hale, "should be critical of every-   *6* thing that seems to him most delightful in his style. He should excise what he most admires, because he wouldn't thus admire it if he weren't...in a sense protecting it from criticism." John Ciardi, the poet, adds, "The last act of the writing must be to become one's own reader. It is, I suppose, a schizophrenic process, to begin passionately and to end critically, to begin hot and to end cold; and, more important, to be passion-hot and critic-cold at the same time."

Most people think that the principal problem is that writers are too proud of   *7* what they have written. Actually, a greater problem for most professional writers is one shared by the majority of students. They are overly critical, think everything is dreadful, tear up page after page, never complete a draft, see the task as hopeless.

The writer must learn to read critically but constructively, to cut what is bad,   *8* to reveal what is good. Eleanor Estes, the children's book author, explains: "The writer must survey his work critically, coolly, as though he were a stranger to it. He must be willing to prune, expertly and hard-heartedly. At the end of each revision, a manuscript may look...worked over, torn apart, pinned together, added to, deleted from, words changed and words changed back. Yet the book must maintain its original freshness and spontaneity."

Most readers underestimate the amount of rewriting it usually takes to produce   *9* spontaneous reading. This is a great disadvantage to the student writer, who sees only a finished product and never watches the craftsman who takes the necessary step back, studies the work carefully, returns to the task, steps back, returns, steps back, again and again. Anthony Burgess, one of the most prolific writers in the English-speaking world, admits, "I might revise a page twenty times." Roald Dahl, the popular children's writer, states, "By the time I'm nearing the end of a story, the first part will have been reread and altered and corrected at least 150 times.... Good writing is essentially rewriting. I am positive of this."

Rewriting isn't virtuous. It isn't something that ought to be done. It is simply   *10* something that most writers find they have to do to discover what they have to say and how to say it. It is a condition of the writer's life.

There are, however, a few writers who do little formal rewriting, primarily   *11* because they have the capacity and experience to create and review a large number of invisible drafts in their minds before they approach the page. And some writers slowly produce finished pages, performing all the tasks of revision simultaneously, page by page, rather than draft by draft. But it is still possible to see the sequence followed by most writers most of the time in rereading their own work.

Most writers scan their drafts first, reading as quickly as possible to catch the   *12* larger problems of subject and form, then move in closer and closer as they read and write, reread and rewrite.

13 The first thing writers look for in their drafts is *information*. They know that a good piece of writing is built from specific, accurate, and interesting information. The writer must have an abundance of information from which to construct a readable piece of writing.

14 Next writers look for *meaning* in the information. The specifics must build to a pattern of significance. Each piece of specific information must carry the reader toward meaning.

15 Writers reading their own drafts are aware of *audience*. They put themselves in the reader's situation and make sure that they deliver information which a reader wants to know or needs to know in a manner which is easily digested. Writers try to be sure that they anticipate and answer the questions a critical reader will ask when reading the piece of writing.

16 Writers make sure that the *form* is appropriate to the subject and the audience. Form, or genre, is the vehicle which carries meaning to the reader, but form cannot be selected until the writer has adequate information to discover its significance and an audience which needs or wants that meaning.

17 Once writers are sure the form is appropriate, they must then look at the *structure*, the order of what they have written. Good writing is built on a solid framework of logic, argument, narrative, or motivation which runs through the entire piece of writing and holds it together. This is the time when many writers find it most effective to outline as a way of visualizing the hidden spine on which the piece of writing is supported.

18 The element on which writers may spend a majority of their time is *development*. Each section of a piece of writing must be adequately developed. It must give readers enough information so that they are satisfied. How much information is enough? That's as difficult as asking how much garlic belongs in a salad. It must be done to taste, but most beginning writers underdevelop, underestimating the reader's hunger for information.

19 As writers solve development problems, they often have to consider questions of *dimension*. There must be a pleasing and effective proportion among all the parts of the piece of writing. There is a continual process of subtracting and adding to keep the piece of writing in balance.

20 Finally, writers have to listen to their own voices. *Voice* is the force which drives a piece of writing forward. It is an expression of the writer's authority and concern. It is what is between the words on the page, what glues the piece of writing together. A good piece of writing is always marked by a consistent, individual voice.

21 As writers read and reread, write and rewrite, they move closer and closer to the page until they are doing line-by-line editing. Writers read their own pages with infinite care. Each sentence, each line, each clause, each phrase, each word, each mark of punctuation, each section of white space between the type has to contribute to the clarification of meaning.

Slowly the writer moves from word to word, looking through language to see   22
the subject. As a word is changed, cut, or added, as a construction is rearranged,
all the words used before that moment and all those that follow that moment
must be considered and reconsidered.

Writers often read aloud at this stage of the editing process, muttering or whis-   23
pering to themselves, calling on the ear's experience with language. Does this
sound right—or that? Writers edit, shifting back and forth from eye to page to ear
to page. I find I must do this careful editing in short runs, no more than fifteen
or twenty minutes at a stretch, or I become too kind with myself. I begin to see
what I hope is on the page, not what actually is on the page.

This sounds tedious if you haven't done it, but actually it is fun. Making some-   24
thing right is immensely satisfying, for writers begin to learn what they are writing about by writing. Language leads them to meaning, and there is the joy of
discovery, of understanding, of making meaning clear as the writer employs the
technical skills of language.

Words have double meanings, even triple and quadruple meanings. Each word   25
has its own potential for connotation and denotation. And when writers rub one
word against the other, they are often rewarded with a sudden insight, an unexpected clarification.

The maker's eye moves back and forth from word to phrase to sentence to   26
paragraph to sentence to phrase to word. The maker's eye sees the need for variety and balance, for a firmer structure, for a more appropriate form. It peers into
the interior of the paragraph, looking for coherence, unity, and emphasis, which
make meaning clear.

I learned something about this process when my first bifocals were prescribed. I   27
had ordered a larger section of the reading portion of the glass because of my work,
but even so, I could not contain my eyes within this new limit of vision. And I still
find myself taking off my glasses and bending my nose towards the page, for my eyes
unconsciously flick back and forth across the page, back to another page, forward
to still another, as I try to see each evolving line in relation to every other line.

When does this process end? Most writers agree with the great Russian writer   28
Tolstoy, who said, "I scarcely ever reread my published writing. If by chance I
come across a page, it always strikes me: all this must be rewritten; this is how
I should have written it."

The maker's eye is never satisfied, for each word has the potential to ignite new   29
meaning. This article has been twice written all the way through the writing
process, and it was published four years ago. Now it is to be republished in a book.
The editors made a few small suggestions, and then I read it with my maker's eye.
Now it has been re-edited, revised, re-read, re-re-edited, for each piece of writing
is to the writer full of potential and alternatives.

A piece of writing is never finished. It is delivered to a deadline, torn out of   30
the typewriter on demand, sent off with a sense of accomplishment and shame

and pride and frustration. If only there were a couple more days, time for just another run at it, perhaps then...♦

1973

Explorations

- Do you believe that "Good writing is essentially rewriting"? If so, do you spend as much time reading your first draft as you do writing it? How many drafts do you usually write?

- Do you read your draft carefully, with a "maker's eye"? Do you feel comfortable reading your work aloud? Are you able to detach yourself from your own writing and accept the criticism of others?

- Do you find that there are practical constraints that prevent you from revising as extensively as Murray suggests? If so, what are they and how might they be overcome?

Andrew Nikiforuk, born in 1955, lives in Calgary, Alberta. He has won four National Magazine Awards, the Atkinson Fellowship in Public Policy, and top honours from the Association of Canadian Journalists for his journalistic work. He has published several books and articles on medicine and educa-tion, including The Fourth Horseman *(1991),* School's Out: The Catastrophe in Public Education and What We Can Do about It *(1993), which was short-listed for the Gordon Montador Award for writing on issues of key social interest, and* If Learning Is So Natural, Why Am I Going to School? *(1994). His highly acclaimed book* Saboteurs *(2001) won the Governor General's Award and the 2002 Arthur Ellis Award for Best True Crime, as well as the W.O. Mitchell City of Calgary Book Prize, and was a national best-seller.*

Beasts, Germs and the Superorganism

Andrew Nikiforuk

One of the most popular books ever written about germs reads like a war manual. *1* The *Microbe Hunters* has more invading, killing and conquering in it than all of *War and Peace*. The title refers to a group of pioneering nineteenth-century scientists, including Louis Pasteur° and Robert Koch°; the book goes on to lionize these men as a band of warrior-saints intent on saving humankind from demonic germs. In every chapter the brave "Tsars of science" rush from lab to lab ambushing anthrax, attacking tubercles or hunting down cholera bacilli, "the terrible little murderers from the Orient." Without "the Super Napoleonic" skills of the "Death Fighters," microbes might have marched all over the earth, brutally murdering women and children. Caught in the urgency of war, assistants to the great microbe hunters obey search-and-destroy instructions: "Find the microbe, kill the microbe." The great struggle against microbial "assassins" and "sub-visible invaders" also had a secret weapon: "the magic bullet" or the antibiotic. Since its publication in 1926, the *Microbe Hunters* has sold millions of copies; new doctors still read it like a boot camp manual.

Not much has changed in the public imagination since the *Microbe Hunters* *2* made germs as popular as sharks. Humans don't like *Escherichia coli°* or aden-oviruses° any more than they have liked wolves, auks or passenger pigeons. If a creature doesn't walk upright or look like a baby seal, humans will probably exter-minate it. Ever since Pasteur first declared that "microbes are a menace" in the 1880s, scientists have been hunting germs like buffalo with one magic bullet after another. Pasteur didn't intend this kind of hostility but his discoveries put biolo-gists on the war-path. The famous French scientist also didn't really believe that "germ theory," the idea that one germ equals one disease, answered all the great questions about infection. From his experiments with silkworms, he knew that the health and even the body temperature of the host, whether worm or human, had as much to say about a microbe's killing ability as the microbe itself. This kind of laborious ecological analysis has never appealed to twentieth-century doctors and scientists on the move. They have preferred the battle-field approach and have wholeheartedly adopted the "germ theory," giving it a more warlike title: "the doctrine of specific etiology." If one germ equals one disease, then one drug should take care of it. Mention the word bacteria and doctors still run for antibiotics as quickly as duck hunters dive for shot-guns. To this day modern medicine is largely based on the training of pill pushers and germ slayers. They have a narrow view of illness and an incredibly distorted view of germs.

3   The real truth about bacteria reads like science fiction and is a lot more exotic than warfare. Bacteria are not only our ancestors but our number one life-support system. They clean our water, prime the atmosphere and take care of the dead. Instead of killing and invading life, they nurture and protect it. As the planet's eldest, brightest and most numerous life-form, bacteria work in teams as one big superorganism. The art of successful living and planet regulating has taken bacteria two and a half billion years to learn. Relatives, no matter how distant or ancient, don't generally go out of their way to murder other relatives unless they have a good reason and this characteristic is particularly true of the superorganism. It has only become a killing machine when people have kicked or trampled its frontiers violating unwritten bacterial codes. No other offspring or dependent species has disturbed and challenged the superorganism as much as we have.

4   Bacteria are not like any other living creature: scientists even put them in their own class. Unlike plants, fungi and animals they are primarily one-celled beings. As such, they remain bacteria and never congregate to form ancillary bodies such as skin, livers or bark. Bacteria even look different than other creatures and come in the shapes of tiny rods, spirals and spheres. Under the eye of a microscope the tubercle bacillus, for example, looks like a maneless sea-horse. The rickettsia of typhoid fever resembles mice stools and the plague bacillus has a jelly bean shape. Syphilis takes the form of a thin slice of corrugated roof metal. Three hundred years ago a Dutch dry goods merchant, Anthonie van Leeuwenhoek, first spied some of these "animalcules" and "wretched beasties" under his home-made microscope. He found them in drinking water, on his teeth, in the stomachs of frogs and horses, on cheese and even in his own excrement after a bout of "looseness." Their behaviour made Leeuwenhoek an ecologist: "Life lives on life—it is cruel, but it is God's will."

5   Much to scientists' eternal discomfort, bacteria will always outnumber the human race in spite of our best reproductive efforts. Each gram of soil houses between 1 and 10 billion bacterial cells, twice the human population on earth. A single hand-held laboratory test tube can grow several billion microbes from one cell in a day. No one knows how many different bacterial species there might be,

but scientists agree that there are more rod-shaped and sphere-shaped creatures in the world than the 1.5 million higher species such as beetles and elephants.

Bacteria's weight of numbers is the product of elementary school math. They 6 reproduce asexually by division, swelling up and splitting in two. With the right amount of food, bacteria can divide every twenty minutes and produce more of themselves in two days than human beings have in their entire history. Bacteria cover the world like a fine invisible crust which is very thick in places. They have been found at heights of thirty-two kilometres and at Pacific depths of eleven kilometres. Their ancient and traditional haunts include hot springs, desert soils, and buffalo stomachs. More recent housing projects include air conditioners, whirlpools, toilets, hospitals and discarded coffee cups. People also make good hosts. Bacteria long ago colonized the human skin, nose, mouth, intestines and genitals where they live as peacefully as grass in a middle-class suburb. Our ancestry can be traced by counting our cells. The human body is held together by 10 quadrillion animal cells and 100 quadrillion (100,000,000,000,000,000) bacterial cells. Humans are made of bacteria, surrounded by bacteria and dependent on bacteria.

Like a troop of Aztec or Mayan gods, microbes are the planet's busiest creators 7 and destroyers. Without them the earth would be a static dung heap of dead animals, plants and humans. The Harvard biologist Lynn Margulis says bacteria can assemble and disassemble all the molecules of modern life except for a few plant hallucinogens and snake venoms. Working in teams, bacteria recycle and transform the dead, whether animal or vegetable, into food for worms and fertile soil for farmers. From the air they fix or capture nitrogen gas and return this life-giver to trees and other creatures. No other life-form can do this. When breathing oxygen they make iron and manganese. In the stomachs of goats and cows they turn half-chewed grasses into digestible sugars. They sour milk, ripen cheese and ferment wine. With the help of algae and other micro-organisms they purify water of the natural human and animal residues. And bacteria don't rest on Sundays.

Aiding bacteria in all of this work are a number of microbial allies, including 8 protozoa (unicellular animals), fungi and viruses. Viruses are floating bits of genetic material and members of the living dead. They don't really come to life until they invade a specific cell belonging to an animal, plant or bacterium and hijack its life-support system to reproduce themselves. As primitive genetic messengers, viruses can provoke evolutionary change in a species and even alter the colour of tulips. Humans contain a lot of genetic information deposited by viruses. Although smaller than bacteria, these tiny microbes are just as ubiquitous. Many keep bacterial communities in check by causing great epidemics and die-offs. The superorganism both respects and employs viruses as freelance evolutionary anarchists.

If a team of bacteria had written the world's history, humans would appear as 9 a period at the end. Earth's very first living creature was a bacterial cell that breast-stroked across the planet's Archean murk. Using rocks, gases and light as energy, bacteria did what they do best over two and a half billion years and multiplied. With their fermenting billions, bacteria changed the earth from a volcanic wasteland into a green land capable of supporting plants, fungi, animals and humans. A bacterial history might also boast that bacteria invented photosynthesis, as well as pigments and vitamin A for protection against ultraviolet light. There is also the heroic story of how fearless armies of bacteria dined on hydrogen and farted oxygen. This gas, combined with bacteria's other explosive wastes (ammonia, carbon dioxide and methyl chloride), created a friendly atmosphere that supports all other living creatures. The planet's very stability still depends on the collective farting, belching, feasting and shitting of bacteria.

10   Throughout history bacteria have witnessed some amazing calamities. Unexpected ecological catastrophes have frozen and warmed the Earth over the millennia but bacteria have always come out smiling. Their indomitable hordes have adapted and increased while dumber creatures such as dinosaurs and woolly mammoths have died off. Ninety-nine percent of the species that have inhabited Earth have ultimately become no more than curious fossil records. Bacteria, however, have resisted extinction as stubbornly as they have resisted antibiotics.

11   The big secret to bacteria's survival is their ability to solve problems. Unlike humans, bacteria share an incredible genetic unity. Faced with a threat to their well-being, bacteria simply order up life-saving genetic information from other bacterial cells, with the same ease that human beings order take-out pizza. Unencumbered by a closet full of genes, bacteria have simply exchanged hereditary life-information whenever necessary. Scientists compare this bacterial gene-pool exchange to consumers using the central data bank of Bell Telephone, Interpol or American Express. The only difference is that bacteria are much better and faster at exchanging information than humans are.

12   Scientists didn't appreciate this genetic unity until doctors started overprescribing penicillin in the 1940s. The primary bacteria under assault were staphylococci, grape-like clusters of germs that poison the blood and lurk in hospitals where unhealthy patients provide them with ample food and warmth. Faced with extinction, the staphylococci put in a call to the great bacterial gene pool where they located an enzyme among a community of soil bacteria that could digest the antibiotic and render it harmless. The life-saving information was quickly relayed back to the staphylococci. This bacterial exchange has been repeated across the globe for almost every antibiotic ever designed. Both tuberculosis and gonorrhea have developed successful drug-resistant strains. Sorin Sonea, a Montreal physician who has great respect for bacteria's resilience, recently observed that any other species needing a similar enzyme "might have required approximately one million years to synthesize it by means of random mutation attempts." In self-defence, bacteria have removed most of the magic from "magic bullets."

Until about ten thousand years ago, humankind and the superorganism lived 13
together in relative peace. In this era of mutual tolerance hunters and gatherers
left few footprints on the land because they kept their numbers at a level the
local jungle (the original grocery store) could sustain. They didn't build great
piles of garbage and they didn't jet from one hunting ground to another, exposing themselves to unfamiliar microbes. Aside from the odd intestinal parasite,
their only fatal encounter with disease may have been food poisoning. To avoid
diarrhea and stomach cramps, hunters gradually learned how to dry and cure
meat. The spear carriers and nut gatherers of old were noble specimens: they
stood tall, had good teeth and were generally so healthy that the only way they
could really control overcrowding was to kill children. The routine drowning,
strangling and abandoning of infants was for hunting people what measles,
malaria and smallpox would later become for farming people. Infanticide kept
the number of mouths roughly equal to the number of four-legged steaks available.

This brief era of bacterial tolerance disappeared as soon as people began their 14
famous "population avalanche" and started to colonize the earth. René Dubos,
the celebrated medical ecologist, calls it an avalanche because the human species
didn't explode, it just started to accumulate dangerously like packed snow on the
side of a mountain. Ten thousand years before Christ, 10 million humans hunted
and gathered on the planet. But after the invention of the plough (and the death
of Christ), more than 200 million had embarked on crusades to civilize the landscape. The agricultural revolution began in earnest when hunters ran short of
woolly mammoths and other big game to kill, and started to tame plants and
animals. In the Middle East they "conscripted" wheat, barley, peas, lentils, donkeys,
sheep, pigs and goats. In Southeast Asia they chose rice, sweet potatoes, taro,
ducks and chickens. Everywhere people started to congregate in great numbers,
they all preached the new gospel of agriculture: thou shalt enslave other species
to help humans multiply and dominate more species.

This aggressive drive didn't take into account the superorganism. By breaking 15
up the soil and taming herds of cattle and goats, humans collided with more
microbes than they had ever met before. Agriculture created a common market of
disease by bringing together all manner of viruses, fungi and bacteria in human
gardens, houses and villages. When the dog became man's best friend so too did
measles. With the cow came tuberculosis and diphtheria. Rhinoviruses (the common cold) probably came riding in on a horse. Anthrax popped out of the soil.
These biological collisions were probably a shock for all species involved.

Thrust into totally new environments, some of the microbes panicked and 16
died while others went on killing sprees. Over time many gradually learned to
live with farmers because dead humans make poor food supplies. After taking an
initial beating, the human immune system also changed and adapted as it became
exposed to more infections. But the Fourth Horseman° wasn't fully roused until
farms allowed increasing numbers of idle people to build cities. Human beehives

have always created enormous opportunities for the superorganism to flourish. A metropolis, by definition and design, excels at constructing garbage heaps, adding feces to water and poisoning the air. When humans started living too close to their own garbage piles, they inadvertently became part of the superorganism's dinner and sprouted an endless variety of skin and gut diseases, including leprosy, cholera and dysentery. To avoid stomach cramps and loose bowels, the Chinese started to boil their tea while the French opted for fermented grape juice.

17   Unlike vigorous hunters and gatherers, sedentary wheat growers and lentil planters were a stooped and hungry lot. They ate too many carbohydrates and their teeth rotted out. Because of foul water supplies, many drank too much wine and became alcoholics. Growing cereals and roots was no more a stable enterprise five thousand years ago than it is now. Periodic droughts, baby booms and greedy ruling élites introduced famine as an historical constant. Humans stressed by hunger can't help but attract germs to do their bacterial duty: to dismember and decay.

18   The ceaseless ploughing of land and chopping of forests, which agricultural empires celebrated as progress, also invited other parasites. The killing of wild lands forced rats, mice, ticks, fleas and mosquitoes to live closer to humans. These scavengers brought genuine surprises such as plague, tularemia, typhus and malaria. As soon as cities of a hundred thousand people began to appear, great die-offs became as common as thunder-storms. To city builders such as the Sumerians, Egyptians and Israelites, pestilence became such a routine event that everyone concluded epidemics were divinely inspired. Horsemen, demons and Pest Maidens appeared everywhere.

19   The constant depopulation of ancient cities by epidemics set in motion a variety of crude biological forces. Because the conditions of urban life exposed humans to more stress, famine and microbes than their immune systems could endure, cities had to import peasants regularly or become ghost towns. To counter rapid urban die-offs, governments, religions and the whip encouraged peasants in rural areas to marry young and have lots of children. Big families still remain a feature of peasant life because great biological lessons take a long time to unlearn.

20   Throughout most of "civilized" history, peasants have been biological fodder for the great microbial communities that cities grew and nurtured. Until the 1600s, most of the world's great metropolises renewed their wealth by swallowing the sons and daughters of soil tillers. Whenever the peasants multiplied too quickly, city states usually disposed of the surplus by enduring a famine or declaring war on a neighbour. The outcome of the war generally depended on which side had accumulated the greatest disease resistance. The Arabs, for instance, defeated the Crusaders with malaria, while the Russians repelled Napoleon's armies with typhoid. One of the reasons the Army of the Union won the American Civil War was that it could afford to lose more men to diarrhea than Confederate troops could. When battling expansive Europeans, nomads, hunters

and New World aboriginals have usually lost the war because of their lower exposure to germs. In this respect, until this century, all warfare has been fought with
germs and won by farm and city people with the tougher immune systems.

Our ancestors took a long time to appreciate the logic of great die-offs. One of   21
the first to notice that war, drought, famine, humidity and even the wind played
a role in these complicated dramas was Hippocrates. He referred to these environmental forces as "air, water and places." The Greek epidemiologist believed
that rapid changes in any of these factors brought about epidemics. He concluded
that a doctor should be "skilled in Nature and must strive to know what man is
in relation to food, drink, occupation and which effect each of these has on the
other." Unlike most of his contemporaries, he recognized that disease didn't
come calling unless there had been either great changes to human health or great
changes made to the health of the land. He didn't know about the superorganism
but he could recognize its handiwork.

The Hippocratic idea that humans make epidemics as easily as bakers bake pies   22
found its wisest disciple in Rudolf Virchow. He was a nineteenth-century bacteria
watcher, doctor, anthropologist, medical reformer and robust Prussian. Virchow
kept so many bones in his office that he had to meet people in a nearby hotel in
order to talk. During a long career of studying microbes, Virchow invented the
best and shortest definition of disease ever written: "life under altered conditions." By altered conditions he meant changes in diet, trade, travel, housing,
clothes and weather—in short, the total environment. Meddle with the conditions of life, predicted Virchow, and the relationship between humans and
microbes will change in unforseen and often fatal ways.

As the modern father of epidemiology, Virchow first assembled these thoughts   23
in 1848 when he went to Upper Silesia, now part of Czechoslovakia and
Germany, to investigate a typhus epidemic among poor cotton workers. His visit
later became the subject of a long and famous report that implicated heavy rains,
bad housing and poverty more than typhus germs. "Epidemics," he concluded,
"resemble great warnings from which a statesman in the grand style can read that
a disturbance has taken place in the development of his people." Virchow's prescription for the people of Upper Silesia had nothing to do with doctors or drugs
but included agricultural reform, self-government, democracy and industrial co-
operatives. To Virchow, medicine was not a matter of hunting microbes but of
uncovering the ecological and social forces that fed disease.

Virchow knew that humans, because they are humans, have a knack of con-   24
stantly changing their living space and uprooting the homes of other species. In
this historical drama people inadvertently construct one "abnormal condition"
after another. The march of civilization is really the story of how changes in
human economy and health have begot abnormal situations and much disease.
Despite what the germ theorists might say, the superorganism merely signals
these social crises with epidemics as part of its ancient mission to maintain the

earth's life-support system in good working order. The earth's first-line defence mechanism will only tolerate so much crowding, pollution and deforestation before some of its members intervene. The superorganism, because it is the super-organism, can't behave any other way.

25   Virchow didn't know about the unity of bacteria but he did understand the meaning of epidemics. Throughout his career he often lamented that the knowl-edge of pestilential disturbances seemed to decrease with each new generation of medical students and politicians. Not much has changed in the last hundred years except that the germ theorists, microbe hunters and pharmaceutical com-panies are now doing an even better job of obscuring the truth: that humans are the aggressive architects of plagues. ◆

1991

Glossary

Louis Pasteur: (1822–1895) French chemist considered to be the founder of microbiology; his discovery that many diseases are caused by specific germs and that the presence of these germs, especially in food and dairy products, can be prevented through a process of sterilization, or "pasteurization," was one of the most important developments in modern medicine.

Robert Koch: (1843–1910) German scientist who discovered the bacterium responsible for tuberculosis in 1882; he was awarded the 1905 Nobel Prize in medicine.

Escherichia coli: also known as *E. coli*, this bacterium inhabits the large intestine of humans and animals.

adenoviruses: any of a number of viruses known to cause respiratory diseases; first found in the adenoid tissue of humans.

the Fourth Horseman: the personification of death in the Book of Revelation (the other three are conquest, slaughter, and famine); the Fourth Horseman, who rides a pale horse, is often associated with death by disease and pestilence.

Explorations

- How do you view germs? Did these views change after reading Nikiforuk's essay?

- Do you see a link between human behaviour and disease? Do you believe that "humans make epidemics"?

- What are some recent epidemics? To what extent do you think ecological and social factors have contributed to their outbreak and spread?

- Do you think it is desirable, or even possible, to try to exterminate dangerous bacteria and viruses?

CHAPTER THREE

Arrangement:
Giving Structure to Ideas

Once you have gathered information and selected the methods of development that will best serve your purpose, you will be faced with the problem of organizing your ideas. Here is a way to put these three steps of the writing process—invention, development, and arrangement—into more concrete terms.

Imagine that you are an architect who wants to travel to Europe in order to study ancient cathedrals. After reading several books, talking to colleagues, and consulting your map (invention), you decide to visit Italy, France, Great Britain, and Spain; you envision these places as being rich with material that will support your research (development). However, you are having difficulty determining the order in which you should visit each country (arrangement). Should you go to France first because it is in a central location, and then go to the surrounding countries? Or should you go to Italy first because the oldest cathedrals are in Rome, and then travel to the countries where the more modern cathedrals are located? In the end, you decide to go to Great Britain first because its cathedrals are of least interest to you, then to France, then to Spain, then to Italy—leaving the best for last.

The strategic planning of a whole journey is just as important to writers as it is to travellers. If you do not give structure to your ideas, if you do not have a master plan, your thoughts may wander aimlessly, leaving your readers feeling lost and disoriented. Your readers will expect you to give them some direction, guiding them from the beginning, through the middle, to the end of your composition. Beginning, middle, end; introduction, body, conclusion. Unfortunately, these divisions are not very useful if you view them as simple boundaries—static, inflexible, and without purpose. This chapter will analyze the structure of the essay in order to help you understand the dynamic function of each part.

Introductions

An introduction, also known as a lead or opening, should do more than just begin an essay; it should capture the interest and imagination of your readers so that they will want to read on, and it should inform them about your subject. Take Carole Corbeil's introduction to "The Advertised Infant: Ivan's Adventures in Babyland" as an example. This introduction is a narrative with a twist; it allows readers to view the world from an infant's point of view, engaging their attention and familiarizing them with the "Big Issues": baby culture and consumerism. Notice that this introduction is more than one paragraph long, as are many introductions.

Like Corbeil, Warren Caragata arouses the interest of his audience with his lead. In "Crime in Cybercity," he begins with the emphatic statement, "It is quite a neighborhood," and proceeds by giving some shocking examples of its residents. After some delay, he puts his subject into focus, surprising readers with a striking comparison or analogy: "The neighborhood is the Internet, and the criminals have moved in." Although his purpose is not stated explicitly, readers know that Caragata intends to talk about criminal activities and the Internet. Indeed, his introduction leads readers smoothly into the debate surrounding cybercrime and law enforcement.

Depending on the situation, you may want to include a clearer statement of purpose before moving into the body of the essay. Emily Martin does this in her scholarly argument, "The Egg and the Sperm: How Science Has Constructed a Romance Based on Stereotypical Male-Female Roles." At the end of her introduction, she states:

> Part of my goal in writing this article is to shine a bright light on the gender stereotypes hidden within the scientific language of biology. Exposed in such light, I hope they will lose much of their power to harm us.

This statement may seem mechanical; however, given the length and the complexity of Martin's article, and considering the academic audience for which she is writing, making a direct reference to what she plans to achieve through her writing is desirable. Because the introduction is the first impression readers have of you, in a scholarly paper you may have to do more than capture your readers' attention; you may have to formally introduce yourself. This shows readers that you have seriously considered the conventions of academic writing.

If your readers do not take you seriously, or if they are skeptical of your position, you may want to begin with an ethical appeal (see Chapter 2: Ethical Appeal). An ethical appeal establishes your authority on the subject and builds up your credibility as a spokesperson. You may also feel that it is necessary to clear yourself of any suspicion. You can do this by countering biases against you or your subject. Martin tries to do this by introducing herself as an anthropologist rather than a feminist; she presents herself as a neutral observer—a social scientist who is analyzing the language of biological scientists—and as a benevolent researcher who wants to free us from harmful gender stereotypes.

If circumstances do not allow you to ingratiate yourself with your readers, you may want to begin more aggressively, attacking opposing viewpoints. Ideally, however, your readers will be friendly rather than hostile. If so, once they are introduced to the subject of your essay, they should be open to the ideas that are to follow in your body paragraphs.

Body Paragraphs: Confirmation

Your body paragraphs should not mechanically list main points; they should provide support or confirmation for your central ideas. Statements of central ideas, also known as "topic sentences," often appear at the beginning of paragraphs, but may be found elsewhere. For instance, a topic sentence may be found near the middle of a paragraph, usually after a transition, or at the end of a paragraph. What you need to keep in mind is that *where* these topic statements are located is less meaningful than *why* they exist: they help readers make connections between ideas, giving them landmarks so that they will not lose sight of main points as they are working through supporting detail.

Organizing your central ideas and supporting details in a way that is effective can be a daunting task because there are no strict rules—there are only patterns of arrangement that you may or may not want to follow. Below are just a few of these well-worn paths.

Spatial and Chronological

A spatial arrangement is used when you describe a person, place, or thing. For example, you may want your readers to view your best friend from head to toe, a picnic area from foreground to background, a sofa from left to right. R. Murray Schafer causes his readers to look from buildings at street level to the towers above in "The Glazed Soundscape": "From the streets we are given views of interiors once private and mysterious; from the towers, executives contemplate the skyline and envision distant goals and objectives."

In this case, Schafer uses a spatial arrangement to confirm that glazed windows have brought about a change in our perception of the world.

To show this change in perception, Schafer also gives the history of glass as a soundscape material. He uses a chronological arrangement, narrating events that take place in time. In a single paragraph, he spans hundreds of years: "About 200 B.C....after 1300.... In 1567....in 1688...." For two more paragraphs, he continues to support his concept of change, providing clear temporal markers such as "For a long time" and "During the twentieth century." Like Schafer, you may want to arrange your narrative in a straightforward, chronological order. But you may also want to vary time sequences, beginning in the middle of a story and flashing back into the past, or beginning in the present time and flashing forward into the future (see Chapter 2: Narration).

Climactic and Inverted

A climactic arrangement begins with the least important point and builds up to the most important point. Corbeil uses this arrangement to lament the separation of Babyland from the "real world":

> The first thing you notice then, when you go through the gates of Babyland, is that you've entered a realm apart, a realm that remains invisible to all but those confined to it. Eventually, you begin to understand, in a visceral way, that the system you live under owes its existence to a rigid separation between the private (home and babies and children) and the public (the "work place").... Most distressing, however, is discovering how we've internalized this division....

In the above paragraph, Corbeil not only heightens our awareness of the division between private and public realities, but she also combines climactic order with chronological order to build up suspense, to show us how she has had a sudden unpleasant realization, a disturbing epiphany, about our society and its polarized values.

An inverted arrangement begins with the most important point and descends to the least important point. Newspaper journalists, who know that most of their readers will skim the page for information, scanning headlines and opening statements rather than doing in-depth readings of whole articles, often use this type of arrangement. While an inverted arrangement is standard for writing newspaper articles, it is uncommon in other forms of writing. More often, writers begin with a relatively strong point, bring in less significant points, and then end with their strongest point.

Block and Alternating

Block and alternating arrangements are used when developing ideas through comparison and contrast. Although they are sometimes used in combination, here we discuss them independently, beginning with the block pattern.

Suppose that you are comparing subject A to subject B. The block pattern requires that you go subject-by-subject, discussing A in full and then B in full. For instance, if you were comparing cats and dogs, you would say everything you wanted to say about cats, such as whether they are loyal, whether they are playful, and then you would say everything you wanted to say about dogs, explaining whether they are, compared with cats, loyal or playful. You may use the pattern of arrangement in a single paragraph, in several paragraphs, or over the course of an entire essay.

The alternating pattern requires that you discuss each subject point-by-point: A and B; A and B; and so on. Again, if you were discussing cats and dogs, you might compare the loyalty of cats with the loyalty of dogs, the playfulness of cats with the playfulness of dogs, and so on. Like the block arrangement this can be done in more than one paragraph:

> Taking a taxi in Peterborough is a very different matter from taking a taxi in Toronto. In the city, the cab drivers are fluently and instantly conversational, a motley collection of men from nearly all corners of the earth. In Peterborough, when they get to know you a little, then they talk.... They do not, as in Toronto, say, "Come in, Number 87654321." They say, "Hey, Ron, where the heck *are* you?"

Notice how in this passage from "Down East," Laurence uses the parallel structure "In the city.... In Peterborough" and the connective phrase "They do not, **as in Toronto**" (our emphasis) to make her contrast clear. Because alternating comparison moves back and forth between ideas, you will want to pay close attention to parallel sentence structure and transitional words, making sure that you are confirming central ideas rather than confusing your readers.

Problem-Solution and Question-Answer

A problem-solution arrangement opens with a statement or detailed description of a problem and follows with suggestions for solving it. In the following excerpt, taken from the end of "The Glazed Soundscape," Murray Schafer uses this pattern to suggest a solution to the problematic effects that glazed windows have had on the modern urban soundscape and, by extension, on the psyche of city-dwellers:

> When the division between 'here' and 'there' is complete, the glass wall will become as impenetrable as the stone wall....And yet one cannot help feeling that the mind-body split of the Western world will only be healed when some of the glass in which we have sheathed our lives is shattered, allowing us again to inhabit a world in which all the senses interact instead of being ranked in opposition.

A question-answer arrangement opens with a probing question and then proceeds to answer it in detail. In "Outports and Outlaws," Kathryn Welbourn answers a common question asked by those who feel rural Newfoundlanders should leave behind their traditional lifestyle based on living off the land:

> Why don't they just pack up and leave or take wage jobs in the tourism industry in their area? Clarence [Laing, a lobster and herring fisherman]

answers the questions with a sigh and a grin: "I don't think I'm made for going around trying to make someone else happy....Fishing, that's what I'm made for."

Both of these patterns of arrangement are useful if you want to reply directly to your readers' concerns.

General-to-Specific and Specific-to-General

A general-to-specific arrangement is commonly used in academic writing. This pattern begins with a general statement, usually the topic sentence, which is supported by specific detail:

> The real mystery is why the male's vast production of sperm is not seen as wasteful. Assuming that a man "produces" 100 million (10^8) sperm per day (a conservative estimate) during an average reproductive life of sixty years, he would produce well over two trillion sperm in his lifetime.

The above example, taken from Emily Martin's article, has an easy-to-follow sequence. The first sentence states the general point—the misconception we have of sperm production—and the next sentence provides statistics that confirm that a man's reproductive system is, in fact, very wasteful.

Specific-to-general arrangement is not as common as general-to-specific arrangement. Because it begins with specific examples and ends with a general statement, it requires readers to work much harder to make sense of detail. The following is a paragraph taken from David Suzuki's "The Prostitution of Academia":

> Scholars in universities represent tiny islands of thought in society. They are sufficiently detached from the priorities of various interest groups like business, government and the military to point out flaws in our current social truths. But by focussing on issues that are socially relevant or economically profitable, we lose sight of the broader context within which that activity falls; we forget history; we become blind to environmental and social costs of our innovations.

In this paragraph, the first two sentences provide detail—the reasons that universities are able to openly criticize industries and government agencies—which lead up to and confirm one of Suzuki's central ideas: that the union between free inquiry and free enterprise has unacceptable costs. (See Chapter 2: Logical Appeal, to learn how these patterns function in argument.)

Body Paragraphs: Refutation and Concession

As well as confirming your central ideas, you may need to refute opposing points of view in your body paragraphs. Even if you are making a compelling argument, you cannot ignore the contrary assumptions and beliefs of your "opponents"—those who do not agree with you. Rather than leaving out objections to your argument, you will want to anticipate and refute them, proving that your opponents' assumptions are false or that their beliefs should be rejected.

At this point, the question of arrangement arises. Should you refute opposing views first and then present your own case, or should you present your own case first and then refute opposing views? Again, there are no strict rules. If you anticipate that opposing points are weak, and if you are confident that your argument is convincing, you may want to establish your own position first and introduce your opponents' arguments later. And even if you think that the counter-arguments are strong, you may want to delay mentioning them, in anticipation that they will trigger and perhaps reconfirm your readers' biases.

More commonly, however, if you anticipate that your opponents' arguments have been well-received, refute them before presenting your own case. David Suzuki does this in "The Prostitution of Academia." Realizing that many academics have accepted what he calls "the Faustian bargain with private industry," Suzuki presents a direct refutation, rejecting former University of B.C. president David Strangway's logic behind exploiting the university for the benefit of free enterprise. He then presents his own case, giving many reasons for objecting to the industrialization of the university.

Like Suzuki, you may want to rely heavily on the direct refutation of your opponent's argument. Keep in mind, however, that direct refutation can seem highly confrontational. In some cases, in order to appear less confrontational, you may acknowledge the validity of some aspect of your opponent's argument, thus building your own credibility, and then go on to refute it. Consider the following concession made by Kathryn Welbourn in "Outports and Outlaws" as she paraphrases the arguments of a local activist, Watson Lane, against Newfoundland's legislation to protect the dwindling cod fishery:

> [Lane] is quick to emphasize that he and most other outporters are not against tourism or environmental protection....The crackdown on rural life, however, has shifted the blame for the province's problems onto outport people, tagging them as abusive and destructive individuals.

In this paragraph, Welbourn shows Lane conceding the importance of environmental concerns and the need for change in the Newfoundland economy; this concession helps to make Lane's later claim that commercial over-fishing is the real source of the decline in Newfoundland fish stocks credible.

Rather than using concession to set up a refutation, at times you may genuinely concede that your opponent has a valid point that cannot be refuted; to try to refute such a point may make you seem insensitive or ignorant. For instance, in murder trials, the defence often concedes the prosecution's argument about the brutality of the crime in order to appear to be reasonable. Whether you choose concession and/or refutation will depend on the particular rhetorical situation.

Conclusions

The situation will also help determine the appropriate ending or conclusion for your essay. When writing an essay for an instructor in a university English course, you may be tempted to follow a routine—to play it safe—by ending with "In conclusion" and a summary. However, a conclusion should do more than repeat introductory points; it should be a continuation of what you have presented in your body paragraphs. While a freshly worded summary may be helpful in reminding readers what your paper is about, particularly in a long essay, it should be accompanied by a memorable finish; you may want to conclude with a reflection on the significance of your main ideas, a narration of an event that sums up your feelings, an apt quotation, or a discussion of the social implications of your argument.

For greater sense of closure, you may want to vary the rhythm of your sentences, stretching out your words, slowing down your pace, until—finally—you are ready to come to a complete stop. Another closing strategy is to arrange your ideas in a circular pattern, rather than a linear one, continuing an idea that is presented at the beginning of your essay in your conclusion. You may also want to end with a direct or indirect reference to your title. The following example is from Evelyn Lau's "An Insatiable Emptiness":

> The last time I forced myself to throw up, it felt like internal surgery. Grief, love, rage, pain—it all came pouring out, yet afterwards it was still there inside me. I had been bulimic off and on for eight years, and in all that vomiting I had not purged myself of any of the things that were making me sick.

Lau's vivid description and her honest reflection on the psychological roots of her illness bring closure to the essay and leave the reader with a powerful image. By indirectly referring to her title, she reinforces the main message of her essay, that eating disorders should not be glamorized, and that their physical effects are real and devastating.

Overview

This chapter presents patterns for arrangement rather than rules to be memorized and regurgitated. Indeed, arrangement is not about following a routine or copying an example; it is about making decisions. You can decide to abbreviate or expand your introduction, combine or rearrange your body paragraphs, vary your conclusion. You can use a single pattern of arrangement to organize a paragraph or to act as a template for your whole essay. Many decisions depend on the situation—the audience, the subject, the purpose, the occasion. The following essays offer varied examples of the choices that nine writers have made.

Warren Caragata, born in 1950, lives in Jakarta, Indonesia, where he is a freelance writer. Until the magazine's closure, he was staff correspondent in Indonesia for Asiaweek. *In Canada, Caragata was a regular correspondent for* Maclean's *magazine and* Business Week. *He has also published a book on trade unions and labour history called* Alberta Labour: A Heritage Untold.

Crime in Cybercity

Warren Caragata

It is quite a neighborhood. *Penthouse* magazine is there, along with amateur 1
pornography purveyors offering graphic portrayals of seemingly every form of sexual activity, from kiddie porn to bestiality. There is Ernst Zundel's proclamation that the Holocaust never happened. And the forbidden secrets of the Karla Homolka case are revealed for those who cannot wait for the evidence to be presented in the Paul Bernardo° murder trial. The neighborhood is the Internet, and the criminals have moved in. Some of the crimes, like obscenity, are familiar, but others have taken new forms, from information theft to the sabotage of computer systems with data-destroying viruses.

Although the neighborhood has much to recommend it, the dark side of the 2
Net has people worried. There have been calls for laws to regulate and censor what moves across the wires. New laws, says Liberal MP Rey Pagtakhan, who is pushing for tighter control, will demonstrate that "we will not tolerate these types of activity." The problem is figuring out how to impose those laws on a computer network originally designed to withstand a nuclear war. "The Internet regards censorship as a hardware failure and just works around it," says Michael Martineau, vice-president of NSTN Inc., a Halifax company that provides Internet connections.

Canada has so far not experienced the kind of cybercrime wave seen in the 3
United States, where most of the reported cases have occurred. In one of the most celebrated U.S. cases, computer hacker Kevin Mitnick was arrested last February in North Carolina and charged with stealing more than $1 million worth of data and thousands of credit-card numbers. In another, Jake Baker, a University of Michigan student, was arrested on threat charges against a fellow student after he wrote a fictitious article about a woman—named after one of his classmates—who was raped and tortured. In Canada, only a last-minute check prevented the on-line version of February's federal budget from spreading an unwanted computer virus. Then, last March, officials at the University of British Columbia in Vancouver found that hackers had broken into the university's computer system and stolen about 3,000 passwords. And in April, Calgary police charged Alan Norton, 52, with multiple counts of possession of child pornography, alleging that he was part of a porn ring linked by international computer networks.

4   The Internet has stretched the concept of what the law means, where it applies and to whom it applies. Copyright law, privacy law, broadcasting law, the law against spreading hate, rules governing fair trials: all are running up against the technology of the Internet. "It presents challenges to the law because of the fact that it is presented in a substantially different form," explains David Johnston, a law professor at Montreal's McGill University who chairs the federal government's advisory council on the information highway. "That form, therefore, requires some adjustment and, some would say, very substantial stretching."

5   Last week in Ottawa, MPs approved Pagtakhan's motion urging the government to get tough with hate on the Internet, with members from all parties voicing their support. "Cyberspace is a free-for-all," says Reform MP Keith Martin. Pagtakhan, a soft-spoken Winnipeg pediatrician, told *Maclean's* that the hate messages he has seen have been "very scary" and would have a hurtful effect on young children. While he acknowledges enforcement would not be easy, he says that is not the point: "To any degree we can, we have to confront this." The government, Pagtakhan believes, will move quickly to set up new rules. The reason for his optimism lies in remarks by Justice Minister Allan Rock—made over the Internet—suggesting that Ottawa was on the verge of action. "We are now considering new laws to establish limits on the use of the Internet and other forms of communication," Rock said. But one justice department official, on condition of anonymity, said that no decision has been taken on how to toughen up enforcement.

6   In fact, the government is still trying to come to grips with the nature of the beast, conscious of the reality that this electronic neighborhood of bits and bytes can be a force of good. Sgt. Craig Hannaford, an RCMP Internet expert in Ottawa, says: "The vast majority of the use of the Internet is totally and completely legitimate." But, he adds, "like any community, you have a small percentage of people who are criminals."

7   Michael Binder, assistant deputy minister at the industry department, asks another key question: "How would you regulate it?" Computer and legal experts all agree that enforcement is difficult. Still, a committee of the Canadian Association of Chiefs of Police has made several recommendations. One would make it illegal to possess computer hacking programs, those used to break into computer systems. Another would make the use of computer networks and telephone lines used in the commission of a crime a crime in itself. The committee also recommends agreements with the United States that would allow police officials in both countries to search computer data banks. But for the time being, Binder says, the government is in no rush to rewrite the statute books. "We don't know how it will evolve," he said. "We don't want to stifle communication. We don't want to shut down the Net."

8   It is pornography that stirs the most controversy. But while there is no doubt that pornography is popular, it amounts to a trickle compared with everything

else available on the Net. And as any walk past a magazine stand will demonstrate, dirty pictures are not automatically obscene under the Criminal Code. David Jones, president of Electronic Frontier Canada and a computer science professor at McMaster University in Hamilton, says the Internet should be governed in the same way as other media. "Pornography is not illegal in Canada," Jones said. "Visit Yonge Street in Toronto or watch cable TV if you have any doubt."

Much of the debate about the Internet arises because it is so new. "We're just sort of waking up to it," says Ian Kyer, president of Computer Law Association Inc. and a lawyer with the Toronto firm of Fasken Campbell Godfrey. "Now that it's an everyday thing, it's coming to the attention of the legislators and police forces, and I think they're not going to like what they see." But the debate is actually age-old and boils down to the limits that society sets on free expression. In an e-mail message, Troy Angrignon, a University of Victoria computer science graduate, told *Maclean's*: "This is NOT a computing issue—it is a civil liberties issue." 9

Freedom of expression is enshrined in the Charter of Rights, and the courts have generally protected it from government encroachment. Although the Supreme Court has not yet ruled on any Internet cases, a speech late last year by Justice John Sopinka gave some hint of how it might respond. While Sopinka observed that rights are not absolute, he made it clear that the court would not easily endorse wide-ranging restrictions. The court had struck down a municipal by-law prohibiting posters on public property, he said, and then tellingly added: "It may be said that the electronic media such as the Internet are the posters of the late 20th century." 10

Almost like posters on telephone poles, the Internet appears to defy regulation, an irony given its roots as a research network for the U.S. defence department, which is no fan of anarchy. No one owns the Net, so no one controls it. Messages are passed from computer system to computer system in milliseconds, and the network literally resembles a web of computers and connecting telephone lines. It crosses borders in less time than it takes to cross most streets, and connections to Australia or Asia are as commonplace as dialling Ottawa or Washington. It is the Net's very lack of frontiers that makes law enforcement so difficult. "One of the real problems with the law of the Internet is deciding, where does the offence occur?" says Kyer. 11

The elusive nature of the Net is illustrated by a recent case in which a postal inspector in Tennessee downloaded pornography from a computer bulletin board in California. The board operator in California was charged and convicted in Tennessee, based on that state's community standards. That decision, says Richard Pitt, CEO of Wimsey Information Services, a Vancouver-based Internet provider, strikes terror into the hearts of computer network operators. They may discover, says Kyer, that the Net may fall subject to regulation in every jurisdic- 12 tion it touches. "It's a frightening prospect to think that we are all then bound by the laws of the most strict and puritanical jurisdictions in the world."

13   The problems of enforcing one nation's laws on the Net are illustrated by the gambling craze. A company called Sports International has established a betting operation on the World Wide Web. For two years, the bookmaker, based on the island of Antigua, has been taking bets on Canadian and American sports events, with bets paid by bank transfers. Next fall, it will become a virtual casino, offering roulette and blackjack to clients—including Canadians—sitting thousands of miles away at their computer screens. Is it illegal? "The question," says Hannaford, "is where is it taking place." On balance, he says, "probably there's not a whole lot that can be done."

14   Zundel, a Toronto publisher with international neo-Nazi credentials, has an outpost on the World Wide Web, an Internet service that combines text and graphics with the seamless ability to move from one database to another using a technology known as hyper-text links. Information about Zundel's cause is posted on an Orange County, Calif., computer by Greg Raven, associated with the Institute for Historical Review. Raven says he set up the Web site to disseminate Zundel's views after a previous site, also in the United States, was shut down by the Internet provider. In addition, the on-line magazine of the white supremacist Heritage Front is found on a Web server in Florida.

15   The saying on the Net is that bits have no boundaries, and that is equally true of smut. Pornography might be sent from a computer in Manitoba to a computer in the United States and then to a computer in Europe, where it may reside, perfectly within the laws of that country. Canadian police forces can ask for help from foreign investigators—but may not get it. A case may not be a priority, especially if the alleged crime is not illegal in that country. "International investigations don't move that quick," Hannaford notes. And Kyer points out that just as some small countries have sometimes set themselves up as money-laundering havens, others could find it profitable to become data havens. The problems are pushing governments to talk about international treaties governing data flows, but so far little has been done.

16   Confronted with the difficulty of trying to grab on to something as amorphous as the Net, some critics and government officials are hoping that Internet service providers—companies like NSTN or Wimsey that, for a fee, will hook up companies and individuals—can police the Net themselves. The information highway council is expected later this month to approve a recommendation that would encourage the providers to develop a code of ethics, in the same way that broadcasters have been "encouraged" to regulate themselves in the transmission of violent television programs. The Net providers say they cannot hope to control what floods over their networks and trust that they will eventually be considered common carriers, as the telephone companies are, freed from liability for what people say and do over the phone. There have been no clear Canadian court

tests. But a U.S. decision suggests that as long as on-line services do not provide content, they may not be liable for the information they carry; in other words, they would be treated as a library or bookstore, not a publisher.

At Wimsey, Pitt says postings in newsgroups—the equivalents of computer-based bulletin boards—add up to more than 100 megabytes a day, the equivalent of maybe 20 million words. On the advice of his lawyers, Wimsey does not provide its subscribers with access to the newsgroups dealing with pedophilia or bestiality. But there is nothing stopping someone from posting an obscene picture to any newsgroup, no matter what the subject.   *17*

Wimsey was overwhelmed in trying to control the newsgroup discussions about the Bernardo-Homolka case, which quickly became a place to exchange information covered by a court-ordered publication ban. It was, says Pitt, like sticking a finger in a leaking dike. "It showed up in so many places on our machines that there was no possibility" that they could control it, he says. As the Supreme Court noted late last year in a decision setting new rules for publication bans: "In this global electronic age, meaningfully restricting the flow of information is becoming increasingly difficult."   *18*

As Canadians try to come to grips with the Internet, one legal expert says the government should tread cautiously to avoid strangling a powerful resource. Jon Festinger, a professor of media law at the University of British Columbia and legal counsel for WIC, Western International Communications Ltd., says the Internet and the debate over it could help Canadians redefine the limits of control. "We should err on the side of tolerance," he says, "and we should err on the side of freedom of expression." ◆   *19*

1995

Glossary

Paul Bernardo: refers to the St. Catharines, Ontario, man who, together with his wife Karla Homolka, was charged with the abduction, rape, torture, and murder of 14-year-old Leslie Mahaffy and 15-year-old Kristen French in 1994; the subsequent trials occasioned what many have called the most publicized legal case in Canadian history. A publication ban was imposed on Homolka's trial in an effort to ensure a fair trial for Bernardo, who was tried after Homolka; however, out-of-country web sites and newspapers made the details of Homolka's trial available.

Explorations

- Do you use the Internet? If so, have you visited any of the problematic sites Caragata refers to? What did you think of them?
- Do reports of increasing cybercrime rates worry you? Why or why not?
- Do you think that the Internet should be regulated by the government? Do you think it can be regulated? What challenges would be involved in regulation?

Carole Corbeil (1956–2000) was born and raised in Montreal, and died in 2000 from ovarian cancer. She was an arts writer and critic for This Magazine, Saturday Night, Canadian Art, *and* The Globe and Mail. *She is the author of the novel* Voice-Over *(1993), which won the City of Toronto Book Award in 1993 as well as the W.H. Smith First Novel Award, and* In the Wings *(1999), which has been adapted for stage by Theatre Passe Muraille.*

The Advertised Infant: Ivan's Adventures in Babyland

Carole Corbeil

1   When Ivan turned three months, the Big Ones took him out of a basket and put him behind bars. Like most babies, Ivan hates to sleep alone so the Big Ones got him a red plastic battery-operated heart which was recommended for "sleep-resistant"[1] infants. The artificial heart beat did, there's no getting around it, remind Ivan of better times.

2   Ivan is napping now, big head close to the red plastic heart, tiny body looking like a little invalid in a terry sleeper. The bars of his Bauhaus° model crib are white, his sleeper is pale blue, and everything around him has the germ-free aura of a new town house. (From the window you can see that the front yard has yet to be sodded, and that a small thin maple awaits burial in a burlap earth bag.) Near Ivan, on the chest of drawers which matches his crib, there is a coffee-coloured plastic contraption with an orange-tipped antenna. The Big One always turns it on before leaving the room. Ivan senses that this is an ear, somehow. There is another ear like it in the kitchen. The unit is, in fact, called "a nursery monitor," or a "nursery listening system for parents' peace of mind." It "lets parents be in two places at once," and it retails for $64.95.

3   Ivan doesn't want the Big One to be in two places at once. He wants to be with, or be carried by, the Big One at all times.

4   The Big One sometimes puts him down on the floor where he can't see a god-damn thing (it's the ceiling if he's on his back, the screaming colours of an "alphabetized learning blanket" if he's on his belly, and he can't turn over yet). The last time the Big One put him on the floor, he managed to hold his head up the whole time, he was so pissed off. Both Big Ones went bananas. They looked at their copy of *The First Twelve Months of Life* and said he was right on time and wasn't that great; they were beginning to worry because Marlene who's such a screamer but the same age was already holding up her head.

5   Now, Ivan is waking up. He opens his eyes. He cries. The happy faces on the "voice-activated crib mobile" above him start to move at a frenetic rate; the more he cries the more the happy faces spin.

He knows the routine. The Big One takes an eternity to come and see him. *6* The Big One winds the music box of another mobile, where clowns this time spin around to sickening music. If he cries in esthetic protest, the Big One sticks an "orthodontic pacifier-exerciser recommended by leading dentists and pediatricians" in his mouth, or a bottle with a silicone nipple which is said to be made "of the same material used for making artificial heart valves."

"Look at those clowns," the Big One says, "those pretty, pretty clowns." There *7* is a tag on the bar from which the clown mobile hangs. "Caution," it says, "mobile for visual entertainment. Not intended to be handled by children."

Now the Big One is going to take him downstairs for a bout with a "shared *8* development system." Babycise, a one hour follow-along video with workout accessories, "was created by leading pediatricians and physical therapists." The Big One identified with this ad: "Chances are you won't be able to spend as much special time with your baby as you want. We're talking about Discovery Time. Learning Time. Doing Things Together Time. It's the time your hectic schedule makes very very scarce." (The Y is part of the Big One's hectic schedule.)

Now the Big One lies Ivan down by the TV, pushes the tape in, hands him a *9* yellow barbell with red, blue and green balls, and one-two-three, they're off on a ride which will help him, at three months, to "develop physically and grow in self-confidence."

By the time he's six months, Ivan sits up and plays with an "activity centre" *10* which is full of things that make "rewarding sounds," and with European-designed objects which spruce up "his eye and hand coordination." He also has numerous encounters with a "glow worm," a strange, worm-shaped object which lights up when it is hugged. It is not until later, when he begins to crawl and then finally to walk, that the Big Ones, anxious and fearful for his safety, get into another major consumeristic panic. (Ivan has let it be known that the playpen, with its "chew-proof vinyl rails," is anathema.)

"BabySafetronics" enter the home. Now when Ivan, using great cunning, man- *11* ages to open the pantry door where foul tasting detergent is kept, a loud, electronic alarm goes off, shaking him to his very foundation. This is called "Door Alert." Occasionally, Ivan is equipped with a beeper, called "The Nanny, an electronic Babysitter." ("The function of The Nanny," in case you haven't guessed, "is to assist in informing you that your child might be out of your immediate presence. It attaches easily to your child and monitors up to 50 feet.")

When the Big One takes Ivan for a walk, Ivan attempts to teach the Big One *12* that private property is a rather odd concept. He explores other people's front yards and ends up on neighbours' front porches. The Big One finds this tiresome and humiliating and therefore buys a "safety harness." ("As your child starts to walk, you have the facility to restrain his movements.") For "a more secure feeling" in "shopping centres, airports, crowded places or anywhere" the Big One handcuffs Ivan to his/her self with Hug & Tug, a multicoloured rope that yanks Ivan from what interests and pleases him.

13   Ivan will probably never know what wondrous things he learned in his first year. He may wonder, when he gets older, why he has to sleep with a walkman, why he wants to suck on artificial heart valves, why going through physical and metaphorical doors fills him with anxiety, why he likes to be restrained during sex, and why he is aflutter with shocks of recognition when he reads Kafka.° But never mind. For now Ivan the Investment is Safe & Secure. And that's what really matters.

14   Babyland is a world of substitutes, a world in which nothing is the real thing, a world where everything is surreal, fantastical, cartoonish, sentimental, exaggerated, excessive. The inhabitants of Babyland moreover are perceived as having the dullest, bluntest, most embryonic senses imaginable. In the daytime, colours not only have to be bold, they have to scream with day-glo pain. At night, everything turns into pastels, with teddies and puppies and tarted-up ABCs dancing on sheets and blankets and nightgowns and sleepers.

15   How, you have to ask yourself, when you first encounter this stuff in baby stores or in the hitherto invisible baby aisle of Shoppers Drug Mart, did Babyland come to be? How did the world of babies come to resemble a derailed acid trip? Why is it that baby ads turn human infants into Disneyfied cuddlies or into chubby ids to be harnessed and restrained?

16   Western technological culture is certainly unique in this respect. No other culture creates such a separate, hermetic, bizarre world for its babies. In tribal and agricultural societies, babies are simply carried about in slings or papooses and take part in the productive life around them through the comfortable mediation of the mother's body.

17   In our society, however, Babyland is so separate from the rest of the world that it is entirely possible to grow to child-bearing age and have no idea how to take care of a baby. Most people now take courses to prepare for the main event, but what happens after the birth is hardly discussed.

18   The first thing you notice then, when you go through the gates of Babyland, is that you've entered a realm apart, a realm that remains invisible to all but those confined to it. Eventually, you begin to understand, in a visceral way, that the system you live under owes its existence to a rigid separation between the private (home and babies and children) and the public (the "work place"). This separation of spheres is economically rooted; it infects every aspect of our lives by organizing what we will experience and how. Most distressing, however, is discovering how we've internalized this division. No matter how many women join the work force, no matter how many babies and young children end up in daycare, the public and the private continue to exist as two distinct realms, with two distinct sets of values, not to mention degrees of reality. "Out in the real" world used to refer to the world of men; now it refers to a world bereft of babies and children.

This definition of reality reminds me of *Who's Real?*, a book I bought for my   *19*
daughter when she was a year old. She was very fond of books with flaps at that
point and *Who's Real?* had plenty of them. It wasn't until I got home that I realized what it was about. An illustration of a toy graces the flap, while underneath,
there is a drawing of the animal the toy is based on. One flap, for example, shows
a rocking horse; lift the flap and you find a so-called real horse. "So-called"
because it is, after all, nothing more than a stylized representation of a horse. A
real horse exists only in the skin-rippling flesh. The question *Who's Real?* obviously can't be answered under these circumstances.

Who's Real? is a kind of paradigm for what goes on in Babyland. The most stun-   *20*
ning thing about baby toys is that they introduce babies to imitations way before
they've had the chance to experience the real thing. All animals, for instance,
are perceived as stuffed first and alive later. Real animals must seem like nastier,
less evolved versions of the prettified, defanged, pastel cuddlies.

The same kind of polarized qualities define the private and the public world.   *21*
It may be that Babyland is the way it is because "the real world" is the way it is.
It may be that Babyland screams with colour and is drenched with sentimentality because it is a split-off; it's the distorted reflection of everything which is
repressed in the "real world." Maybe if the two worlds were more integrated,
we'd start to see true colour in both realms. It's just a theory, mind you, just a
theory.

According to critic Raymond Williams, the early uses of the word culture all   *22*
had something to do with process; culture referred to the tending of something,
crops or animals. So baby culture can be defined as how we tend to tend babies
in the heated, isolated boxes we call home, or in the more heavily populated
boxes we call daycare centres. ("Tend to tend" because there are a lot of variations here—there's a mainstream, high tech baby culture, an alternate, low tech
baby culture, and an achievement-oriented baby-yuppie culture. The mainstream
is most likely to use the products Ivan is subjected to.)

While in our society fashions of baby tending come and go, human infants   *23*
don't; they have strict biological expectations which are either frustrated by the
fashions of the day, or fulfilled. The history of western infants is of necessity tied
to the history of women, and the technologically oriented obstetrics and pedi-
atrics of modern medicine have made both unconscionably miserable. (Male
doctors invented formula—an "improvement on breast-milk," for example, or
drove both baby and mother crazy by advising scheduled feedings every four
hours.) What newborns expect is simple—to be held, carried, to feel the same
motion and heartbeat as in the womb, to be fed from the breast whenever hunger
strikes, and, as they get older, to learn from the activity of those around them,
while returning periodically to the mock-womb protection of the parents' arms.
(It is a product of our evolution that babies expect to be carried at all times; predators would have made mincemeat out of them otherwise.)

24   The expectation of taking part in a culture is also a product of our evolution, and the mores we absorb from the earliest moments of life correspond to the inborn ways of other species. What babies first encounter, in other words, is "imprinted" as rigidly as the instincts of animals. (In the rare instances where children have been raised by animals, they cannot be broken from their first imprintings; animals raised by different animals, however, are much more flexible when it comes to adapting to their own species because so many of their responses are innate.)

25   How a baby is cared for, then, is crucial. It is certainly more crucial than the objects and toys that make up Babyland. (Babies, in any case, are rarely interested in toys. They're interested in playing with what adults play with, or use, and adults rarely use baby toys. Wooden spoons, pots and pans, little brooms, real telephones, and especially tape decks are big hits.)

26   In terms of marketing, however, what fascinates a baby is irrelevant. Babies don't buy baby products; adults do. And it's not just anxious, insecure, learning on the job first-time parents who buy baby products. The triumph of consumerism is that it has transformed life into a series of stackable markets (the baby, kid, teen, marriage, middle age, senior, dying markets), and transformed all rituals with orgies of product giving.

27   Baby toys are not, moreover, the most lucrative part of the baby market. The lion's share of the baby market goes to "instruments of infant care," as one manufacturer of high chairs, swingomatics, playpens and walkers, puts it. These products are aimed at people, you understand, who are in a profound state of shock (nothing has prepared them for the bloody sensorama of birth) and who now spend most of their waking hours obsessing about crib death (some have been known to dangle feathers in front of their babies' mouths to make sure they're "still breathing").

28   Today's parents, moreover, are in an unenviable and historically unique situation. They must bring up children without the physical and emotional support of an extended family. An awful lot of baby products "extend" or try to duplicate the mother's body because an extra pair of arms, or eyes, or ears, are rarely available. In fact, a baby store is a kind of body shop. (All the body parts, not too surprisingly, are recommended by leading white male pediatricians.)

29   Baby culture is, in fact, a lot like sports culture. In sports culture it is impossible to do the simplest thing, like running, without buying lots of equipment (head bands, track suits, wrist guards), and most activities depend on the validation of medical experts for their pleasure.

30   A baby store, moreover, is not just a body shop, it's also a projection shop. Baby products perfectly reflect the neuroses, obsessions and trends of this, our twilight zone. Even the twin preoccupation of the eighties—"security systems" and "fitness systems"—have found their way into baby culture.

31   Looked at from an infant's point of view, however, baby products are a very poignant kind of code. What products proclaim, if they are used as advertised, is

that it is preferable and "safer" to bond with objects than with human beings because objects do not disappear the way human beings do; that the body is inadequate and must be supplemented if not supplanted by technology; that the visual sense is the most important sense; that knowing how to use tools—beep horns, push levers, dial phones, rattle bells—is the foundation of human society; that approval and therefore well-being is dependent on the mastery of such skills. Last but not least, the restraining equipment makes it clear that the Big One's agenda is vastly more important than one's own.

You have to admit that the above provides a masterful kind of imprinting.   *32* Looked at from this perspective, the baby market could set in motion the obsessive-compulsive attachment to objects which makes all other markets possible. An added feature of this advertised baby tending is that infants are so traumatized by the cold void they encounter that memory of those early years is completely wiped out. As adults they are likely to scoff at the notion that babies have real feelings and real expectations; the cycle may then perpetuate itself.

It's just a theory, mind you, just a theory. ◆   *33*

1987

Endnote

1. All the products in Ivan's world are real, and all quotes are from advertising or packaging material.

Glossary

Bauhaus: a school of art and architecture founded in Germany by Walter Gropius (1883–1969). Bauhaus is characterized by a geometric, hard-edged style.

Kafka: Franz Kafka (1883–1924), German-Austrian novelist and story writer who lived and worked in Prague. Kafka's works centre on the atomized existence of modern society, where people encounter grotesque and fantastic daily occurrences in a dream-like world of unreality.

Explorations

- Do you think that Ivan's experience is representative of most infants in North America? Why or why not?

- What baby products are currently being marketed? Why do parents buy these products—for the child's sake or for their own?

- Looking at different stages of life, can you find evidence to support Corbeil's theory that after living in Babyland, "a world in which nothing is the real thing, a world where everything is surreal, fantastical, cartoonish, sentimental, exaggerated, excessive," we are prone to having an obsessive-compulsive attachment to objects?

Mark Kingwell, born in 1963, is an assistant professor of philosophy at the University of Toronto at Scarborough and writes a regular column in the Commentary section of the National Post. *He is also the author of a number of books, including the national best-seller* Better Living: In Pursuit of Happiness from Plato to Prozac, *which won the 1998 Drummer General's Award for Non-Fiction;* A Civil Tongue: Justice, Dialogue, and the Politics of Pluralism, *winner of the 1996 Spitz Prize in Political Theory; and* Dreams of Millennium: Report from a Culture on the Brink *(1996).*

The Goods on the Tube

Mark Kingwell

1   It is the medium we most love to hate. The glowing black cube, the cathode-ray cyclops lodged in our living rooms. We regard it with fascinated horror, feel powerless before it, sucked into its evil vortex. We use it, in the resonant phrase of the critic Neil Postman, to amuse ourselves *to death.* Television: bane of our lives, the hardest of hard drugs.

2   Except it isn't. It is, instead, one of the most powerful, useful, and aesthetically advanced media humans have ever created, rivalling print in its flexibility and easily outdistancing all other visual media—plays, opera, even movies—in its influence. It brings ordinary people entertainment, information, even (not to be sneered at) a form of company—at a price well below what it takes to see a movie a week. Why, then, are we forever bent on demonizing it?

3   A good question, especially for those people who watch television regularly and in fairly large amounts. TV fans are made to feel ashamed of their "weakness." They become furtive and skulking, resorting to misdirection, vagueness, even denial, when the subject arises in polite company.

4   *Television? Well, yes, I own one. Of course. For the news. And PBS. But I don't watch it a lot. Not really. Steven Bochco?°* I tell you, I don't know the man.

5   It's about time we put an end to this cravenness and defended the medium that has the greatest impact on most of our lives. The first step is to expose some of the myths surrounding television, those pieces of conventional wisdom that crop up whenever people get into a good self-justifying lather of TV disapproval. Contrary to received opinion, watching television is not bad for you. It might even be good. To see why, take a few of the myths in turn.

6   *Watching television makes you stupid.* Like a lot of things that are supposed to "make" you stupid, television can only highlight what nature or God has already rendered. Of course, there are stupid shows on television. Watching these shows may be annoying; it is not debilitating.

7   Nor does watching television mean you can't have a full, productive life. Are there better things to do than watch TV? Of course there are. If you can convince

yourself that you will bake bread, write sonnets, or build houses for the poor when you're not watching TV, more power to you. (Unless your sonnets are no good; a bad sonnet is worse than no sonnet at all.)

But if you're thinking, as in a recent Aptiva computer ad, that surfing the Internet is somehow morally superior to watching television, think again. The bulk of log-on time is not spent in the selfless pursuit of knowledge we see depicted in those ads, with bright kids soaking up the world's best encyclopedia. In fact, it's mostly spent trolling the wires for useless information and inane conversation. That's not better than TV; it's just TV carried on by other means. 8

Liking television means hating print. TV and print are media, systems of delivering ideas and information. Each has advantages and disadvantages; each does some things better than the other. 9

You can't do any serious philosophizing on TV, because that requires the discipline of linear text and intricate argument; but neither can you fully integrate text and images in a book the way you can in a masterly TV documentary like, say, Ken Burns's landmark *Civil War* series or in the brilliant "Secret Life of Machines" and "Connections" programmes on The Learning Channel, in which oddball British intellectuals trace the development of the photocopier or explain why modern astronomy began with the military need to measure cannonball trajectories. 10

There are, for that matter, junk books just as there's junk TV, and television programmes as searching and moving, in their way, as great works of narrative art. The success of television has not harmed book culture, either—on the contrary. There are more books being published now than ever before in human history. In short, there is no evolutionary struggle afoot between television and print, no hard choice to be made between them. 11

But television warps the minds of children. Like all good things, TV should be taken in moderation. But parents bent on limiting access to TV might want to consider whether the warping they fear might happen in the opposite direction. Kids who don't watch TV *at all* are likely to find themselves alienated from their own culture. 12

One of the reasons parents worry so much about TV, of course, is that they fear cop shows and explosion-filled movies will confuse children so that they can't tell the real from the invented. Or that they'll then imitate what they see. But this shows a surprising lack of confidence in their own parenting skills. Violent television is just one part of a world that, along with school-yard bullies and rewarded greed, makes teaching the basic lessons of morality difficult. Children have to be taught why violence is not a good way to solve problems. Violence depicted realistically on TV is probably more effective in this task than the apparently painless violence of "Roadrunner" cartoons. 13

There still exists no consensus evidence that observing violence on television leads to actual violence. And if you don't want your kids watching it, you can switch the channel when one of those plentiful warnings about violence and bad 14 language comes on. Or, when the time comes, you can install the signal-blocking "V-chip."°

15   Should we deplore TV violence in a blanket fashion anyway, just to be on the safe side? I don't think so. Depictions of violence can serve an artistic, as well as an educational, purpose. Consider the devastating opening sequence on "Homicide" last season that showed a boy killed in crossfire at a mall. We should be wary of bureaucratic control that would rule out something so aesthetically effective. Warnings are one thing; censorship is another.

16   *Television distorts the world.* Like any medium, television stands between us and what it depicts, sometimes rendering the thing itself shadowy and distant. It can create bizarre expectations and twisted notions of reality. TV news, for example, does tend to manipulate the world and deliver it, packaged and slick, into our living rooms in handy thirty-minute parcels.

17   But we should also acknowledge that TV news forces us to see what's going on around us in a way otherwise impossible. We see the anguish on the faces of the war-torn, the grim looks of suffering. Is this just voyeurism? Not if we force ourselves to make it the occasion for moral insight. The incongruity of searing images of war and famine broken up by, say, ads for Depends adult diapers, is unsettling in an important way. Sitting in our comfortable rooms, we cannot ignore our own security, the smallness of our concerns set against those of the globe's majority. In a sense, it is precisely because television news can't offer the detached analysis of print that it is more disturbing to personal equilibrium than any newspaper.

18   *Television undermines democracy.* Anti-TV critics think TV is Aldous Huxley's deadening "soma,"° but in more powerful form. TV is a mental syringe: entertainment slips into our brains and delivers a payload of consumer culture that destroys our sense of civic obligation, our interest in participating in the life of our own communities. Thus we become channel-changing morons at the mercy of Nike and Procter & Gamble, marching out zombie-like, past the homeless and sick, to buy Air Jordans or Tide.

19   On the whole, though, these critics tend to underestimate the critical faculties of people, even as they overestimate their desire for "better" programmes and political criticism. There is no clamouring unmet need for in-depth political analysis, and the one sense in which most people are highly intelligent is in knowing exactly what they want. If they don't get it—on television, in the marketplace, or in politics—they will simply change the channel. In the end, it's not advertisers that get good shows cancelled; it's the Nielsen numbers.°

20   So unless we're prepared to argue that we know what people want better than they do themselves, we cannot say that TV is undemocratic. On the contrary, it's the most democratic medium we have, and getting more so: proliferating channels, more access, a greater range of niche markets. Television is us. That may be alarming to intellectuals, as lowest-common-denominator things generally are, but it's all part of the democratic bargain.

Okay, but the numbers mean that television programming is uniformly bad. No, it   *21*
isn't. Television is not, contrary to what we are often told, an undifferentiated
sludge of infotainment that should be judged by a single standard. TV is more like
one of those mega-bookstores, where you can find everything from sports and
warplanes, cooking and lifestyle advice, to Proust° and Nietzsche° and Jane
Austen.° It's absurd to say anything about the "general" standard of television.
There is no such thing.

There is, in fact, a lot of good television on the air now, not all of it educa-   *22*
tional documentaries or the high-minded British drama to be found on "Mystery"
and "Masterpiece Theatre." Network TV offers a number of edgy, well-crafted
shows that make staying in more than a matter of avoiding the Arctic chill: "Law
and Order," "The X-Files," and "Homicide." Distinguished by acting and writing
of surprising excellence, these shows share a compelling aesthetic of darkness
owing as much to *film noir* as to the jumpy, hand-held photographic techniques
now so much in vogue. ("NYPD Blue" goes too far; watching it is like trying to
read on a bus.) They are as dramatically accomplished as much of the literary
canon, as socially conscious as anything by Dickens° or Brecht.°

In comedy, "Seinfeld" has recently regained its sharpness, now that George   *23*
is once more in a manic phase, and the gentle humour of "Frasier" and "The
Drew Carey Show" are nice counterpoints (from upper-middle and lower-middle
classes respectively) to the bleak, nihilistic hilarity of "The Larry Sanders Show."
The late, lamented "My So-Called Life" is in reruns on Showcase, which also
snagged some good Australian exports, while those great old Brit espionage
shows—"The Saint," "The Avengers"—are on Bravo.

Those with a taste for camp can tune in to the Fox Network's flagship,   *24*
"Melrose Place," arguably the funniest show on television, an explosion of the
soap-opera genre that just keeps going further over the top. Or the CBC's "Rita
& Friends," for those delicious moments when the Nova Scotia crooner intro-
duces the week's obligatory alterna-pop guests. "And now, my good friends, uh,
Treble Charger will do their hit single, um…"

In short, there is wheat amongst the chaff. Within the boundaries of the   *25*
medium, or sometimes stretching those boundaries, these shows are saying
important things, telling stories, arousing emotions, and making us laugh—
intentionally or otherwise. It is not absurd to call them art, for by any reasonable
definition they are. And it is not silly to find them worthwhile. ◆

1996

Glossary

Steven Bochco: (b. 1943) American screenwriter and television producer responsible for creating such hit series as *Hill Street Blues*, *L.A. Law*, *NYPD Blue*, and
Murder One.

V-chip: Canadian-developed micro-computer chip that enables television viewers to block out programs they do not want to see.

Aldous Huxley's deadening "soma": Aldous Huxley (1894–1963), an English novelist, essayist, and satirist best known for the dystopic vision of the future and scientific progress he evoked in the novel *Brave New World* (1932); in that novel "soma" is the euphoric and hallucinogenic drug dispensed by the state in order to condition its citizens toward passivity, collectivity, and bland social harmony.

Nielsen numbers: the registered system for tracking and monitoring how many viewers regularly tune in to certain television programs.

Proust: Marcel Proust (1871–1922), French novelist best known for his mammoth 16-volume *Remembrance of Things Past* (1913–1927).

Nietzsche: Friedrich Nietzsche (1844–1900), German philosopher, classical scholar, and poet who rejected Christian doctrine, rationalist philosophy, and systemic thought in his investigations into human will and the "irrational."

Jane Austen: (1775–1817) English novelist whose works include *Sense and Sensibility*, *Pride and Prejudice*, *Mansfield Park*, *Emma*, and *Persuasion*.

Dickens: Charles Dickens (1812–1870), English novelist known for his evocative portraits of 19th-century London in books like *Oliver Twist*, *Nicholas Nickleby*, *Great Expectations*, *Bleak House*, and *David Copperfield*.

Brecht: Bertolt Brecht (1898–1956), German expressionist poet and influential playwright whose plays include *Mother Courage*, *The Good Woman of Setzuan*, *The Caucasian Chalk Circle*, and, with Kurt Weill, *The Threepenny Opera*.

Explorations

- Would you feel ashamed of telling people how much TV you watch? Why or why not?

- Do you view those who watch a fair amount of TV as leading unproductive lives? Do you consider anyone you know to be "addicted" to television?

- Which television shows do you consider to be stupid, tasteless, or overly violent? Which shows do you think are intelligent, tasteful, or educational?

Evelyn Lau was born in Vancouver, British Columbia, in 1970. After spending much of her youth on the street, she gained international fame at age 18 with the publication of her first work, Runaway: Diary of a Street Kid (1989), *which was adapted into a TV movie. Since then, she has published numerous volumes of poetry and prose, including* You Are Not Who You Claim (1990), *which won the Milton Acorn People's Poetry Award,* Oedipal Dreams (1992), Fresh Girls (1993), Other Women (1996), *and* Inside Out: Reflections on a Life So Far (2001). *In 1992 Lau became the youngest poet to have been nominated for a Governor General's Award.*

An Insatiable Emptiness

Evelyn Lau

I no longer clearly remember the first time I forced myself to throw up. What I do remember is how inexpert I was and how long it took before I succeeded in actually vomiting instead of just gagging and retching. I began by sticking my finger down my throat and wiggling it around, but this produced few results; it wasn't until articles about bulimia appeared in women's magazines that I finally thought to use the handle of a toothbrush instead of my forefinger. It became easy after that. 1

In my mid-teens, I was too young to believe I was anything but immortal. It didn't occur to me that what I was doing was dangerous—instead, it seemed a smart and practical way of coping with things. I went through months of throwing up once or twice a day, then brief periods when I did not throw up at all, when I seemed to have broken the pattern. Surely this meant I was in control. But by the time I turned 18, the months of not throwing up had diminished to weeks, and when I *was* vomiting I was doing it four, five, six times a day. I had become addicted to the sensation. It was no longer a penance I had to perform after eating, but the reward at the end of a binge. I loved the feeling I had after purging, of being clean and shiny inside like a scrubbed machine, superhuman. I would rise from the bathroom floor, splash my face with cold water, vigorously brush the acid from my mouth. I would take a wet cloth, wipe off the vomit that had spattered my arms, and feel as energized as someone who had just woken from a nap or returned from an invigorating jog around the block. I felt as if everything disgusting inside me had been displaced so that it was now outside myself. Not only all the food I had eaten, but my entire past. 2

No one could tell me to stop, not even my friends who eventually knew what I was doing. They could not control this part of my life or any other. This was mine alone—the chemical flower smell of the blue water in the toilet, the vomit that shot out as a burning liquid, drenching the sides of the bowl. After a session in the bathroom, a certain emptiness would sing inside me, a sensation of having 3 become a cage of bones with air rushing through it. I craved this feeling so much I no longer cared what I had to eat in order to vomit—I would cram clusters of bananas into my mouth, or tubs of ice cream that lurched back up my throat in a thin and startlingly sweet projectile.

4   When I left the bathroom, I felt like someone who had achieved some great thing—climbed a mountain, written a book—and survived. I was overweight by only 10 pounds or so, but when I looked in the mirror all I saw was buttery flesh covering my body. My stomach had become swollen and globular from the gorging and purging; I had earned it the way other women earn washboard stomachs and lean waists from hours of sit-ups and crunches at the gym.

5   As a child, I had been thin and healthy, with a flat belly and limbs that turned brown in the summer. I had my first period when I was 11, and for the next several years the blood welled out of me in thick, rust-coloured gouts that no tampons or pads could contain. My body had somehow become a vessel filled with secret, terrible workings, and I longed to make it translucent, pared-down, clean as a whistle. But the blood spread in the shapes of clouds on my skirts and pants, for 10 or 12 days each month, and my hips and breasts pressed outwards. I hated what was happening to my body, once so straight and uninflected. I attracted the attention of one of my parents' friends, who stared at the fuzzy-dark crook at the top of my thighs when I sat cross-legged in front of him, who asked me to perform somersaults and splits while his thick lips hung open with desire. My own father grew awkward around me, refusing to touch me or meet my eyes, driven away by this growing body that forced him out like a giant balloon expanding in a small room. I was in despair. I wanted to trick my body back into childhood by starving it, but I was hungry all the time; I craved food during the week prior to my traumatic periods. Sometimes I would consume a whole bag of shortbread cookies or three chocolate bars; the sugar and fat would induce a heavy, mucousy lethargy.

6   My breasts continued to develop, horrifying my mother, who frequently made me undress in front of her so she could ridicule them. Her actions convinced me there was something wrong with my body. She decided to put the whole family on a diet, serving small portions of steamed fish and vegetables, chicken with the skin removed. During dinner, and in the hungry hours of the evening that followed, she would say over and over again, "It's because of you we didn't get enough to eat, that we're going to bed hungry. Look at the sacrifices we're making for you." I would sit at the dinner table, staring down at my plate with tears in my eyes, grief forming a hot, choking knot in my throat. I would watch my father slowly raise his fork to his mouth while my eagle-eyed mother watched me triumphantly, eating only half of what was on her plate in order to set an example.

7   My mother was so thin and white that whenever I glimpsed her undressing behind a half-closed door, her thighs looked like those of the Holocaust survivors I examined in photographs in history class at school. Meanwhile, I began to put

on weight, growing chubby beneath sweatshirts and loose jeans. I stole chocolates from the drugstore, bought greasy bags of day-old cookies from the bakery, consumed candies in a blind rush on the mile-long walk from school to home. I crammed myself with food, yet I hated food: its veils of grease, its sauces like paste. I hated its fragility beneath my hands, could not bear the delicacy of pastry. But once I started eating, I could not stop, and after I gave in I would again have to cope with the horrible feeling of satiation—a feeling so uncomfortable and guilt-ridden it threatened to annihilate me.

I hated the unaccustomed thickness of my body, yet I took a secret, perverse 8
pride in the space I was filling up, the air I was pushing aside in the family home in order to make room for myself. I looked in scorn upon my mother, who wore tiny pink sweaters with pearl buttons, size XS. Her legs were like bleached sticks, the skin white and crepey; her hipbones jutted visibly beneath her skirts, and she reminded me of a starving cow, its ribs and hips holding up the tent of skin. At 13, I had grown to match my father's weight. But at 130 pounds, he was small for a man, his arms straight, the biceps undefined. He was weak, useless in the battle that had sprung up between my mother and myself. He would not protect me, he took no sides in the daily tug-of-war for power. He merely absented himself, took the coward's way out. For this, I knew, one day I would make him suffer.

I thought that if I were to physically fight my mother I could break her dry 9
arms like twigs. I could twist her skeleton between my hands; I could sit on her and suffocate her. But it never came to that. Instead, with each pound I gained, my mother became more controlling. I felt that in my entire world there was only one thing my mother could not take away from me: my body. She was trying, of course, with her diets and carefully calibrated meals and calorie counters set up around the kitchen. She wanted to watch me day and night, but in this she inevitably encountered frustration and failure: she could not see the junk food I snuck between meals and hid between textbooks and in my locker at school.

And it was driving my mother crazy, I began to realize. She turned to the only 10
thing she could control 24 hours a day: her own body. For every pound I gained, she lost one. In Grade 9, when I came home from school I found her doing jumping jacks and skipping rope in the living room, or following an aerobics show on television. She had virtually stopped eating, complaining that I was doing enough eating for us both. Her eyes grew large in her face, and her hair began to fall out in swirls that clogged up the drain in the sink and the shower. When I stood up from the table and looked down at my mother's skull, I could see the wide, white swathe of the part in her hair.

For a while, my father insisted that she eat, but he soon gave up and came 11
home less and less, always too late for the dinner hour, fraught as it was with its agonizing tensions: my mother staring at me with fascination as I ate, her eyes transfixed with hunger. I thought I could no longer stand it; I was as guilty as a murderer with every bite. At night, I lay in my room contemplating suicide and

listening to the footsteps of my father pacing his study, waiting for his wife to fall asleep before daring to enter their bedroom. When I trespassed there, I saw pink walls, pink curtains, a pink throw on the queen-sized bed. The bedroom faced south, and all day the sun shone relentlessly through the gauze curtains, revealing the motes of dust in the air. When I opened the dresser drawers, I found beautiful, tiny clothes, beaded and jewelled, carefully folded and wrapped in plastic, as if their owner had already died. I knew these clothes would never again be worn by my mother, and I would never be small enough to wear them. I knew this was a source of bitterness in my mother's life—she could not pass herself on to me; she could not live her life again through me. In order to survive, I would have to deny my mother this second life and claim my own.

12   In the en suite bathroom I found orange lipsticks dried to hard, wax nubs, cakes of powder that crumbled at a touch, an old tube of KY Jelly squeezed from the bottom like toothpaste. All of it seemed a shrine to my mother's glamorous past. She had been a beauty in her youth, with thick hair that hung down to her waist, so much hair it was almost impossible to bind into ponytails. She had pale skin and pink cheeks like apple blossoms, and she wore short skirts and high heels to work.

13   What my mother didn't know was that I was already beginning to incorporate her inside me. She didn't know that she was winning and that for the rest of my life I would contain aspects of her—both the young beauty turning men's heads and the wasted figure doing sit-ups on the living room floor. I would grow up to wear contact lenses and to put a wave in my hair; I would admire myself in mirrors and spend small fortunes on clothes and cosmetics. Beneath this evidence of self-esteem, though, I would learn to cultivate a parallel self-hatred: my thoughts would repeat themselves obsessively; I would become compulsive in my behaviour, desperate for control; I would avoid other women because I was afraid they would be like my mother; and I would live at the mercy of my emotions, the endless stream of hatred that poured out of my mouth when I bent over the toilet.

14   "You will never succeed at anything," my mother told me day after day. "You're like your father—spineless, weak, good for nothing."

15   The last time I saw them, when I was 17 and they were in their 50s, he seemed bewildered by what had happened to our family. She had become a confused, agitated woman who plucked ceaselessly at the strap of her purse with an anguished tic. She had become powerless to control me, this piece of herself that had separated from her. She had lost me in her attempt to keep me forever.

16   I was 20 years old when I began to lose the feeling of immortality. I thought my body would regenerate itself in time, that once again everything would be new and resilient. But it only got worse. My body began showing signs of wear— my throat constantly ached from throwing up, and when I opened my mouth I saw in the mirror a red, inflamed pendulum dangling behind rows of teeth softened and eroded by acid. My own teeth, once so enamel white—the sort of teeth

parents thank God for; the sort of teeth a man meeting me for the first time would go away remembering—had, overnight it seemed, turned pitted and yellow, the back ones worn down to shrunken saddles. When I looked in the mirror, they were translucent as X-rays, made, it seemed, of water and putty. I began to brush more vigorously after each purge, not knowing then that I was accelerating the process, scrubbing my teeth with my own stomach acid.

I waited for the day when I would throw up blood. Already I could taste it at 17
the back of my throat, inching farther upward with each heartbeat. Now after vomiting, I would rise shakily from my knees, gripping the edge of the counter for balance, my heart knocking wildly in my chest. A column of flame speared me from my stomach to my throat—my esophagus a two-edged blade in my chest, a tunnel set on fire, a steel pole thrust through me.

Now when I threw up, I reeled from the pain. I was not throwing up half- 18
digested food, as I had for years, but what felt like complete objects—plastic balls, pieces of Lego, nuts and bolts that tore at me as they came out of my body. Afterwards, my stomach would hurt so much that for the rest of the evening any sustenance I sought would have to be the sort given to a convalescent or a starvation victim: thin porridge, vegetable soup, herbal tea.

I no longer thought of myself as a girl or a woman. I no longer felt sexual desire. 19
I was an "it," a conduit for a constant stream of ugliness that had to pass through it in order for me to stay pure.

In some dim part of me, I knew that when I left my apartment to go out into 20
the street, other people did not see me as I saw myself. They did not recoil from me in horror, as I expected. I knew I was a reasonably attractive young woman, like so many young women in the city, neither fat nor thin. But I felt somehow grotesque and abnormal. Strangers knew nothing of my secret; friends were helpless; my dentist would only shake his head over my open mouth and tap his pencil along my teeth to track the path of corrosion the vomit had left in its wake.

Once, in a determined moment, I called the Eating Disorders Clinic at St. 21
Paul's Hospital, but the waiting list meant I would not get in for a year. At that time, a year seemed forever, so I did not add my name to the list. Surely in a year's time everything would change, resolve itself. Twelve months later I called again, but by this time the list was even longer, and again I did not add my name.

I finally stopped being bulimic nearly two years ago, when I was 22. It ended 22
not because of willpower or therapy or something so banal as an increased sense of self-esteem. It ended because the pain from throwing up rendered the pleasure slight by comparison. It ended when my softened teeth cringed at every mouthful and when I woke several times each night with cramps wracking my stomach from one side of my waist to the other. It ended when I arrived at the point where I could no longer feel my feet. Months later, when I went to the doctor, he would diagnose it as an electrolyte imbalance caused by the vomiting up of so many vitamins and minerals. But for a long time, I didn't know what it was, and it

frightened me—sometimes when I stood up, I nearly fell over. My feet were like dead fish, cold and clammy, disconnected from the rest of my body. Once in a while they flared suddenly to life, a constellation of pins and needles, so that I could not bear to press my soles to the floor. When I tried to go to the bathroom in the middle of the night, I felt in the underwater light of that hour as if I had transformed into the fairy-tale mermaid who had chosen her lover over the sea: with each step, I landed on knife points.

23   By then I had also developed a hiatus hernia—a portion of my stomach pro-truded through my esophagus—and my teeth became so compromised that one day one of them simply disintegrated under pressure.

24   "Your tooth isn't going to grow back," the dentist said flatly, and it was then I understood for the first time that my body did not possess some secret store of replacement parts, that physical damage, like its psychological counterpart, left marks that could remain a lifetime.

25   The last time I forced myself to throw up, it felt like internal surgery. Grief, love, rage, pain—it all came pouring out, yet afterwards it was still there inside me. I had been bulimic off and on for eight years, and in all that vomiting I had not purged myself of any of the things that were making me sick. ◆

1995

Explorations

- Do you know anyone who has had an eating disorder such as bulimia or anorexia nervosa? If so, how did you deal with the situation? How did other friends and family members react?

- Why do you think most people see their dysfunctional eating behaviours as desirable? What does it take to change their minds?

- Do you think that those of a particular gender or a particular culture are more prone to eating disorders? Why or why not?

Margaret Laurence (1926–1987) was born in Neepawa, Manitoba. She attended United College (now the University of Winnipeg) and was awarded her B.A. in arts in 1947. After marrying John Fergus Laurence, a civil engineer, she lived in many countries, including British Somaliland (present-day Somalia), where she began her writing. An acclaimed Canadian novelist and short-story writer, she is best known for her Manawaka series, including The Stone Angel, The Fire-Dwellers, A Bird in the House, A Jest of God, *and* The Diviners. *Margaret Laurence's writing won many awards, including two Governor General's awards; she was made a Companion of the Order of Canada in 1971, and she received honorary degrees from more than a dozen Canadian universities.*

Down East

Margaret Laurence

My geographical grasp of Canada was not learned at school. It came straight from   1
the semantic roots of what I now perceive to have been my folk culture, and it
was many years before I suspected that in textbook terms it might not be totally
accurate. It was, however, very accurate psychologically. A quick glance at the
geographical terminology of my youth will reveal my prairie origins.

The West, of course, meant us, that is, the three prairie provinces, especially   2
Manitoba and Saskatchewan. Alberta just barely qualified—it was a little too
close to those mountains for our entire trust. We sometimes suspected that
Albertans had more in common with *The Coast* than they did with us. *The Coast*
meant only one thing—British Columbia. As far as we were concerned, there was
only one coast. The eastern coast, presumably, was so distant as to be beyond our
ken. *The Coast* was a kind of Lotus Land° which we half scorned and half envied.
All prairie people, as was well known, wanted to retire there. Think of it—a land
with no winter, semi-tropical beaches, breezes which were invariably balmy; a
land where the apricots and apples virtually dropped into your mouth. Jerusalem
the Golden,° with milk and honey blest   that was how we thought of it. At the
same time, we considered in our puritanical hearts that our climate was healthier,
as we sneezed our way through the desperate winter and thawed our white-frozen
ears and knees gently, not too close to the stove, as we had been taught.

Apart from *The West* and *The Coast*, our country contained only one other   3
habitable area (*The North*, in our innocent view, being habitable only by the
indigenous Eskimo and the occasional mad trapper), and that was *Down East*.
This really meant Ontario. Quebec and the Maritimes existed in geography
books but not in our imaginations, a sad lack of the teaching of Canadian literature, I now think, being partly responsible. Everyone born on the prairies has a

sense of distance, but there were limitations even to our horizon-accustomed eyes. *Down East* was within our scope, and upon it we foisted our drought-and-depression fantasies. The people *Down East* did not know what it meant to be hard up—like most depressed areas, we had the illusion of solitary suffering. I did not personally suffer very much, if at all, from the depression of the thirties, but I certainly imbibed the dominant myths of my culture. *Down East* was mainly composed of banks and mortgage companies, and the principal occupation of most Ontario people was grinding the faces of the poor. In their spare time, they attended cocktail parties and made light scornful banter of their impoverished relatives out west. My only relative *Down East* was an aunt married to a man who had once, glamorously, been a bush pilot, but of course that was different. This same aunt told me not long ago that she lived in Ontario for years before the prairie chip finally fell from her shoulders.

4   As the years passed, I grew to understand that my early impressions of Ontario were somewhat distorted, to put it mildly. But something of the old antagonism towards Upper Canada remained until the past year when I lived there and discovered something of Ontario for the first time.

5   Yes, there were many things I didn't like, chief among them the virtually cannibalistic advance of what we are pleased to term, with stunning inaccuracy, Progress. Toronto, it is true, has more banks than even I dreamed possible in my youthful condemnation, and one has to drive seemingly endless miles even to begin to get away from the loathsome high-rise apartments going up everywhere. Yes, you listen to the radio in the morning and hear the city's air-pollution index and wonder if you should venture as far as Yonge and Bloor° without a gasmask. Yes, water pollution wades deeper and deeper into the Great Lakes. But there are other areas still left, and one prays for their survival.

6   *The land around Bancroft in the fall.* I had never seen the hardwood maples in autumn before. The prairie maples turn yellow, marvellously clear and clean-coloured. But these scarlet flames of trees, a shouting of pure colour like some proclamation of glory, have to be seen to be believed. Words won't make a net to catch that picture; nor, I think, will paint. But suddenly I could see why the Group of Seven° was so obsessed with trying to get it down, this incredible splendour, and why, for so long, many Canadian writers couldn't see the people for the trees. With trees like these, no wonder humans felt overwhelmed. The maples stretched along ridge after ridge, with yellow poplar and speared pine for the eye's variety, as though God had planned it this way. A friend and I walked over the clumps of coarse grass, over the slabs of exposed bronze-brown rock, and there in the small valley was a beaver lake, the camouflaged lodges barely discernible, and only the wind and the birds to be heard, the cold air gold with sun and azure with sky.

7   "This is my heartland," my friend said, simply and without embarrassment. She did not visualize herself as a wordsmith, yet when she talked about the country

around Bancroft, she enabled me to see beyond the trees to the roots which exist always within the minds of humans. Her people farmed this land for generations. Cousins and uncles still lived here, in the farmhouses half hidden away from the gravel or dirt roads. I began to realize that most of the prairie towns and farms I remembered were in fact relatively new compared with this part of the land.

Later, months later, thinking of the blazing cold conflagration of the maples in *8* fall, and the sense of history, of ancestors buried here, I thought of one of Margaret Atwood's poems about Susanna Moodie,° when that prickly, over-proud pioneer lady's son was drowned. The last line of one poem will always haunt the mind—"I planted him in this country like a flag."

Kitchener and/or Waterloo. I never did discover which part of the town was *9* which, or what to call each. Two towns have merged, but both seem to maintain their separate identities. This is Mennonite country, and in the markets on week-ends you can buy homemade sausage and cheese. I visited a friend who has lived there most of her life, and who writes about the Mennonite people,° their customs, their cooking, and, more than anything, their life-view, which is to us amazingly untouched by this century, amazingly simple and related to one another. Naturally, outsiders tend to regard their way of life as archaic, but sometimes one wonders if their view won't endure longer than ours.

Morning came early in the country just outside Kitchener, and I got up despite *10* my hatred of early rising, drawn by the sun on the snow. I tramped along the paths beside Sunfish Lake, thinking that people in Canada really ought to be told that not everywhere does the winter come like this, with this brightness of both air and snow. Through the woods, tangled in among the bushes, a small river tried to take its course, and flowed despite the ice, making bizarre carvings on the frozen parts of itself. Back at the house, looking out the window, I saw a whole contingent of red cardinals, coming for birdseed my friend put out. Arrogant crimson feathers, sleek against the snow. I never imagined that I would be much of a bird-watcher. But there are moments when one is struck with a sudden intense awareness of the beauty of creatures, and wishes their continuance could be guaranteed. I would like my grandchildren, when they exist, to be able to see cardinals like these.

Peterborough. To me, this small city on the Otonabee river meant Robertson *11* Davies' country—some of his books, *The Diary of Samuel Marchbanks* and others, and himself those years ago as the fiery editor of *The Peterborough Examiner*. The area remains so related, but now I see it as the historical home of Susanna Moodie as well, that snobbish composer of dreadful patriotic poems and writer of *Roughing It in the Bush*, that genteel and self-dramatizing English lady who never really came to terms with what was a very raw land when she settled here in the 1830's. More especially the area now evokes Catharine Parr Traill,° who made this land her own, who named many of the wildflowers, and who lived here-abouts until she died at a very old age—a woman both gentle and strong.

12   Many of the Peterborough streets are maple-edged, and the old houses are square, solid, dignified, redbrick, some with wooden lacework around their elegant verandas. The houses sit in the shade of their trees, cogitating on the past, which in some cases is more than a century. Not long for Europe, but long enough in our terms. These streets do seem to be from another era. One almost expects little kids in knickerbockers or frilly gingham gowns to spring out of the next hedge with homemade stands and one-cent lemonade signs.

13   In nearby Lakefield, you can buy pine blanket chests made by someone's great-grandfather, and if you're lucky you can hear an old-timer reminiscing about the last of the great paddlewheel steamers that used to ply these waters. In Lakefield, too, they make excellent cheese. You can buy it, in three degrees of sharpness, from the place where it is produced, and the giant cheese wheels smell and taste like your childhood. There is also a place where they still make their own ice-cream, in a dozen flavours.

14   Taking a taxi in Peterborough is a very different matter from taking a taxi in Toronto. In the city, the cab drivers are fluently and instantly conversational, a motley collection of men from nearly all corners of the earth. In Peterborough, when they get to know you a little, then they talk. Most seem to be local men. When they talk over the intercom, it is to people who are their known neighbours. They do not, as in Toronto, say, "Come in, Number 87654321." They say, "Hey, Ron, where the heck *are* you?" Sometimes a despatcher [*sic*] loses his temper and addresses a particular driver as "sir." "Well, sir, if you can't find that address on Charlotte Street, you've got to have been born yesterday." I listened to these exchanges for quite some time before it dawned on me that "sir" in these parts could sometimes mean an ironic reproach. A legacy, perhaps, from the hordes of bloody-minded Irish who settled this area? The well-driller who divined with a willow wand (yes, it really works) the well for my cottage near Peterborough, also had an inflection of those Irish. When asked about the well's potential, he replied, "Lard,° woman, you got enough water there to supply halfa Trona." And I was reminded of James Joyce°—"Hail Mary, full of grease, the Lard is with thee...."

15   Probably I will be accused of sentimentality and nostalgia, writing affectionately about these towns *Down East* and this countryside, but I don't think this accusation would be entirely true. No era that is gone can ever return, nor would one want it to. I will, however, admit that in looking at towns where some quietness and sense of history remain I am looking at them at least partly as a tourist. I'm aware that under the easily perceivable surface there lurk the same old demons of malice and man's persistent misunderstanding of man. I was born in a small town—I *know* all that. But I would venture to suggest my own theory about such places.

16   Are they really anachronisms? Or may they possibly turn out to be to our culture what the possession of manuscripts in monasteries was to mediaeval

Europe during the dark ages? Maybe some of them will survive, and maybe we will need them. Whatever their limitations, it is really only in communities such as these that the individual is known, assessed, valued, seen, and can breathe without battling for air. They may not be our past so much as our future, if we have one. ◆

1976

Glossary

Lotus Land: the fabled home of the "lotus-eaters" in Alfred, Lord Tennyson's 1832 poem of the same name; it is a place of ease and delight, where one can partake of dreamy luxury.

Jerusalem the Golden: in the Book of Revelation, the description of the New Jerusalem, the city that will emerge from the destruction of the coming Apocalypse, as a paradise of golden sunlight and plenty; this image has become a metaphor for an ideal or heavenly city throughout English literature, most notably in William Blake's 1804 poem *Jerusalem*.

Yonge and Bloor: main intersection of downtown Toronto where the north-south Yonge and east-west Bloor arteries cross.

Group of Seven: a loose organization of modern Canadian painters formed in Toronto in 1920; original members were Franklin Carmichael, Lawren Harris, A.Y. Jackson, Franz Johnston, Arthur Lismer, J.E.H. Macdonald, and F.H. Varley.

Margaret Atwood's poems about Susanna Moodie: reference to *The Journals of Susanna Moodie* (1970), in which the 19th-century Canadian pioneer and author of *Roughing It in the Bush* (1852) becomes the archetypal colonial entering the unknown wilderness of the New World.

Mennonite people: a Protestant religious-cultural group dating from the Anabaptist movement of the early 16th-century Reformation, and primarily of Dutch and North German descent; Mennonites first came to Canada from Pennsylvania after the American Revolution and many settled in the Kitchener-Waterloo area of southern Ontario, later immigrants settled in the prairies.

Catharine Parr Traill: (1802–1899) English-born writer and sister of Susanna Moodie, Traill immigrated to Canada in 1832; her 1836 book, *The Backwoods of Canada*, chronicles her life on a farm in present-day Lakefield, Ontario.

"Lard": Irish dialect for "Lord."

James Joyce: (1882–1941) Irish novelist, short-story writer, and poet whose greatest works—*A Portrait of the Artist as a Young Man*, *Ulysses*, and *Finnegan's Wake*—secured him a place at the forefront of the modernist movement in literature.

Explorations

- What region of Canada do you most identify with? What are the boundaries of this region?

- How do you distinguish between different regions of Canada? Do you use the same geographical terminology as Laurence?

- Have you ever realized that your impressions of a certain region have been distorted? If so, what made you come to this realization?

Emily Martin, born in 1944, is professor of anthropology at New York University, New York. She received her Ph.D. from Cornell University in 1971. She has received many academic honours and awards and sits on a number of editorial advisory boards. She is the author of a number of books on Chinese culture, reproduction, and the history of immunology. Her works include The Woman in the Body: A Cultural Analysis of Reproduction *(1987) and* Flexible Bodies: The Role of Immunity in American Culture from the Days of Polio to the Age of AIDS *(1994).*

The Egg and the Sperm: How Science Has Constructed a Romance Based on Stereotypical Male-Female Roles

Emily Martin

The theory of the human body is always a part of a world-picture....The theory of the human body is always a part of a fantasy.

(James Hillman, The Myth of Analysis)[1]

As an anthropologist, I am intrigued by the possibility that culture shapes how   1
biological scientists describe what they discover about the natural world. If this were so, we would be learning about more than the natural world in high school biology class; we would be learning about cultural beliefs and practices as if they were part of nature. In the course of my research I realized that the picture of egg and sperm drawn in popular as well as scientific accounts of reproductive biology relies on stereotypes central to our cultural definitions of male and female. The stereotypes imply not only that female biological processes are less worthy than their male counterparts but also that women are less worthy than men. Part of my goal in writing this article is to shine a bright light on the gender stereotypes hidden within the scientific language of biology. Exposed in such a light, I hope they will lose much of their power to harm us.

Egg and Sperm: A Scientific Fairy Tale

At a fundamental level, all major scientific textbooks depict male and female   2
reproductive organs as systems for the production of valuable substances, such as egg and sperm.[2] In the case of women, the monthly cycle is described as being designed to produce eggs and prepare a suitable place for them to be fertilized and grown—all to the end of making babies. But the enthusiasm ends there. By extolling the female cycle as a productive enterprise, menstruation must necessarily be viewed as a failure. Medical texts describe menstruation as the "debris"

of the uterine lining, the result of necrosis, or death of tissue. The descriptions imply that a system has gone awry, making products of no use, not to specification, unsalable, wasted, scrap. An illustration in a widely used medical text shows menstruation as a chaotic disintegration of form, complementing the many texts that describe it as "ceasing," "dying," "losing," "denuding," "expelling."[3]

3   Male reproductive physiology is evaluated quite differently. One of the texts that sees menstruation as failed production employs a sort of breathless prose when it describes the maturation of sperm: "The mechanisms which guide the remarkable cellular transformation from spermatid to mature sperm remain uncertain....Perhaps the most amazing characteristic of spermatogenesis is its sheer magnitude: the normal human male may manufacture several hundred million sperm per day."[4] In the classic text *Medical Physiology*, edited by Vernon Mountcastle, the male/female, productive/destructive comparison is more explicit: "Whereas the female *sheds* only a single gamete each month, the somniferous tubules *produce* hundreds of millions of sperm each day" (emphasis mine).[5] The female author of another text marvels at the length of the microscopic somniferous tubules, which, if uncoiled and placed end to end, "would span almost one-third of a mile!" She writes, "In an adult male these structures produce millions of sperm cells each day." Later she asks, "How is this feat accomplished?"[6] None of these texts expresses such intense enthusiasm for any female process. It is surely no accident that the "remarkable" process of making sperm involves precisely what, in the medical view, menstruation does not: production of something deemed valuable.[7]

4   One could argue that menstruation and spermatogenesis are not analogous processes and, therefore, should not be expected to elicit the same kind of response. The proper female analogy to spermatogenesis, biologically, is ovulation. Yet ovulation does not merit enthusiasm in these texts either. Textbook descriptions stress that all of the ovarian follicles containing ova are already present at birth. Far from being *produced*, as sperm are, they merely sit on the shelf, slowly degenerating and aging like overstocked inventory: "At birth, normal human ovaries contain an estimated one million follicles [each], and no new ones appear after birth. Thus, in marked contrast to the male, the newborn female already has all the germ cells she will ever have. Only a few, perhaps 400, are destined to reach full maturity during her active productive life. All the others degenerate at some point in their development so that few, if any, remain by the time she reaches menopause at approximately 50 years of age."[8] Note the "marked contrast" that this description sets up between male and female: the male, who continuously produces fresh germ cells, and the female, who has stockpiled germ cells by birth and is faced with their degeneration.

5   Nor are the female organs spared such vivid descriptions. One scientist writes in a newspaper article that a woman's ovaries become old and worn out from ripening eggs every month, even though the woman herself is still relatively

young: "When you look through a laparoscope...at an ovary that has been through hundreds of cycles, even in a superbly healthy American female, you see a scarred, battered organ."[9]

To avoid the negative connotations that some people associate with the female [6] reproductive system, scientists could begin to describe male and female processes as homologous. They might credit females with "producing" mature ova one at a time, as they're needed each month, and describe males as having to face problems of degenerating germ cells. This degeneration would occur throughout life among spermatogonia, the undifferentiated germ cells in the testes that are the long-lived, dormant precursors of sperm.

But the texts have an almost dogged insistence on casting female processes in [7] a negative light. The texts celebrate sperm production because it is continuous from puberty to senescence, while they portray egg production as inferior because it is finished at birth. This makes the female seem unproductive, but some texts will also insist that it is she who is wasteful.[10] In a section heading for *Molecular Biology of the Cell*, a best-selling text, we are told that "Oogenesis is wasteful." The text goes on to emphasize that of the seven million oogonia, or egg germ cells, in the female embryo, most degenerate in the ovary. Of those that do go on to become oocytes, or eggs, many also degenerate, so that at birth only two million eggs remain in the ovaries. Degeneration continues throughout a woman's life: by puberty 300,000 eggs remain, and only a few are present by menopause. "During the 40 or so years of a woman's reproductive life, only 400 to 500 eggs will have been released," the authors write. "All the rest will have degenerated. It is still a mystery why so many eggs are formed only to die in the ovaries.[11]

The real mystery is why the male's vast production of sperm is not seen as [8] wasteful.[12] Assuming that a man "produces" 100 million (10^8) sperm per day (a conservative estimate) during an average reproductive life of sixty years, he would produce well over two trillion sperm in his lifetime. Assuming that a woman "ripens" one egg per lunar month, or thirteen per year, over the course of her forty-year reproductive life, she would total five hundred eggs in her lifetime. But the word "waste" implies an excess, too much produced. Assuming two or three offspring, for every baby a woman produces, she wastes only around two hundred eggs. For every baby a man produces, he wastes more than one trillion (10^{12}) sperm.

How is it that positive images are denied to the bodies of women? A look at [9] language—in this case, scientific language—provides the first clue. Take the egg and the sperm.[13] It is remarkable how "femininely" the egg behaves and how "masculinely" the sperm.[14] The egg is seen as large and passive.[15] It does not *move* or *journey*, but passively "is transported," "is swept,"[16] or even "drifts"[17] along the fallopian tube. In utter contrast, sperm are small, "streamlined,"[18] and invariably active. They "deliver" their genes to the egg, "activate the developmental program of the egg,"[19] and have a "velocity" that is often remarked upon.[20] Their tails are "strong" and efficiently powered.[21] Together with the forces of ejaculation, they can "propel the semen into the deepest recesses of the vagina."[22] For this they need "energy," "fuel,"[23] so that with a "whiplash-like motion and strong lurches"[24] they can "burrow through the egg coat"[25] and "penetrate" it.[26]

10   At its extreme, the age-old relationship of the egg and the sperm takes on a royal or religious patina. The egg coat, its protective barrier, is sometimes called its "vestments," a term usually reserved for sacred, religious dress. The egg is said to have a "corona,"[27] a crown, and to be accompanied by "attendant cells."[28] It is holy, set apart and above, the queen to the sperm's king. The egg is also passive, which means it must depend on sperm for rescue. Gerald Schatten and Helen Schatten liken the egg's role to that of Sleeping Beauty: "a dormant bride awaiting her mate's magic kiss, which instills the spirit that brings her to life."[29] Sperm, by contrast, have a "mission,"[30] which is to "move through the female genital tract in quest of the ovum."[31] One popular account has it that the sperm carry out a "perilous journey" into the "warm darkness," where some fall away "exhausted." "Survivors" "assault" the egg, the successful candidates "surrounding the prize."[32] Part of the urgency of this journey, in more scientific terms, is that "once released from the supportive environment of the ovary, an egg will die within hours unless rescued by a sperm."[33] The wording stresses the fragility and dependency of the egg, even though the same text acknowledges elsewhere that sperm also live for only a few hours.[34]

11   In 1948, in a book remarkable for its early insights into these matters, Ruth Herschberger argued that female reproductive organs are seen as biologically interdependent, while male organs are viewed as autonomous, operating independently and in isolation:

> At present the functional is stressed only in connection with women: it is in them that ovaries, tubes, uterus, and vagina have endless interdependence. In the male, reproduction would seem to involve "organs" only.
>
> Yet the sperm, just as much as the egg, is dependent on a great many related processes. There are secretions which mitigate the urine in the urethra before ejaculation, to protect the sperm. There is the reflex shutting off of the bladder connection, the provision of prostatic secretions, and various types of muscular propulsion. The sperm is no more independent of its milieu than the egg, and yet from a wish that it were, biologists have lent their support to the notion that the human female, beginning with the egg, is congenitally more dependent than the male.[35]

12   Bringing out another aspect of the sperm's autonomy, an article in the journal *Cell* has the sperm making an "existential decision" to penetrate the egg: "Sperm

are cells with a limited behavioral repertoire, one that is directed toward fertilizing eggs. To execute the decision to abandon the haploid state, sperm swim to an egg and there acquire the ability to effect membrane fusion."[36] Is this a corporate manager's version of the sperm's activities—"executing decisions" while fraught with dismay over difficult options that bring with them very high risk?

There is another way that sperm, despite their small size, can be made to loom   13
in importance over the egg. In a collection of scientific papers, an electron micrograph of an enormous egg and tiny sperm is titled "A Portrait of the Sperm."[37] This is a little like showing a photo of a dog and calling it a picture of the fleas. Granted, microscopic sperm are harder to photograph than eggs, which are just large enough to see with the naked eye. But surely the use of the term "portrait," a word associated with the powerful and wealthy, is significant. Eggs have only micrographs or pictures, not portraits.

One depiction of sperm as weak and timid, instead of strong and powerful—   14
the only such representation in western civilization, so far as I know—occurs in Woody Allen's movie *Everything You Always Wanted To Know About Sex* *But Were Afraid to Ask*. Allen, playing the part of an apprehensive sperm inside a man's testicles, is scared of the man's approaching orgasm. He is reluctant to launch himself into the darkness, afraid of contraceptive devices, afraid of winding up on the ceiling if the man masturbates.

The more common picture—egg as damsel in distress, shielded only by her   15
sacred garments; sperm as heroic warrior to the rescue—cannot be proved to be dictated by the biology of these events. While "facts" of biology may not *always* be constructed in cultural terms, I would argue that in this case they are. The degree of metaphorical content in these descriptions, the extent to which differences between egg and sperm are emphasized, and the parallels between cultural stereotypes of male and female behavior and the character of egg and sperm all point to this conclusion.

New Research, Old Imagery

As new understandings of egg and sperm emerge, textbook gender imagery is   16
being revised. But the new research, far from escaping the stereotypical representations of egg and sperm, simply replicates elements of textbook gender imagery in a different form. The persistence of this imagery calls to mind what Ludwik Fleck termed "the self-contained" nature of scientific thought. As he described it, "the interaction between what is already known, what remains to be learned, and those who are to apprehend it, go to ensure harmony within the system. But at the same time they also preserve the harmony of illusions, which is quite secure within the confines of a given thought style."[38] We need to understand the ways in which cultural content in scientific descriptions changes as biological discoveries unfold, and whether that cultural content is solidly entrenched or easily changed.

17   In all of the texts quoted above, sperm are described as penetrating the egg, and specific substances on a sperm's head are described as binding to the egg. Recently, this description of events was rewritten in a biophysics lab at Johns Hopkins University—transforming the egg from the passive to the active party.[39]

18   Prior to this research, it was thought that the zona, the inner vestments of the egg, formed an impenetrable barrier. Sperm overcame the barrier by mechanically burrowing through, thrashing their tails and slowly working their way along. Later research showed that the sperm released digestive enzymes that chemically broke down the zona; thus, scientists presumed that the sperm used mechanical *and* chemical means to get through to the egg.

19   In this recent investigation, the researchers began to ask questions about the mechanical force of the sperm's tail. (The lab's goal was to develop a contraceptive that worked topically on sperm.) They discovered, to their great surprise, that the forward thrust of sperm is extremely weak, which contradicts the assumption that sperm are forceful penetrators.[40] Rather than thrusting forward, the sperm's head was now seen to move mostly back and forth. The sideways motion of the sperm's tail makes the head move sideways with a force that is ten times stronger than its forward movement. So even if the overall force of the sperm were strong enough to mechanically break the zona, most of its force would be directed sideways rather than forward. In fact, its strongest tendency, by ten-fold, is to escape by attempting to pry itself off the egg. Sperm, then, must be exceptionally efficient at *escaping* from any cell surface they contact. And the surface of the egg must be designed to trap the sperm and prevent their escape. Otherwise, few if any sperm would reach the egg.

20   The researchers at Johns Hopkins concluded that the sperm and egg stick together because of adhesive molecules on the surfaces of each. The egg traps the sperm and adheres to it so tightly that the sperm's head is forced to lie flat against the surface of the zona, a little bit, they told me, "like Br'er Rabbit° getting more and more stuck to tar baby the more he wriggles." The trapped sperm continues to wiggle ineffectually side to side. The mechanical force of its tail is so weak that a sperm cannot break even one chemical bond. This is where the digestive enzymes released by the sperm come in. If they start to soften the zona just at the tip of the sperm and the sides remain stuck, then the weak, flailing sperm can get oriented in the right direction and make it through the zona—provided that its bonds to the zona dissolve as it moves in.

21   Although this new version of the saga of the egg and sperm broke through cultural expectations, the researchers who made the discovery continued to write papers and abstracts as if the sperm were the active party who attacks, binds, penetrates, and enters the egg. The only difference was that sperm were now seen as performing these actions weakly.[41] Not until August 1987, more than three years after the findings described above, did these researchers reconceptualize the process to give the egg a more active role. They began to describe the zona as an

aggressive sperm catcher, covered with adhesive molecules that can capture a sperm with a single bond and clasp it to the zona's surface.[42] In the words of their published account: "The innermost vestment, the *zona pellucida*, is a glyco-protein shell, which captures and tethers the sperm before they penetrate it....The sperm is captured at the initial contact between the sperm tip and the *zona*.... Since the thrust [of the sperm] is much smaller than the force needed to break a single affinity bond, the first bond made upon the tip-first meeting of the sperm and *zona* can result in the capture of the sperm."[43]

Experiments in another lab reveal similar patterns of data interpretation. *22* Gerald Schatten and Helen Schatten set out to show that, contrary to conventional wisdom, the "egg is not merely a large, yolk-filled sphere into which the sperm burrows to endow new life. Rather, recent research suggests the almost heretical view that sperm and egg are mutually active partners."[44] This sounds like a departure from the stereotypical textbook view, but further reading reveals Schatten and Schatten's conformity to the aggressive-sperm metaphor. They describe how "the sperm and egg first touch when, from the tip of the sperm's triangular head, a long, thin filament shoots out and harpoons the egg." Then we learn that "remarkably, the harpoon is not so much fired as assembled at great speed, molecule by molecule, from a pool of protein stored in a specialized region called the acrosome. The filament may grow as much as twenty times longer than the sperm head itself before its tip reaches the egg and sticks."[45] Why not call this "making a bridge" or "throwing out a line" rather than firing a harpoon? Harpoons pierce prey and injure or kill them, while this filament only sticks. And why not focus, as the Hopkins lab did, on the stickiness of the egg, rather than the stickiness of the sperm?[46] Later in the article, the Schattens replicate the common view of the sperm's perilous journey into the warm darkness of the vagina, this time for the purpose of explaining its journey into the egg itself: "[The sperm] still has an arduous journey ahead. It must penetrate farther into the egg's huge sphere of cytoplasm and somehow locate the nucleus, so that the two cells' chromosomes can fuse. The sperm dives down into the cytoplasm, its tail beating. But it is soon interrupted by the sudden and swift migration of the egg nucleus, which rushes toward the sperm with a velocity triple that of the movement of chromosomes during cell division, crossing the entire egg in about a minute."[47]

Like Schatten and Schatten and the biophysicists at Johns Hopkins, another *23* researcher has recently made discoveries that seem to point to a more interactive view of the relationship of egg and sperm. This work, which Paul Wassarman conducted on the sperm and eggs of mice, focuses on identifying the specific molecules in the egg coat (the zona pellucida) that are involved in egg-sperm interaction. At first glance, his descriptions seem to fit the model of an egalitarian relationship. Male and female gametes "recognize one another," and "interactions....take place between sperm and egg."[48] But the article in *Scientific American* in which those descriptions appear begins with a vignette that presages the dominant motif of their presentation: "It has been more than a century since Hermann Fol, a Swiss zoologist, peered into his microscope and became the first person to see a sperm penetrate an egg, fertilize it and form the first cell of a new embryo."[49] This portrayal of the sperm as the active party—the one that *penetrates* and *fertilizes* the egg and *produces* the embryo—is not cited as an example of an earlier, now outmoded view. In fact, the author reiterates the point later in the article: "Many sperm can bind to and penetrate the zona pellucida, or outer coat, of an unfertilized mouse egg, but only one sperm will eventually fuse with the thin plasma membrane surrounding the egg proper (*inner sphere*), fertilizing the egg and giving rise to a new embryo."[50]

24   The imagery of sperm as aggressor is particularly startling in this case: the main discovery being reported is isolation of a particular molecule *on the egg coat* that plays an important role in fertilization! Wassarman's choice of language sustains the picture. He calls the molecule that has been isolated, ZP3, a "sperm receptor." By allocating the passive, waiting role to the egg, Wassarman can continue to describe the sperm as the actor, the one that makes it all happen: "The basic process begins when many sperm first attach loosely and then bind tenaciously to receptors on the surface of the egg's thick outer coat, the zona pellucida. Each sperm, which has a large number of egg-binding proteins on its surface, binds to many sperm receptors on the egg. More specifically, a site on each of the egg-binding proteins fits a complementary site on a sperm receptor, much as a key fits a lock."[51] With the sperm designated as the "key" and the egg the "lock," it is obvious which one acts and which one is acted upon. Could this imagery not be reversed, letting the sperm (the lock) wait until the egg produces the key? Or could we speak of two halves of a locket matching, and regard the matching itself as the action that initiates the fertilization?

25   It is as if Wassarman were determined to make the egg the receiving partner. Usually in biological research, the *protein* member of the pair of binding molecules is called the receptor, and physically it has a pocket in it rather like a lock. As the diagrams that illustrate Wassarman's article show, the molecules on the sperm are proteins and have "pockets." The small, mobile molecules that fit into these pockets are called ligands. As shown in the diagrams, ZP3 on the egg is a polymer of "keys"; many small knobs stick out. Typically, molecules on the sperm would be called receptors and molecules on the egg would be called ligands. But Wassarman chose to name ZP3 on the egg the receptor and to create a new term, "the egg-binding protein," for the molecule on the sperm that otherwise would have been called the receptor.[52]

26   Wassarman does credit the egg coat with having more functions than those of a sperm receptor. While he notes that "the zona pellucida has at times been viewed by investigators as a nuisance, a barrier to sperm and hence an impediment to fertilization," his new research reveals that the egg coat "serves as a sophisticated biological security system that screens incoming sperm, selects only

those compatible with fertilization and development, prepares sperm for fusion with the egg and later protects the resulting embryo from polyspermy [a lethal condition caused by fusion of more than one sperm with a single egg]."[53] Although this description gives the egg an active role, that role is drawn in stereotypically feminine terms. The egg *selects* an appropriate mate, *prepares* him for fusion, and then *protects* the resulting offspring from harm. This is courtship and mating behavior as seen through the eyes of a sociobiologist: woman as the hard-to-get prize, who, following union with the chosen one, becomes woman as servant and mother.

And Wassarman does not quit there. In a review for *Science*, he outlines the   27 "chronology of fertilization."[54] Near the end of the article are two subject headings. One is "Sperm Penetration," in which Wassarman describes how the chemical dissolving of the zona pellucida combines with the "substantial propulsive force generated by sperm." The next heading is "Sperm-Egg Fusion." This section details what happens inside the zona after a sperm "penetrates" it. Sperm "can make contact with, adhere to, and fuse with (that is, fertilize) an egg."[55] Wassarman's word choice, again, is astonishingly skewed in favor of the sperm's activity, for in the next breath he says that sperm *lose* all motility upon fusion with the egg's surface. In mouse and sea urchin eggs, the sperm enters at the *egg's* volition, according to Wassarman's description: "Once fused with egg plasma membrane [the surface of the egg], how does a sperm enter the egg? The surface of both mouse and sea urchin eggs is covered with thousands of plasma membrane-bound projections, called microvilli [tiny 'hairs']. Evidence in sea urchins suggests that, after membrane fusion, a group of elongated microvilli cluster tightly around and interdigitate over the sperm head. As these microvilli are resorbed, the sperm is drawn into the egg. Therefore, sperm motility, which ceases at the time of fusion in both sea urchins and mice, is not required for sperm entry."[56] The section called "Sperm Penetration" more logically would be followed by a section called "The Egg Envelops," rather than "Sperm-Egg Fusion." This would give a parallel—and more accurate—sense that both the egg and the sperm initiate action.

Another way that Wassarman makes less of the egg's activity is by describing   28 components of the egg but referring to the sperm as a whole entity. Deborah Gordon has described such an approach as "atomism" ("the part is independent of and primordial to the whole") and identified it as one of the "tenacious assumptions" of Western science and medicine.[57] Wassarman employs atomism to his advantage. When he refers to processing going on within sperm, he consistently returns to descriptions that remind us from whence these activities came: they are part of sperm that penetrate an egg or generate propulsive force. When he refers to processes going on within eggs, he stops there. As a result, any active role he grants them appears to be assigned to the parts of the egg, and not to the egg itself. In the quote above, it is the microvilli that actively cluster around the sperm. In another example, "the driving force for engulfment of a fused sperm comes from a region of cytoplasm just beneath an egg's plasma membrane."[58]

Social Implications: Thinking Beyond

29   All three of these revisionist accounts of egg and sperm seem to escape the hierarchical imagery of older accounts. Even though each new account gives the egg a larger and more active role, taken together they bring into play another cultural stereotype: woman as a dangerous and aggressive threat. In the Johns Hopkins lab's revised model, the egg ends up as the female aggressor who "captures and tethers" the sperm with her sticky zona, rather like a spider lying in wait in her web.[59] The Schatten lab has the egg's nucleus "interrupt" the sperm's dive with a "sudden and swift" rush by which she "clasps the sperm and guides its nucleus to the center."[60] Wassarman's description of the surface of the egg "covered with thousands of plasma membrane-bound projections, called microvilli" that reach out and clasp the sperm adds to the spiderlike imagery.[61]

30   These images grant the egg an active role but at the cost of appearing disturbingly aggressive. Images of woman as dangerous and aggressive, the femme fatale who victimizes men, are widespread in Western literature and culture.[62] More specific is the connection of spider imagery with the idea of an engulfing, devouring mother.[63] New data did not lead scientists to eliminate gender stereotypes in the descriptions of egg and sperm. Instead, scientists simply began to describe egg and sperm in different, but no less damaging, terms.

31   Can we envision a less stereotypical view? Biology itself provides another model that could be applied to the egg and the sperm. The cybernetic model°— with its feedback loops, flexible adaptation to change, coordination of the parts within a whole, evolution over time, and changing response to the environment—is common in genetics, endocrinology, and ecology and has a growing influence in medicine in general.[64] This model has the potential to shift our imagery from the negative, in which the female reproductive system is castigated both for not producing eggs after birth and for producing (and thus wasting) too many eggs overall, to something more positive. The female reproductive system could be seen as responding to the environment (pregnancy or menopause), adjusting to monthly changes (menstruation), and flexibly changing from reproductivity after puberty to nonreproductivity later in life. The sperm and egg's interaction could also be described in cybernetic terms. J.F. Hartman's research in reproductive biology demonstrated fifteen years ago that if an egg is killed by being pricked with a needle, live sperm cannot get through the zona.[65] Clearly, this evidence shows that the egg and sperm *do* interact on more mutual terms, making biology's refusal to portray them that way all the more disturbing.

32   We would do well to be aware, however, that cybernetic imagery is hardly neutral. In the past, cybernetic models have played an important part in the imposition of social control. These models inherently provide a way of thinking

about a "field" of interacting components. Once the field can be seen, it can become the object of new forms of knowledge, which in turn can allow new forms of social control to be exerted over the components of the field. During the 1950s, for example, medicine began to recognize the psychosocial *environment* of the patient: the patient's family and its psychodynamics. Professions such as social work began to focus on this new environment, and the resulting knowledge became one way to further control the patients. Patients began to be seen not as isolated, individual bodies, but as psychosocial entities located in an "ecological" system: management of "the patient's psychology was a new entrée to patient control."[66]

The models that biologists use to describe their data can have important social   33
effects. During the nineteenth century, the social and natural sciences strongly influenced each other: the social ideas of Malthus° about how to avoid the natural increase of the poor inspired Darwin's *Origin of Species*.[67] Once the *Origin* stood as a description of the natural world, complete with competition and market struggles, it could be reimported into social science as social Darwinism, in order to justify the social order of the time. What we are seeing now is similar: the importation of cultural ideas about passive females and heroic males into the "personalities" of gametes. This amounts to the "implanting of social imagery on representations of nature so as to lay a firm basis for reimporting exactly that same imagery as natural explanations of social phenomena."[68]

Further research would show us exactly what social effects are being wrought   34
from the biological imagery of egg and sperm. At the very least, the imagery keeps alive some of the hoariest old stereotypes about weak damsels in distress and their strong male rescuers. That these stereotypes are now being written in at the level of the *cell* constitutes a powerful move to make them seem so natural as to be beyond alteration.

The stereotypical imagery might also encourage people to imagine that what   35
results from the interaction of egg and sperm—a fertilized egg—is the result of deliberate "human" action at the cellular level. Whatever the intentions of the human couple, in this microscope "culture" a cellular "bride" (or femme fatale) and a cellular "groom" (her victim) make a cellular baby. Rosalind Petchesky points out that through visual representations such as sonograms, we are given "*images* of younger and younger, and tinier and tinier, fetuses being 'saved'." This leads to "the point of viability being 'pushed back' *indefinitely*."[69] Endowing egg and sperm with intentional action, a key aspect of personhood in our culture, lays the foundation for the point of viability being pushed back to the moment of fertilization. This will likely lead to greater acceptance of technological developments and new forms of scrutiny and manipulation, for the benefit of these inner "persons": court-ordered restrictions on a pregnant woman's activities in order to protect her fetus, fetal surgery, amniocentesis, and rescinding of abortion rights, to name but a few examples.[70]

36   Even if we succeed in substituting more egalitarian, interactive metaphors to describe the activities of egg and sperm, and manage to avoid the pitfalls of cybernetic models, we would still be guilty of endowing cellular entities with personhood. More crucial, then, than what *kinds* of personalities we bestow on cells is the very fact that we are doing it at all. This process could ultimately have the most disturbing social consequences.

37   One clear feminist challenge is to wake up sleeping metaphors in science, particularly those involved in descriptions of the egg and the sperm. Although the literary convention is to call such metaphors "dead," they are not so much dead as sleeping, hidden within the scientific content of texts—and all the more powerful for it.[71] Waking up such metaphors, by becoming aware of when we are projecting cultural imagery onto what we study, will improve our ability to investigate and understand nature. Waking up such metaphors, by becoming aware of their implications, will rob them of their power to naturalize our social conventions about gender. ◆

1991

Endnotes

1. James Hillman, *The Myth of Analysis* (Evanston, Ill.: Northwestern University Press, 1972), 220.

2. The textbooks I consulted are the main ones used in classes for undergraduate premedical students or medical students (or those held on reserve in the library for these classes) during the past few years at Johns Hopkins University. These texts are widely used at other universities in the country as well.

3. Arthur C. Guyton, *Physiology of the Human Body*, 6th ed. (Philadelphia: Saunders College Publishing, 1984), 624.

4. Arthur J. Vander, James H. Sherman, and Dorothy S. Luciano, *Human Physiology: The Mechanisms of Body Function*, 3d ed. (New York: McGraw Hill, 1980), 483–84.

5. Vernon B. Mountcastle, *Medical Physiology*, 14th ed. (London: Mosby, 1980), 2:1624.

6. Eldra Pearl Solomon, *Human Anatomy and Physiology* (New York: CBS College Publishing, 1983), 678.

7. For elaboration, see Emily Martin, *The Woman in the Body: A Cultural Analysis of Reproduction* (Boston: Beacon, 1987), 27–53.

8. Vander, Sherman, and Luciano, 568.

9. Melvin Konner, "Childbearing and Age," *New York Times Magazine* (December 27, 1987), 22–23, esp. 22.

10. I have found but one exception to the opinion that the female is wasteful: "Smallpox being the nasty disease it is, one might expect nature to have designed antibody molecules with combining sites that specifically recognize the epitomes on smallpox virus. Nature differs from technology, however: it thinks nothing of wastefulness. (For example, rather than improving the chance that a spermatozoan will meet an egg cell,

nature finds it easier to produce millions of spermatozoa.)" Niels Kaj Jerne, "The Immune System," *Scientific American* 229, no. 1 (July 1993): 53. Thanks to a *Signs* reviewer for bringing this reference to my attention.

11. Bruce Alberts et al., *Molecular Biology of the Cell* (New York: Garland, 1983), 795.

12. In her essay "Have Only Men Evolved?" in *Discovering Reality: Feminist Perspectives on Epistemology, Metaphysics, Methodology, and Philosophy of Science*, ed. Sandra Harding and Merrill B. Hintikka (Dordrecht, The Netherlands: Reidel, 1983), 45–69, esp. 60–61, Ruth Hubbard points out that sociobiologists have said the female invests more energy than the male in the production of her large gametes, claiming that this explains why the female provides parental care. Hubbard questions whether it "really takes more 'energy' to generate the one or relatively few eggs than the large excess of sperms required to achieve fertilization." For further critique of how the greater size of eggs is interpreted in sociobiology, see Donna Haraway, "Investment Strategies for the Evolving Portfolio of Primate Females," in *Body/Politics*, ed. Mary Jacobus, Evelyn Fox Keller, and Sally Shuttleworth (New York: Routledge, 1990), 155–56.

13. The sources I used for this article provide compelling information on interactions among sperm. Lack of space prevents me from taking up this theme here, but the elements include competition, hierarchy, and sacrifice. For a newspaper report, see Malcolm W. Browne, "Some Thoughts on Self Sacrifice," *New York Times* (July 5, 1988), C6. For a literary rendition, see John Barth, "Night-Sea Journey," in his *Lost in the Funhouse* (Garden City, N.Y.: Doubleday, 1968), 3–13.

14. See Carol Delaney, "The Meaning of Paternity and the Virgin Birth Debate," *Man* 21, no. 3 (September 1986): 494–513. She discusses the difference between the scientific view that women contribute genetic material to the fetus and the claim of long-standing Western folk theories that the origin and identity of the fetus comes from the male, as in the metaphor of planting a seed in soil.

15. For a suggested direct link between human behavior and purportedly passive eggs and active sperm, see Erik H. Erikson, "Inner and Outer Space: Reflections on Womanhood," *Daedalus* 93, no. 2 (Spring 1964): 582–606, esp. 591.

16. Guyton (n. 3), 619; and Mountcastle (n. 5), 1609.

17. Jonathan Miller and David Pelham, *The Facts of Life* (New York: Viking Penguin, 1984), 5.

18. Alberts et al., 796.

19. Ibid., 796.

20. See, e.g., William F. Ganong, *Review of Medical Physiology*, 7th ed. (Los Altos, Calif.: Lange Medical Publications, 1975), 322.

21. Alberts et al. (n. 11), 796.

22. Guyton, 615.

23. Solomon (n. 6), 683.

24. Vander, Sherman, and Luciano (n. 4), 4th ed. (1985), 580.

25. Alberts et al., 796.

26. All biology texts quoted use the word "penetrate."

27. Solomon, 700.

28. A. Beldecos et al., "The Importance of Feminist Critique for Contemporary Cell Biology," *Hypatia* 3, no. 1 (Spring 1988): 61–76.

29. Gerald Schatten and Helen Schatten, "The Energetic Egg," *Medical World News* 23 (January 23, 1984): 51–53, esp. 51.

30. Alberts et al., 796.

31. Guyton (n. 3), 613.

32. Miller and Pelham (n. 17), 7.

33. Alberts et al. (n. 11), 804.

34. Ibid., 801.

35. Ruth Herschberger, *Adam's Rib* (New York: Pelligrini & Cudaby, 1948), esp. 84. I am indebted to Ruth Hubbard for telling me about Herschberger's work, although at a point when this paper was already in draft form.

36. Bennett M. Shapiro, "The Existential Decision of Sperm," *Cell* 49, no. 3 (May 1987): 293–94, esp. 293.

37. Lennart Nilsson, "A Portrait of the Sperm," in *The Functional Anatomy of the Spermatozoan*, ed. Bjorn A. Afzelius (New York: Pergamon, 1975), 79–82.

38. Ludwik Fleck, *Genesis and Development of a Scientific Fact*, ed. Thaddeus J. Trenn and Robert K. Merton (Chicago: University of Chicago Press, 1979), 38.

39. Jay M. Baltz carried out the research I described when he was a graduate student in the Thomas C. Jenkins Department of Biophysics at Johns Hopkins University.

40. Far less is known about the physiology of sperm than comparable female substances, which some feminists claim is no accident. Greater scientific scrutiny of female reproduction has long enabled the burden of birth control to be placed on women. In this case, the researchers' discovery did not depend on development of any new technology. The experiments made use of glass pipettes, a manometer, and a simple microscope, all of which have been available for more than one hundred years.

41. Jay Baltz and Richard A. Cone, "What Force is Needed to Tether a Sperm?" (abstract for Society for the Study of Reproduction, 1985), and "Flagellar Torque on the Head Determines the Force Needed to Tether a Sperm" (abstracted for Biophysical Society, 1986).

42. Jay M. Baltz, David F. Katz, and Richard A. Cone, "The Mechanics of the Sperm-Egg Interaction at the Zona Pellucida," *Biophysical Journal* 54, no. 4 (October 1988): 643–54. Lab members were somewhat familiar with work on metaphors in the biology of female reproduction. Richard Cone, who runs the lab, is my husband, and he talked with them about my earlier research on the subject from time to time. Even though my current research focuses on biological imagery and I heard about the lab's work

from my husband every day, I myself did not recognize the role of imagery in the sperm research until many weeks after the period of research and writing I describe. Therefore, I assume that any awareness the lab members may have had about how underlying metaphor might be guiding this particular research was fairly inchoate.

43. Ibid., 643, 650.

44. Schatten and Schatten (n. 29), 51.

45. Ibid., 52.

46. Surprisingly, in an article intended for a general audience, the authors do not point out that these are sea urchin sperm and note that human sperm do not shoot out filaments at all.

47. Schatten and Schatten, 53.

48. Paul M. Wassarman, "Fertilization in Mammals," *Scientific American* 259, no. 6 (December 1988): 78–84, esp. 78, 84.

49. Ibid., 78.

50. Ibid., 79.

51. Ibid., 78.

52. Since receptor molecules are relatively *immotile* and the ligands that bind to them relatively *motile*, one might imagine the egg being called the receptor and the sperm the ligand. But the molecules in question on egg and sperm are immotile molecules. It is the sperm as a *cell* that has motility, and the egg as a cell that has relative immotility.

53. Wassarman, 78–79.

54. Paul M. Wassarman, "The Biology and Chemistry of Fertilization," *Science* 235, no. 4788 (January 30, 1987): 553–60, esp. 554.

55. Ibid., 557.

56. Ibid., 557-58. This finding throws into question Schatten and Schatten's description (n. 29 above) of the sperm, its tail beating, diving down into the egg.

57. Deborah R. Gordon, "Tenacious Assumptions in Western Medicine," in *Biomedicine Examined*, ed. Margaret Lock and Deborah Gordon (Dordrecht, The Netherlands: Kluwer, 1988), 19–56, esp. 26.

58. Wassarman, "The Biology and Chemistry of Fertilization," 558.

59. Baltz, Katz, and Cone (n. 42 above), 643, 650.

60. Schatten and Schatten, 53.

61. Wassarman, "The Biology and Chemistry of Fertilization," 557.

62. Mary Ellman, *Thinking about Women* (New York: Harcourt Brace Jovanovich, 1968), 140; Nina Auerbach, *Woman and the Demon* (Cambridge, Mass.: Harvard University Press, 1982), esp. 186.

63. Kenneth Alan Adams, "Arachnophobia: Love American Style," *Journal of Psychoanalytic Anthropology* 4, no. 2 (1981): 157–97.

64. William Ray Arney and Bernard Bergen, *Medicine and the Management of Living* (Chicago: University of Chicago Press, 1984).

65. J.F. Hartman, R.B. Gwatkin, and C.F. Hutchison, "Early Contact Interactions between Mammalian Gametes In Vitro," *Proceedings of the National Academy of Sciences* (U.S.) 69, no. 10 (1972): 2767–69.

66. Arney and Bergen, 68.

67. Ruth Hubbard, "Have Only Men Evolved?" (n. 12 above), 51–52.

68. David Harvey, personal communication, November 1989.

69. Rosalind Petchesky, "Fetal Images: The Power of Visual Culture in the Politics of Reproduction," *Feminist Studies* 13, no. 2 (Summer 1987), 263–92, esp. 272.

70. Rita Arditti, Renate Klein, and Shelley Minden, *Test-Tube Women* (London: Pandora, 1984); Ellen Goodman, "Whose Right to Life?" *Baltimore Sun* (November 17, 1987); Tamar Lewin, "Courts Acting to Force Care of the Unborn," *New York Times* (November 23, 1987), A1 and B10; Susan Irwin and Brigitte Jordan, "Knowledge, Practice, and Power: Court Ordered Cesarean Sections," *Medical Anthropology Quarterly* 1, no. 3 (September 1987): 319–34.

71. Thanks to Elizabeth Fee and David Spain, who in February 1989 and April 1989, respectively, made points related to this.

Glossary

Br'er Rabbit: character in the "Uncle Remus" series of children's books authored by Joel Chandler Harris (1848–1908).

cybernetic model: model relating to the theory or study of communication and control in living organisms or machines.

Malthus: Thomas Robert Malthus (1766–1834), British economist and sociologist whose 1798 edition of *An Essay on the Principle of Population* prompted Darwin to explore the patterns of evoluton.

Explorations

- Do you usually view scientific language as being objective and therefore free from gender bias? Why or why not?

- Can you give examples of ways that gender bias in language can be harmful?

- In what ways do you think cultural stereotypes have shaped the discourse of scholars in your field of study?

R. Murray Schafer was born in Sarnia, Ontario, in 1933. He received his LRSM (Licentiate of the Royal Schools of Music) in 1952 from Carleton University. In 1961 he began 12 years of teaching at Memorial University as artist-in-residence and then at Simon Fraser University where he set up the World Soundscape Project *dedicated to the study of the relationships between people and their acoustic environment. He is a highly regarded composer who has received many honours, including becoming the first recipient of the triennial Glenn Gould award in 1971. A well-known Canadian composer and writer, he is the author of* The Composer in the Classroom, The New Soundscape, The Tuning of the World, *and* The Thinking Ear.

The Glazed Soundscape

R. Murray Schafer

In the Tunisian restaurant in Montreal, the proprietor and his wife share a carafe of wine fitted with a spout from which they pour the wine directly into their mouths by raising and tipping it, in exactly the way the old wineskin would have worked. The sensation of drinking is entirely different when the liquid is squirted into the mouth rather than sipped out of a glass or sucked through a straw, and so are the accompanying sounds, on this occasion a bright burbling as the air seeks to replace the liquid through the twisted thin spout. Nothing touches the mouth but the liquid. It is probably the purest way to drink, yet it has been replaced by the glass as individual proprietorship has replaced tribal sharing. Slurping liquids through straws from bottles or cans represents an even greater degree of privatization—the hidden elixir. The glass, replacing more tuneful receptacles, is raised and chimed at the beginning of the meal, partly in compensation for mute consumption, an exercise denied its prophylactic successor, the plastic cup. Materials change, sounds change, social customs change.

The soundscape of every society is conditioned by the predominant materials from which it is constructed. Thus we may speak of bamboo, wood, metal, glass, or plastic cultures, meaning that these materials produce a repertoire of sounds of specific resonance when touched by active agents, by humans or wind or water. The containers and conveyances for water could make a nice dossier of keynote sounds for cross-cultural study. In modern times water forms a strong domestic keynote in the presence of taps, toilets and showers; in other cultures the sounds of water are more clearly marked at the village fountain or pump where all washing is done and from which all water is drawn to the household.

Unlike water, stone does not make a sound on its own; rather only when brushed, chipped, scraped or crushed. The various methods in which this happens have characterized cultures in many parts of the world. Before roads began to be macadamized in the nineteenth century, wagon wheels over cobblestones provided one of the clearest keynotes of all stone cultures, often rising to the level of annoyance, so that straw was often spread over the roads near hospitals or around the homes of the sick to mute the sound of the horses' hooves and the grating of the wagon wheels.[1] Europe was a stone culture and to a large extent still is, particularly in its smaller, less-touched communities. When stones were piled up to build cathedrals, palaces and homes, they affected the reflection of sounds both within and without their surfaces, fortifying spoken rhetoric and amplifying music and military parades. North America was originally a wood culture, passing, like modern Europe, to cement and glass during the twentieth century.

4   Glass is the most imperceptible soundscape material and therefore needs special treatment. Its history goes back possibly nine thousand years or more,[2] though its prominence is much more recent. About 200 B.C. Roman glassmakers learned how to roll out slabs of glass to make mosaics and also to close small window surfaces, though their semi-opacity admitted only feeble light. The manufacturing of glass was improved by the Venetians after 1300 but it was not until the seventeenth century that the glazing of windows began on a large scale. In 1567 Jean Carré, a merchant from Antwerp, had received a twenty-one-year license from Queen Elizabeth I for making window glass in Britain, but it was Louis Lucas de Nehan's new method of casting in 1688 that for the first time permitted the production of large polished plates of flat glass of relatively uniform thickness from which it was possible to make excellent mirrors and fill large window openings.

5   For a long time there was a tax on glazed windows. In Britain the occupier of a house with ten windows had to pay an annual tax of 8s.4d. in 1776, rising to £2.16.0 in 1808. The high rate continued until 1825 when the tax was halved and houses with seven or fewer windows were declared exempt. When the excise duties on glass were repealed in 1845 the industry immediately entered a period of rapid growth. A symbol of its triumph was the Crystal Palace° of 1851, containing a million square feet of glass.

6   During the twentieth century the commercial streets of all cities have gradually suffered their romantic stone work to be chipped away to provide larger display windows, while above them tower buildings that have altogether abolished windows, replacing them with skins of glass. From the streets we are given views of interiors once private and mysterious; from the towers, executives contemplate the skyline and envision distant goals and objectives. None of this is new. We have lived with it for some time. Our concern is with the change of perception brought about by glazing.

7   The glazed window was an invention of great importance for the soundscape, framing external events in an unnatural phantom-like 'silence.' The diminution of sound transmission, while not immediate and occurring only gradually with

the thickening of glazing, not only created the notion of a 'here' and a 'there' or a 'beyond,' but also introduced a fission of the senses. Today one can look at one's environment, while hearing another, with a durable film separating the two. Plate glass shattered the sensorium, replacing it with contradictory visual and aural impressions.

With indoor living, two things developed antonymously: the high art of music, and noise pollution—for the noises were the sounds that were kept outside. After art music had moved indoors, street music became an object of particular scorn. Hogarth's° celebrated print *The Enraged Musician* shows the conflict in full view. A professional musician indoors clamps his hands over his ears in agony while outside his workroom a multitude of sonorous activities are in progress: a baby is screaming, a man is sharpening knives on a grindstone, children are playing with ratchets and drums, several hawkers are selling wares assisted by bells and horns, and one shabbily-dressed beggar has targeted the musician's window for an oboe serenade. The developing antagonism between music and the soundscape can be more clearly sensed by comparing Hogarth's print with Brueghel's° town square of a century earlier. Hogarth's print contains glass windows. Brueghel's painting does not. Brueghel's people have come to the open windows to listen; Hogarth's musician has come to the window to shut it.

In a study of fairy tales, Marie-Louise von Franz points out that glass 'cuts you off, as far as your animal activity is concerned... Mentally you are not cut off. You can look at everything through glass practically undisturbed, for you can see as well as though it were not there... but it cuts off the animal contact... People very often say, "It feels as if there were a glass wall... between me and my surroundings. That means I see perfectly well what is going on, I can talk to people, but the animal and feeling contact, the warmth contact is cut off by a glass wall..."[3] The world of sounds and textures, the palpitating, kinetic world, is zoned out; we still watch it move, but from our (generally seated) position indoors our physical contact with it has ceased. The physical world is 'there'; the world of reflection and speculation is 'here.' Without our participation 'there' tends to become: a) deserted (as around modern apartment houses); or b) squalid (as in dense urban areas); or c) romanticized (as from a resort window).

One could actually argue that noise in the city increases in accordance with the thickness of glazing. The beautiful French windows along the eighteenth- and nineteenth-century avenues of European cities, now frosted over as their prosperous former tenants desert them for quieter residences, document° how such windows, sufficient at one time to resist street noise, have long since become inadequate. Those windows were intended to be opened; they did not seal off the environment totally as do the unopenable windows of the modern hotel room.

When the space within is totally insulated it craves reorchestration: this is the era of Muzak° and of the radio, a form of interior decoration, designed or absent-mindedly introduced to reenergize the space and render it more sensorially com-

(margin numbers: 8, 9, 10, 11)

plete. Now the interior and exterior can become totally contradictory. The world seen through the window is like the world of a movie set with the radio as sound-track. I recall travelling in the dome car of a train passing through the Rocky Mountains with schmaltzy music on the public address system and thinking: this is a travelogue movie about the Rocky Mountains—we are not here at all.

12   When the division between 'here' and 'there' is complete, the glass wall will become as impenetrable as the stone wall. Even thieves will respect it. Shattered glass is a trauma everyone is anxious to avoid. 'He shall rule them with a rod and shatter them like crockery,' is a potent acoustic image in Revelation (2:27). A keynote of the Middle-Eastern soundscape under normal circumstances, crockery became a violent signal when broken. For us the same is true of glass. And yet one cannot help feeling that the mind-body split of the Western world will only be healed when some of the glass in which we have sheathed our lives is shat-tered, allowing us again to inhabit a world in which all the senses interact instead of being ranked in opposition. ◆

1993

Endnotes

1. There are numerous allusions to this in European literature, for instance in chapter 19 of Thackeray's *Vanity Fair* where the street is laid knee deep in straw and the knocker of the door is removed when Miss Crawley is ill.

2. According to Sir W.M. Flinders Petrie, glaze was known from 12,000 B.C. in ancient Egypt, though the earliest pure glass dates from 7,000 B.C. See: G.W. Morey, *The Properties of Glass* (New York, 1938), p. 12.

3. Marie-Louise von Franz, *Individuation in Fairy Tales* (Boston and London, 1990), p. 15.

Glossary

The Crystal Palace: the architectural showpiece and crowning achievement of the 1851 Great Exhibition in London, England.

Hogarth: William Hogarth (1697–1764), influential British artist whose satirical graphic work highlights a variety of 18th-century themes, including the ills of the modern city and issues of race, class, and taste.

Brueghel: Pieter Brueghel the Elder (1525–1569), Flemish artist who is famous for his paintings and drawings of landscapes and peasant life.

Muzak: the corporate name for a licensed system of recorded music dating from the 1930s that is piped in to factories, restaurants, supermarkets, and hotel ele-vators; the term is also used generically (with a lower-case "m") to designate any pre-recorded light background music.

Explorations

- Are you sensitive to your culture's soundscape? How would you describe your soundscape at home, at school, and/or at work?

- Do you usually notice how different materials in your surroundings create different sounds? How do these sounds affect you?

- Do you ever feel as though windows cut you off from the physical world? In what way do windows affect your senses?

David Suzuki, born in Vancouver, B.C., in 1936, is an award-winning scientist, environmentalist, broadcaster, and writer. He graduated from Amherst College in 1958 with an honours B.A. in biology and earned his Ph.D. in zoology from the University of Chicago. He was a full professor at the University of British Columbia from 1969 until his retirement in 2001 and has published several books, including Inventing the Future *(1989) and* Wisdom of the Elders *(1992). He hosts CBC's* The Nature of Things, *and is the head of the David Suzuki Foundation, an internationally renowned environmental non-profit organization.*

The Prostitution of Academia

David Suzuki

1   All governments of industrialized countries wish to emulate Japanese success in the high-tech industries, so they are attempting to capitalize on the creative energies of scientists in universities.

2   Responding to pressure from the government and industry, Canadian universities are encouraging academics to develop ties with the private sector, thereby accelerating the transfer of basic knowledge to industry. The unique role of academic scholars as a group without a vested interest in business or government is thus terribly compromised.

3   In a glossy advertisement for the University of British Columbia entitled "Engine of Recovery," President David Strangway states on the first page: "Universities are a major source of free enquiry, providing the ideas that can later be exploited by free enterprise. We need both the push of free enquiry and the pull of free enterprise for success in our society." The rest of the brochure is filled with examples of people, primarily scientists, ostensibly solving practical problems in medicine, industry and society.

4   Across Canada, universities are rushing to become part of the industrial enterprise, as faculty are being encouraged to become entrepreneurs who exploit their discoveries for profit. There have been few objections to or questions raised about this process. I, for one, do not agree with President Strangway's political-economic analysis of the societal role of universities and I have grave concerns about the headlong rush to industrialize the university. Let me explain.

5   Historically, universities were never meant to be places where people prepared for jobs or where specialists aimed to benefit the "private sector." The university has traditionally been a community of people sharing in the exploration of human thought and creativity. The common assumption since universities became public enterprises has been that if the best minds of our youth are an important natural resource, then universities will maximize their development.

A good university is a place where scholars, dreamers, artists and inventors can 6
exist with no more justification than excelling at what they do and sharing their
skills and knowledge. The full range of human thought is encompassed within a
university. One consequence is that such knowledge often leads to criticism of
government and industry. University scholars can be a pain in the neck to people in power. That's why academics have fought for *tenure* as a means of protection from harassment for their ideas and social critiques. Society needs objective
critics if it is to have more than parochial, self-centred goals. Sadly for most
Canadian academics, tenure has become a sinecure rather than a privilege and
opportunity.

The industrialization of the university is a mistake for many reasons, one of the 7
most trivial being that it will not do what its proponents claim. In rushing to welcome investment from companies to exploit new ideas and discoveries, scientists
seem to have forgotten or are unaware that most of our current hotshot ideas will
in time prove to be wrong, irrelevant or unimportant. Science is mainly in the
business of invalidating the latest concepts. So why the rush to apply them?

But I have much deeper reasons for objecting to the industrialization of the 8
university. The essence of an academic community is the free exchange of ideas,
a sharing of knowledge. The formation of private companies within universities
and with their faculty runs counter to this spirit. Private companies encourage a
destructive kind of competitiveness that can be petty and mean. Secrecy becomes
a priority when patenting ideas is a primary goal. And the lure of profit can result
in both shoddy science and a narrow focus that ignores broader questions of
social responsibility and impact.

My most serious concern is with the vital role of the academic as both critic 9
and source of knowledge for society. Without an axe to grind, the scholar is in a
unique position to provide a balanced point of view with data to back him or her
up. During the Vietnam War, two of the most visible activists among scientists
were MIT's David Baltimore (who later earned a Nobel Prize) and Harvard's
Mark Ptashne. They were critical of companies like Dow Chemical and
Monsanto for their production of napalm, defoliants and tear gas. Today, both
Baltimore and Ptashne have their own biotechnology companies while Dow and
Monsanto are heavily involved in biotechnology. Do you think for a minute that
Baltimore and Ptashne would be as critical of those industries today? Not on your
life.

In the seventies, after the Arab oil embargo,° I was involved in a film on the 10
massive deposit of oil in Alberta's Tar Sands. At the time, with oil prices sky-
rocketing, there was talk of perhaps ten more oil extraction plants as big or bigger than Syncrude.° Each would produce at least fifty tons of sulphur dioxide a
day. That's a lot of acid rain. So we tried to find a university ecologist in the area
who would speak to us on camera about the environmental consequences of such
development. We were unsuccessful because no one wanted to jeopardize his

grant from the oil companies! Yet it is precisely for that knowledge that society supports such experts in a university.

11   I don't deny a role for university faculty in the application of new ideas. Our top-notch people are Canada's eyes and ears to the world's research, and good people will have ideas that can eventually be exploited. But the deliberate and urgent push to economic payoff distorts scholarship within the university and subverts its thrust to the will of those who have the money. Profit and destruction are the major reasons for the application of science today, while environmental and social costs are seldom seriously addressed. That's why we need scholars who are detached from those applications.

12   I remain a faculty member of UBC and because I care so much for the university I am compelled to speak out in criticism. Tenure confers the obligation to do so.

13   I don't condone but can understand why university scientists, who have been underfunded for so long, are welcoming the Faustian bargain° with private industry. But I fail to comprehend why philosophers, historians and sociologists who should know better are acquiescing so easily.

14   The headlong rush to industrialize the university signals the implicit acceptance of many assumptions that have in the past been questioned by academics themselves. For example, free enterprise, like most economic systems, is based on the unquestioned necessity for steady growth—growth in GNP, consumption and consumer goods.

15   Steady incremental growth within a given interval is called "exponential growth," and any scientist knows that nothing in the universe grows exponentially indefinitely. Yet economists, business people and politicians assume the explosive increase in income, consumer goods and GNP (and inflation) of the past decades must be maintained to sustain our quality of life. Historians know that this growth is an aberration, a blip that must inevitably stop and reverse itself. But how can the fallacy of maintainable exponential growth be seriously challenged when the university is busy selling the myth that it can help maintain such growth?

16   Scholars in universities represent tiny islands of thought in society. They are sufficiently detached from the priorities of various interest groups like business, government and the military to point out flaws in our current social truths. But by focussing on issues that are socially relevant or economically profitable, we lose sight of the broader context within which that activity falls; we forget history; we become blind to environmental and social costs of our innovations.

17   In the U.S., a significant portion of the budgets of universities like MIT, Harvard, Cal Tech and Stanford now comes from private investment. This has split their faculties in debate over whether there should be such close ties with private enterprise. But while those institutions are private, Canada's major universities are all publicly supported. Yet there has been little debate in Canada over the imminent industrialization of academia. The activity and knowledge of

our university scientists is paid for by the public and should be available for their benefit, not hidden behind a curtain of classified information, profit priorities or patent secrecy. Academics who accept grants or investments from the military or the pharmaceutical, forestry and computer industries, for example, will be reluctant to jeopardize that support by criticizing those industries when necessary.

There is another consequence of the increased industrialization of our univer-   18
sities that originates in the mentality of scientists themselves. Among scientists there is a hierarchy of position that is directly correlated to grant size and continued research output. A scientist has to keep his "hand in" to maintain status and credibility with his peers. Anyone who decides to look at a wider range of social, environmental or ethical matters, instead of focussing with tunnel vision on specific problems at the cutting edge of research, loses status in the scientific pecking order. Nobel laureates like George Wald of Harvard and Cal Tech's Linus Pauling and Roger Sperry who have become social activists and critics of some areas of science are often referred to disparagingly as "senile," "over the hill" or "out of his area." As university scientists become bound to private enterprise more tightly, their horizons will be restricted even more and they will be far less patient with those who raise social and ethical implications of their work.

Let me be specific by considering one of the hottest areas of applied science—   19
biotechnology—genetic engineering of organisms for commercial purposes. Biotech companies have been sprouting up on campuses like mushrooms. In a number of international meetings held at universities to discuss the future of biotechnology, none has seriously considered the potential misuse or hazards of the technology. Surely an academic community of scholars who maintain an arm's-length relationship with vested interests of society should be expected to raise those questions. Who else will do it?

One of the claims made to encourage greater investment in biotechnology is   20
its potential to "feed the world's hungry." It is a self-serving, shallow justification. Starvation on this planet is a consequence more of political and technological factors than a shortage of food. Even if it weren't, the exponential growth of our species' numbers, which has already doubled the global population twice in the past century, will far outstrip any increase in food production brought about by biotechnology. Scientists anxious to justify their research for more support will resist such objections.

Canadians should be wary of the uncritical push to increase the links between   21
university academics and private industry because there are unacceptable "costs." ◆

1989

Glossary

Arab oil embargo: result of a meeting in Kuwait in October 1973, just after the outbreak of the Yom Kippur War, when leaders of several Arab oil-exporting countries in the Middle East (collectively known as OPEC) decided to impose production and export cutbacks on Western countries politically sympathetic to Israel; what followed was a near-total embargo on oil exports to the U.S. and its allies that lasted until March 1974 and provoked a world-wide energy crisis.

Syncrude: Syncrude Canada Ltd., the world's largest producer of synthetic crude oil.

Faustian bargain: quite literally, a "deal made with the devil." It derives from the central premise of the Faust, or Doctor Faustus, legend, in which a German spiritualist sells his soul to the devil (Mephistopheles) in exchange for infinite knowledge and power. The legend has inspired numerous literary treatments, including plays by Christopher Marlowe (*Doctor Faustus* [1604]) and J.W. von Goethe (*Faust* [1808; 1832]), and a novel by Thomas Mann (*Doctor Faustus* [1947]).

Explorations

- Do you believe that the industrialization of the university is a mistake? Why or why not?

- As a tenured professor, Suzuki feels obligated to criticize the members of his own university. As a student, do you feel the same obligation?

- Would you criticize a private industry if it was acting unethically? Would you criticize the same industry if it was giving you thousands of dollars in financial support?

Kathryn Welbourn, born in Quebec and raised in Ontario, is an award-winning print journalist and radio documentary maker. She has won national, international, and regional awards for her work, and founded the regional newspaper The Northeast Avalon Times. *Welbourn has always had a special interest in writing about the rights of rural people and their increasing struggle for survival, including the Dene/Metis land claim agreement in the N.W.T., the fishery crisis in Newfoundland, and the problems of farmers in Alberta and Newfoundland. Welbourn lives in Newfoundland with her husband and two sons.*

Outports and Outlaws

Kathryn Welbourn

Jig a few cod or bag a moose for the winter larder? If you're a rural Newfoundlander,   1
think again. Thanks to environmental crackdowns, your way of life is a crime.

Amid the black swells of a murderously cold October sea, Frank McCarthy   2
leans straight into the North Atlantic wind, ball cap pointed toward the sky, hazel eyes searching for sunkers. Standing fast against the oncoming weather, he expertly guides the tiller of the small wooden boat he borrowed from a neighbour. She's cracked and chipped, stripped of both paint and, until Frank was in need of her, usefulness. She's just good enough to be out on the water, nothing more. Despite the forbidding weather we pass several other small boats—local fishermen jigging for cod. They pull their lines with ease, and given the customs of Newfoundland outport life, I assume we'll pull up alongside for a bit of gossip. When we wave a welcome, however, the men look up sharply and speed off in the opposite direction. With a resigned shrug, Frank explains that they don't know me; after all, I could be an undercover fisheries officer.

"No, they wouldn't stop for you now," he says of neighbours too fearful to pass   3
a civil word. "They don't know who's in the boat with you. But you can't blame them."

We pull up smoothly by Dolly's Rock, a small knob of land on Newfoundland's   4
northeast coast that's separated from the tiny village of Too Good Arm by this thin stretch of rock-spiked water. Settling in at his chosen spot, Frank, a lean slip of a man, begins flicking his jigger into the sea, testing the water for cod. It's hard to believe something so simple is such a serious crime. "Yeah, this is illegal, catching a few cod for your supper," he says. "Take it home and eat it and be called a criminal for that."

Frank McCarthy is in big trouble with the law. If the 49-year-old fisherman   5
had slapped his wife or driven around town drunk, he would be in less trouble than he is in right now. Frank was convicted of doing what comes naturally— jigging a few codfish for his winter supply. He was fined $3500, which he can not

afford to pay. Neither can he serve 90 days in jail, because he would lose the weekly payments of about $200 his family receives as compensation for the closure of the cod fishery. His wife, Ruby, and their two teenagers would have to go on welfare. The 17-foot fishing boat Frank's been working on all year will probably be repossessed. Frank could have escaped the fisheries officers when they came to arrest him here on the water. He saw them trying to sneak in around the cove in their fast boat. Frank laughs at the idea of the "fish police" going undercover in a community as small as Too Good Arm, population 162. As he pulls in a nice-sized cod for his dinner, he recalls that he made no effort to get away.

6   "I kept fishing while they were there reading me my rights. 'You have the right to remain silent,'" Frank laughs darkly, pulls out his knife, and bleeds his fish. "Well I'm not silent, I'm jigging." For the rest of Canada, the dominant story out of Newfoundland in the past few years has been the collapse of the Northern cod stocks and the subsequent closure of the food fishery in the summer of 1994. For the first time in nearly 400 years, Newfoundlanders no longer have the right to feed their families from the sea. And for the more than 250 000 rural Newfoundlanders who populate the hundreds of tiny outports snugged into coves straddling the rocky arms of the island's coasts, a more insidious trend is developing, one that cuts closer to their way of life. The locals have been read the environmental riot act, a sweeping assault on their traditional subsistence activities. Firewood and saw-log quotas have been cut. Controversial limits on the use of all-terrain vehicles keep outporters away from rabbit runs, berry patches, and moose trails.

7   Even the childhood pleasure of fishing conners and tom cods—small inshore fish—off the wharf is now against the law. In one of the most bizarre cases, a young man was fined more than $1000 for "molesting" a salmon. He was one of two boys throwing rocks at a large fish in a river.

8   From the outside, the zealous enforcement by federal and provincial governments of a battery of fisheries and wildlife regulations appears to be a legitimate conservation campaign, a sad but necessary evil. Rabbit populations are low, salmon stocks are slowly coming back, and the cod stocks remain depleted. "When you have a major problem with the conservation of resources, you just cannot carry on with traditions," says Ernie Collins, the recently retired chief of enforcement for the Department of Fisheries and Oceans (DFO) in Newfoundland. "Traditions will sometimes have to be curtailed or, indeed, ended."

9   But it is also true that corporate trawlers continue to drag up cod as a by-product of other activities, and which sells as a luxury item in the local supermarket. Pulp and paper companies clear-cut and spray huge tracts of Newfoundland forest, citing historic 90-year agreements. Outfitters and their wealthy, trophy-hunting clientele track their prey with the provincial government's active encouragement. For outporters being chased over the water and through the woods, the crackdown is traumatic. This is, after all, a population with the highest number

of hunters per capita in Canada, a place where woodstoves heat homes, and winter larders are filled with bottled moose, salted fish, and wild-berry preserves. Norman Okihiro, a professor of sociology at Mount Saint Vincent University in Halifax, Nova Scotia, describes the government campaign as the criminalization of rural Newfoundland. "The way of life in outport Newfoundland depends, in large part, on people being able to sustain themselves from the land and from the sea," he says. "To have such severe penalties basically outlaws the way of life."

Jim Overton, a sociologist at Memorial University of Newfoundland in St.   10 John's, sees the enforcement as part of a government effort to resettle the outports, shifting people out of the old economy and into supposedly more lucrative ventures such as tourism. "There's a very heavy hand, which is part of a war on people's traditional activities," he says. "The sentences are very harsh compared with the kinds of sentences that are handed out for, say, shoplifting or sexual abuse. The only way to interpret them is that the state has decided to teach people a lesson."

Resettlement is an old story in rural Newfoundland. The first time it came up   11 was in the early 1600s, when English fish merchants persuaded the monarchy to enact laws to discourage and even stop outport settlements. Settlers from Britain, desperate to escape poverty and unemployment, had begun building permanent homes in small groups scattered thinly along the rocky coasts of the Southern shore and Conception Bay. Although there were fewer than 1000 permanent residents at the time, the fish merchants were annoyed by the settlers' presence. The merchants wanted a monopoly on the island's fabulous cod stocks, so the British government declared it illegal to bring new settlers over on fishing vessels, to allow fishermen to stay once the cod season was over, or to settle within 10 kilometres of the coast. The laws were repealed only in the late 1670s when Britain needed settlers to establish its sovereignty over the island.

In modern days, forcing people to move from the outports is a common trick   12 of governments that want to reallocate the island's natural resources. In the 1950s through to the 1970s, Premier Joey Smallwood's° resettlement program aimed to bring outporters into the mainstream by evacuating 440 small communities. Smallwood thought outporters' way of living was too backward for the 20th century. He wanted to modernize the small-boat fishing family and bring in high-tech, intensive fishing techniques such as draggers. He offered roads and services in larger centres and compensation for people who left their homes behind or who agreed to put them on floats and ferry them over to places like St. John's. More recently, the federal government offered relocation money as part of the federal fish aid package to entice at least half the coastal fishery workers to find employment elsewhere. The provincial government, meanwhile, is desperate for new economic development, such as big-game outfitting or foreign garbage disposal. Although nearly half the island's population lives in rural areas, the province is now cutting back essential services, such as snow clearing, in these regions—a subtle, yet effective, message that depopulating the outports is now under way.

13   Watson Lane knows all about resettlement. A retired school principal from Twillingate, just a few kilometres from Too Good Arm, Lane was raised in the traditional life of the outports on Bragg's Island in Bonavista Bay. Coming from a long line of fishermen, Lane gravitated to Memorial University in St. John's to pursue his interests in theology and the arts, but he chose to move back to work in rural schools. "The outport is the place where we play," he says. "It's our park, our back garden. Being part of all that gives you a big feeling. When I get to Bragg's Island, I'm lord and master, just like when I was a boy skipping 'round."

14   In the modest home he built for his retirement in nearby Glovertown, Lane seems the last person one would expect to thumb his nose at the authorities; but he sees no other option: "Our ingenuity, our self-respect, is being undermined. They have moved right into our living room," Lane says, his lilting voice tinged with contempt. "It puts me in mind of Victor Hugo's *Les Misérables* where the laws are such that you have to watch your back, be suspicious of the police. It puts shivers through you … men out at night so they can jig a few cod."

15   The changes have been slow and steady but became strikingly apparent after the cod fishery was closed in 1992. A policy of zero tolerance for poaching of any kind was adopted, and governments began talking about new ways to use rural Newfoundland and its resources for tourism and industry. Most startling to outporters such as Lane was DFO's use of the term "recreational fishery" for what had always been known as the food fishery. In keeping with the new environmental attitude, regulations once ignored are now enforced. Lane recounts a litany of Orwellian regulations°: he can cut a decreasing amount of firewood, but he can't give it to an aging neighbour; he can shoot a moose if he has a licence, but he can't sell the meat, even if he doesn't need it all; he can give the meat as a gift, but he must wrap it in a note to prove it came from legal hunting, like a report card pinned to the pocket of a wayward child.

16   To channel local frustrations, Lane started an outport lobby group. About 30 people attended the first meeting, and Lane says membership is growing. He is quick to emphasize that he and most other outporters are not against tourism or environmental protection. These days, for example, Lane is helping a friend build a wharf out on the ice for a new charter boat. As well, his lobby group is not protesting the closure of commercial industries such as the fishery. Inshore communities have been demanding and predicting the closure for years. The crackdown on rural life, however, has shifted the blame for the province's problems onto outport people, tagging them as abusive and destructive individuals. "It is not the Newfoundland man and woman and child going out in the boat on Sunday afternoon that did this," he says. "This is the price we're paying for the greedy money grubbers that swept the ocean floor clean."

Lane is not interested in going back to the old days of kerosene lamps. Modern   *17*
outport life is a clever combination of the old and the new; outboard motors in
place of the old make-and-break engines, all-terrain vehicles instead of horses in
the woods, wages for work rather than payment in supplies. "My way of life
includes having a lobster on the beach and building my own home," says Lane.
"A 55-year-old man sits on his wharf, and the ocean is just in front of him. What
will he do? Don't ask me the question about whether I'll jig a fish or no."

Ernie Collins begs to differ. As the former chief of the DFO's enforcement in   *18*
Newfoundland, Collins does not sympathize with poachers of any kind. "We're
very proud of those fines," Collins says. "Traditions die hard, but we have no sympathy for these people. We've learned our lesson from the cod." Fisheries and
wildlife officers have been told to be just as tough on those people out getting a
bit of food as on those taking hundreds of pounds of fish for sale. The DFO has
hooked up with provincial wildlife officers and the RCMP in an effort to crack
down on local offenders. Enforcement officers now use DNA samples in courts
and infrared glasses and cameras in the field. Wildlife officials admit it is difficult
for officers to police their neighbours and sometimes their friends, but Collins
says the laws must be enforced. "The message that's out there is, if you break
these laws we're going to hit you where it hurts," he says.

But locals are hearing a different message. With the closure of the commercial   *19*
fishery and commercial boats tied up, many believe that enforcement officers are
at a loss for something to do. "So here you're having people watching the local vil-
lagers," says Norman Okihiro. "If somebody decides to go down the bay and just
take a look around, you have a wildlife officer follow them. This is harassment."
He illustrates his point with a true scenario: A family picnic on the beach, showing visiting relatives a good time. They lay out the food and settle in to eat, but
the day is spoiled when they realize they are being watched by a fisheries officer.
"Fisheries and wildlife officers have powers which most people would be surprised
at," he says. "They can search your car, and they have powers of seizure. These
authority figures are feared and may be given a bit too much respect. People have
told me of searches of entire villages looking for poached meat—things that would
not go on in the city, where you have lawyers and not as much fear."

In fact, some of the sentences being handed out seem to violate the *Charter of*   *20*
Rights and Freedoms. A fisherman charged with lobster poaching was ordered by
a judge not to buy, possess, or eat any lobster at all. Then there is the case of 24-
year-old Troy Gilbert from St. Fintan's, on the island's west coast. The young man
had been playing a large salmon with a single hook for three hours when he got
fed up and put on a jigger (a kind of lure)—illegal now because its two hooks
make it too efficient. Troy wanted the fish for his mother's table, and knew he
couldn't miss with a double hook. When he pulled his catch out of the water,
some fisheries officers who had been watching him for three hours came out of
the woods and chased him through the bush. Troy takes a young man's pride in

his escape that day, although one wonders what kind of shape the officers were in. Troy, after all, has a pronounced limp from a childhood illness; but then, he knows the woods so well, fishing and hunting since he was 10 years old.

21   In the end, the officers had taken pictures, and Troy was convicted of jigging a salmon instead of catching it on a regular fly. He makes only about $150 per week at a local dairy farm, so he cannot pay the $4000 fine. Even worse is his probation order: for three years he is not allowed within 300 metres of an inland river. "I'd have to stay home and sit on my step all day just to keep the probation," he says in disgust. "I have to go to work—it's too close to the river. I have to cut wood for Mom—cross the river again. If I was to get sick tomorrow, I'd have to die on the doorstep or cross the river. So I have to watch out for the wildlife officers all the time."

22   It is a calm and warm evening in Sally's Cove, at the base of the Great Northern Peninsula. The water and sky form a seamless match, erasing the line of the horizon. Clarence Laing, a lobster and herring fisherman, heaves his boat down a roll of logs into the water, while his wife Margaret, and their youngest child, Jamie, 12, ready the herring nets. There is laughter and shouting as the boat hits the sea with a splash.

23   Clarence starts the motor, and the family moves out to their fishing berth. Tonight Jamie is getting a lesson in setting the net. He makes a few mistakes at the tiller, but his father rights the boat and Jamie tries again. His father, a 50-ish man with a bodybuilder's physique, smiles. Later, in the Laings' neat wooden home just steps from the sea, Margaret spreads out the family dinner of moose meat, homemade bread, fish, and vegetables. Like all of their neighbours, the Laings built their home themselves, harvesting the lumber from the woods. Most people in the area also build their own homes from raw logs, a skill passed down through generations. Hunting and trapping and berry picking are part of the cycle of work. Even the community store is heated with firewood to save on electric bills, which run up to $300 per winter month for the average saltbox house. Back in the early 1960s, the Laings started out with a tar-paper shack right on the beach and then built on as they could afford to. "I never borrowed anything in my life. I waited until I had a dollar," says Clarence, sitting back comfortably at the dinner table. "We went without many's the time. I kept my money and spent it on my (fishing) gear. I built up and built up until I got what I wanted. No dear, I don't owe no one. Not a cent."

24   Sally's Cove is one of the most beautiful places on the island. There are flat cleared fields leading to the beach, and the Long Range Mountains brood in the background. Parks Canada liked the area so much it offered in the 1970s to relocate the 54 families who lived there. When at least 12 families, including the Laings, refused to move, the government set aside about 13 square kilometres of land as a community enclave and built Gros Morne National Park around Sally's Cove. Now, Margaret says, it is like living in a zoo. Residents are fenced in by the

rules and regulations of the park, which ban all hunting and set out inadequate rabbit-snaring and woodcutting areas for local people. The Laings had to get rid of their sheep because the park did not want them grazing near the road or on the meadows. Two young men up the road have been banned from the park for refusing to give up their chain saw as evidence when they were investigated for allegedly cutting trees to build their new fishing boats. An 80-year-old trapper had his snowmobile confiscated for setting his trapline back in the hills on park land. For their part, Clarence and Margaret do not see anything wrong with such activities.

"No, I couldn't follow all the regulations," says Clarence. "I don't know if any- 25 body knows what they all are, because they keep changing all the time. I say most people just goes on and does what they always do and hopes they don't get caught."

Wardens say they are just enforcing the rules set out by Parks Canada. You can 26 not advertise as a wilderness reserve and have tourists see moose entrails by the side of the road or locals cutting trees in the woods. The Laings, however, have different priorities. "A good citizen is a man who makes sure his family is warm and comfortable, a man who helps keep his neighbours and his community going," says Clarence. "Every law they're making now is making it harder to live."

A few kilometres up the road, the park has set up a fisherman's interpretive 27 centre to show tourists how fishing families lived "30 years ago." The Laings only find it insulting, a parody of their daily work down on the beach.

The combination of the park and new provincial and federal crackdowns is 28 almost enough to put the Laings out of business. Why don't they just pack up and leave or take wage jobs in the tourism industry in their area? Clarence answers the question with a sigh and a grin: "I don't think I'm made for going around trying to make someone else happy, make sure tourists, if they want their slice of bread, they got it, and their jam is on the right of their plate, their bed is made up right. Fishing, that's what I'm made for. They'll be no punching a clock and begging a boss for me."

There has been a lot of charged writing about the death of the outports since 29 the closure of the Northern cod fishery in 1992. National columnists, such as *The Globe and Mail*'s William Thorsell, have even gone so far as to claim it is immoral for people like the Laings to raise their children in rural Newfoundland. In subsequent media coverage, Newfoundlanders were called a burden on the rest of Canada. Michael Asch has heard this discourse before. The University of Alberta anthropology professor worked on the Mackenzie Valley Pipeline Inquiry in the 1970s, examining land use by native peoples in the Northwest Territories. The Canadian government, he says, is treating outport Newfoundland with the same disrespect that characterized its dealings with the Northern Dene.

"There was a presumed respect for a different way of life when we signed our 30 treaties with native peoples, and the same for when Newfoundland joined confederation. We're forgetting what our commitments were to these people and trying to force them into assimilation." The broken faith is based on ignorance about the lives of the people being regulated, he adds. "If people do not make a lot of money, then they're not considered to be up to some kind of modernizing concept of what a standard of living ought to be. It's part of an assumption about the outporters, that they're just savages who are plundering the resources."

31   Back in Too Good Arm, Frank McCarthy is trying to put together an appeal of his conviction. He cannot afford a lawyer nor can he get legal aid for a fisheries offence. "I'm going to tell the judge I was fishing out of necessity," he says. "Not just necessity, something I've always done. Something I wants to do. You can't call this justice." Taking a stand against DFO has exacted a big cost. Frank's marriage, already strained by unemployment, has disintegrated since his conviction. Ruby wanted Frank to stop jigging. "I'm not used to having the officers coming to the door," she said when Frank was first arrested. She wanted him to stay out of trouble. "I don't agree with what they done to Frank, but I want things to go back to the way they were."

32   But Frank just could not stop. In the room he has rented above an abandoned store in nearby Virgin Arm, he sounds tired—a man who has lost everything.

33   "I don't know why it hurts me so much," he says with resignation. "A whole way of life taken from you. I couldn't stand still for that."

◆ ◆ ◆

34   Since this award-winning article was first published in *Equinox Magazine* in October 1995, not much has changed in outport Newfoundland. A small cod fishery has been reopened. Inshore fishermen in some parts of the island asked DFO to allocate individual quotas so fishermen could take their time, fishing where and when it was best. Offshore boats voted for a competitive fishery— everybody fishes until the stock quota is taken—and that's what DFO agreed to. Far fewer than the half of the inshore fishermen the federal government hoped would leave the fishery have actually gone. Instead, inshore fishermen have diversified—fighting for crab and other permits. They have been refused the right to purchase bigger boats and so are forced to take their inshore boats offshore and pull crab pots under perilous conditions. As well, some fear the dragger shrimp fishery is destroying the crab fishery. Newfoundlanders are now allowed to fish cod for food one or two weekends a year. This has led to at least one drowning and fears of other tragedies as people go out in any weather during the "recreational fishery weekend." In Nova Scotia, New Brunswick, P.E.I., and Quebec, the food fishery is open year round. Since the cod stocks are the same, there has been no reasonable explanation given for this. Still, many Newfoundlanders eat fresh cod all summer. Some locals even take their cell phones out on the water, and when the fisheries officers leave the wharf, someone just gives them a ring. ◆

2001

Glossary

Joey Smallwood (1900–1991): a controversial figure who worked hard to help bring Newfoundland into Confederation in 1949 and served as the province's premier from 1949 until 1972.

Orwellian regulations: refers to George Orwell's novel *Nineteen Eighty-Four*, in which a totalitarian government imposes severe limitations on people's behaviours and thoughts.

Explorations

- Do you agree with Welbourn that outport fishers in Newfoundland are being unfairly persecuted by conservation legislation, or do you think that the need to conserve fish stocks should take precedence? Why? Do you see any middle ground in this conflict? In what circumstances should the rights and freedoms of individuals be limited for the good of the state?

- What conflicts exist between traditional ways of life and new lifestyles in your community? What is the impact of these conflicts on you and your community as a whole? What solutions do you see?

- Many people around the world feel that globalization (marked in part by the increase in the power of capitalist, multinational corporations and the decrease in the power of national governments) has happened at the expense of local communities and the autonomy of the individuals who live in these communities. Do you agree or disagree? What examples can you use to support your views?

CHAPTER FOUR

Style: Pushing the Boundaries

Some students think of style as an innate skill over which they have no control, or as ornamentation to be added after an essay is written. In fact, style—the words you choose and the way you arrange them—can be controlled, and it permeates every aspect of the writing process. Other students believe that style is— to borrow the words of 18th-century satirist Jonathan Swift—putting "proper words in proper places" and is based on a set of conventions. What Jonathan Swift thought might be "proper words" is difficult to discern, and almost certainly different from what might seem proper to you, or your parents, or your instructors, or your friends. What is "proper" depends on who you are writing for and where, when, and why you are writing.

The important thing to remember is that while you should keep conventions and rules in mind, such as the rules of grammar, these rules can be deliberately altered for stylistic purposes; for instance, you might convey to your audience a sense of fragmentation by using sentence fragments, a sense of weakness or passivity by using weak expletives or passive voice, or you might offer insight by creating a striking image. Indeed, style is pushing the boundaries of convention so that your ideas become meaningful and memorable to your audience.

American essayist Annie Dillard, in her essay "Push It," offers some valuable advice to writers:

> There is something you find interesting, for a reason hard to explain. It is hard to explain because you have never read it on any page; there you begin. You were made and set here to give voice to this, your own astonishment. Write as if you were dying. At the same time, assume you write for an audience of terminal patients. That is, after all, the case. What would you begin writing if you knew you would die

soon? What could you say to a dying person that would not enrage by its triviality?

Perhaps Dillard's advice seems a little extreme, particularly if you have given little thought to style; her point is that you should not hesitate to use your own voice to say what you feel compelled to say, whether or not it has been said before. This chapter will encourage you to experiment with words in the hope that the new places you discover will astonish you.

Diction

Levels of Language

Sometimes we worry—even lose sleep—about presenting the appropriate linguistic persona in a special situation—a job interview, dinner with a new supervisor, a presentation. We're usually unaware, though, of how immediately the appropriate linguistic persona pops up during a routine day—the way we switch instantly from the language and tone appropriate in conversation with a close friend to that appropriate with a professor or police officer or dentist.

Just as we establish an appropriate face-to-face persona for effective communication, we must establish an appropriate "written" persona for each essay. The best place to start is to recognize the different levels of formality and the particular conventions attached to each of these levels. Levels of diction include the range from very formal to very informal, and are usually characterized as "formal," "informal," "colloquial," and "slang." The level of formality of an essay's diction and syntax will determine for the audience the author's attitude both to the topic and to them; that is, an essay's level of language will both reflect and help establish the closeness of the relationship between author and audience.

Thomas King juxtaposes different levels of language—even in the title of his essay, "How I Spent My Summer Vacation: History, Story, and the Cant of Authenticity." The beginning of the title is familiar, friendly, known, but the words after the colon are academic, colder and more distant, the diction more commonly found in scholarly writing. Note the differences in levels of diction in the following passage:

> "Well, for instance," I said, "Stanley Fish suggests that there are interpretative communities composed of groups of people who share commonalities, who agreed on how things such as history and myth are interpreted, how the universe is ordered."
>
> "That so?" said Bella.
>
> "And Adrienne Rich talks about the politics of location and how your subject position, your gender, race, class all determine what you see and how you interpret what you see."

> "Okay," Bella said with a sigh. "There were these two guys from France came to visit us. They wanted to hear old stories, so Latisha told them about Old Man and Old Woman and how death came to the world."

Some of the humour of King's essay derives from the juxtaposition of different levels of language; Gary Genosko surprises his audience when he writes about Canada's national sport with formal diction in "Hockey and Culture": the discrepancy between language and topic encourages the reader to rethink hockey not just as a sport but as form of cultural expression. For instance,

> Discussions of hockey all too often suffer from normopathic tendencies that assume both standard or normative definitions of how to participate, in some measure, in its manifestations and a pathological attachment to such norms. Such assumptions crush plurality and all creative combinations and applications of the game in the expanded field of culture.

Personal Pronouns

Most students have been discouraged from using first and second person pronouns in their academic writing. However, this attitude is slowly changing. Until recently, the appearance of objectivity, often achieved by the invocation of the apparently unbiased pronoun "one," has been prized over subjectivity and personal experience. But more and more, scholars are seeing personal experience as central to intellectual inquiry. For instance, in her essay "Sex and Death and the Rational World of Defense Intellectuals," an academic analysis of the language of the military, Carol Cohn draws on her own experience, which she presents in the first person: "Although I was startled by the combination of dry abstraction and odd imagery that characterizes the language of defense intellectuals, my attention was quickly focused on decoding and learning to speak it." In foregrounding her own experience and her own reactions, Cohn avoids invoking the all-knowing voice of "one" that too often allows writers to present opinion as fact, and the audience feels that she has shared with them, which strengthens her appeal to ethos.

While it has become more acceptable to incorporate personal pronouns into scholarly essays, practices differ: you should always determine your instructor's or discipline's expectations regarding formality in essays you are submitting for grades.

Gender-Neutral Language

Using the masculine pronoun "he" to refer to both women and men is a long-standing tradition. Often, students believe that they must adhere to this convention in order to write academically acceptable essays. Language, however, has an impact on the way you perceive reality, and your perceptions affect the way you see yourself and others. You can see how exclusive gender-specific language is in the following example from "Of Studies." Francis Bacon writes of the importance of a well-rounded education: "…if a man write little, he had need have a great memory; if he confer little, he had need have a present wit: and if he read little, he had need have much cunning.…" Bacon uses "men" and "he" because he was writing about men only; women did not attend school in the Renaissance. If they were taught at all, they were taught womanly pursuits, such as needlework, drawing, singing, and piano, in their homes. Because women's roles in society have changed significantly since Bacon's time, and continue to change today, our language must reflect the change. Adhering to a tradition that has its roots in the oppression of women preserves that oppression.

Figurative Language

Figurative language is a way to push words beyond their everyday uses in order to clarify your ideas and to make your prose memorable. The following is far from an exhaustive list, but it indicates the figurative devices most common in non-fiction prose.

Alliteration and Assonance

Alliteration and assonance are both sound devices by which a writer can communicate the emotions associated with a concept simply by repeating certain sounds. Alliteration is the repetition of initial consonant sounds, assonance the repetition of vowel sounds. For instance, Michael Ondaatje's aunt Dolly's brain "leaps like a spark plug" (the "l" sound flows so the phrase is quick and nimble—like Dolly's brain). In "The Disposable Rocket," John Updike says that the space for the male is "the fly ball high against the sky," the long "i" sounds stretching to create a sense of upward movement.

Irony

Irony reveals levels of contrasting meaning. Verbal irony can be conveyed in a word; for instance, you might say "Wonderful! I have three exams on December 20th"—the "wonderful" is ironic, since your audience knows that you do not think it is wonderful. Irony can also be evident in a circumstance or situation. For example, in "The Female Body," Margaret Atwood disparages the kind of glamorized female body men usually prefer. Yet in her Barbie doll example, it is, ironically, the girl's father who insists that he will not allow such a doll in his house, not the mother.

Metaphor

A metaphor describes an idea or an object in terms of another idea or object. Writers use metaphors in order to make abstract concepts concrete, to help their readers better grasp their ideas. For instance, Michael Ondaatje's aunts "knit the story together, each memory a wild thread in the sarong." The knitting metaphor underscores the complexity of family relationships and histories; it encourages the audience to envision the intricate weave of the sarong and to associate that weave with the abstract concept of family relationships.

Dead Metaphors

Clichés are expressions that have been used over and over so often that they have lost their meaning. "As dry as a bone," "as old as the hills," and "I am so hungry I could eat a horse" are examples of clichés. Unless you can find a way to revitalize a cliché, do not use it. Refer to Annie Dillard's essay "Living like Weasels" in Chapter 2 and note how she adds new life to old sayings. For instance, she transforms the clichés "hold on for dear life" into "I should have...held on for a dearer life" and "down and out" into "Down is out, out of your ever-loving mind...." By taking old and dead metaphors and breathing new life into them, Dillard causes her reader to pause and ponder the actual meaning—both of the cliché and of its revitalization. This is a particularly effective device: Dillard's main point—that humans are too willing to settle for the "shoulds" in their lives, that it would be better to, like weasels, grasp life fully—is echoed in her ability to grasp old and dead images and renew them.

Personification

Personification allows a writer to imbue inanimate objects with human characteristics. Because we are familiar with human characteristics, applying them to inanimate objects allows a reader to more easily perceive a writer's feelings: inanimate objects "come alive" with meaning when they are personified. Daphne Marlatt, in "Difference (em)bracing," makes poetry come alive by saying that it "speaks in corresponding differences."

Simile

Like a metaphor, a simile considers one idea in terms of another, but in a simile, the comparison is overtly presented using "like" or "as." John Updike begins "The Disposable Rocket," "Inhabiting a male body is like having a bank account; as long as it's healthy, you don't think much about it." By comparing a healthy male body to a healthy bank account, Updike immediately conveys to his readers his sense of the body as functional but distant, something that serves a purpose but needs little care. His use of financial imagery also evokes a sense of the earning potential of the male.

Tone

Your attitude towards your subject and audience can be revealed through your tone of voice. Tone can be created through word choice and arrangement; indeed, connotative language and turns of phrase can make your writing voice sound sympathetic, condescending, amazed, or frustrated. The tones you can create are as numerous as the feelings you want to convey. The tone you choose will give voice to an attitude, allowing your ideas to move beyond the one-dimensional surface of the page. For instance, note the cynicism with which Atwood begins "The Female Body." Asked by the *Michigan Quarterly Review* to submit an essay on the female body, Atwood responds by using a cynical tone to express her discomfort with having the female body objectified as a "capacious topic": "I dump in the fuel and away goes my topic, my topical topic, my controversial topic, my capacious topic...." Thomas King uses a humorous tone through most of "How I Spent My Summer Vacation." For example, he tells his audience about his attempt to voice to Bella his belief in the distinction between history and myth:

> "That's history," Bella told me when she had finished the fourth telling of the story. "You got any questions?"
>
> I was dying to tell Bella that this wasn't history at all, that this was...well...myth. But I didn't get a chance.
>
> "Some of those white people call this story myth because they figure it never happened. Is that what you're thinking?"
>
> I was in full retreat by now and was willing to do or say anything to get out of the way.

The tone of this passage, gentle and tinged with humour, conveys to the audience a growing realization that this "simple" storyteller, this elderly woman, is far wiser and more intuitive than a simple description of her could convey. Tone can, with few words, help a writer clarify a point or convey an attitude that might otherwise take a paragraph to express.

Sentence Variety

Writers often choose a particular sentence type to underscore or emphasize a point. Simple sentences, which contain one independent clause, dramatize a point. Compound sentences consist of two or more independent clauses and are particularly useful for combining parallel ideas. Complex sentences, which have one independent clause and one or more dependent clauses, reveal levels of importance among ideas. Compound-complex sentences, those with two or more independent and one or more dependent clauses, are appropriate for expressing complex relationships among ideas.

Margaret Atwood effectively employs a variety of sentence types in "The Female Body" in order to achieve particular purposes. She writes of the two halves of the female brain, "[T]hey're joined together by a thick cord; neural pathways flow from one to the other, sparkles of electric information washing to and fro." This compound sentence, in which the independent clauses are joined by a semicolon, not only combines parallel ideas—that the halves of the brain are joined by a cord and that neural pathways flow between them—but the sentence also emulates the subject matter: the independent clauses, like the brain, are connected. Atwood follows this sentence with a sentence fragment, "Like light on waves," which foregrounds the fragmentation of the image of light reflecting on waves. Two simple sentences complete the paragraph: "She listens. She listens in." These sentences are startling—they stand out because of their simplicity—and they echo, just as overheard voices echo in the mind. Do not underestimate the power of sentence structure: it can help you create meaning.

Balanced Sentences

Sentences that are balanced deliberately repeat a word, a phrase, or a clause structure and therefore tend to be memorable. For instance, Bacon says, "Reading maketh a full man, conference a ready man, and writing an exact man." The rhythm of this sentence amplifies its impact. Balanced sentences may also present an antithesis such as in American president John F. Kennedy's famous line, "Ask not what your country can do for you; ask what you can do for your country."

Anaphora

Anaphora is similar to the balanced sentence in that there is repetition, but in anaphora, which is frequently used in oral delivery, a word, phrase, or clause is repeated at the beginning of several consecutive sentences. Martin Luther King, Jr., whose essay "Letter from Birmingham Jail" appears in Chapter 2, frequently uses this device.

Paragraph Length

Paragraph length, like sentence length, can be varied to create interesting effects. Margaret Atwood's paragraphs are fairly short compared with Carol Cohn's or John Updike's; the abruptness of the shortest, "Snails do it differently. They're hermaphrodites and work in threes," maintains the often sarcastic tone of the essay while demanding that the audience consider these biological oddities.

Overview

As you experiment with the above devices in your own writing, you will find your images and ideas coming alive. You may have some difficulty at first overcoming your own inhibitions and broadening the scope of your prose, but as you persevere, you will, indeed, be astonished with the way the various devices invigorate the written word and help you to clearly communicate your voice to your reader. The readings in this chapter have been chosen to illustrate various stylistic devices and their effects. As you read through these essays, and through essays in other chapters, pay particular attention to the ways in which the writers are able to allow you to see their ideas, and to hear their voices.

Margaret Atwood was born in Ottawa, Ontario, in 1939; she studied with Northrop Frye at Victoria College, and earned an M.A. at Radcliffe. Atwood has published several novels, including The Edible Woman, Surfacing, Lady Oracle, Life Before Man, Cat's Eye, Alias Grace, The Blind Assassin, *and* Oryx and Crake, *published in April 2003. She was awarded the Governor General's Award for one of her several collections of poetry,* The Circle Game, *and for her novel* The Handmaid's Tale, *and the 1996 Giller Prize for* Alias Grace. *Her novels explore diverse themes, often focusing on alienation, particularly of women. Atwood's* Survival: A Thematic Guide to Canadian Literature, *published in 1972, broke new ground in the field of criticism of Canadian literature.*

The Female Body

Margaret Atwood

...entirely devoted to the subject of "The Female Body." Knowing how well you have written on this topic...this capacious topic...

letter from Michigan Quarterly Review

1

I agree, it's a hot topic. But only one? Look around, there's a wide range. Take my own, for instance. 1

I get up in the morning. My topic feels like hell. I sprinkle it with water, brush parts of it, rub it with towels, powder it, add lubricant. I dump in the fuel and away goes my topic, my topical topic, my controversial topic, my capacious topic, my limping topic, my nearsighted topic, my topic with back problems, my badly behaved topic, my vulgar topic, my outrageous topic, my aging topic, my topic that is out of the question and anyway still can't spell, in its oversized coat and worn winter boots, scuttling along the sidewalk as if it were flesh and blood, hunting for what's out there, an avocado, an alderman, an adjective, hungry as ever. 2

2

The basic Female Body comes with the following accessories: garter belt, pantigirdle, crinoline, camisole, bustle, brassiere, stomacher, chemise, virgin zone, spike heels, nose ring, veil, kid gloves, fishnet stockings, fichu, bandeau, Merry Widow, weepers, chokers, barrettes, bangles, beads, lorgnette, feather boa, basic black, compact, Lycra stretch one-piece with modesty panel, designer peignoir, flannel nightie, lace teddy, bed, head. 3

3

The Female Body is made of transparent plastic and lights up when you plug it in. You press a button to illuminate the different systems. The circulatory system is red, for the heart and arteries, purple for the veins; the respiratory system is blue; the lymphatic system is yellow; the digestive system is green, with liver and 4 kidneys in aqua. The nerves are done in orange and the brain is pink. The skeleton, as you might expect, is white.

5   The reproductive system is optional, and can be removed. It comes with or without a miniature embryo. Parental judgment can thereby be exercised. We do not wish to frighten or offend.

4

6   He said, I won't have one of those things in the house. It gives a young girl a false notion of beauty, not to mention anatomy. If a real woman was built like that she'd fall on her face.

7   She said, If we don't let her have one like all the other girls she'll feel singled out. It'll become an issue. She'll long for one and she'll long to turn into one. Repression breeds sublimation. You know that.

8   He said, It's not just the pointy plastic tits, it's the wardrobes. The wardrobes and that stupid male doll, what's his name, the one with the underwear glued on.

9   She said, Better to get it over with when she's young. He said, All right, but don't let me see it.

10   She came whizzing down the stairs, thrown like a dart. She was stark naked. Her hair had been chopped off, her head was turned back to front, she was missing some toes and she'd been tattooed all over her body with purple ink in a scrollwork design. She hit the potted azalea, trembled there for a moment like a botched angel, and fell.

11   He said, I guess we're safe.

5

12   The Female Body has many uses. It's been used as a door knocker, a bottle opener, as a clock with a ticking belly, as something to hold up lampshades, as a nutcracker, just squeeze the brass legs together and out comes your nut. It bears torches, lifts victorious wreaths, grows copper wings and raises aloft a ring of neon stars; whole buildings rest on its marble heads.

13   It sells cars, beer, shaving lotion, cigarettes, hard liquor; it sells diet plans and diamonds, and desire in tiny crystal bottles. Is this the face that launched a thousand products? You bet it is, but don't get any funny big ideas, honey, that smile is a dime a dozen.

14   It does not merely sell, it is sold. Money flows into this country or that country, flies in, practically crawls in, suitful after suitful, lured by all those hairless pre-teen legs. Listen, you want to reduce the national debt, don't you? Aren't you patriotic? That's the spirit. That's my girl.

15   She's a natural resource, a renewable one luckily, because those things wear out so quickly. They don't make 'em like they used to. Shoddy goods.

6

16   One and one equals another one. Pleasure in the female is not a requirement. Pair-bonding is stronger in geese. We're not talking about love, we're talking about biology. That's how we all got here, daughter.

Snails do it differently. They're hermaphrodites, and work in threes.   *17*

7

Each Female Body contains a female brain. Handy. Makes things work. Stick   *18*
pins in it and you get amazing results. Old popular songs. Short circuits. Bad
dreams.

Anyway: each of these brains has two halves. They're joined together by a   *19*
thick cord; neural pathways flow from one to the other, sparkles of electric information washing to and fro. Like light on waves. Like a conversation. How does
a woman know? She listens. She listens in.

The male brain, now, that's a different matter. Only a thin connection. Space   *20*
over here, time over there, music and arithmetic in their own sealed compart-
ments. The right brain doesn't know what the left brain is doing. Good for aiming through, for hitting the target when you pull the trigger. What's the target?
Who's the target? Who cares? What matters is hitting it. That's the male brain
for you. Objective.

This is why men are so sad, why they feel so cut off, why they think of them-   *21*
selves as orphans cast adrift, footloose and stringless in the deep void. What void?
she asks. What are you talking about? The void of the universe, he says, and she
says Oh and looks out the window and tries to get a handle on it, but it's no use,
there's too much going on, too many rustlings in the leaves, too many voices, so
she says, Would you like a cheese sandwich, a piece of cake, a cup of tea? And he
grinds his teeth because she doesn't understand, and wanders off, not just alone
but Alone, lost in the dark, lost in the skull, searching for the other half, the twin
who could complete him.

Then it comes to him: he's lost the Female Body! Look, it shines in the gloom,   *22*
far ahead, a vision of wholeness, ripeness, like a giant melon, like an apple, like
a metaphor for "breast" in a bad sex novel; it shines like a balloon, like a foggy
noon, a watery moon, shimmering in its egg of light.

Catch it. Put it in a pumpkin, in a high tower, in a compound, in a chamber,   *23*
in a house, in a room. Quick, stick a leash on it, a lock, a chain, some pain, settle it down, so it can never get away from you again. ◆

1992

Explorations

- How do you think most women view their bodies? Where do you think this
  perception of themselves stems from?

- How do you think most men view women's bodies? Do you think that their
  perceptions stem from the same places as those of their female counterparts?

- How do you view your own body? As a model of perfect health? As an object
  of constant disappointment? What do you do (or what lengths are you willing
  to go to) to maintain a positive body image?

Francis Bacon, a Renaissance author and philosopher regarded as the father of inductive reasoning, was born in London in 1561. He was educated at Trinity College, Cambridge, and became a barrister. Bacon became a Member of Parliament in 1584, a post he held for 36 years. He was one of the earliest English essayists, and several of his essays and discourses were published during his lifetime. He died in 1626.

Of Studies

Francis Bacon

1   Studies serve for delight, for ornament, and for ability. Their chief use for delight is in privateness and retiring; for ornament, is in discourse; and for ability, is in the judgment and disposition of business. For expert men can execute and perhaps judge of particulars, one by one, but the general counsels and the plots and marshalling of affairs come best from those that are learned. To spend too much time in studies is sloth; to use them too much for ornament is affectation; to make judgment wholly by their rules is the humour of a scholar. They perfect nature, and are perfected by experience, for natural abilities are like natural plants, that need proyning by study; and studies themselves do give forth directions too much at large, except they be bounded in by experience. Crafty men contemn studies; simple men admire them; and wise men use them, for they teach not their own use, but that is a wisdom without them and above them, won by observation. Read not to contradict and confute, nor to believe and take for granted, nor to find talk and discourse, but to weigh and consider. Some books are to be tasted, others to be swallowed, and some few to be chewed and digested; that is, some books are to be read only in parts; others to be read, but not curiously; and some few to be read wholly and with diligence and attention. Some books also may be read by deputy, and extracts made of them by others, but that would be only in the less important arguments and the meaner sort of books; else distilled books are like common distilled waters, flashy things. Reading maketh a full man, conference a ready man, and writing an exact man. And therefore, if a man write little, he had need have a great memory; if he confer little, he had need have a present wit: and if he read little, he had need have much cunning, to seem to know that he doth not. Histories make men wise, poets witty, the mathematics subtile, natural philosophy deep, moral grave, logic and rhetoric able to contend. *Abeunt studia in mores.*° Nay there is no stond or impediment in the wit but may be wrought out by fit studies, like as diseases of the body may have appropriate exercises. Bowling is good for the stone and reins; shooting for the lungs and breast; gentle walking for the stomach; riding for the head; and the like. So if a man's wit be wandering, let him study the mathematics, for in

demonstrations, if his wit be called away never so little, he must begin again. If his wit be not apt to distinguish or find differences, let him study the schoolmen, for they are *cymini sectores*.° If he be not apt to beat over matters, and to call up one thing to prove and illustrate another, let him study the lawyers' cases. So every defect of the mind may have a special receipt. ◆

1625

Glossary

Abeunt studia in mores: from Ovid's *Heroides*, this can be translated as "Studying helps form character."

cymini sectores: literally means "hair splitters."

Explorations

* What purposes do your studies serve? How do the purposes of your studies compare to Bacon's purposes?

* Do you make a solid effort to read, write, and exchange ideas? If so, what have been the results of your hard work?

Carol Cohn, born in 1951, is a Human Rights Fellow and a senior research scholar in the Department of Political Science at Wellesley College. She received her B.A. from the University of Michigan (1973) and her Ph.D. in social and political theory from the Union Graduate School (1988). "Sex and Death and the Rational World of Defense Intellectuals" was written when Cohn was in graduate school. Her current scholarly interests include exploring national security discourse as a linguistic creation that perpetuates gender stereotypes. She is currently, with support from the Ford Foundation, examining gender mainstreaming in international security institutions.

Sex and Death and the Rational World of Defense Intellectuals

Carol Cohn

1   My close encounter with nuclear strategic analysis started in the summer of 1984. I was one of 48 college teachers attending a summer workshop on nuclear weapons, strategic doctrine, and arms control that was held at a university containing one of the nation's foremost centers of nuclear strategic studies, and that was cosponsored by another institution. It was taught by some of the most distinguished experts in the field, who have spent decades moving back and forth between academia and governmental positions in Washington. When at the end of the program I was afforded the chance to be a visiting scholar at one of the universities' defense studies center, I jumped at the opportunity.

2   I spent the next year immersed in the world of defense intellectuals—men (and indeed, they are virtually all men) who, in Thomas Powers's words, "use the concept of deterrence to explain why it is safe to have weapons of a kind and number it is not safe to use." Moving in and out of government, working sometimes as administrative officials or consultants, sometimes in universities and think tanks, they create the theory that underlies U.S. nuclear strategic practice.

3   My reason for wanting to spend a year among these men was simple, even if the resulting experiences were not. The current nuclear situation is so dangerous and irrational that one is tempted to explain it by positing either insanity or evil in our decision makers. That explanation is, of course, inadequate. My goal was to gain a better understanding of how sane men of goodwill could think and act in ways that lead to what appear to be extremely irrational and immoral results.

4   I attended lectures, listened to arguments, conversed with defense analysts, interviewed graduate students throughout their training, obsessed by the question, "How *can* they think this way?" But as I learned the language, as I became more and more engaged with their information and their arguments, I found that

my own thinking was changing, and I had to confront a new question: How can *I* think this way? Thus, my own experience becomes part of the data that I analyze in attempting to understand not only how "they" can think that way, but how any of us can.

This article is the beginning of an analysis of the nature of nuclear strategic 5
thinking, with emphasis on the role of a specialized language that I call "technostrategic." I have come to believe that this language both reflects and shapes the American nuclear strategic project, and that all who are concerned about nuclear weaponry and nuclear war must give careful attention to language—with whom it allows us to communicate and what it allows us to think as well as say.

I had previously encountered in my reading the extraordinary language used to 6
discuss nuclear war, but somehow it was different to hear it spoken. What hits first is the elaborate use of abstraction and euphemism, which allows infinite talk about nuclear holocaust without ever forcing the speaker or enabling the listener to touch the reality behind the words.

Anyone who has seen pictures of Hiroshima burn victims may find it perverse 7
to hear a class of nuclear devices matter-of-factly referred to as "clean bombs." These are weapons which are largely fusion rather than fission and they release a somewhat higher proportion of their energy as prompt radiation, but produce less radioactive fallout than fission bombs of the same yield.

"Clean bombs" may provide the perfect metaphor for the language of defense 8
analysts and arms controllers. This language has enormous destructive power, but without emotional fallout; without the emotional fallout that would result if it were clear one was talking about plans for mass murder, mangled bodies, human suffering. Defense analysts don't talk about incinerating cities: they talk about "countervalue attacks." Human death, in nuclear parlance, is most often referred to as "collateral damage"; for, as one defense analyst said, with just the right touch of irony in his voice and twinkle in his eye, "the Air Force doesn't target people, it targets shoe factories."

Some phrases carry this cleaning up so far as to invert meaning. The MX mis- 9
sile will carry ten warheads, each with the explosive power of 300 to 475 kilotons of TNT: *one* missile the bearer of destruction approximately 250 to 400 times that of the Hiroshima bombing. Ronald Reagan has christened the MX missile "the Peacekeeper." While this renaming was the object of considerable scorn in the community of defense analysts, some of these very same analysts refer to the MX as a "damage limitation weapon."

Such phrases exemplify the astounding chasm between image and reality that 10
characterizes technostrategic language. They also hint at the terrifying way in which the existence of nuclear devices has distorted our perceptions and redefined the world. "Clean bombs" as a phrase tells us that radioactivity is the only "dirty" part of killing people.

11   It is hard not to feel that one function of this sanitized abstraction is to deny the uncontrolled messiness of the situations one contemplates creating. So that we not only have clean bombs but also "surgically clean strikes": "counterforce" attacks that can purportedly "take out"—that is, accurately destroy—an opponent's weapons or command centers, without causing significant injury to anything else. The image is unspeakably ludicrous when the surgical tool is not a delicately controlled scalpel but a nuclear warhead.

12   Feminists have often suggested that an important aspect of the arms race is phallic worship; that "missile envy," to borrow Helen Caldicott's phrase, is a significant motivating force in the nuclear buildup. I have always found this an uncomfortably reductionist explanation and hoped that observing at the center would yield a more complex analysis. Still, I was curious about the extent to which I might find a sexual subtext in the defense professionals' discourse. I was not prepared for what I found.

13   I think I had naively imagined that I would need to sneak around and eavesdrop on what men said in unguarded moments, using all my cunning to unearth sexual imagery. I had believed that these men would have cleaned up their acts, or that at least at some point in a long talk about "penetration aids," someone would suddenly look up, slightly embarrassed to be caught in such blatant confirmation of feminist analyses.

14   I was wrong. There was no evidence that such critiques had ever reached the ears, much less the minds, of these men. American military dependence on nuclear weapons was explained as "irresistible, because you get more bang for the buck." Another lecturer solemnly and scientifically announced, "To disarm is to get rid of all your stuff." A professor's explanation of why the MX missile is to be placed in the silos of the newest Minuteman missiles, instead of replacing the older, less accurate missiles, was "because they're in the nicest hole—you're not going to take the nicest missile you have and put it in a crummy hole." Other lectures were filled with discussion of vertical erector launchers, thrust-to-weight ratios, soft lay downs, deep penetration, and the comparative advantages of protracted versus spasm attacks—or what one military adviser to the National Security Council has called "releasing 70 to 80 percent of our megatonnage in one orgasmic whump."[1]

15   But if the imagery is transparent, its significance may be less so. I do *not* want to assert that it somehow reveals what defense intellectuals are really talking about, or their motivations; individual motives cannot necessarily be read directly from imagery, which originates in a broader cultural context. The history of the atomic bomb project itself is rife with overt images of competitive male sexuality, as is the discourse of the early nuclear physicists, strategists, and members of the Strategic Air Command.[2] Both the military itself and the arms manufacturers are constantly exploiting the phallic imagery and promise of sexual domination that

their weapons so conveniently suggest. Consider the following, from the June 1985 issue of *Air Force Magazine*: Emblazoned in bold letters across the top of a two-page advertisement for the AV-8B Harrier II—"Speak Softly and Carry a Big Stick." The copy below boasts "an exceptional thrust-to-weight ratio," and "vectored thrust capability that makes the...unique rapid response possible."

Another vivid source of phallic imagery is to be found in descriptions of nuclear   *16* blasts themselves. Here, for example, is one by journalist William Laurence, who was brought by the Army Air Corps to witness the Nagasaki bombing.

> Then, just when it appeared as though the thing had settled down into a state of permanence, there came shooting out of the top a giant mushroom that increased the size of the pillar to a total of 45,000 feet. The mushroom top was even more alive than the pillar, seething and boiling in a white fury of creamy foam, sizzling upward and then descending earthward, a thousand geysers rolled into one. It kept struggling in an elementary fury, like a creature in the act of breaking the bonds that held it down.[3]

Given the degree to which it suffuses their world, the fact that defense intel-   *17* lectuals use a lot of sexual imagery is not especially surprising. Nor does it, by itself, constitute grounds for imputing motivation. The interesting issue is not so much the imagery's possible psychodynamic origins as how it functions—its role in making the work world of defense intellectuals feel tenable. Several stories illustrate the complexity.

At one point a group of us took a field trip to the New London Navy base   *18* where nuclear submarines are home-ported, and to the General Dynamics Electric Boat yards where a new Trident submarine was being constructed. The high point of the trip was a tour of a nuclear-powered submarine. A few at a time, we descended into the long, dark, sleek tube in which men and a nuclear reactor are encased underwater for months at a time. We squeezed through hatches, along neon-lit passages so narrow that we had to turn and press our backs to the walls for anyone to get by. We passed the cramped racks where men sleep, and the red and white signs warning of radioactive materials. When we finally reached the part of the sub where the missiles are housed, the officer accompanying us turned with a grin and asked if we wanted to stick our hands through a hole to "pat the missile." *Pat the missile?*

The image reappeared the next week, when a lecturer scornfully declared that   *19* the only real reason for deploying cruise and Pershing II missiles in Western Europe was "so that our allies can pat them." Some months later, another group of us went to be briefed at NORAD (the North American Aerospace Defense Command). On the way back, the Air National Guard plane we were on went to refuel at Offutt Air Force Base, the Strategic Air Command headquarters near

Omaha, Nebraska. When word leaked out that our landing would be delayed because the new B-1 bomber was in the area, the plane became charged with a tangible excitement that built as we flew in our holding pattern, people craning their necks to try to catch a glimpse of the B-1 in the skies, and climaxed as we touched down on the runway and hurtled past it. Later, when I returned to the center I encountered a man who, unable to go on the trip, said to me enviously, "I hear you got to pat a B-1."

20   What is all this patting? Patting is an assertion of intimacy, sexual possession, affectionate domination. The thrill and pleasure of "patting the missile" is the proximity of all that phallic power, the possibility of vicariously appropriating it as one's own. But patting is not only an act of sexual intimacy. It is also what one does to babies, small children, the pet dog. The creatures one pats are small, cute, harmless—not terrifyingly destructive. Pat it, and its lethality disappears.

21   Much of the sexual imagery I heard was rife with the sort of ambiguity suggested by "patting the missiles." The imagery can be construed as a deadly serious display of the connections between masculine sexuality and the arms race. But at the same time, it can also be heard as a way of minimizing the seriousness of militarist endeavors, of denying their deadly consequences. A former Pentagon target analyst, in telling me why he thought plans for "limited nuclear war" were ridiculous, said, "Look, you gotta understand that it's a pissing contest—you gotta expect them to use everything they've got." This image says, most obviously, that this is about competition for manhood, and thus there is tremendous danger. But at the same time it says that the whole thing is not very serious—it is just what little boys or drunk men do.

22   Sanitized abstraction and sexual imagery, even if disturbing, seemed to fit easily into the masculine world of nuclear war planning. What did not fit was another set of words that evoked images that can only be called domestic.

23   Nuclear missiles are based in "silos." On a Trident submarine, which carries 24 multiple-warhead nuclear missiles, crew members call the part of the sub where the missiles are lined up in their silos ready for launching "the Christmas tree farm." In the friendly, romantic world of nuclear weaponry, enemies "exchange" warheads; weapons systems can "marry up." "Coupling" is sometimes used to refer to the wiring between mechanisms of warning and response, or to the psychopolitical links between strategic and theater weapons. The pattern in which a MIRVed missile's nuclear warheads land is known as a "footprint." These nuclear explosives are not dropped; a "bus" "delivers" them. These devices are called "reentry vehicles," or "RVs" for short, a term not only totally removed from the reality of a bomb but also resonant with the image of the recreational vehicles of the ideal family vacation.

24   These domestic images are more than simply one more way to remove oneself from the grisly reality behind the words; ordinary abstraction is adequate to that

task. Calling the pattern in which bombs fall a "footprint" almost seems a willful distorting process, a playful, perverse refusal of accountability—because to be accountable to reality is to be unable to do this work.

The images evoked by these words may also be a way to tame the uncontrol- 25 lable forces of nuclear destruction. Take the fire-breathing dragon under the bed, the one who threatens to incinerate your family, your town, your planet, and turn it into a pet you can pat. Or domestic imagery may simply serve to make every-one more comfortable with what they're doing. "PAL" (permissive action links) is the carefully constructed, friendly acronym for the electronic system designed to prevent the unauthorized firing of nuclear warheads. The president's annual nuclear weapons stockpile memorandum, which outlines both short- and long-range plans for production of new nuclear weapons, is benignly referred to as "the shopping list." The "cookie cutter" is a phrase used to describe a particular model of nuclear attack.

The imagery that domesticates, that humanizes insentient weapons, may also 26 serve, paradoxically, to make it all right to ignore sentient human beings. Perhaps it is possible to spend one's time dreaming up scenarios for the use of massively destructive technology, and to exclude human beings from that tech-nological world, because that world itself now includes the domestic, the human, the warm and playful—the Christmas trees, the RVs, the things one pats affectionately. It is a world that is in some sense complete in itself; it even includes death and loss. The problem is that all things that get "killed" happen to be weapons, not humans. If one of your warheads "kills" another of your war-heads, it is "fratricide." There is much concern about "vulnerability" and "sur-vivability," but it is about the vulnerability and survival of weapons systems, rather than people.

Another set of images suggests men's desire to appropriate from women the 27 power of giving life. At Los Alamos, the atomic bomb was referred to as "Oppenheimer's baby"; at Lawrence Livermore, the hydrogen bomb was "Teller's baby," although those who wanted to disparage Teller's contribution claimed he was not the bomb's father but its mother. In this context, the extraordinary names given to the bombs that reduced Hiroshima and Nagasaki to ash and rub-ble—"Little Boy" and "Fat Man"—may perhaps become intelligible. These ulti-mate destroyers were the male progeny of the atomic scientists.

The entire history of the bomb project, in fact, seems permeated with imagery 28 that confounds humanity's overwhelming technological power to destroy nature with the power to create: imagery that converts men's destruction into their rebirth. Laurence wrote of the Trinity test of the first atomic bomb: "One felt as though he had been privileged to witness the Birth of the World." In a 1985 interview, General Bruce K. Holloway, the commander in chief of the Strategic Air Command from 1968 to 1972, described a nuclear war as involving "a big bang, like the start of the universe."

29   Finally, the last thing one might expect to find in a subculture of hard-nosed realism and hyper-rationality is the repeated invocation of religious imagery. And yet, the first atomic bomb test was called Trinity. Seeing it, Robert Oppenheimer thought of Krishna's words to Arjuna in the *Bhagavad Gita*: "I am become death, destroyer of worlds." Defense intellectuals, when challenged on a particular assumption, will often duck out with a casual, "Now you're talking about matters of theology." Perhaps most astonishing of all, the creators of strategic doctrine actually refer to their community as "the nuclear priesthood." It is hard to decide what is most extraordinary about this: the arrogance of the claim, the tacit admission that they really are creators of dogma; or the extraordinary implicit statement about who, or rather what, has become god.

30   Although I was startled by the combination of dry abstraction and odd imagery that characterizes the language of defense intellectuals, my attention was quickly focused on decoding and learning to speak it. The first task was training the tongue in the articulation of acronyms.

31   Several years of reading the literature of nuclear weaponry and strategy had not prepared me for the degree to which acronyms littered all conversations, nor for the way in which they are used. Formerly, I had thought of them mainly as utilitarian. They allow you to write or speak faster. They act as a form of abstraction, removing you from the reality behind the words. They restrict communication to the initiated, leaving the rest both uncomprehending and voiceless in the debate.

32   But being at the center revealed some additional, unexpected dimensions. First, in speaking and hearing, a lot of these terms are very sexy. A small supersonic rocket "designed to penetrate any Soviet air defense" is called a SRAM (for short-range attack missile). Submarine-launched cruise missiles are referred to as "slick'ems" and ground-launched cruise missiles are "glick'ems." Air-launched cruise missiles are magical "alchems."

33   Other acronyms serve in different ways. The plane in which the president will supposedly be flying around above a nuclear holocaust, receiving intelligence and issuing commands for where to bomb next, is referred to as "Kneecap" (for NEACP—National Emergency Airborne Command Post). Few believe that the president would really have the time to get into it, or that the communications systems would be working if he were in it—hence the edge of derision. But the very ability to make fun of a concept makes it possible to work with it rather than reject it outright.

34   In other words, what I learned at the program is that talking about nuclear weapons is fun. The words are quick, clean, light; they trip off the tongue. You can reel off dozens of them in seconds, forgetting about how one might interfere with the next, not to mention with the lives beneath them. Nearly everyone I observed—lecturers, students, hawks, doves, men, and women—took pleasure in using the words; some of us spoke with a self-consciously ironic edge, but the

pleasure was there nonetheless. Part of the appeal was the thrill of being able to manipulate an arcane language, the power of entering the secret kingdom. But perhaps more important, learning the language gives a sense of control, a feeling of mastery over technology that is finally not controllable but powerful beyond human comprehension. The longer I stayed, the more conversations I participated in, the less I was frightened of nuclear war.

How can learning to speak a language have such a powerful effect? One *35* answer, discussed earlier, is that the language is abstract and sanitized, never giving access to the images of war. But there is more to it than that. The learning process itself removed me from the reality of nuclear war. My energy was focused on the challenge of decoding acronyms, learning new terms, developing competence in the language—not on the weapons and wars behind the words. By the time I was through, I had learned far more than an alternate, if abstract, set of words. The content of what I could talk about was monumentally different.

Consider the following descriptions, in each of which the subject is the after-   *36* math of a nuclear attack.

> Everything was black, had vanished into the black dust, was destroyed. Only the flames that were beginning to lick their way up had any color. From the dust that was like a fog, figures began to loom up, black, hairless, faceless. They screamed with voices that were no longer human. Their screams drowned out the groans rising everywhere from the rubble, groans that seemed to rise from the very earth itself.[4]

> You have to have ways to maintain communications in a nuclear environment, a situation bound to include EMP° blackout, brute force damage to systems, a heavy jamming environment, and so on.[5]

There is no way to describe the phenomena represented in the first with the   *37* language of the second. The passages differ not only in the vividness of their words, but in their content: the first describes the effects of a nuclear blast on human beings; the second describes the impact of a nuclear blast on technical systems designed to secure the "command and control" of nuclear weapons. Both of these differences stem from the difference of perspective: the speaker in the first is a victim of nuclear weapons, the speaker in the second is a user. The speaker in the first is using words to try to name and contain the horror of human suffering all around her; the speaker in the second is using words to insure the possibility of launching the next nuclear attack.

Technostrategic language articulates only the perspective of the users of   *38* nuclear weapons, not the victims. Speaking the expert language not only offers distance, a feeling of control, and an alternative focus for one's energies; it also offers escape from thinking of oneself as a victim of nuclear war. No matter what one deeply knows or believes about the likelihood of nuclear war, and no matter what sort of terror or despair the knowledge of nuclear war's reality might inspire, the speakers of technostrategic language are allowed, even forced, to escape that awareness, to escape viewing nuclear war from the position of the victim, by virtue of their linguistic stance.

39   I suspect that much of the reduced anxiety about nuclear war commonly experienced by both new speakers of the language and longtime experts comes from characteristics of the language itself: the distance afforded by its abstraction, the sense of control afforded by mastering it, and the fact that its content and concerns are those of the users rather than the victims. In learning the language, one goes from being the passive, powerless victim to being the competent, wily, powerful purveyor of nuclear threats and nuclear explosive power. The enormous destructive effects of nuclear weapons systems become extensions of the self, rather than threats to it.

40   It did not take long to learn the language of nuclear war and much of the specialized information it contained. My focus quickly changed from mastering technical information and doctrinal arcana, to an attempt to understand more about how the dogma I was learning was rationalized. Since underlying rationales are rarely discussed in the everyday business of defense planning, I had to start asking more questions. At first, although I was tempted to use my newly acquired proficiency in technostrategic jargon, I vowed to speak English. What I found, however, was that no matter how well informed my questions were, no matter how complex an understanding they were based upon, if I was speaking English rather than expert jargon, the men responded to me as though I were ignorant or simpleminded, or both. A strong distaste for being patronized and a pragmatic streak made my experiment in English short-lived. I adopted the vocabulary, speaking of "escalation dominance," "preemptive strikes," and one of my favorites, "sub-holocaust engagements." This opened my way into long, elaborate discussions that taught me a lot about technostrategic reasoning and how to manipulate it.

41   But the better I became at this discourse, the more difficult it became to express my own ideas and values. While the language included things I had never been able to speak about before, it radically excluded others. To pick a bald example: the word "peace" is not a part of this discourse. As close as one can come is "strategic stability," a term that refers to a balance of numbers and types of weapons systems—not the political, social, economic, and psychological conditions that "peace" implies. Moreover, to speak the word is to immediately brand oneself as a soft-headed activist instead of a professional to be taken seriously.

42   If I was unable to speak my concerns in this language, more disturbing still was that I also began to find it harder even to keep them in my own head. No matter how firm my commitment to staying aware of the bloody reality behind the

words, over and over I found that I could not keep human lives as my reference point. I found I could go for days speaking about nuclear weapons, without once thinking about the people who would be incinerated by them.

It is tempting to attribute this problem to the words themselves—the 43 abstractness, the euphemisms, the sanitized, friendly, sexy acronyms. Then one would only need to change the words: get the military planners to say "mass murder" instead of "collateral damage," and their thinking would change. The problem, however, is not simply that defense intellectuals use abstract terminology that removes them from the realities of which they speak. There *is* no reality behind the words. Or, rather, the "reality" they speak of is itself a world of abstractions. Deterrence theory, and much of strategic doctrine, was invented to hold together abstractly, its validity judged by internal logic. These abstract systems were developed as a way to make it possible to, in Herman Kahn's phrase, "think about the unthinkable"—not as a way to describe or codify relations on the ground.

So the problem with the idea of "limited nuclear war," for example, is not only 44 that it is a travesty to refer to the death and suffering caused by *any* use of nuclear weapons as "limited," or that "limited nuclear war" is an abstraction that obfuscates the human reality beneath any use of nuclear weapons. It is also that limited nuclear war is itself an abstract conceptual system, designed, embodied, and achieved by computer modeling. In this abstract world, hypothetical, calm, rational actors have sufficient information to know exactly what size nuclear weapon the opponent has used against which targets, and adequate command and control to make sure that their response is precisely equilibrated to the attack. No field commander would use the tactical nuclear weapons at his disposal at the height of a losing battle. Our rational actors would have absolute freedom from emotional response to being attacked, from political pressures from the populace. They would act solely on the basis of a perfectly informed mathematical calculus of megatonnage. To refer to limited nuclear war is to enter a system that is de facto abstract and grotesquely removed from reality. The abstractness of the entire conceptual system makes descriptive language utterly beside the point.

This realization helped make sense of my difficulty in staying connected to 45 concrete lives as well as of some of the bizarre and surreal quality of what people said. But there was still a piece missing. How is it possible, for example, to make sense of the following:

> The strategic stability of regime A is based on the fact that both sides are deprived of any incentive ever to strike first. Since it takes roughly two warheads to destroy one enemy silo, an attacker must expend two of his missiles to destroy one of the enemy's. A first strike disarms the attacker. The aggressor ends up worse off than the aggressed.[6]

46   The homeland of "the aggressed" has just been devastated by the explosions of, say, a thousand nuclear bombs, each likely to be at least 10 to 100 times more powerful than the bomb dropped on Hiroshima, and the aggressor, whose homeland is still untouched, "ends up worse off"?

47   I was only able to make sense of this kind of thinking when I finally asked myself: Who—or what—is the subject? In technostrategic discourse, the reference point is not human beings but the weapons themselves. The aggressor ends up worse off than the aggressed because he has fewer weapons left; any other factors, such as what happened where the weapons landed, are irrelevant to the calculus of gain and loss.

48   The fact that the subjects of strategic paradigms are weapons has several important implications. First, and perhaps most critically, there is no real way to talk about human death or human societies when you are using a language designed to talk about weapons. Human death simply *is* collateral damage—collateral to the real subject, which is the weapons themselves.

49   Understanding this also helps explain what was at first so surprising to me: most people who do this work are on the whole nice, even good, men, many with liberal inclinations. While they often identify their motivations as being concern about humans, in their work they enter a language and paradigm that precludes people. Thus, the nature and outcome of their work can utterly contradict their genuine motives for doing it.

50   In addition, if weapons are the reference point, it becomes in some sense illegitimate to ask the paradigm to reflect human concerns. Questions that break through the numbing language of strategic analysis and raise issues in human terms can be easily dismissed. No one will claim that they are unimportant. But they are inexpert, unprofessional, irrelevant to the business at hand. The discourse among the experts remains hermetically sealed. One can talk about the weapons that are supposed to protect particular peoples and their way of life without actually asking if they are able to do it, or if they are the best way to do it, or whether they may even damage the entities they are supposedly protecting. These are separate questions.

51   This discourse has become virtually the only response to the question of how to achieve security that is recognized as legitimate. If the discussion of weapons was one competing voice in the discussion, or one that was integrated with others, the fact that the referents of strategic paradigms are only weapons might be of less note. But when we realize that the only language and expertise offered to those interested in pursuing peace refers to nothing but weapons, its limits become staggering. And its entrapping qualities—the way it becomes so hard, once you adopt the language, to stay connected to human concerns—become more comprehensible.

52   Within a few weeks, what had once been remarkable became unnoticeable. As I learned to speak, my perspective changed. I no longer stood outside the impen-

etrable wall of technostrategic language and once inside, I could no longer see it. I had not only learned to speak a language: I had started to think in it. Its questions became my questions, its concepts shaped my responses to new ideas. Like the White Queen, I began to believe six impossible things before breakfast—not because I consciously believed, for instance, that a "surgically clean counterforce strike" was really possible, but because some elaborate piece of doctrinal reasoning I used was already predicated on the possibility of those strikes as well as on a host of other impossible things.

My grasp on what I knew as reality seemed to slip. I might get very excited, for   53
example, about a new strategic justification for a no-first-use policy and spend time discussing the ways in which its implications for the U.S. force structure in Western Europe were superior to the older version. After a day or two I would suddenly step back, aghast that I was so involved with the *military* justifications for not using nuclear weapons—as though the moral ones were not enough. What I was actually talking about—the mass incineration of a nuclear attack— was no longer in my head.

Or I might hear some proposals that seemed to me infinitely superior to the   54
usual arms control fare. First I would work out how and why these proposals were better and then ways to counter the arguments against them. Then it might dawn on me that even though these two proposals sounded different, they still shared a host of assumptions that I was not willing to make. I would first feel as though I had achieved a new insight. And then all of a sudden, I would realize that these were things I actually knew before I ever entered this community and had since forgotten. I began to feel that I had fallen down the rabbit hole.

The language issues do not disappear. The seductions of learning and using it   55
remain great, and as the pleasures deepen, so do the dangers. The activity of trying to out-reason nuclear strategists in their own games gets you thinking inside their rules, tacitly accepting the unspoken assumptions of their paradigms.

Yet, the issues of language have now become somewhat less central to me, and   56
my new questions, while still not precisely the questions of an insider, are questions I could not have had without being inside. Many of them are more practical: Which individuals and institutions are actually responsible for the endless "modernization" and proliferation of nuclear weaponry, and what do they gain from it? What role does technostrategic rationality play in their thinking? What would a reasonable, genuinely defensive policy look like? Others are more philosophical, having to do with the nature of the "realism" claimed for the defense intellectuals' mode of thinking and the grounds upon which it can be shown to be spurious. What would an alternative rationality look like?

My own move away from a focus on the language is quite typical. Other recent   57
entrants into this world have commented that while the cold-blooded, abstract

discussions are most striking at first, within a short time you get past them and come to see that the language itself is not the problem.

58   I think it would be a mistake, however, to dismiss these early impressions. While I believe that the language is not the whole problem, it is a significant component and clue. What it reveals is a whole series of culturally grounded and culturally acceptable mechanisms that make it possible to work in institutions that foster the proliferation of nuclear weapons, to plan mass incinerations of millions of human beings for a living. Language that is abstract, sanitized, full of euphemism; language that is sexy and fun to use; paradigms whose referent is weapons; imagery that domesticates and deflates the forces of mass destruction; imagery that reverses sentient and nonsentient matter, that conflates birth and death, destruction and creation—all of these are part of what makes it possible to be radically removed from the reality of what one is talking about, and from the realities one is creating through the discourse.

59   Close attention to the language itself also reveals a tantalizing basis on which to challenge the legitimacy of the defense intellectuals' dominance of the discourse on nuclear issues. When defense intellectuals are criticized for the cold-blooded inhumanity of the scenarios they plan, their response is to claim the high ground of rationality. They portray those who are radically opposed to the nuclear status quo as irrational, unrealistic, too emotional—"idealistic activists." But if the smooth, shiny surface of their discourse—its abstraction and technical jargon—appears at first to support these claims, a look below the surface does not. Instead we find strong currents of homoerotic excitement, heterosexual domination, the drive toward competence and mastery, the pleasures of membership in an elite and privileged group, of the ultimate importance and meaning of membership in the priesthood. How is it possible to point to the pursuers of these values, these experiences, as paragons of cool-headed objectivity?

60   While listening to the language reveals the mechanisms of distancing and denial and the emotional currents embodied in this emphatically male discourse, attention to the experience of learning the language reveals something about how thinking can become more abstract, more focused on parts disembedded from their context, more attentive to the survival of weapons than the survival of human beings.

61   Because this professional language sets the terms for public debate, many who oppose current nuclear policies choose to learn it. Even if they do not believe that the technical information is very important, some believe it is necessary to master the language simply because it is too difficult to attain public legitimacy without it. But learning the language is a transformative process. You are not simply adding new information, new vocabulary, but entering a mode of thinking not only about nuclear weapons but also about military and political power, and about the relationship between human ends and technological means.

The language and the mode of thinking are not neutral containers of infor- *62* mation. They were developed by a specific group of men, trained largely in abstract theoretical mathematics and economics, specifically to make it possible to think rationally about the use of nuclear weapons. That the language is not well suited to do anything but make it possible to think about using nuclear weapons should not be surprising.

Those who find U.S. nuclear policy desperately misguided face a serious *63* quandary. If we refuse to learn the language, we condemn ourselves to being jesters on the sidelines. If we learn and use it, we not only severely limit what we can say but also invite the transformation, the militarization, of our own thinking.

I have no solutions to this dilemma, but I would like to offer a couple of *64* thoughts in an effort to push it a little further—or perhaps even to reformulate its terms. It is important to recognize an assumption implicit in adopting the strategy of learning the language. When we outsiders assume that learning and speaking the language will give us a voice recognized as legitimate and will give us greater political influence, we assume that the language itself actually articulates the criteria and reasoning strategies upon which nuclear weapons development and deployment decisions are made. This is largely an illusion. I suggest that technostrategic discourse functions more as a gloss, as an ideological patina that hides the actual reasons these decisions are made. Rather than informing and shaping decisions, it far more often legitimizes political outcomes that have occurred for utterly different reasons. If this is true, it raises serious questions about the extent of the political returns we might get from using it, and whether they can ever balance out the potential problems and inherent costs.

I believe that those who seek a more just and peaceful world have a dual task *65* before them—a deconstructive project and a reconstructive project that are intimately linked. Deconstruction requires close attention to, and the dismantling of, technostrategic discourse. The dominant voice of militarized masculinity and decontextualized rationality speaks so loudly in our culture that it will remain difficult for any other voices to be heard until that voice loses some of its power to define what we hear and how we name the world.

The reconstructive task is to create compelling alternative visions of possible *66* futures, to recognize and develop alternative conceptions of rationality, to create rich and imaginative alternative voices—diverse voices whose conversations with each other will invent those futures. ◆

1987

Endnotes

1. General William Odom, "C³I and Telecommunications at the Policy Level," incidental paper from a seminar, *Command, Control, Communications and Intelligence*

(Cambridge, Mass.: Harvard University Center for Information Policy Research, Spring 1980), p. 5.

2. See Brian Easlea, *Fathering the Unthinkable: Masculinity, Scientists and the Nuclear Arms Race* (London: Pluto Press, 1983).

3. William L. Laurence, *Dawn over Zero: The Study of the Atomic Bomb* (London: Museum Press, 1974), pp. 198–99.

4. Hisako Matsubara, *Cranes at Dusk* (Garden City, N.Y.: Dial Press, 1985).

5. General Robert Rosenberg, "The Influence of Policy Making on C^{3}I," speaking at the Harvard seminar, *Command, Control, Communications and Intelligence*, p. 59.

6. Charles Krauthammer, "Will Star Wars Kill Arms Control?" *New Republic*, January 21, 1985, pp. 12–16.

Glossary

EMP: electromagnetic pulse.

Explorations

- Have you ever used a specialized language? If so, when conversing with others, did you notice any changes in your attitude towards your subject matter?

- Do you feel that it is necessary to use jargon in your faculty or field of study? What functions do you think such language serves in areas such as medicine, law, psychology, forestry, economics, literary criticism, or computer science?

- Do you agree with Cohn's belief that language shapes thought? Why or why not?

Gary Genosko, born in 1959, is an assistant professor in the Department of Sociology at Lakehead University in Ontario, and the general editor of The Semiotic Review of Books. *He has published on topics such as semiotics, communications, and cultural studies and writes about sports in the alternative Canadian press. A collection of his columns and articles can be found in* Contest: Sports/Politics/Culture *(1999).*

Hockey and Culture

Gary Genosko

From the mainstream to the avant-garde, hockey has served as an all-terrain vehicle for the aesthetic explorations of English and French Canadians. Whether it is Roch Carrier's famous short story "Une abominable feuille d'érable sur la glace" ("The Hockey Sweater") or Serge Morin and Serge Dufaux's 1983 film *De l'autre côté de la glace* (a still from this film featuring a whimsical goaltender appeared on the cover of the art magazine *Parallélogramme* [vol. 19, no. 4 (1994)]), cultural and political allegiances have been registered through hockey's potent symbols. Indeed, for a poignant and sporting expression of Québécois nationalism, one need look no further than Rick Salutin's *Les Canadiens* (1977), in which the election of the Parti Québécois on November 15, 1976, lifts the burden of political expression from the backs of the players onto those of the Péquistes.° Still, I want to break apart this Canadian binarism, without diminishing the importance of artistic accomplishments based upon it, and in so doing, let all the hockey being played across the country and beyond the rink, to be sure, engage a broader understanding of the subjectivities, cultures, and rituals of the game, with tolerance and respect. Discussions of hockey all too often suffer from normopathic tendencies that assume both standard or normative definitions of how to participate, in some measure, in its manifestations and a pathological attachment to such norms. Such assumptions crush plurality and all creative combinations and applications of the game in the expanded field of culture.

1

What Is the Plural of Hockey?

When the New York weekly the *Village Voice* (March 9, 1993) ran excerpts from the libretto of Torontonian Brad Walton's hockey opera *The Loves of Wayne Gretzky*, in which the author stages an affair between the Great One and the Pittsburgh Penguins star Mario Lemieux, the routine subjective formations (masculine, white, nationalistic) that have typified hockey culture were queered. Gay hockey opera may be a fleeting genre, but its implications for making the hockey subject aware of his/her homoerotic investments in the game are substantial. This fictional episode led to further coverage in the *Voice* (August 16, 1994) of

2

Vancouver-based reporter Daniel Gawthrop's articles in *Xtra West* and the *Vancouver Sun* extolling the virtues of Vancouver Canuck star Pavel Bure: "androgynous, fawn-like features ... lips like rose petals, bedroom eyes and fashionably coiffed hair." Coverage of hockey fans in Canadian gay communities, in the *Globe and Mail* and by CBC Television colour-commentator Don Cherry—whose televisual performances during intermissions are tied to shifting constructions of hockey consumers, enabling him, out of one side of his mouth, to refer to foreign players as "sissies" and, out of the other side, to welcome gay fans into the fold—during a *Hockey Night in Canada* broadcast brought the issue of the diverse constituencies of hockey to the fore and further invested the game with a remarkable pluralism.

3   If one were to look for these kinds of openings to new, plural hockey subjectivities in recent books such as Richard Gruneau and David Whitson's *Hockey Night in Canada: Sport, Identities, and Cultural Politics* (1993), one would only be disappointed. The tired, singular, heterosexual hockey masculinity and, in certain importance instances, the breakthroughs, and how they are not so subtly devalued, of young women such as goaltender Manon Rheaume at the professional level are rehearsed by social scientists Gruneau and Whitson. While the authors are better prepared, in methodological terms, to understand labour issues, they lack the expertise to speak convincingly of culture and identity. A few references to cultural theory appear here and there in the text, but these only enable Gruneau and Whitson to conclude that hockey is part of a global, post-modern, capitalist culture, even though it offers "new spaces for identity formation" to so-called new groups, about whom they have nothing to say.

Hockey Night on the Rez

4   Tomson Highway understands well the strange effects a hockey game can have on a community. In his play *Dry Lips Oughta Move to Kapuskasing*, the fictional reserve of Wasaychigan Hill experiences a "revolution" when, in Zachary Jeremiah Keechigeesik's dream, the women of the reserve form a hockey team called the Wasy Wailerettes: The "particular puck" with which they eventually play circulates throughout the play, finding its way at one point into the bosom of Gazelle Nataways, only to be shaken loose later in the action, before the final game sequence (which is really a dream sequence) can unfold. The repetition of the question "Where's the puck?" heralds a nightmare sequence in the first game sequence in which Nanabush (in this instance as the spirit of Black Lady Halked—a parody of the pseudo-native emblem of the Chicago Black Hawks) sits upon a "giant luminescent puck." It needs to be recalled that in the opening sequence of the play it was Nanabush (as the spirit of Gazelle Nataways) who, with a bump of her hip, turned on the television to *Hockey Night in Canada*. Later, when Zachary wakens from his dream to return to the reality of his wife, Hera, and their new baby, he remarks how much the moon looked like a puck

last night (harking back to the vision of Nanabush) and asks his wife whether she has ever thought of playing hockey, to which she replies: "Yea right. That's all I need is a flying puck right in the left tit, neee. . . ." With the hockey game long over and the Smurfs on the television screen before him, all Zachary can do is point out that Smurfs don't play hockey! You won't find Tomson Highway in *Hockey Night in Canada*. And you won't hear about Maple Leaf great George Armstrong, whose mother was part Ojibway and French Canadian and who was subjected to the kind of racism that almost every hockey writer covering the "original six"°—not nations, but NHL teams—considered inevitable: he was nicknamed "Chief." In hockey it is through all-too-common stereotypes, through nicknames, emblems, mascots, and marketing imagery of all kinds, that cultural differences and traditions are rendered benign and slightly ridiculous. Stereotypes of these sorts are the currency of the dominant hockey discourse, and they are also commodities, the exchange of which fosters belonging ("my team") but creates an impoverished cultural identity because it is defined by the marketplace.

Gruneau and Whitson confess that they grew up in the 1950s and 1960s in 5 Toronto. They do not tell us if they remember Armstrong's nickname, nor what it meant to them to have the name of Tim Horton loosen itself from hockey and become just another doughnut shop (well, not just another shop, since Eddie Shack opened his doughnut shop in Caledon, northwest of Toronto, thereby moving the well-established cultural bond between doughnuts and cops into the hockey realm). A further, more general bond needs to be investigated, one that I call "fast ice, fast food." The investments of hockey players, both during their athletic careers and upon retirement, have pointed towards fast food outlets: does anyone remember Bobby Orr pizza? How about John Anderson burgers? I've already mentioned doughnuts. What do you think they serve at Gretzky's? And the food at Don Cherry's Grapevine was not much to write home about. Round, tepid, greasy food sitting in pools of fat, like pucks on melting ice. Anyway, Gruneau and Whitson meticulously avoid analyses of specific products (see my remarks below on Nike). Remarkably, Gruneau and Whitson even avoid the important matter of collecting in hockey circles.

They claim that "'communities' formed around acts of consumption ... are 6 not political communities in any meaningful sense of the word." One can agree that capitalist subjectivity requires reductions and limitations and still understand that the pursuit of hockey through consumption needs to be freed from spectatorship and the caps-and-shirts analyses in order to move into areas of "social identification" that are less obvious but no less political. The very notions of "social" and "public" and "community" have rendered identification problematic. The paths of subject formation and identification are tangled up in doughnuts and memories and the fictional fact that Dry Lips oughta move to the Kap because she fell down, blocking the slap shot of her teammate Hera Keechigeesik and denying her a sure goal.

Heroes at the Bar

7   Labour conflict in sports inevitably leaves sportscasters and reporters in the difficult position of making the transition to the labour and even legal beats. This
is an awkward situation at the best of times, as their airtime and word quotas
prove to be difficult to fill with anything other than platitudes about the "history
and future of the game," the "fans," the "nation," and themselves (the latter is
more important than one might think, since the expression of indignation about
labour strife is a subgenre unto itself in sports reporting that provides the occasion for the reporter to "sound off"). The issue is one of competence for the
sportswriter. The boundaries of sports journalism are confused by labour and legal
issues. The point is that labour issues are perceived by many covering sports to
intrude upon the sporting domain like unwelcome visitors, interlopers, as it were,
trespassing upon well-marked home turf. Perhaps this is why, after several recent
labour disputes and the legal proceedings against influential hockey player agent
Alan Eagleson,° there has been such a deafening silence concerning the recent
legal victory of retired hockey players with regard to a pension fund surplus to
which they had been denied access. Long-retired stars who are still household
names and many also-rans subsist on tiny pensions and in some cases operate
small businesses, like the very visible Eddie Shack, graduating from selling
Christmas trees to selling doughnuts.

8   The main issue concerns the judicial interpretation of a technical legal contract: specifically, a pension plan. A further issue involved the question of when
a trustee could be removed from its position. Law has, of course, its own codes
about which sports reporters are often not competent to comment.

9   Inflation in the early and mid-1980s gave rise to huge surpluses in the National
Hockey League pension plan. This situation was not unique to hockey pensions.
These surpluses arose for nurses, factory workers, and others, and had been
unforeseen when such pension plans were established. Approximately $21 million
of the league's pension surplus was directed by the board of the National Hockey
League Pension Society towards the league to support collective-bargaining
agreements and to provide a "holiday" from pension contributions. (In the pen-
sion/insurance industry "surpluses" arise from "experience rate credits"—which
are like cash, as they can purchase holidays from contributions for employers and
additional pension benefits for employees.) Some cash was also given to the six
original clubs. Seven players challenged the allotment of funds, arguing that,
according to the pension plan, any excess generated by the plan had to be applied
exclusively for the benefit of player participants. They also challenged the ability
of the Pension Society (owing to earlier agreements, there were no longer any
player representatives on its board) to continue as trustee.

10   At trial, the judge found that the original language of the 1947 pension plan
and its regulations, as well as agreements and memorandums between the league
and the players throughout the 1960s and 1970s, required that "all monies" and

"any benefits" be held "for the benefit of the Participant exclusively." The Pension Society was not free to assign the excesses to the benefit of the league. The trial judge did not remove the Pension Society as trustee, finding that its direction of funds was based on legal and actuarial advice that appeared sound.

The National Hockey League Pension Society appealed the part of the trial 11 decision that required it to pay the surplus back into the pension fund. The players appealed the part of the decision that allowed the Pension Society to remain as trustee. The Ontario Court of Appeal upheld the decision of the trial judge on both the surplus issues and the trustee issue. Finally, on July 28, 1994, the Supreme Court of Canada refused to grant the Pension Society leave to appeal.

For lawyers, this case is about reading the language of pension agreements, and 12 it will be used to support the claim of both employees and employers to pension surpluses. If sportscasters were able to comment on the legal matters influencing the business of gaming, hockey fans would be able to appreciate that this case produced a reward for retired hockey players who worked for so little and that the league went all the way to the Supreme Court trying to do these players out of a decent pension.

The player participants are, then, owed their additional benefits, including 13 costs and pre- and post-judgment interest on $21 million. Perhaps this scenario will make it to the stage like John P. Moore's *The Lindros Trial: Extracts from Regina v. Eric Bryan Lindros*, the text of which was culled from the transcripts of the trial concerning an alleged incident of spitting beer at a Whitby, Ontario, nightclub. But this time it won't be played for laughs.

Minor History

The colour barrier was finally broken in the National Hockey League in 1958. 14 This was rather late compared to major league baseball, for example, into which Jackie Robinson had broken 11 years earlier, in 1947. Hockey was, in fact, the last North American sport to have black athletes enter its ranks. On January 18, 1958, left winger William "Willie" O'Ree took to the ice for the Boston Bruins. A native of Fredericton, O'Ree had played semi-pro hockey for the Quebec Aces in 1956–57 before being called up by Boston general manager Lynn Patrick. He played only two games for the Bruins in 1958, scoring no points. He played again for the Bruins in the 1960–61 season, appearing in 43 games and earning 14 points.

During the 1959–60 season, O'Ree was sent to Kingston to play for the 15 Frontenacs, the Bruins' farm team in the Eastern Professional Hockey League. At the beginning of the season, it was noted without any further comment in the local press that O'Ree, one of coach Cal Gardner's "veterans" on what was not a particularly successful team, "was the first Negro to play in the NHL." In 50 games O'Ree tallied a very respectable 46 points. Although Kingston's claim to being the birthplace of hockey is still hotly contested by Montreal, Kingston can claim for itself an important place in black hockey history, and not only in the case of the trail-blazing O'Ree. A smart hockey historian might stir the pot a little by arguing that the Quebec Senior Hockey League of the mid- to late 1940s was richer in black hockey talent, citing the all-black forward line (Manny McIntyre and the Carnegie brothers, Herb and Ossie) iced by Sherbrooke in 1947 as evidence. That the brilliant playmaker and triple-time MVP (most valuable player) of the Quebec league Herb Carnegie wasn't drafted is evidence, as sports reporter James Christie argued in the *Globe and Mail* (April 1997), of the NHL's—specifically Conn Smythe's—backwardness and conservatism. This is further evidence that the myth of the halcyon days of the original six needs to be finally debunked for the sake of a critical understanding of the game's history and politics.

16   O'Ree's career was mostly spent in the minors playing for Western Hockey League teams in Los Angeles and San Diego. Despite the obscurity that such a career path normally entails, he is widely known as "the Jackie Robinson of hockey" and has received civic honours from San Diego, honouring him as the first black in the NHL, and recognition of his historic role from the New Brunswick Sports Hall of Fame in his hometown of Fredericton. Additionally, the NHL's Diversity Task Force sponsored a Willie O'Ree All-Star Weekend in 1991, arranging for disadvantaged youths from the Chicago area to meet the players and develop their skills. In 1998 it was the fortieth anniversary of O'Ree's breakthrough. Despite the impetus of the fiftieth anniversary of Jackie Robinson's accomplishment, which was celebrated in 1997 and generated sufficient interest for sportswriters to turn their attention to the minor histories of the major professional leagues, it is unclear whether or not the same interest will be given to O'Ree's story.

17   Black hockey history has a further Kingston connection, since another left winger, Tony McKegney, arguably the most successful black forward in the NHL to date, played OHA Junior A hockey for several seasons with the Kingston Canadians, from 1974–75 through 1977–78, before he was drafted by the Buffalo Sabres. He was captain of the Canadians and scored prolifically as a junior.

18   McKegney was exposed to the virulent racism of the Old South when John Bassett drafted him in 1977 for the World Hockey Association's Birmingham Bulls. The threats by Bulls' season ticket holders to cancel their subscriptions if the team iced a black hockey player convinced Bassett to release McKegney outright from his contract. McKegney's signing and release took place in less than a week's time. McKegney was not the first black player signed by a WHA team. Already in 1972 Alton White had played for the New York Raiders, making him the first black in the league, followed closely by Bill Riley and Mike Marson of the Washington Capitals, who played together in 1974. McKegney's experience in Kingston had certainly not prepared him for the racism he encountered in Birmingham. When he was captain of the Frontenacs, his picture was regularly in the press and his hockey exploits were followed with intense interest.

I have not mentioned all of the black NHLers (think about goaltenders for a   *19*
moment and who comes to mind?—obviously, the first black goalie, Grant Fuhr,
who broke in with Edmonton in 1981, and then, more obscurely, Eldon "Pokey"
Reddick, who played for the Jets in Winnipeg for a season and a half in the late
1970s), but the list is short. The more general point is that the telling of hockey
history through its minoritarian elements expands the cultural field of the game
and the potential for new subjective formations that are not limited by the standard accounts—either of the history of the game or of the supposedly normal
identities of those who play and watch it in the "Great White North."

Athletes as Pets

In *Landscape of Modern Sport* (1994), John Bale advances the provocative idea   *20*
that "the sportscape or athlete to which we show affection is the athletic analogue of the garden or the pet." Maple Leaf Gardens, he points out, doesn't contain any shrubs, but it nonetheless remains a garden, if only euphemistically, as a
sportscape aestheticized through horticultural and architectural imagery. This
garden is full of "pets" that are disciplined, functionalized, steroid-enhanced, and
exhaustively trained to perform. These athletic pets are dominated so that they
may best receive the affection of the spectators, their owners, and even, in
extreme cases, their parents. Hockey netminders often adopt animal motifs when
having their masks painted; Toronto Maple Leaf goaltender Felix Potvin is nicknamed "The Cat," for example. Just as animals are used in military contexts (in
advertisements for weapons and equipment in professional magazines and the
decoration of airplanes), a single attribute (stealth, strength, speed, agility) is
abstracted from a given species, exaggerated, and reconnected with a new thing
or activity. We should not, however, expect all animal motifs to be used positively. Distortions are commonplace—think of mascots whose imbecility is supposed to provide light entertainment between breaks in the action. But what is
being played for its amusement value is the representation of an animal as a mentally and physically challenged child. This kind of mascot is in a direct genealog-
ical line with cartoon characters whose flaws defined their characters.

The training thesis has been in circulation in less developed forms for some   *21*
time now. In his discussion of the ambiguous healthiness of sports in "Sports
Chatter," from *Travels in Hyperreality* (1986), Umberto Eco maintained that one
of the "first degenerations of the contest" involves "the raising of human beings
dedicated to competition. The athlete is already a being who has hypertrophied
one organ, who turns his body into the seat of an exclusive source of continuous
play. The athlete is a monster." The dedication to "total instrumentalization"
makes the athlete a monster or, better, to follow Bale, a pet. But pets, while often
distorted through selective breeding and the aesthetic determinations of what
features are desirable for a given species on the show circuit, are also dearly loved,
especially when they perform for their caretakers. While Eco recognizes that the

athlete is dedicated to sports training regimes, however brutal and unhealthy they may be, Bale elides the matter of dedication. There has never been a greyhound, to use other words, that was dedicated to being trained to over-race and starve. Many people do, however, submit to exhaustive and repetitive training routines. Neither athletes nor pets submit to the kind of abuse that is common in such training.

22   By changing the register of the analogy ever so slightly, however, we are thrown back to the identification of black slaves and domesticated farm animals and slaveholders as wild predators, poignantly employed in the classic American slave narrative of Frederick Douglass, *Narrative of the Life of Frederick Douglass, An American Slave: Written by Himself* (orig. 1845; Franklin 1989). What this autobiographical narrative reveals is the prevailing nineteenth-century image of the black slave as a healthy animal who, if needs be, will be broken through labour, tortured and/or murdered, and selectively bred. It is not very far from the racism of the Old South to contemporary stereotyped representations of black athletes, that is, from animalization to the petishism of focusing the so-called naturally expressive black body. Indeed, consciousness, as we learned in the case of Canadian sprinter Ben Johnson after the debacle in Seoul, was denied to the black male insofar as he was figured as a "primitive," an animal-machine. Race and, indeed, gender oppression function through animalization, as does economic exploitation. As Patricia Hill Collins puts it in *Black Feminist Thought* (1990), "a race of 'animals' can be treated as such—as victims or pets."

Disciplining Road Hockey

23   The town of Gananoque in eastern Ontario recently tightened up its By-law No. 83–32 concerning the regulation of traffic and parking. In addition to what you might expect to find in a traffic by-law, there is the following subsection on the matter of "Playing on Roadway Prohibited": "1. No person shall play or take part in any game or sport upon a roadway."

24   Sociologists of sport in Germany, such as Lüder Bach (1993), for instance, have shown a keen interest in the study of informal sports activities and facilities. The informality of such sports means the absence of a wide variety of prerequisites: institutional, individual, and organizational. The proliferation of informal sports occurs generally in the context of the absence of legal prohibition, which is only to say that the facilities being put to use allow for a secondary use above and beyond their primary uses. To put this more forcefully, primary uses are decoded for the sake of new practices that remake and remodel rules of participation. For generations of Canadian boys and girls, roadways have been places for playing road or "ball" hockey, skipping, playing hopscotch, or just throwing around any number of balls, Frisbees, and so on. Of course, quiet roads are preferred to busy routes, but no matter, since there is usually a safety protocol in effect: when a car appears, its presence is announced, the action stops, equipment is moved. The

smallest, the weakest, and the least well equipped often get to play, although there is no denying the effects of neighbourhood pecking/picking orders.

Recently, I took up the matter of informal sporting activities in one of my sports   *25* columns for *Borderlines* magazine (Genosko 1996). Existing single-use leisure sites are being put to other uses—ski slopes are being invaded by snowboarders, bicycle paths and lanes are full of in-line skaters, and drained swimming pools are haunted by skateboarders. While the sportscape is changing, it is also being generalized. The sportscape is the city itself. Just as mountain bikers surmounted to some degree certain obstacles of the streetscape, culminating in the kamikaze subculture of the bike courier, skateboarders and in-line skaters are rediscovering these and other obstacles—curbs, stairs, hand and guard rails, gaps, edges, trash bins, parked cars, benches—and turning them into the found tools of street skating. Skateboarding is urban studies on wheels. Surrealists and situationalists may have perfected urban drifting, but boarders and skaters are refinishing the cityscape with street-style high jinks by grinding on rails, pipes, and ledges of all sorts, riding walls, or flying over vehicles after being launched by jump ramps.

In effect, the Gananoque by-law makes road hockey a traffic offence, not to   *26* mention further eroding the rights of pedestrians. Moreover, it pushes informal street sports towards more formal frames, perhaps not all the way to the boarded iceless surface and the ball hockey association, but at least into parking lots and playgrounds, thereby displacing other activities. This legal re-territorialization of the roadway is designed to enable the cops actually to trap and deform the flows of unorganized sporting desire and its fuzzy, neighbourhood aggregates. The push is on towards organization and commercial interests: join the league, pay a fee, buy this equipment, consume! If you won't cooperate: pay a fine!

Down and Out in the NHL

Deprivation has reached a new low. Goaltenders are begging—in transit shelters   *27* and subway stations around Maple Leaf Gardens, as well as on TV spots broadcast during games, not to mention in Nike's promotional booklets distributed in the Gardens to launch an ad campaign.

But these are not just any goalies. These are humiliated, down-and-out goalies   *28* reduced to scratching together a living by panhandling, cab driving, breakdancing, cycle messengering, janitorial work, and hot dog vending.

Sure, they've kept their equipment, 30-odd pounds of rawhide, high-tech plas-   *29* tic, wire-enforced padding, clunky skates, and heavy sticks. But times are tough for these guys because, after all, have you ever tried to pedal a bike or break-dance or drive a cab in full goalie gear? These goalies haven't learned to translate their skills, let alone change their equipment.

We are far, far away from Ken Danby's iconic goalie as a study in concentra-   *30* tion, as well as from the anthropological noodling of the Hockey Hall of Fame, with its wall of "ritually" decorated goalie masks.

31   Why goalies? The advertising campaign is in support of a line of hockey skates promoted by fast-skating and powerful-shooting forwards, all in a sponsorship deal with Nike. In the campaign's narrative, the formidable skills of these forwards have resulted in the dismissal of a series of goalies from their respective teams. The collective story told by these goalies is printed awkwardly on torn pieces of cardboard and held up for passersby to read: "I am a former NHL netminder. Please help. Read my story. Read my other goalie friends' stories. Read why you should never send either Mats Sundin, Jeremy Roenik, or Sergei Federov a birthday card."

32   Beaten goalies with dull skates and broken sticks have a hard time translating their netminding skills: "Will stop pucks for food," the sign of one reads; another offers private goaltending lessons and novel entertainment for parties. The insignias of their former teams represent an NHL merchandizing tie-in. Team logos are copyrighted property, after all. These goalies are licensed failures.

33   There are legions of homeless in New York and Toronto who are living evidence of the effects of Reaganomics° and Ontario's current brand of economic and social Harrisment.° There is supposed to be humour in the incongruity between the outfits and tasks performed by Nike's goalies. This humour is at the expense of the homeless and, especially, of the working poor. As manufacturing jobs leave the country, skills that once made a person employable become as useless as goalie equipment at a hot dog stand. The campaign implies that the fall from grace is a result of a personal shortcoming. No hint of structural matters here—neither a defenceman nor a right-wing ideologue in sight!

34   Tucked away in some of the images—on the hot dog wagon and the janitor's bucket—is the Nike logo. It isn't that the equipment of the working poor has a sponsor; rather, it is that no one can be independent, perhaps work at all, even panhandle, because everything is already owned by someone else, and hence, they must have their fee. Despite itself, Nike brings home the fact that we are living in the hell of a perpetual advertising event. Welcome to Nike Town, where even the soiled cardboard of the homeless bears a logo.

35   Nike's corporate luxury is to turn poverty and homelessness into an advertising icon, courtesy of its ad agencies, in the name of ice skates. No goalie I've ever seen could possibly stop a company like Nike when it is breaking full speed for the net. The market for hockey equipment is beginning to see some serious competition as footwear manufacturers get into the game.

36   This is the season of the goalie in advertising. Molson's, too, has its 12-armed goalie monster in the "I Am Canadian" print campaign. Molson's goalie is not exactly the Hindu deity Krishna in a Maple Leafs uniform, as we have come to expect since the film *Masala* (directed by Srinivas Krishna) rearranged hockey theology, but more like Kali having a bad day. Like Nike, however, Molson's thinks of hockey in terms of a showdown: a forward in alone on a goalie. "Showdown" was a gimmicky individual skills competition developed in the late

1970s to keep hockey fans glued to the screen during breaks between periods, the heaviest times of advertising during broadcasts. Despite Molson's ad copy about the pursuit of goals not involving any "corporate boxes, five dollar hot dogs or million dollar scoreboards"—just the sort of things that a beer company with a vested interest in hockey actually aspires to—it's still just "me versus the monster." No team, no help, and the only one cheering if you beat the goalie is yourself. "I Am Canadian" is, in the advertising life, another way of saying that not even you are your own, anymore.

The Temple of Hockey

The floor plan of the Hockey Hall of Fame reveals a great deal about the meta-   *37* physics and ethics underwriting the current representations of the game. Essentially, the Hall sprawls along the east end of the concourse level of BCE Place, in the bowels of Toronto's financial district. It is an extension of the underground shopping concourse; in fact, the final stop on the official self-guided walk of the Hall (presented by John Armstrong in the Hockey Hall of Fame magazine) is a souvenir shop called the Spirit of Hockey. This shop cannot be avoided because it is also the Hall's exit. Commerce is the spirit of hockey, and its wares crystallize this spirit better, we are told, than "great memories" of the Hall and hockey itself.

The Hall presents one wave after another of history, internationalism, frag-   *38* ments of empire, family affairs, interactivity, and video-induced passivity in the name of sponsorships; someone unfamiliar with the game might be fooled into thinking that this is a temple devoted to the *Toronto Sun*, Ford, Esso, Blockbuster Video, Speedy Muffler, Molson's, TSN, Coca-Cola, and so forth. Commercial history is not only well provided for but intimately tied to the history of the game itself. Commercial ephemera originally tied to specific products—plastic buttons and instant desserts, coupons and gasoline, cards and bubble gum—become collectibles in heavily overcoded micro-markets but also serve as markers of historical phases (from the original six to expansion, the very idea representing the expansion of capital with the discovery of a wider American market and concomitant merchandising opportunities). Indeed, involvement in some aspect of the game can be demonstrated through souvenirs and, even better, through the ever-expanding universe of merchandise. The "family zone" figures the nuclear family as a consumption machine designed in the 1950s but built to last or at least accrue value as its own material history is translated into the obscure codes uttered by collectors in the throes of acquiring yet another piece of the puzzle. This vulgar capitalist ethics is but a warm-up to weightier justifications.

The hustle and bustle of the concourse gives way to the only part of the Hall   *39* at street level. The ascent to the Bell Great Hall is billed as the highlight of any visit. The Great Hall provides a direct line to the transcendental unity of hockey. It is the "core sanctuary of hockey's proud history" articulated by the presence of

Lord Stanley's Cup, the focal point of the room, bathed in the kaleidoscopic light of the stained glass of the 45-foot-high dome. This rococo sanctuary was the head office of the Bank of Montreal until 1949, and a branch until 1982, later to be rescued from disuse when the Hall opened in 1993. The bank vault is still in use, housing the original silver cup donated by Lord Stanley in 1893. Hockey and banking history bleed together in a glorious vision of nation and culture building. The Great Hall is a trophy room commemorating great hockey men (inducted members of the Hockey Hall of Fame), a male preserve to be sure, of the Great White North. The architecture of banking still dominates the skyline of Toronto, just as it shaped the streetscape of the city in the nineteenth century. What would be more appropriate than an MBANX commercial featuring Stompin' Tom's "The Hockey Song"? This makes the symbolic economy of hockey obvious to everyone, even to so-called hockey purists sunk in their anti-labour meditations on the creation of the Lord. The Great Hall is described as a "quiet place in which to reflect on the richness of our past." Perhaps "the riches of the past" would have streamlined the message. It is a place of pilgrimage, with the cup itself playing the role of sacred relic. It is the sort of thing upon which one is compelled to lay hands. There are no annoying busy signals here. The connection is always clear as the cup soars towards the heavens, held aloft by the great heights of the city's towers of finance. Inspired by the French translation of Hockey Hall of Fame as "Le Temple de Renommée du Hockey," I said a silent prayer for the Maple Leafs, since only a god can save them now. "Oh Lordie," as Molson Canadian would have us utter. ◆

1999

References

Bach, Lüder. "Sports without Facilities: The Use of Urban Spaces by Informal Sports." *International Review for Sociology of Sport* 28 (1993): 281–96.

Bale, John. *Landscapes of Modern Sport*. London: Leicester University Press, 1994.

Bathgate et al v. National Hockey League Pension Society et al. (1993) 11 *Ontario Reports* (3d): 449ff.

Collins, Patricia Hill. *Black Feminist Thought*. Boston: Unwin Hyman, 1990.

Eco, Umberto. *Travels in Hyperreality*. San Diego: Harcourt Brace Jovanovich, 1986.

Franklin, H. Bruce. *Prison Literature in America*. New York: Oxford University Press, 1989.

Gananoque, Town of. By-law No. 83–32: Being a by-law to regulate traffic and parking on highways, Subsection 64.

Gawthrop, Daniel. "Desperately Seeking Pavel." *Xtra West* 6 (5 November 1993).

Genosko, Gary. "What Is the Plural of Hockey?" *Fuse* 18, no. 4 (1995): 46–47.

——. "Hell on Wheels." *Borderlines* 41 (1996): 40–42.

——. "Kingston's Links to Black Hockey History." *Kingston Whig-Standard*, 23 April 1997.

Grierson, Bruce. "Hockey Nike in Canada." *Saturday Night*, April 1997: 64–73.

Gruneau, Richard, and David Whitson. *Hockey Night in Canada: Sport, Identities, and Cultural Politics*. Toronto: Garamond Press, 1993.

Highway, Tomson. *Dry Lips Oughta Move to Kapuskasing*. Saskatoon: Fifth House, 1989.

Salutin, Rick. *Les Canadiens*. Vancouver: Talon Books, 1977.

Glossary

Péquistes: members of the Parti Québécois (PQ-ist, pronounced pay keest').

"original six": the NHL's six original teams: the Boston Bruins, New York Rangers, Chicago Black Hawks, Detroit Red Wings, Toronto Maple Leafs, and Montreal Canadiens.

Alan Eagleson: (b. 1933) a Toronto lawyer, an agent, and the first executive director of the NHL's Players' Association (1967–1990). Eagleson pleaded guilty to charges in 1994 of racketeering and defrauding the NHL Players' Association; he served six months, and in 1998 resigned from the Hockey Hall of Fame.

Reaganomics, Harrisment: slang terms used to describe policies and politics developed by the Reagan government in the United States, and by former premier Mike Harris in Ontario.

Explorations

- Are you a devoted fan, a hockey-hater, or somewhere in between? To what extent does hockey define your sense of Canadian identity?

- Do you agree with Genosko's claim that "Discussions of hockey all too often suffer from normopathic tendencies"? Can you think of times when these norms have been challenged? What was your reaction?

Thomas King, who is of Cherokee, Greek, and German descent, was born in Alberta in 1943. He received his Ph.D. in English literature at the University of Utah and chaired the University of Minnesota's American Indian Studies program. His publications include an anthology of Native writing, All My Relations, *three novels—*Medicine River; Green Grass, Running Water; *and* Truth and Bright Water—*and a collection of short stories,* One Good Story, That One. *He has also written books for children, and a popular CBC radio series,* The Dead Dog Café Comedy Hour. *He published his most recent work,* Dreadful Water Shows Up, *under the pseudonym Hartley Goodweather. King's stories, gently humorous, often focus on the conflation of Western and Native myths and cultures. King is currently a professor of creative writing at the University of Guelph.*

How I Spent My Summer Vacation: History, Story, and the Cant of Authenticity

Thomas King

1   According to the 1991 Neiman Marcus Christmas catalog, you can buy a custom carved totem pole or a painting by Rosie the Elephant. These two advertisements did not sit on opposing pages, although they should for they form a wonderful cultural diptych; the poles are carved by an authentic Native carver, and the paintings are rendered by an authentic elephant.

2   This has little to do with my essay, which is not available in the catalog, but it did suggest certain things to me about the power of advertising, the value of authenticity, and the need for essential Truths. And it reminded me of my summer vacation.

3   Last summer, I was at the Sun Dance° on the Blood reserve° in southern Alberta. Old friends had invited me up. I had never been to a Sun Dance before. When I told several of my neighbours in St. Paul where I was going, their eyes slowly glazed over and I imagined them conjuring up images of Catlin's romantically rendered Indians hanging about by their pectorals from poles.

4   In all honesty, I was not sure what to expect myself, but I was reasonably sure that I would have better luck seeing this kind of white-male eroticism at the theatre than I would on the Alberta prairies.

5   As it turned out, I was right. If my neighbours had gone with me that July, they probably would have been disappointed for the major activities at the Sun Dance involved an incessant coming and going: go to the store to get bread; take the kids in for a doctor's appointment; grab another load of wood; run to town for more ice; drive the bags of garbage to the dumpster in Standoff; duck home and take a shower.

And constant preparations. Each lodge had coffee. Food was everywhere. Not   6
a conspicuous show of food, just its constant presence—a pot of stew, soup, a picnic ham, bread, apples and bananas. And all around, elders, adults, and children
were on the move, circling the camp, visiting. You can sit in one lodge all day,
and, in between the preparations, and the dances, you will be able to meet and
greet many of the people in the camp, for the Sun Dance is a consummate social
ceremony as well as a religious one, and that is the way it should be. It is also an
occasion for storytelling.

I was sitting in my friend's lodge enjoying yet another cup of coffee, minding   7
my own business, when the flap of the teepee was pulled to one side and two elderly women and a younger man entered. We greeted each other; the women settled themselves on their side of the lodge and the man and I settled ourselves on
our side. For a while, no one said a word.

Finally, one of the women, a woman named Bella, leaned forward, looked at   8
me, looked at the ground, and looked back at me.

"I hear you're a historian," she said.   9

I quickly told her it wasn't true, that I was a writer, a novelist, a storyteller. But   10
she waved me off.

"Same thing," she said, and she began to tell this story.   11

There was a young man who came to the reserve to talk to elders. He was from   12
a university (Bella didn't say where) but when she said the word university, she
slowed down and stretched out each syllable as if she were pulling on an elastic
and the man sitting next to me started to laugh as if he had just heard an excellent joke. Bella waited until he stopped and then she continued.

The man, Bella explained, wanted to hear old stories, stories from back in the   13
olden days, stories about how Indians used to live. So she told him about how
death came into the world, how Old Man and Old Woman had argued over
whether human beings should live forever or whether they should die. Old Man
thought they should live. Old Woman thought they should die.

So they made a wager, a bet. Old Man got a buffalo chip and they agreed that   14
if they threw the chip in the river and it sank, then human beings would live forever. If it floated, the human beings must die.

There are no surprises here. The chip floated, and, as Bella explained to the   15
man, that was how death came into the world.

At this point in her story, Bella told me that the young man, all eager and full   16
of sound, jumped in and said that whites had the same sort of story. And before
anyone could stop him, he began a recitation of Genesis, how everything was
perfect in the garden, how there was no death, how Eve found the apple, how
she ate the apple, how she seduced Adam, how Adam and Eve acquired knowledge, and how, from then on, things got gloomy. He concluded by noting what
a coincidence it was that women, in both cases, were responsible for these dis-
asters.

17   After he finished, the elders thanked him for his remarks and the man from the university thanked the elders and everyone went their own way.

18   When Bella finished telling this story, she settled back in her chair and drank some coffee. Then she looked right at me, and she said, "And that's why he never heard the rest of the story."

19   The first thing that flashed through my mind was Paul Harvey. The second was to keep my mouth shut, for I understood that attached to the story Bella had just told was a caution to mind my manners and not to interrupt as the other man had done.

20   So I shut up, and I waited. Bella finished her coffee and had another cup. There was some soup in the pot and that was passed around with bread and more coffee.

21   Then Bella said, "So you see Old Woman was right. If there had been no death, there would have been so many people, the world would have sunk into the ocean. Just look at it now! Old Woman understood the need for balance."

22   I think I started to smile, but Bella cut me off quickly. "And that Eve woman was right, too," she said. "No point in being stupid all your life."

23   We sat in the lodge for a long time and talked about family and children, the price of gas, the weather, Martin's new van, Dixie's cellular telephone, and Thelma's new boyfriend from Calgary.

24   Finally, the three of them got up to leave and move to the next lodge.

25   "You work at a university just like that young man?" Bella asked me.

26   I told her that I did.

27   "It's real frustrating, you know, to have to keep telling that story. Maybe you can find that young man and tell him he should get it right.

28   "Tell him," she continued, "to remember that Eve woman of his and to use the brains she gave him."

29   I followed Bella outside. The rains had been heavier than usual that July and the prairie grass was tall. Here and there in the distance, sections of canola were in full bloom, bright gold against the deeper greens and blues, and from the camp on the Belly Buttes, you could see the sky in all directions and watch the land roll into the mountains.

30   "You write stories?" Bella asked me.

31   "Yes, I do."

32   "About us Indians?"

33   "Most of the time."

34   She smiled and shook her head. "You're kinda young to be a historian."

35   I had to leave that day to go down into eastern Oregon for a writers' conference and all the way down, I chewed on what Bella had suggested about story and history. I was, of course, able to dismiss her contention that story and history were the same, knowing that she had never studied history, knowing that she was not aware of the fine distinctions that separated the two. Of course, history *was* a

story, and, as with all stories, it carried with it certain biases that proceeded from culture, language, race, religion, class, gender. It was burdened with the demands of nationalism, subject to the vagaries of scholarship, and wrapped up in the myth of literacy. Nonetheless, as one of my professors told me, history dealt with a series of facts rather than fictions, and, while the interpretations of those facts will vary, these small truths would remain.

I was comforted by that. I am not sure why, but I was.   *36*

When I finished the conference at Lake Wallowa, I headed back to the Sun   *37* Dance. I wanted to get there in time to see the men dance. But the first thing I did was to look up Bella. I found her sitting in a folding chair outside one of the lodges enjoying the panorama of the prairies and the Rockies.

"You again!" she said.   *38*

She motioned me to sit down beside her and I did. I did not know what to   *39* say or how to start. I wanted to tell her about history and story, but instead, we sat there and watched Chief Mountain turn blue and then purple as the light deepened.

"You know," Bella said, "there was this guy about your age came out to visit us.   *40* He was from Ottawa. Reporter. Wanted to know what we thought about Meech Lake, so Florence told him about how Coyote won a bet with Old Woman and how death came into the world. You know the story?"

I said I thought she had told me a story like that several days ago.   *41*

But did I remember it, she wanted to know. Could I tell it, again?   *42*

I made the mistake of saying that I thought I could. Bella settled into the chair,   *43* waved at the mosquitoes, put her hands in her lap, and closed her eyes.

I thought she was going to sleep. But she wasn't.   *44*

"You waiting for winter?"   *45*

So I began to tell the story, and I thought I did a pretty good job. When I fin-   *46* ished, I settled in the grass, put my hands in my lap, and closed my eyes. As I sat there, I could hear Bella shifting her weight in the chair.

"Okay," said Bella. "There was this Mormon guy from Cardston came to visit   *47* us. Wilma brought him by. He was an old guy, had a bad leg, you know. He said he was collecting oral history for the church. So Francis told him about how Duck and Buffalo had a bet and how Duck won the bet and how death came into the world."

And Bella proceeded to tell the story once again. It was the same basic tale,   *48* but each time she told it, some of the facts changed. First it was Old Man and Old Woman who had made the bet. Then it was Old Woman and Coyote. Duck and Buffalo got into the act in a third telling. Sometimes it was a rock that was supposed to float. Once the bet involved a feather. The man from a universi-ty/Ottawa/Cardston changed, too. First he was young, then middle-aged, and finally, old. The only thing that remained truly constant was that death came to the world.

49   "That's history," Bella told me when she had finished the fourth telling of the story. "You got any questions?"

50   I was dying to tell Bella that this wasn't history at all, that this was...well...myth. But I didn't get a chance.

51   "Some of those white people call this story myth because they figure it never happened. Is that what you're thinking?"

52   I was in full retreat by now and was willing to do or say anything to get out of the way.

53   "Maybe it's a little of both," I said.

54   "You think that, do you?"

55   "Well, for instance," I said, "Stanley Fish suggests that there are interpretative communities composed of groups of people who share commonalities, who agreed on how things such as history and myth are interpreted, how the universe is ordered."

56   "That so?" said Bella.

57   "And Adrienne Rich talks about the politics of location and how your subject position, your gender, race, class all determine what you see and how you interpret what you see."

58   "Okay," Bella said with a sigh. "There were these two guys from France came to visit us. They wanted to hear old stories, so Latisha told them about Old Man and Old Woman and how death came to the world."

59   It was almost dark when I left Bella.

60   I do not know exactly what Bella was trying to tell me about history and story. Indeed, I do not know if she was trying to tell me anything at all. Perhaps, as she said, she just wanted to make sure I got the story straight.

61   But I do not believe this. The elements of her story were too well placed. The conflict too cleverly organized. The resolution too pointed and axiomatic. I even suspect that the frame of the story—the man coming to hear a story—is apocryphal. But curiously, while the supporting facts changed in each telling of the story, the essential relationships—the relationship of humans to death and the relationship of balance to chaos—remained intact. Bella had begun here and crafted a set of facts to support these relationships, to create a story, to create a history.

62   Then, too, the language itself shifted as ceremony gave way to instruction. Metaphor, imagery, the rhythmic and repetitive syntaxes, the rhetorical interrogatories gave way to more didactic structures that marched lockstep from beginning to end, from premise to conclusion. These shape changes were not a product of frustration, the having to tell a story again and again, making it progressively simpler and simpler, but rather the concern with purpose, allowing Bella, as she told one version all full of colour and motion, to declare that this was story, and as she told another version all full of instance and example, to insist that this was history.

Of course, we know we cannot trust authorial intent, and you should be rightly   *63*
appalled that I bring it up at all.

Yet in considering what Bella told me and what I know, I am struck by how   *64*
thin the line between history and story is, resting as it appears to do on a single
question, a single concern—did it happen/is it authentic/can it be verified/is it
real—and on the assumption of the preeminence of literacy within non-Native
culture. Patricia Limerick, in her fine critical study of the West, *The Legacy of
Conquest*, questions this very assumption. Speaking specifically about history and
anthropology and the West, Limerick says that "human differences that hinged
on literacy assumed an undeserved significance." This significance that Limerick
speaks of is, I believe (and I think Limerick would agree), not merely a function
of the ability to read but rather the blind belief in the efficacy of the written
word.

As an example, let's take my own trip to Alberta. When I am famous, some   *65*
bright graduate student in search of a thesis or an assistant professor in search of
tenure might consider a history of my life as a writer. Chapter five might start out
with several paragraphs that recount my journey in July of 1991 to the Sun
Dance in southern Alberta where I met with a Blood woman named Bella; how
over a period of days, with a short break during which I went to eastern Oregon
to attend a writers' conference, Bella and I discussed the relationship of history
to story and how that discussion inspired a most interesting paper that I later
gave at the American Studies Coffee Hour in November of 1991.

Ah, history. Ah, story. What if I never went to the Sun Dance? What if I made   *66*
all this up? What if I went to the Sun Dance, but Bella is a fiction? What if I went
to the Sun Dance and talked to a woman named Bella, but I completely made up
our conversation on history and story. What if I went to the Sun Dance, met a
woman named Bella, had a conversation such as I describe, and could produce
trustworthy witnesses to swear that my account of that conversation is accurate?

Perhaps what really happened was that someone, say a historian, said some-   *67*
thing in passing about history that set me thinking and that during my stay at the
Sun Dance and talking with some of the people and listening to the stories they
told, I decided to use that particular setting as a backdrop to give my personal
thoughts and remarks an authentic context.

We like our history to be authentic. We like our facts to be truthful. We are   *68*
suspicious of ambiguity, uneasy with metaphor. We are not concerned with essential relationships. We want cultural guarantees, solid currencies that we can take
to the bank.

I tried to explain this to Bella with one example that I knew would carry the   *69*
day. As we were sitting there on the Alberta prairies, I turned to the east and said
in my best matter-of-fact voice, "It's the facts that separate history from story. For
instance," I droned on, "the sun rises every day in the east."

Bella half-turned, smiled, and nodded her head. "Has so far," she said.   *70*

71   So that is it. Bella, if she exists, believes that history and story are the same. She sees no boundaries, no borders, between what she knows and what she can imagine. Everything is story, and all the stories are true. Whereas I am forced to try to separate them. To put fancy in one pile, facts in another, so the two will not get mixed up. By training (and I am speaking here of culture and society rather than just the university) I go forth into the world, not to question the presence of God in the universe, nor to confront the mysteries of birth and death, nor to consider the complexities of being, but simply to ascertain what is authentic and what is not.

72   Harry Truman and Paul Revere for instance.

73   Harry Truman, when he was President, ordered the military to drop two atomic bombs on Japan, one on Hiroshima and one on Nagasaki. We can read about it. We can go to Hiroshima and see the monument. We can see the aftermath of the destruction.

74   Paul Revere, when he was a young silversmith in Boston, rode through the city streets to alert the citizenry to the impending British invasion. We can read about it. We can go to Boston and see the Old North Church. We can walk the path he took that fateful night, and follow the drama in Longfellow's poem.

75   Well, so much for literacy.

76   Thank God, then, for Neiman Marcus and the Christmas catalog and the certificates of authenticity they provide. While questions of history and story may continue to plague me, I can tell you I sleep easier knowing that I own a painting by a real elephant, and that the totem pole in my back yard was not chainsawed into existence by an out-of-work lumberjack. Bella probably wouldn't care, but then she wouldn't care that Paul Revere never made his ride, either.

77   All levity aside, I want to assure you that this essay is, in the best sense of the word, authentic. In a world which believes that wisdom is, in the main, a matter of keeping facts and fictions straight, it's the least I can do. ◆

1997

Glossary

Sun Dance: a yearly summer dance common to such Plains and Plateau tribes as the Lakota, Dakota, Cheyenne, Kiowa, and Blackfoot that lasts three to four days; it has central religious significance for the spiritual health and strength of the participants and their families.

Blood Reserve: located in southwestern Alberta, near the United States border, this is the largest Native reserve in Canada, numbering more than 7000 members of the Blood Tribe of the Blackfoot Nation.

Explorations

- As a student, have you been taught to make a clear distinction between history and story, fact and fiction? If so, have you ever questioned this distinction?

- What if King never went to the Sun Dance or never talked to a woman named Bella? Would you view his writing as being less authentic? Why or why not?

Daphne Marlatt was born in Melbourne, Australia, in 1942 and spent the early part of her childhood in Malaysia before immigrating to Vancouver, British Columbia, in 1951. A pioneering experimental lesbian-feminist poet and novelist, she is the author of more than a dozen books crossing from non-fiction to fiction prose and poetry. Her non-fiction works are Steveston Recollected: A Japanese-Canadian History *(1975) and* Opening Doors: Vancouver's East End *(1980), and she has written many works of fiction, including* Ana Historic *(1988) and* Taken *(1996).*

Difference (em)bracing

Daphne Marlatt

In Not the Same Person

1   What is it makes some words essential, relevant to one woman writer and irrelevant to another? and can we communicate then? what is communication but a sharing of our visions of what is essential? And by that i don't mean to refer to essence but to necessity, that which motivates us as writers. Sometimes in reading as in writing the shift from inessential to essential occurs in the same person (and is she, are you then the same?)—that certain space where words turn from abstraction and, not uncertainty exactly, but a kind of unspecificity where they have existed somewhere out there as objects in flight (UFO's even) in the world you read or listen in on, and then in a flash wing in to the core of your being and you recognize all that they stand for and that you have a stake in them, a share as speaker / writer / reader / listener, all of you there in that active complex. This is very different from being taken up by aliens, since it involves your own assertion of what is meaningful to you.

2   The difference writing makes where, caught in the act so to speak, you ask yourself questions and discover the words you can stand by are words that stand that ground you have a share in. Feminist, for instance, subject, mother, lesbian—words i recognize and have a stake in. They set up currents of meaning that establish this you i also am (not third person, as in totally other, and not quite the same as me). 'You' is a conduit, a light beam to larger possibility, so large it fringes on the other without setting her apart from me. Because we speak about 'her' in the third person, 'she' is where exclusion takes place. 'Feminist,' 'lesbian' take on other meanings then, even other qualities as words—they suddenly limit, they suddenly objectify. But in the first or second person i see who you are, feminist, lesbian: your historicity, your meaning-potential is what i grow into.

3   So i recognize certain words that constitute my body (not exclusive of the psychic terrain my body stands in)—the body of my writing. As any of us does over

time. 'Getting to know you' words out there—maybe as other as the King of Siam—written from a white colonial point of view.° Those dated words which excited my fifteen-year-old imagination under cloudy skies backlit by the foots and spots of Theatre Under the Stars in Stanley Park, still run through my forty-seven year old mind. But now i suspect a hidden imperialism in them: making the other the same and therefore plausible, i.e., plausibly me. This script lies at the heart of fiction and is not what i'm trying to get at, which is the plausible implausibility of living difference as both other *and* not-other. Another besides me.

As Virginia Woolf has written of 'the sixty or seventy times which beat simul-   4 taneously in every normal human system' and how rarely we manage to synchronize them, or again of 'the perfect rag-bag of odds and ends within us—a piece of a policeman's trousers lying cheek by jowl with Queen Alexandra's wedding veil'[1] (this is a distinctly English cultural rag-bag). Or as Hélène Cixous has written of writing as 'precisely working (in) the in-between, inspecting the process of the same and of the other without which nothing can live, undoing the work of death—to admit this is first to want the two, as well as both...'[2] Women keep trying to write it, what we sense which language resists, structured as it is on the basis of difference as black + (read *or*) white, men or women, straight or gay, absolute difference which cannot bear the weight of both / and.

It is poetry which pushes the limits of this system, speaks in corresponding dif-   5 ferences (differences which speak to each other). Not the same as 'same difference,' that childhood taunt of dismissal which collapsed difference into an identical same. How to find the words that will stand the corresponding differences of this complexity we glimpse ourselves living, despite the monocultural stereotypes that delude us into thinking difference means an opposition, the utterly singular on one side of a great divide.

Difference is where the words turn depending on who reads them and how we   6 bring who we are to that reading. When we each bring our differences into that reading, the multiple nature of the real begins to be heard.

Arriving at Shared Ground Through Difference

It wasn't sharing but difference in a multiplicity of ways i felt first as a child in   7 Malaya where i was taught the King's (it was then) English, to mind my P's & Q's, to behave and speak 'properly,' when all the while i was surrounded by other languages that were not proper at all for a white colonial child, but which nevertheless i longed to understand, filled as they were with laughter, jokes, calls, exclamations, comfort, humming. Sometimes rocked to sleep, sometimes teased or scolded, sometimes ignored by the sounds of Cantonese, Malay, Thai, i stood on the fringe and longed to know what the stories were that produced such laughter, such shakings of the head. When my Amahs spoke only English, they knew and i knew it was not the same, it meant we had to be 'proper.' O the complexities of the power dynamic between colonial children and their mother-

substitutes, these women who had given up the possibility of families for themselves but who nevertheless led other lives, barely heard between the lines proper
to their servant roles, and who illicitly imparted some of that culture, some of
that life-experience to their Mem's° children. I grew up loving the emotive sound
of women's voices and distrustful of a system that dismissed women's experience
in general, and some women's more than others', depending on the colour of
their skin and the language(s) they spoke—and many spoke more than the single-
minded ruling one.

8   Then there was my mother's mother tongue: English English with its many
intensifiers, its emphatic sentence pitches, its ringing tones of boarding-school
elocution lessons. Learning to speak properly—'Don't drawl like that, it sounds
so dreadfully American. Why can't you pronounce the ends of your words?' The
trouble was i had become embarrassed by the language i spoke which branded me
as both excessive (those intensifiers) and excessively polite in Canadian school-
yards. My speech sounded exaggerated: 'Wha'd ya mean "awfully sorry" You're
not awful are you?' It sounded pretentious: 'listen, *nobody* walks on the *grawss*.'
At first 'wanna,' and 'movies' and 'you guys' sounded funny in my mouth, as if i
were trying to speak counterfeit words. But imitation cut both ways: there was
now a whole new level of my own vocabulary, words that sounded false on the
street: cinema, rubbish, being sent to Coventry,° not to mention that give-away,
Mummy, a world away from Mom. And so i engaged in long battles with my
mother, each of us trying to correct the other, she correcting for purity of origin,
while i corrected for common usage—each of us with different versions of 'the
real thing.' The struggle over reality is a deadly one that cuts to the root of being.
Words were always taken seriously in my house because they were the weapons
of that struggle. But a woman's sense of herself in the language she speaks can
only be denied so long before it transforms into a darker (side of the moon), a
more insistent ir-reality, not *un*real because its effects are felt so devastatingly in
its subject and those around her. Her words, her very style of speaking derided by
her own children, her colonial manners and English boarding-school mores dismissed as inappropriate by Canadianized daughters who denied any vestige of
them in their own behaviour and speech, she withdrew into chronic depression
and hypochondria. 'Unbalanced.' 'Loony.' But to deny: to completely say no to.
A powerful mechanism. A form of colonialism at work within the family.

9   By the time I entered the University of British Columbia in the first year of the
sixties, Canadian was something i had mastered—and i use that word deliberately.
As a student of literature, almost all my literary models, quite literally 'the masters'
of English (or American—at that time we didn't study Canadian) literature were
men. As a young writer, the contemporary poetry other writers pointed me to was
largely written by men. My own 'masters' (in that sense of mentors) were Charles
Olson, Robert Duncan, Robert Creeley and their masters, William Carlos
Williams, Ezra Pound, Louis Zukofsky. Somehow reading 'the poet, he' to include

me, i trained myself in that poetic, the injunctions to get rid of the lyric ego, not
to 'sprawl' in loose description or emotion ungrounded in image, to pay strict
attention to the conjoined movement of body (breath) and mind in the movement of the line, though it didn't occur to me then to wonder whether my somewhat battered female ego was anything like a man's, or whether my woman's body
had different rhythms from his, or whether my female experience might not give
me an alternate 'stance' in the world (one that wasn't so much 'in' as both in &
outside of a male-dominated politic & economy).

But there were cracks, fissures that led me to another writing world. Through   10
Robert Duncan's prose poems and Charles Olson's essays i remembered my original delight in the extendable and finely balanced nature of the sentence
ungoverned by line breaks (a different sort of sprawl). Duncan led me to Gertrude
Stein and her play with emphasis, with difference in repetition, with the passionate nature of the loopy speaking sentence, peculiarly a woman's in her work.
Duncan led me to H.D. too, another sort of passion, the passion of vision, of
interwoven imageries lifted live from a wealth of spiritual traditions, the H.D. of
her long poems and now the H.D. of her novels documenting the inner struggles
of a woman living very much in her time.

Impossible to list here all the reading paths (as divergent as Anaïs Nin, Maxine   11
Hong Kingston, Phyllis Webb, Marguerite Duras, Zora Neale Hurston, Nicole
Brossard among others) which led me to the hidden and astonishingly varied tradition of women's writing—the other side of that man-in-the-moon face polished
and presented to us as the shining side of 'Contemporary Literature' when i was
in school. The dark side, a wonderful colloquy of women's voices writing about
the 'trivial,' taboo and tacit: solitude verging on madness, women's social roles
and loss of self, excessive passion, a whole female erotic, daily doubts that give
the lie to philosophic certainties, companionship with animals and trees,
women's companionship despite double standards in (and within) sex and race,
double standards everywhere and women speaking of and writing on that double
edge, in touch with one another's difficult balance there. And that was the
excitement, the lifting of a horizon, that here was an ongoing dialogue where
women were central, not marginal, where women were delighting in writing the
complex i (fem.), not trying to write like 'the poet, he' in all his singular authority.

The Singularly Complex

This dialogue that our writing enters is a singularly (as in deviating from the   12
norm) complex one because it includes, it must include, voices from so many
fringes, not just that fringe, women (translated as white, middle-class, heterosexual, Anglo-Canadian/American) that has been gradually getting so legiti-
mated it would seem to be moving into centre. Becoming aware of this dialogue
on the (many) fringes, listening to other women's words/realities, is to engage in
a delicate balance between recognition of difference and recognition of shared

ground. The balance between i and we, neither capitalized nor capitalizing on the other.

13   To begin with, to write I, to assume our own centrality as ground, goes against all our gender-conditioning and is a frightening first step in autobiography and journal-writing. We do it because we must. But when we write I we discover that this singular column with its pedestal and cap, this authorized capital letter, far from being monolithically singular is full of holes a wind blows through, whispering contradictory images, echoing others' words. I am not myself, or we are not myself, *or* each of us is our selves in the plural, struggling to speak the difference we sense through rigid assumptions of sameness and identity in the language we have inherited.

14   I becomes a kind of shorthand for a complex of such fractured identity, with a corresponding urge to write we to include others. But at the same time this i, fraught with inner difference, cannot simply graph those inner differences onto others. A recognition of real differences of life-experience, privilege and accessibility to the centre is essential here. Without that, i simply co-opt others' experiences in attempting to make them mine in the writing, in attempting to make my we cover their i.

15   There are many we's which any i might feel included in, just as there are many we's which any i might feel excluded from, colour, class and sexual orientation being the broadest of distinctions/groupings. We cross over many borderlines, we inhabit many borderlands (as Gloria Anzaldúa°3 and Joy Kogawa°4 have both recently attested to). The complex of these for each one of us is not the same as for any other. This makes the differences in our language and in our sense of our selves crucial. It makes attention to difference in the work of others essential, and collaboration rather than assimilation an essential writing practice. Only then can we learn not to dominate one another with our claims to reality. ◆

1990

Endnotes

[With thanks to Nicole Brossard, Betsy Warland, Joy Kogawa and Lee Maracle for their analyses.]

1.   Virginia Woolf, *Orlando* (London: Granada, 1977), p. 191, p. 49.

2.   Hélène Cixous, 'The Laugh of the Medusa' in *New French Feminisms*, eds. Elaine Marks and Isabelle de Courtivron (New York: Schocken, 1981), p. 254.

3.   At the Third International Feminist Book Fair, Montreal, June 1988.

4.   At Telling It: Women and Language Across Cultures, Simon Fraser University Downtown, November 1988.

Glossary

white colonial point of view: a legacy of European imperialism, this world view often deems racial and ethnic minorities socially "inferior" and culturally "other."

Mem: abbreviation of memsahib, an Anglo-Indian term referring to a European married woman, or one who acts like a European woman.

sent to Coventry: a British phrase that means "to be shunned or ignored." Coventry is a city in England that housed prisoners during the British Civil War. The people of Coventry shunned the prisoners, and thus the phrase "being sent to Coventry" was born.

Gloria Anzaldúa: a chicana (Mexican-American) lesbian feminist writer and cultural theorist whose works include the book *Borderlands/La Frontera: The New Mestiza* (1987), which combines Spanish and English poetry and prose.

Joy Kogawa: a second-generation Japanese-Canadian who is known for her novels, poetry, and essays. Her novel *Obasan* focuses on Japanese-Canadians and the injustices they experienced during and after World War II.

Explorations

- How do different pronouns such as "I," "you," "she," and "we" and different words such as "feminist," "mother," and "lesbian" affect your attitude towards other people's writing?

- How do personal differences such as gender, sexual orientation, class, age, race, and ethnicity affect your own "body of writing"?

- Do you think that you can communicate with others who do not share your experiences? If so, how?

Michael Ondaatje, born in 1943 in Sri Lanka (then Ceylon), immigrated with his mother to England in 1954 before moving to Canada in 1962. He currently teaches English at York University's Glendon College. An award-winning poet and novelist, Ondaatje's many books include Running in the Family; There's a Trick with a Knife I'm Learning to Do; Coming Through Slaughter; In the Skin of a Lion; *the Booker Award–winning* The English Patient, *which was adapted for a film that won nine Academy Awards; and* Anil's Ghost, *winner of the Governor General's Award and co-winner of the Giller Prize. Ondaatje lives in Toronto with his wife, Linda Spalding, where together they edit the literary journal* Brick.

Aunts

Michael Ondaatje

1   How I have used them....They knit the story together, each memory a wild thread in the sarong. They lead me through their dark rooms crowded with various kinds of furniture—teak, rattan, calamander, bamboo—their voices whispering over tea, cigarettes, distracting me from the tale with their long bony arms, which move over the table like the stretched feet of storks. I would love to photograph this. The thin muscle on the upper arms, the bones and veins at the wrist that almost become part of the discreet bangle, all disappearing into the river of bright sari or faded cotton print.

2   My aunt Dolly stands five foot tall, weighing seventy pounds. She has not stopped smoking since the age of fifteen and her 80-year-old brain leaps like a spark plug bringing this year that year to life. Always repeating the last three words of your question and then turning a surprising corner on her own. In the large house whose wings are now disintegrating into garden and bush she moves frail as Miss Havisham.° From outside the house seems incapable of use. I climb in through the window that frames her and she greets me with "I never thought I'd see you again," and suddenly all these journeys are worth it, just to be able to hug this thin woman who throws her cane onto the table in order to embrace me.

3   She and her brother Arthur were my father's close friends all his life. He knew that, whatever he had done, Arthur would be there to talk him out of madness, weakness, aloneness. They introduced most of the children of our generation to the theatre, dressing us up in costumes for *The Mikado, A Midsummer Night's Dream*—all of which Dolly made herself. Although her family was not excessive in their affairs, they shielded anyone who was in the midst of a passion. "Affairs were going on all around us, even when we were children...so we were well trained."

4   Today is one of Dolly's deaf days but the conversation rolls with the pure joy of the meeting. "Oh I looked after you several times when you were in

Boralesgamuwa, do you remember?" "Yes, yes." "WHAT?" "*Yes*." The frailty does not stop her stories though she pauses now and then to say, "God if you quote me I'm dead. I'll be caught for libel and *killed*....You see they liked their flirtations. All the wives met their beaux in the Cinnamon Gardens, that's where they went to flirt, then they'd come here and use us as an alibi. Your grandmother Lalla for instance had lots of relationships. We could never keep up with her. We almost had to write the names down to remember who she was seeing. My advice you see is to get on with everybody—no matter what they do."

The conversation is continually halted by a man lying just below the ceiling   5 hammering nails into it—hoping to keep it propped up for a few more years. Outside loud chickens fill in the spaces between Dolly's words. Eyes squint in the smoke. "I wish I could see you properly but my glasses are being fixed this week."

As I prepare to leave she walks with me, half deaf and blind, under several lad-   6 ders in her living room that balance paint and workmen, into the garden where there is a wild horse, a 1930 car splayed flat on its axles and hundreds of flowering bushes so that her eyes swim out into the dark green and unfocussed purple. There is very little now that separates the house from the garden. Rain and vines and chickens move into the building. Before I leave, she points to a group photograph of a fancy dress party that shows herself and my grandmother Lalla among the crowd. She has looked at it for years and has in this way memorized everyone's place in the picture. She reels off names and laughs at the facial expressions she can no longer see. It has moved tangible, palpable, into her brain, the way memory invades the present in those who are old, the way gardens invade houses here, the way her tiny body steps into mine as intimate as anything I have witnessed and I have to force myself to be gentle with this frailty in the midst of my embrace. ◆

1982

Glossary

Miss Havisham: a character in Charles Dickens's *Great Expectations* (1860). Jilted on her wedding day, she becomes a bitter old woman who locks herself in her house and trains her ward, Estella, to manipulate and destroy men.

Explorations

- Do you have memories of an elderly relative—an aunt, an uncle, a grandmother or grandfather? Are these memories clear, or have they been blurred by time?

- Do you remember any of the stories told by members of your family or by those who were close to them? If so, why do you think these stories have remained in your mind?

*Pierre Trudeau (1919–2000) was born in Montreal, Quebec. He practised
and taught labour law in Montreal until the early 1960s. In 1971 he married Margaret Sinclair, and they had three sons, Justin, Sasha, and Michel.
In 1965 Trudeau was elected to the Canadian Parliament as a Liberal M.P.
He remained in federal politics for the next two decades, being re-elected
in 1968, 1972, 1974, 1979, and 1980. He was leader of the Liberal Party
from 1968 until 1984, and prime minister of Canada between 1968 and
1979, and between 1980 and 1984. He died at the age of 80, a highly
respected, charismatic leader.*

    *The pieces below come from a collection of Trudeau's writings and
speeches over time, organized thematically (The Essential Trudeau, ed.
Ron Graham, published in 1998). For each section, Trudeau wrote an
informal commentary, which is shown in italics to distinguish it from the
main text.*

On Bilingualism

Pierre Trudeau

1   French Quebec's "state of siege" mentality was usually expressed along these lines:
"We're still being attacked on all sides by the Anglos, the Protestants, the Jews, the for-
eigners, and anybody who goes and works with them is not to be trusted." The reason
I was so happy to go to Ottawa in Jean Marchand's° wake was that he was obviously a
man who had spent his entire adult life working to benefit the people of Quebec. Those
who thought that Quebec should separate naturally saw us as enemies and called us traitors. But I think we ended up getting so much support from Quebec because people realized we weren't traitors, we were just trying to do our best in a larger pond.

2   True, Ottawa in those days was very English. You could hardly speak French one
minute a day. If you were writing a memo to your colleague who was equally French,
you both had to communicate in English. We had the BNA Act,° which said that the
laws and debates in Parliament must be in both languages and so on, but in practice it
was an English city. Across the river was the French city Hull but it was an industrial
town dominated by the belching smokestacks of a paper mill.

3   As soon as we got in power, we were determined to change all that. We sent half the
civil servants to Hull, we tore down the paper mill, we built a fine museum. I'm a func-
tionalist in politics, but as rational as I try to be, I realize that people are impressed by
these images. Before, when Quebec was a backward state with a largely uneducated
people weak in business and the sciences, it had nowhere to go. But I knew that it would
modernize someday and then it would have some place to go: it could go out of
Confederation.

4   The enemies of bilingualism propagated the myth that everyone in Canada would
have to speak French. In fact, bilingualism only meant that the federal government had

to serve Canadians in both official languages. The Official Languages Act never caused anyone who wasn't bilingual to be fired. But when we started recruiting people at the bottom, we began demanding that they have a knowledge of the other language. Not everybody has an automatic right to work in the civil service of Canada. You have to have certain skills, such as reading and writing, perhaps some math and a familiarity with computers. And we said that you now have to know English and French if you want to go to the higher ranks, though not if you want to be, say, a civil servant in a post office in Moose Jaw. It was a long-term plan, and those who wanted to learn English or French were offered all kinds of costly programs.

There wasn't the same kind of backlash in Quebec about bilingualism, but there was   5 a subtle opposition to it. The strongest argument behind the separatist and nationalist° cause was that Canada was an unjust country, that Quebeckers couldn't even speak their own language in Ottawa or the courts, and so on. Well, the Official Languages Act was a terrible demolition of that argument. Never mind what happened in Manitoba in 1896; never mind what happened in Ontario before the First World War; never mind what happened in New Brunswick. Now things have changed.

At the very time we were working hard to sell the idea of two official languages in   6 Canada, Robert Bourassa° chose to make French the only official language in Quebec. If he had talked about principal language or working language, it wouldn't have done so much damage. Even so, I never considered using the power Ottawa had under the constitution to disallow his legislation. The way to change laws is to change governments, I've always believed, so it was up to the people to be better informed and their politicians more open-minded.

Despite the enormous progress the French language has made in Canada since the   7 1920s, you could argue that it still needs some protection from the onslaught of North American culture. But do you defend it by once again closing doors and coercing people or do you defend it by making it a matter of pride and excellence? Laws that promote the use of French, the excellence of it, the teaching of it to immigrants, are good laws, because they give people choices and opportunities to learn. That's what happened when a lot of English children began going to French immersion classes across the country because they thought of Quebec as an exciting province and French as one of the great vehicles of culture in the world. But you can hardly expect the rest of the country to respect French if English is being stamped out in Quebec.

Forcing people to do something is contrary to my nature. I believe in freedom of   8 choice. Anyone who comes to Canada comes believing it's a free country. Yet the first thing they're told is that their kids can't go to English schools. Even René Lévesque° was ashamed of it, and my government only allowed Quebec to do it under the Charter as a kind of temporary linguistic tariff, however much I disliked the spirit of it. Meanwhile, many of our own French-Canadian university students can't write proper French and can barely speak it properly. That surely isn't the fault of the British conquest or the North American environment. So why not reform the school system as a first step to make sure the language is taught properly?

9   *At one point in history everybody was using French as the language of diplomacy, culture, science. Today English is the international language of business, technology, and so on. That's a given. If you try to fight it artificially, you'll condemn your people to a new dark age. Instead, you have to counter this reality with superiority. The Swedes, for example, aren't losing their language, despite being just a small country in Europe: they're keeping it while picking up two or three others. Similarly, I believe in promoting the French language by promoting the excellence of the people who speak it. A proud people will keep their language precisely because they're proud of it. But if you have to scare or threaten them into keeping it, you're never going to have a proud people who are determined to preserve their language and preserve it freely rather than by coercion.*

10   *There are still some people in Canada who want to turn the clock back, who say it's so much simpler to run the country with one part speaking French and the other speaking English. But you won't run a country very long that way. At some point one part will say that it doesn't need the other, that it's less expensive not to translate everything, that we might as well just separate.*

◆ ◆ ◆

11   My friends and I entered federal politics for the precise purpose of proving that French Canadians could be at home in Canada outside Quebec and could exercise their rights in the federal capital and throughout the country. This was also the purpose of the Official Languages Act and of the emergence of what the English-speaking press was soon calling "French power."

12   The separatists of both Quebec and the West well understood what was happening. Conscious that their ultimate goal presupposed an exclusively English-speaking Canada and an exclusively French-speaking Quebec, they abandoned their minorities in other provinces—French-speaking and English-speaking—and fought tooth and nail against the policy of bilingualism, which in their terms was the work of traitors and double-dealers.

◆ ◆ ◆

13   As far back as memory serves, French Canadians had been essentially asking for one thing: respect for the French fact in Canada and incorporation of this fact into Canadian civil society, principally in the areas of language and education, and particularly in the federal government and provinces with French-speaking minorities. After two centuries of struggle and a few symbolic victories (bilingual money and stamps, for example), the Official Languages Act was passed in 1969 and minority-language education rights were entrenched in the Charter of 1982. The gates had suddenly opened and institutional bilingualism was recognized in Canada.

14   Then, equally suddenly, the Quebec *nationalists* no longer wanted the French language to be made equal with English throughout Canada. They denounced bilingualism as utopic at the very moment it was becoming a reality. With Bills 22 and 101, Quebec declared itself *unilingually* French and abandoned the cause of French-speaking minorities in other provinces, the better to marginalize the

English-speaking minority in Quebec; the Quiet Revolution° had suddenly empowered us to become indifferent to the first minority and intolerant of the second. It is as if we had practised virtue only out of weakness or hypocrisy.

◆ ◆ ◆

The issue at stake is not the mere survival of the French language and of the cul- 15
tural values relating to it. Their survival is already assured. French is spoken in Quebec by an ever-increasing number of persons. If one discounts the possibility of genocide or of some major cataclysm, it seems certain that in this part of America French will continue to be spoken regardless of what happens to the constitution.

The problem is therefore to stimulate our language and culture so that they are 16
alive and vital, not just fossils from the past. We must realize that French will only have value to the extent that it is spoken by a progressive people. What makes for vitality and excellence in a language is the collective quality of the people speaking it. In short, the defence of the French language cannot be suc-cessful without accomplishments that make the defence worthwhile.

◆ ◆ ◆

The day of language barriers is finished, at least as far as science and culture are 17
concerned; and if Quebec's intellectuals refuse to master a language other than their own, if they will recognize no loyalty but to their *nation*, then they may be renouncing forever their place among the world's intellectual élite.

◆ ◆ ◆

The French language will be able to express progressive values only if North 18
Americans who speak it are themselves in the forefront of progress, that is to say, if they compete on an equal basis with English-speaking Canadians.

But the competition *must* be on an equal basis. Otherwise, the French popula- 19
tion is in danger of becoming paralysed by an excess of defensive mechanisms. We shall develop the mentality of a beleaguered people, withdrawing into Quebec the better to sustain the siege. In other words, French Canadians may be forced by *English*-speaking *nationalism* to push Quebec nearer to a *national* state and sooner or later to independence.

◆ ◆ ◆

I am afraid that excessive preoccupation with the future of the language has made 20
certain people forget the future of the person speaking it. A working man may care about his language and cultural values; he also cares very strongly about hav-ing a decent life without the risk of losing the little he has through some mis-guided political adventure.

◆ ◆ ◆

Bilingualism unites people; dualism divides them. Bilingualism means you can 21
speak to the other; duality means you can live in one language and the rest of Canada will live in another language.

◆ ◆ ◆

22   Quebec experiences the diversity of Canada where it lives; it is part of its deepest self. If Quebec were to deny, or to claim to lessen or neglect this vital dimension of its being, it would commit an injustice, a betrayal of its responsibility which would result in continuing self-improvement.

◆ ◆ ◆

23   Languages have two functions. They act both as a vehicle of communication, and as a preservation of culture. Governments can support languages in either or both of these roles, but it is only in the communication role that the term "official" is employed. An overwhelming number of Canadians use either English or French in their day-to-day communications with one another and with government. It is for this practical reason—not some rationalization about races—that these two languages have attained an official character in Canada. French and English are not superior to or more precise than any other language. They are simply used more in Canada.

◆ ◆ ◆

24   If French Canadians are able to claim equal partnership with English Canadians, and if their culture is established on a coast-to-coast basis, it is mainly because of the balance of linguistic forces within the country. Historical origins are less important than people generally think, the proof being that neither Inuit nor Indian dialects have any kind of privileged position. On the other hand, if there were six million people living in Canada whose mother tongue was Ukrainian, it is likely that this language would establish itself as forcefully as French. In terms of realpolitik, French and English are equal in Canada because each of these linguistic groups has the power to break the country. ◆

1998

Glossary

Jean Marchand: one of the "three wise men" (with Trudeau and Gérard Pelletier) invited by the federal Liberals to run for Parliament in the 1960s. All three won their seats in the 1965 election, and Trudeau became leader of the party when Pearson resigned in 1968. Marchand played a central role in the 1981 constitutional debate as Speaker of the Senate and as a strong defender of Quebec federalism. He was appointed in 1986 to the Order of Canada.

BNA Act: the British North America Act (1867), which said that the laws and debates in Parliament must be in both languages.

nationalist: italicized by Trudeau in this collection (together with *nation, national, nationalism* and their variants) "whenever he mean[t] them in the ethnic or sociological sense, as a way of clearly differentiating them from the same words used (without italics) in the political or social sense" (Graham, *The Essential Trudeau*, p. xii). In italic passages, these words appear in roman type.

Robert Bourassa: Liberal premier of Quebec, 1970–1976 and 1985–1993.

René Lévesque: (1922–1985) one of the founders (in 1968) and the first leader of the Parti Québécois (PQ). The PQ won the provincial election of 1976, and Lévesque became premier.

Quiet Revolution: a social and cultural revolution in Quebec (1960–1966). Termed "quiet" because it was not brought about through traditional violent revolutionary means.

Explorations

- Arguments over official bilingualism have raged for decades. What attitudes toward bilingualism have you heard? Which positions do you agree with and why? Has Trudeau's essay affected your own position? How?

- Do you agree that if Canada were not officially bilingual, Quebec and Canada might just as well separate; that official bilingualism has helped keep Quebec in Canada?

- Culture and language are inseparable. Do you agree that lack of pride in one's culture can lead to the erosion of that culture's language? Can you think of examples, besides Quebec, in which pride in culture has affected language, either positively or negatively?

John Updike was born in 1932 in Shillington, Pennsylvania. A novelist, critic, short-story writer, poet, and playwright, he has published more than 50 books and won numerous awards, including the Pulitzer Prize, the American Book Award, and the National Book Critics Circle Award. Updike is perhaps best known for his ongoing saga of Harry "Rabbit" Angstrom, which currently comprises a cycle of four novels: Rabbit, Run (1960), Rabbit Redux (1971), Rabbit Is Rich (1981), and Rabbit at Rest (1990). His novel Seek My Face was published in November, 2002.

The Disposable Rocket

John Updike

1   Inhabiting a male body is like having a bank account; as long as it's healthy, you don't think much about it. Compared to the female body, it is a low-maintenance proposition: a shower now and then, trim the fingernails every ten days, a haircut once a month. Oh yes, shaving—scraping or buzzing away at your face every morning. Byron,° in *Don Juan*, thought the repeated nuisance of shaving balanced out the periodic agony, for females, of childbirth. Women are, his lines tell us,

> Condemn'd to child-bed, as men for their sins
> Have shaving too entail'd upon their chins,—

> A daily plague, which in the aggregate
>   May average on the whole with parturition.

From the standpoint of reproduction, the male body is a delivery system, as the female is a mazy device for retention. Once the delivery is made, men feel a faint but distinct falling-off of interest. Yet against the enduring female heroics of birth and nurture should be set the male's superhuman frenzy to deliver his goods: He vaults walls, skips sleep, risks wallet, health, and his political future all to ram home his seed into the gut of the chosen woman. The sense of the chase lives in him as the key to life. His body is, like a delivery rocket that falls away in space, a disposable means. Men put their bodies at risk to experience the release from gravity.

2   When my tenancy of a male body was fairly new—of six or so years' duration—I used to jump and fall just for the joy of it. Falling—backwards, or down stairs—became a specialty of mine, an attention-getting stunt I was still practicing into my thirties, at suburban parties. Falling is, after all, a kind of flying, though of briefer duration than would be ideal. My impulse to hurl myself from high windows and the edges of cliffs belongs to my body, not my mind, which resists the

siren call of the chasm with all its might; the interior struggle knocks the wind from my lungs and tightens my scrotum and gives any trip to Europe, with its Alps, castle parapets, and gargoyled cathedral lookouts, a flavor of nightmare. Falling, strangely, no longer figures in my dreams, as it often did when I was a boy and my subconscious was more honest with me. An airplane, that necessary evil, turns the earth into a map so quickly the brain turns aloof and calm; still, I marvel that there is no end of young men willing to become jet pilots.

Any accounting of male-female differences must include the male's superior   3 recklessness, a drive not, I think, toward death, as the darkest feminist cosmogonies would have it, but to test the limits, to see what the traffic will bear—a kind of mechanic's curiosity. The number of men who do lasting damage to their young bodies is striking; war and car accidents aside, secondary-school sports, with the approval of parents and the encouragement of brutish coaches, take a fearful toll of skulls and knees. We were made for combat, back in the postsimian, East-African days, and the bumping, the whacking, the breathlessness, the pain-smothering adrenaline rush form a cumbersome and unfashionable bliss, but bliss nevertheless. Take your body to the edge, and see if it flies.

The male sense of space must differ from that of the female, who has such   4 interesting, active, and significant inner space. The space that interests men is outer. The fly ball high against the sky, the long pass spiraling overhead, the jet fighter like a scarcely visible pinpoint nozzle laying down its vapor trail at forty thousand feet, the gazelle haunch flickering just beyond arrow-reach, the uncountable stars sprinkled on their great black wheel, the horizon, the mountaintop, the quasar—these bring portents with them and awaken a sense of relation with the invisible, with the empty. The ideal male body is taut with lines of potential force, a diagram extending outward; the ideal female body curves around centers of repose. Of course, no one is ideal, and the sexes are somewhat androgynous subdivisions of a species: Diana° the huntress is a more trendy body type nowadays than languid, overweight Venus,° and polymorphous Dionysus° poses for more underwear ads than Mars.° Relatively, though, men's bodies, however elegant, are designed for covering territory, for moving on.

An erection, too, defies gravity, flirts with it precariously. It extends the dia-   5 gram of outward direction into downright detachability—objective in the case of the sperm, subjective in the case of the testicles and penis. Men's bodies, at this junction, feel only partly theirs; a demon of sorts has been attached to their lower torsos, whose performance is erratic and whose errands seem, at times, ridiculous. It is like having a (much) smaller brother toward whom you feel both fond and impatient; if he is you, it is you in curiously simplified and ignoble form. This sense, of the male body being two of them, is acknowledged in verbal love play and erotic writing, where the penis is playfully given a pet name, an individuation not even the rarest rapture grants a vagina. Here, where maleness gathers to a quintessence of itself, there can be no insincerity, there can be no hiding; for sheer nakedness, there is nothing like a hopeful phallus; its aggressive shape is indivisible from its tender-skinned vulnerability. The act of intercourse, from the point of view of a consenting female, has an element of mothering, of enwrapment, of merciful concealment, even. The male body, for this interval, is tucked out of harm's way.

6   To inhabit a male body, then, is to feel somewhat detached from it. It is not an enemy, but not entirely a friend. Our being seems to lie not in cells and muscles but in the traces that our thoughts and actions inscribe on the air. The male body skims the surface of nature's deeps wherein the blood and pain and mysterious cravings of women perpetuate the species. Participating less in nature's processes than the female body, the male body gives the impression—false—of being exempt from time. Its powers of strength and reach descend in early adolescence, along with acne and sweaty feet, and depart, in imperceptible increments, after thirty or so. It surprises me to discover, when I remove my shoes and socks, the same paper-white, hairless angles that struck me as pathetic when I observed them on my father. I felt betrayed when, in some tumble of touch football twenty years ago, I heard my tibia snap; and when, between two reading engagements in Cleveland, my appendix tried to burst; and when, the other day, not for the first time, there arose to my nostrils out my own body the musty attic smell my grandfather's body had.

7   A man's body does not betray its tenant as rapidly as a woman's. Never as fine and lovely, it has less distance to fall; what rugged beauty it has is wrinkleproof. It keeps its capability of procreation indecently long. Unless intense athletic demands are made upon it, the thing serves well enough to sixty, which is my age now. From here on, it's chancy. There are no breasts or ovaries to admit cancer to the male body, but the prostate, that awkwardly located little source of seminal fluid, shows the strain of sexual function with fits of hysterical cell replication, and all that male-bonding beer and potato chips add up in the coronary arteries. A writer, whose physical equipment can be minimal as long as it gets him to the desk, the lectern, and New York City once in a while, cannot but be grateful to his body, especially to his eyes, those tender and intricate sites where the brain extrudes from the skull, and to his hands, which hold the pen or tap the keyboard. His body has been, not himself exactly, but a close pal, potbellied and balding like most of his other pals now. A man and his body are like a boy and the buddy who has a driver's license and the use of his father's car for the evening; one goes along, gratefully, for the ride. ◆

1993

Glossary

Byron: George Gordon, Lord Byron (1788–1824), English Romantic poet who, in both his work and life, created the prototype of the "Byronic hero," a defiant, melancholy young man who broods on some mysterious sin in his past.

Diana: Roman goddess of the hunt.

Venus: Roman goddess of love.

Dionysus: Greek god of wine and fertility.

Mars: Roman god of war.

Explorations

- Have you ever thought of the male body as a bank account or disposable rocket? What other metaphors would you use to describe it?

- How would you account for the male-female differences that Updike identifies, such as "the male's superior recklessness" and interest in outer space?

- Do you think that, generally speaking, men feel more detached from their bodies than women do? Why or why not?

Jacob Ward is a former staff writer for The Industry Standard *and senior editor at* Architecture *magazine. He has written for the magazine* Wired, *as well as for* Metropolis, eDesign, *and other magazines. He is currently writing his first novel.*

Crime Seen

Jacob Ward

1   It's 2:30 pm on the fourth day of Michael Serge's murder trial. In a wood-paneled room of the county court house in Scranton, Pennsylvania, Judge Terrance Nealon gives the jury a brief speech on the difference between art and fact, then motions for the prosecution to begin.

2   At the back of the courtroom, a crowd of onlookers from the local legal community crane their necks as a technician cues up a 72-second video. It's an animated re-creation of Serge, a retired police detective, shooting and killing his wife of 35 years, Jennifer. The picture appears on a 5-foot screen positioned near the jury box.

3   The family's living room comes into focus around Serge's wife, realistically rendered with sandy-blond hair and wire-rimmed glasses, and wearing animal-print pajamas. Serge appears, gun in hand. What follows is a second-by-second breakdown of the three shots he's alleged to have fired. First, a bright blue line extends from Serge's gun, leaving behind a frozen rope of red. The blue passes through Jennifer's lower torso and into a stereo cabinet. Next, Serge fires into the wall. In a dramatic ending, he again takes aim at his wife, who is crouched on the floor. The shot pierces her from right arm to left rib in deadly cartoon green. The screen goes black.

4   Serge, 55, blinks at the digital image of himself. His son, seated behind him in the courtroom, weeps silently. Jennifer's sister clutches a cardboard-backed photograph of herself with the victim. Standing with the spectators is Paul Walker, a local defense attorney, who marvels at the effectiveness of the animation. Walker has worked either with or against most of the lawyers present and happens to be a close friend of the victim's brother. But today, like so many others, he's here just to watch. "I've seen a lot of photos of people lying bloody on the ground," he says later. "But when I saw the animation, it was eerie. If a coroner says the victim had a posterior entrance wound, that doesn't mean anything to a jury. When you see her shot in the back and then down on her knees, that brings it to life."

5   What the jury saw is known as forensic animation—the computerized illustration of events recounted by courtroom testimony (in this case, the coroner's report and the state trooper's on-scene analysis). It's the newest in a chain of

technologies—from lie-detector tests to handwriting analysis and DNA sampling—that is transforming the world of litigation. And while it's nothing more than pixels on a monitor, this legal tool is proving remarkably effective.

David Golomb, a Manhattan attorney who has served as president of the New   6
York State Trial Lawyers Association, calls it "devastating evidence," saying, "If you have a good animation, it's such a difficult thing for the other side to fight."

The first animation was presented to a Bronx jury in a 1984 auto accident case.   7
It was crudely done, with block graphics on an Apple II. Eight years later, the technique was employed in a high-profile criminal trial for the first time and helped convict San Francisco porn king Jim Mitchell of murdering his brother. Over the past decade, as computing power has grown faster and cheaper, forensic animation—used to illustrate everything from baby shakings to product malfunctions—has become increasingly common.

In an age when the courts are clogged with litigation, the acceptance of foren-   8
sic animation reflects more than the need to find the truth. Judges seem eager to admit any valid evidence that can shorten the duration of a trial. In barely a minute, the jury comes away with information that would otherwise require two days of overwrought oratory. "This is a video country," Golomb explains. "People are used to getting information from the television." In the half-dozen cases in which he has used computer animation, opposing counsel settled almost immediately.

The new procedure has spawned a thriving industry worth about $30 million   9
annually. There are some 100 firms around the country that specialize in forensic animation, not to mention countless studios that create films as well as provide other types of litigation consulting—among the biggest: Engineering Animation, Decision Quest, and Animators at Law.

To make the video as realistic as possible, the animators begin with raw data   10
culled from the site by accident reconstructionists. To get a digital representation of the crime scene, they sometimes use laser-transit survey devices to shoot beams over every inch of the area. "We present everything to one-thirtieth of a second on an x, y, and z axis," says Andre Stuart, CEO of 21st Century Forensic Animation, the company that produced the clip in the Serge case. Then, relying on supplementary data such as photographs, ballistics information, and a coroner's report, they fill in the holes and craft a narrative.

A 3-D animation of even the simplest two-vehicle accident, produced using   11
the fairly unsophisticated CAD° program 3D StudioMax, will cost a client no less than $5,000, Stuart estimates. High-end work can climb to as much as $180,000. But even then, this isn't your glossy Hollywood production. Frequently, 21st Century assembles its worlds using libraries of mix-and-match premodeled people, vehicles, and furniture. The company has roughly 25 cases on its docket, and since its inception in 1989 more than 400 clients have retained its services, among them Johnnie Cochran.° Cochran hired Stuart's firm

in two high-profile cases: Anthony Dwain Lee, the young African-American actor who was shot to death by a Los Angeles police officer in 2000, and Amadou Diallo, the Guinean immigrant who was killed in 1999 by plainclothes New York cops.

12   For all of its impact on judges and juries, forensic animation borders on pseudoscience. Consider a typical auto accident. Skid marks, paint samples, and scattered glass yield reliable and scientifically acceptable computer images. Still, much of the moviemaking process comes down to guesswork. How hard did the driver brake? How foggy was the road? As a result, the quest for accuracy is sometimes compromised. Lawyers will often act as executive producers, overseeing the making of the film and calling for changes—in visual tone, for instance—where they believe it may help the case. By changing a single camera angle, Golomb claims he won a multimillion-dollar settlement in a car crash.

13   Critics have argued that forensic animation is more prejudicial than illuminating—that it possesses an unjustified ring of truth and may cause jurors to overlook other evidence. Serge's attorney, Joseph D'Andrea, scorned the animation, calling it a cartoon and demanding it be excluded from the trial. He feared its cause-and-effect starkness would inalterably cast his client as a murderer. But Judge Nealon chose to admit it, writing that "an animated exhibit should not be regarded as unfairly prejudicial merely because it enables a party to demonstrate a point more effectively."

14   The prosecution's decision to commission an animation in such an open-and-shut case had more to do with defining the future than with winning. As the first animation ever admitted into a criminal trial in Pennsylvania, it sets a powerful precedent. "We're not known for being trailblazers around here," says Jennifer Henn, a staff reporter for the local *Scranton Times.* "It's amazing the judge allowed the animation in."

15   Back in the courtroom, the prosecution rests. Walking to his hotel, Randy Matzkanin, a mechanical engineer who managed the animation team behind the Serge case, admits he was nervous at the trial. During a recess the previous day, Matzkanin learned he and a state trooper—the DA's key witness—had miscommunicated about a detail concerning the arrangement of the body in the room. As a result, the video was flawed. "It wasn't inaccurate, strictly speaking," Matzkanin points out, "but it should have been done differently."

16   A few days later, the jury deliberates for less than two hours before convicting Michael Serge of first-degree murder. Thirty minutes after that, he's sentenced to life in prison without parole. ◆

2002

Glossary

CAD program: computer-aided design program. Software used for drafting in areas such as architecture and woodworking.

Johnnie Cochran: a well-known American lawyer, Cochran defended O.J. Simpson against charges of murdering his ex-wife and her companion.

Explorations

- Think of two or three news stories you've read in the newspaper or heard on the radio before you saw footage on television at a later date. How did the visuals affect your reception of the story? Did they change how the story affected you?

- Some students learn most effectively by listening, some through reading, and some by seeing visual aids. How do you learn best? Why do you think that is?

CHAPTER FIVE

Delivery: Creating a Public Voice

As a student, you are probably most used to writing in isolation, and your voice is thus probably heard only by your instructor and a few people close to you. In this age of rapidly advancing technology, however, it is worth remembering that most cultures have their roots in oral traditions. For example, much of western culture is based on knowledge passed on by the ancient Greek philosopher/orators such as Plato and Aristotle. First Nations people in North America passed on—and still pass on—their traditions and cultures orally. Yet, despite our history, many of us have lost touch with the spoken word. As a result, we tend to be hesitant when asked to share our ideas with a wider audience.

While many of you will never have the chance to stand behind a podium with a microphone speaking to thousands of people as Martin Luther King, Jr. or Pierre Elliott Trudeau often did, you may be given the opportunity to publish a letter in a newspaper, make a speech at a formal celebration, or present your research at an academic conference. Projecting your personal voice into realms beyond the classroom will allow you to engage more freely in public debate. This chapter will give you guidelines for creating a public voice and adapting it to any situation, written or spoken.

Guidelines for Creating a Public Voice

The most critical aspect of creating a public voice is to be able to foreground your credibility as a writer or speaker. You can do this by knowing your subject well, and by identifying and engaging your audience.

Your Subject

The better you know your subject, the more effective your voice will be. When you read an essay or listen to a public address, you expect the voice you hear to be confident and knowledgeable. Your audience expects the same from you. Have the facts of your subject at hand, and be prepared to defend your views.

Your Audience

Getting a clear picture of your audience will allow you to tailor your material to its needs. The following questions will help you to profile your audience:

- What is the age of the members of your audience? Their racial background? Their gender? Their sexual orientation?

- What are their socio-economic and educational levels?

- Are the members of your audience affiliated with any social, political, professional, or religious organizations?

- What do your audience members value (money, health, and so on)?

- How knowledgeable is your audience about your subject?

Once you identify your audience's main characteristics, you can choose the delivery strategies that are most appropriate.

Your Delivery

Delivery involves using voice and gesture to engage your audience: in your writing you can do this figuratively through the stylistic choices you make. Figures of speech such as anaphora, alliteration, and assonance help you to project your voice in a memorable way, and other figures of speech such as metaphor, simile, and personification gesture to concrete images (see Chapter 4). While stylistic considerations are important in all writing, they are particularly important when articulating ideas in a public forum.

In an oral presentation, there are additional strategies that will help you deliver your ideas to your audience. Speaking clearly, modulating the speed and tone of your voice, and making eye contact with your audience will ensure that you project to every member of the audience. Short sentences, clear transitional words, and the judicious use of repetition will also help your audience remember key points. Working with notes in point form will allow you to focus on the audience rather than on the page, giving you the freedom to use non-verbal gestures as well as verbal cues to communicate ideas: handouts and overhead transparencies provide your audience with useful visual cues.

Body language can further affect your audience's perception of your delivery; however, you need to use it wisely. If you wave your arms around aimlessly, it can hinder your delivery by distracting your audience from your material. But if your stance is confident and you move purposefully, gestures can help you to appear self-assured and provide emphasis.

Overview

Speaking to a wide audience is often intimidating, but it can also be liberating. Creating a public voice can take your private thoughts to a new level—a level that has social and political implications. By expressing your ideas publicly, you are accepting the responsibility not only to voice but to act upon your beliefs; you thereby empower yourself by engaging with the world around you. Many essays in this chapter address a wide audience. Some are actually speeches; others reflect on the implications of speaking in a public forum. All are interesting examples of the possibilities of voice and gesture in delivering messages to the public.

Aristotle, a Greek philosopher, was born in Stagira in 384 BC. In 367 he became a pupil of the philosopher Plato at Plato's Academy in Athens; he remained there as a student and a teacher for 20 years. Later, he founded his own school, the Lyceum. Most of Aristotle's unpublished writings survive, and include lecture notes and treatises, many of which are published in Rhetoric; *work published in his lifetime exists now only in fragments recorded by other writers. When Alexander the Great died, Aristotle was forced to flee to Euboea, where he died in 322 BC.*

From *Rhetoric*

Aristotle

Rhetoric may be defined as the faculty of observing in any given case the available means of persuasion. This is not a function of any other art. Every other art can instruct or persuade about its own particular subject matter; for instance, medicine about what is healthy and unhealthy, geometry about the properties of magnitudes, arithmetic about numbers, and the same is true of the other arts and sciences. But rhetoric we look upon as the power of observing the means of persuasion on almost any subject presented to us; and that is why we say that, in its technical character, it is not concerned with any special or definite class of subjects. 1

Of the modes of persuasion some belong strictly to the art of rhetoric and some do not. By the latter I mean such things as are not supplied by the speaker but are there at the outset—witnesses, evidence given under torture, written contracts, and so on. By the former I mean such as we can ourselves construct by means of the principles of rhetoric. The one kind has merely to be used, the other has to be invented. 2

Of the modes of persuasion furnished by the spoken word there are three kinds. The first kind depends on the personal character of the speaker; the second on putting the audience into a certain frame of mind; the third on the proof, or apparent proof, provided by the words of the speech itself. Persuasion is achieved by the speaker's personal character when the speech is so spoken as to make us think him credible. We believe good men more fully and more readily than others; this is true generally whatever the question is, and absolutely true where exact certainty is impossible and opinions are divided. This kind of persuasion, like the others, should be achieved by what the speaker says, not by what people think of his character before he begins to speak. It is not true, as some writers assume in their treatises on rhetoric, that the personal goodness revealed by the speaker contributes nothing to his power of persuasion; on the contrary, his character may almost be called the most effective means of persuasion he possesses. Secondly, persuasion may come through the hearers, when the speech stirs their 3 emotions. Our judgments when we are pleased and friendly are not the same as when we are pained and hostile. It is towards producing these effects, as we maintain, that present-day writers on rhetoric direct the whole of their efforts. This subject shall be treated in detail when we come to speak of the emotions. Thirdly, persuasion is effected through the speech itself when we have proved a truth or an apparent truth by means of the persuasive arguments suitable to the case in question.

4   There are, then, these three means of effecting persuasion. The man who is to be in command of them must, it is clear, be able (1) to reason logically, (2) to understand human character and goodness in their various forms, and (3) to understand the emotions—that is, to name them and describe them, to know their causes and the way in which they are excited. ◆

(c. 336 BC/First published in English 1637)

Explorations

- Do you ever hear the word "rhetoric" being used? If so, in what context?

- Do you view Aristotle's modes of persuasion as being effective? Why or why not?

- Do you consciously use "the available means of persuasion"—*logos*, *ethos*, and *pathos*—in your own writing?

Tommy Douglas was born in 1904 in Falkirk, Scotland. In 1911, his family moved to Winnipeg. Shortly after settling in Winnipeg, Douglas was diagnosed with osteomyelitis in his right leg. Because Douglas' family was not wealthy, they could not pay for the best or most immediate treatment, resulting in the near loss of his leg. This experience likely sparked the beginning of Douglas' mission for universal public health care. He began his career as a minister, but after working with local parties, Douglas was elected to Parliament under the banner of the Co-operative Commonwealth Federation, which later became part of the New Democratic Party of Canada. Douglas was premier of Saskatchewan and leader of the NDP, during which time he made universal medicare his priority. He died in 1986.

Douglas was also well known for his opposition to the death penalty. He delivered the speech reprinted below in the House of Commons on April 5, 1966.

Capital Punishment

Tommy Douglas

There are times, Mr. Speaker, when the House of Commons rises to heights of grandeur and becomes deeply conscious of its great traditions. I think this debate has been one of those rare occasions. There has been a minimum of rancour and there has been no imputation of motives because I think that the abolitionists and retentionists alike have been sincerely searching their consciences to see if we can honestly resolve a moral problem. This problem is, how can we abolish a brutal punishment without endangering the safety of society? 1

I am in favour of the motion to abolish capital punishment and I am also supporting the amendment to put it on a five-year trial basis. I doubt that there is much new that can be said in this debate. The entire field has been well covered but I should like to put very briefly four reasons for my opposition to capital punishment. The first is that capital punishment is contrary to the highest concepts of the Judaic Christian ethic. I do not propose to go into theological arguments, but both in this debate and in the discussions which have taken place outside the House many people have been quoting Scripture in support of retaining the death penalty. 2

It is always a dangerous practice to quote isolated passages of Scripture. The Bible has been quoted in times past to support slavery, child labour, polygamy, the burning of witches, and subservience to dictators. The Scriptures have to be viewed as a whole. The Bible is not one book; it is many books. It does not have a static concept. It represents man's emerging moral concepts as they have grown through the centuries. 3

4   It is true that the Mosaic law° provided the death penalty for murder. It is equally true, if one looks particularly at the 20th chapter of the book of Leviticus, that the Mosaic law provided the death penalty for 33 crimes including such things as adultery, bestiality, homosexuality, witchcraft and sacrificing to other gods than Jehovah. It seems to me that those who want to pick out isolated texts from the Bible in support of retaining the death penalty for murder have to be equally consistent and ask that the death penalty be retained for all the other crimes listed in the Mosaic law.

5   Of course, those who take this position overlook several facts. They overlook, first of all, the fact that the Mosaic law was an advanced law for the primitive times in which it was formulated. It was later succeeded by the Hebrew prophets who introduced the idea of justice superseded by mercy, the possible redemption and reestablishment of the individual. They overlook the fact that if any nation in the world ought to feel itself bound by Mosaic law it should be the state of Israel. The state of Israel abolished the death penalty many years ago except for Nazi war criminals and for treason committed in times of war. The religious hierarchy of the state of Israel enthusiastically supported the Knesset° in abolishing the death penalty in that country.

6   But for those of us who belong to the Christian religion it seems to me we have to remember also that the Christian religion went far beyond the Mosaic law. In the days of the founder of Christianity the Mosaic law still obtained. This law decreed that a woman taken in adultery could be stoned to death. We should remember the statement of Jesus of Nazareth when he came upon a group of people preparing to stone such a woman to death. He said, Let him who is without sin among you cast the first stone.

7   When the crowd had dwindled away so that only the woman was left he said to the woman, "Go and sin no more." It seems to me that this is the ultimate culmination of the Christian concept of the application of mercy and the possible redemption of the individual.

8   My second reason for opposing capital punishment is that I believe capital punishment brutalizes the society that uses it without providing any effective deterrent that cannot be provided equally well by life imprisonment. I believe that any society that practises capital punishment brutalizes itself. It has an effect upon that society and I do not believe that society can rid itself of murderers by itself becoming a murderer. Surely if brutality would deter the committing of a crime Great Britain should have been a place of law-abiding citizens because a little over 150 years ago there were over 200 crimes for which an individual could be put to death. Instead of making Britain a nation of law-abiders it was a country where crime abounded, where human sensibilities were dulled by the public execution of criminals. It is rather significant that in that day, as in this, it was often the juries who were more humane than the lawmakers. It was only because juries refused to convict, knowing the terrible punishment which would follow,

that the lawmakers were forced 150 years ago to remove the death penalty from a great many of the crimes for which it had been prescribed.

All of the evidence which can be gathered seems to indicate that the death 9 penalty is not a unique deterrent and that life imprisonment can be equally effective....

I readily agree, Mr. Speaker, that quoting endless statistics is not going to prove 10 either the case for abolition or the case for retention, but there certainly seems to be no convincing volume of evidence which would satisfy any unbiased individual that abolishing the death penalty has resulted in an upsurge of homicide or that those states which have retained the death penalty are any freer of capital crimes than those which have not.

After all, Mr. Speaker, who is it that the death penalty deters? It has certainly 11 not deterred the man who commits murder. Will it deter him in the future? Surely he can be deterred in the future by being incarcerated for the remainder of his life. Who is deterred if this man is hanged? Is he to be hanged as an example to the rest of the community? I can conceive of nothing more immoral than to break a man's neck as an example to other people, but if that is the argument then surely, as the Leader of the Opposition (Mr. Diefenbaker) said yesterday, we ought to have public executions.

The hon. member for Winnipeg South Centre (Mr. Churchill) said that the 12 fear of death will deter men. The fear of death will deter normal men but when a man commits murder, is he normal? Can we understand the motivation that causes a man to take a human life? When a man commits homicide, does he sit down and assess whether he is committing it in a state that has capital punishment or in a state that has abolished capital punishment? I think not. In the main the man who commits homicide is the man who is mentally ill; the man who kills does not make the common, rational judgments that are made by the average individual.

An individual who has become so mentally sick that he will take another life 13 or ravage a child is certainly not a mentally healthy or normal individual.

The third reason I am opposed to capital punishment, Mr. Speaker, is that I 14 believe there are better ways to ensure the safety of society. I completely agree with the hon. member for Winnipeg South Centre who argued that we must be concerned about the safety of the public. When he asks which is the more important, the life of an innocent person who may be killed or the life of a murderer, there is no doubt that the life of the innocent person is the more important. But is the fact that we break a man's neck any guarantee that innocent people will not be hurt?

We are not suggesting removing the penalty. We are saying that the penalty 15 which ought to be retained is one that will do the two things which are important. First of all, it must be a penalty which will remove the convicted person from human society as long as that person is likely to be a menace to the safety and well-being of his fellow-men. Second, that person should be given an opportunity to receive whatever psychiatric treatment and rehabilitation is possible in the light of his own particular circumstances.

16   What we have to decide is what we are trying to do, Mr. Speaker. Are we thinking purely of punishing somebody because they have done wrong? Are we thinking purely in punitive terms? Are we thinking purely in terms of vengeance or retribution? Or are we thinking of the two things I have mentioned, first, the safety of society by incarcerating the convicted murderer for life and, second, the possible rehabilitation and redemption of that individual. There is additionally the third great advantage that if society has made a mistake it is possible to rectify the mistake because justice is a human institution and like all human institutions it is liable to error.

17   I maintain that society has no right to take from a man something which it cannot restore to him. If society makes a mistake and confines a man to prison, depriving him of his freedom, when that mistake is found out society can at least restore to him his freedom and provide him with some compensation for the years he has been incarcerated. But if we hang a man and then find that a mistake has been made there is nothing at all which can be done to make amends.

18   My quarrel with the death penalty is that it is purely a negative attempt to promote the safety of society. We need to adopt positive measures to promote the safety of society. For instance, we need better law enforcement. In both Canada and the United States every year a great many unsolved crimes are committed. One of the best deterrents is for the criminal to know that if he does commit a crime he will be found out, that he will be incarcerated and put in a place where he can no longer be a menace to the community. We need quicker crime detection methods. For some types of crimes, particularly for those involving psychotics, there ought to be indeterminate sentences.

19   We all recall a case a few years ago in which a man sexually assaulted a child. He was sentenced to five years in jail. To my mind this was ridiculous because it was based purely on the punitive concept and not out of regard for the safety of the community. It was assumed that at five years less one day, when he was in jail, he was a menace but at five years plus one day he was no longer a menace. Such an individual ought to be sentenced to be kept out of circulation until such time as a panel of judges, psychiatrists and social workers are as certain as a human person can be that the individual is no longer a menace to the safety of the community. I think that in many cases indeterminate sentences to keep out of circulation psychotics who are likely to commit crimes would be of great advantage. In the case I referred to the man got out of jail after five years. Within six months he had not only assaulted another child but had killed the child in the process. Had that individual been sentenced to an indeterminate sentence in the first instance he would not have committed this second heinous crime.

If we want genuine deterrents in this country we need a program of penal   *20*
reform for the segregation of prisoners and for their rehabilitation so that young
first offenders do not go to jail to take what is virtually a postgraduate course in
crime.

Let us face the fact that when we talk about retaining capital punishment as a   *21*
deterrent we are really trying to take the easy way out from solving our problems.
In the long run society often gets the criminals it deserves.

Why do we have criminals? What is wrong with the society that produces   *22*
criminals? Some years ago when I was attending Chicago University I remember
that every newspaper in the United States had a heading, "Where Is Crawley?"
Crawley was a young gunman who was being hunted across the United States for
a series of murders.

A very great columnist in the United States wrote a column which he headed,   *23*
"Why Is Crawley?" He said that the people of the United States, instead of asking
"Where Is Crawley?", ought to take a little time out to ask, "Why Is Crawley?"
The columnist went over his history. He came from a broken home which the
father had deserted and where the mother was out working all day. The boy lived
on the streets. He was part of a gang of hoodlums. He was sent to a reformatory
and then was back on the streets. He was without proper education and without
any counselling. He was sent to jail and associated with hardened criminals. He
came out of jail twice as tough as when he went in. By 19 he was a hardened
criminal. By the time he was 21 he was a killer. He was finally shot down by the
police who were trying to capture him.

I suppose one of the most lamentable murders in our time has been the killing   *24*
of President John F. Kennedy. Yet, when one reads the story of the man who is
believed to have been responsible for his death, we find that when Lee Oswald
was a boy in school he was recommended to undergo psychiatric treatment
because of the dangerous psychotic tendencies he then displayed. But there were
not enough psychiatrists to look after all the children in that particular part of
New York City and this boy was not treated. This boy grew up with his psychotic
tendencies expanding, and he is believed to have been responsible for extin-
guishing one of the brightest lights of our generation.

If we really want to tackle the problem of eliminating crime, we must tackle   *25*
the problem of the slums which breed crime and we must tackle the problem of
the lack of psychiatric clinics to take care of psychotics and persons who may
become criminally dangerous. We need the kind of penal reform that will make
possible the rehabilitation of first offenders with proper probation and parole. We
need to go to the roots of the cause of crime and to ask ourselves what it is that
produces the murderer in society....

My final point is that I am opposed to capital punishment because I believe   *26*
that the measure of a nation is the manner in which it treats its misfits and its
offenders. Capital punishment has already been abolished in most of the

advanced nations of the Western world. The abolition of capital punishment has come to be taken as the hallmark of a nation's conscience. I want to see Canada take this great forward step, and I want to make a special appeal to the members of the House to consider how important for Canada and for its future will be the vote we shall take tonight.

27   I should not want to be in the shoes of the Prime Minister and the members of his cabinet who have to face up to this very difficult problem. Nobody has been hanged in Canada since 1962. If the motion tonight is defeated the government is going to be in an awkward position. Either it will have to commute those sentenced to death to life imprisonment, knowing that the House of Commons has just rejected a motion suggesting the abolition of the death penalty, or it will have to take the defeat of the motion as an expression of opinion and allow the death sentences to be carried out.

28   I urge the members of the House to consider the predicament which faces the Prime Minister and the cabinet. I want to urge the House to give a five-year trial to the abolition of the death penalty. If the fears that have been expressed prove to be warranted, if there is an upsurge in the rate of homicide, if we are faced with an increase in crime rate, then in five years the members of the House of Commons who are here then can allow the death penalty to become effective again simply by taking no action. But I would urge that we give this a chance, that we step into line with the progressive countries of the world which have already abolished the death penalty.

29   What I plead for is that we pass this resolution tonight, with the amendment, which will declare in principle that the House is in favour of abolishing capital punishment and replacement with life imprisonment [*sic*]. If we do that then I believe the House of Commons will have won a great victory, not a victory that will be accompanied by the blaring of trumpets or the rolling of drums but a victory in that we will have taken a forward, moral step and left behind one of the last relics of barbarianism. We will be moving forward to a more humane approach in dealing with crime. ◆

1966

Glossary

Mosaic law: the ancient law of the Hebrews, ascribed to Moses.

Knesset: the Israeli parliament.

Explorations

- According to Douglas, "All of the evidence which can be gathered seems to indicate that the death penalty is not a unique deterrent and that life imprisonment can be equally effective." Do you agree with Douglas' claim that the death penalty is not a unique deterrent? Would you favour the death penalty if it deterred crimes more effectively than other punishments? Why or why not?

- Douglas' speech was written in 1966. How do you think the arguments for and against capital punishment differ in present-day debate?

Stephen Jay Gould, born in 1941, grew up in New York City and graduated from Antioch College, and received his Ph.D. from Columbia University in 1967. He was professor of geology, zoology, and paleontology at Harvard University and renowned in the field of evolutionary biology. He was also a regular columnist for Natural History *magazine. Among his many books are* Ever Since Darwin *(1974);* The Panda Thumb *(1980), winner of an American Book Award;* The Mismeasure of Time *(1981), winner of a National Book Critics Circle Award; and* Dinosaur in a Haystack *(1996). Gould died of lung cancer in 2002 at the age of 60.*

Dinomania

Stephen Jay Gould

I

1   Macbeth's soliloquy on his intended murder of King Duncan provides our canonical quotation for the vital theme that deeds spawn unintended consequences in distant futures. "If it were done," Macbeth muses, "'twere well it were done quickly." The act must be swift, but, even more important the sequelae must be contained, as Macbeth hopes to "trammel up the consequence, and catch, with his surcease, success; that but this blow might be the be-all and the end-all here." Yet Macbeth fears that big events must unleash all the genies of unknowable futures—for "bloody instructions, which being taught, return to plague the inventor."

2   I doubt that Henry Fairfield Osborn° considered these lines, or imagined any popular future for his new discoveries, when he published a conventionally dull, descriptive paper in 1924 on three genera of dinosaurs recently found in Mongolia on the famous Gobi Desert expedition. In this paper, titled "Three New Theropoda, *Protoceratops* Zone, Central Mongolia," Osborn named, and described for the first time, the "skull and jaws, one front claw and adjoining phalanges" of a small but apparently lithe and skillful carnivore. He called his new creature *Velociraptor mongoliensis* to honor these inferred skills, for *Velociraptor* means "quick seizer." *Velociraptor*, Osborn wrote, "seems to have been an alert, swift-moving carnivorous dinosaur." He then describes the teeth as "perfectly adapted to the sudden seizure of...swift-moving prey...The long rostrum and wide gape of the jaws indicate that the prey was not only living but of considerable size."

3   Osborn was America's greatest vertebrate paleontologist, but he was also the politically conservative, socially prominent, imperious president of the American Museum of Natural History in New York. He would, I think, have been quite surprised, and not at all amused, to learn that, nearly seventy years later, his creature

would win a new, and vastly extended, status as the primary dinosaur hero (or villain, depending on your modes of rooting) in the blockbuster film *Jurassic Park*.

Public fascination has always followed these prehistoric beasts. Just ten years 4 after Richard Owen coined the word *dinosaur* in 1840, sculptor Waterhouse Hawkins was hard at work on a series of full-scale models to display in the Crystal Palace during the Great Exhibition of 1851. (The Crystal Palace burned in 1936, but Hawkins's dinosaurs, recently spruced up with a coat of paint, can still be seen in Sydenham, south of London.)

But the popular acclaim of dinosaurs has been fitful and episodic. We saw them 5 in *King Kong* (thanks to Willis O'Brien and his brilliant technique of stop-motion photography using small models, later magnified). We filled our cars under the sign of a giant green *Brontosaurus*, the logo of Sinclair Oil (who also provided a fine exhibit at the 1939 World's Fair in New York). But dinosaurs never became a pervasive cultural icon, and some decades largely ignored the great beasts. I was a "dinosaur nut" as a kid growing up in New York during the late forties and early fifties. Hardly anyone knew or cared about these creatures, and I was viewed as a nerd and misfit on that ultimate field of vocational decision—the school playground at recess. I was called "Fossil Face"; the only other like-minded kid in the school became "Dino" (I am pleased to report that he also became a professional natural historian). The names weren't funny, and they hurt.

During the last twenty years, however, dinosaurs have vaulted to a steady level 6 of culturally pervasive popularity—from gentle Barney who teaches proper values to young children on a PBS television series, to ferocious monsters who can promote films from "G" to "R" ratings. This dinosaurian flooding of popular consciousness guarantees that no paleontologist can ever face a journalist and avoid what seems to be the most pressing question of the nineties: Why are children so fascinated with dinosaurs?

The question may be a commonplace, but it remains poorly formulated in 7 conflating two quite separate issues. The first—the Jungian or archetypal theme,° if you will—seeks the universal reason that stirs the soul of childhood (invariably fatuous and speculative, hence my dislike of the question). To this inquiry, I know no better response than the epitome proposed by a psychologist colleague: big, fierce, and extinct—in other words, alluringly scary, but sufficiently safe.

Most questioners stop here, supposing the inquiry resolved when they feel satisfied about archetypal fascination. But this theme cannot touch the heart of current dinomania, culminating in the extraordinary response to *Jurassic Park*, for an obvious, but oddly disregarded, reason: dinosaurs were just as big, as fierce, and as extinct forty years ago, but only a few nerdy kids, and even fewer professional paleontologists, gave a damn about them. We must therefore pose the second question: Why now and not before?

We might propose two solutions to this less general, but more resolvable, ques- 9 tion—one that I wish were true (but almost cannot be), and one that I deeply regret (but must surely be correct). As a practicing paleontologist, I would love to believe that current dinomania arose as a direct product of our research, and all the fascinating new ideas that our profession has generated about dinosaurs. The slow, lumbering, stupid, robotic, virtually behaviorless behemoths of my childhood have been replaced by lithe, agile, potentially warm-blooded, adequately smart, and behaviorally complex creatures. The giant sauropods were mired in ponds during my youth, for many paleontologists regarded them as too heavy to hold up their own bodies on land. Now they stride across the plains, necks and tails outstretched. In some reconstructions they even rear up on their hind legs to reach high vegetation, or to scare off predators. (They are so depicted in the first *Brachiosaurus* scene of *Jurassic Park*, and in the full-scale fiberglass model of *Barosaurus* recently installed in the rotunda of the American Museum of Natural History—though most of my colleagues consider such a posture ridiculously unlikely.) When I was a child, ornithopods laid their eggs and then walked away forever. Today, these same creatures are the very models of maternal, caring, politically correct dinosaurs. They watch over their nests, care for their young, form cooperative herds, and bear such lovely, peaceful names as *Maiasaura*, the "earth mother lizard" (in contrast with such earlier monikers as *Pachycephalosaurus*, the "thick bonehead lizard"). Even their extinction now appears in a much more interesting light. They succumbed to vaguely specified types of "climatic change" in my youth; now we have firm evidence for extraterrestrial impact as the trigger for their final removal.

10   But how can this greening of dinosaurs be the major reason for present faddishness—for if we credit the Jungian theme at all, then the substrate for fascination has always been present, even in the bad old days of dumb and lumbering dinosaurs (who were, after all, still big, fierce, and extinct). What promotes this substrate to overt and pervasive dinomania? To such questions about momentary or periodic fads, one quintessentially American source usually supplies a solution—recognition and exploitation of commercial possibilities.

11   When I was growing up on the streets of New York City, yo-yo crazes would sweep through kiddie culture every year or two, usually lasting for a month or so. These crazes were not provoked by any technological improvement in the design of yo-yos (just as more-competent dinosaurs do not engender dinomania). Similarly, a Jungian substrate rooted in control over contained circular motion will not explain why every kid needed a yo-yo in July 1951, but not in June 1950 (just as dinosaurs are always available, but only sometimes exploited).

12   The answer, in short, must lie in commercialization. Every few years, someone figured out how to make yo-yos sell. As some point about twenty years ago, some set of forces discovered how to turn the Jungian substrate into profits from a plethora of products. You just need a little push to kick the positive feedback machine of human herding and copying behavior into its upward spiral (especially powerful in kids with disposable income).

I'd love to know the source of the initial push (a good theme for cultural his-   *13*
torians). Should we look to the great expansion of museum gift shops from holes-
in-the-wall run by volunteers to glitzy operations crucial to the financial health
of their increasingly commercialized parent institutions? Or did some particular
product, or character, grip enough youthful imaginations at some point? Should
we be looking for an evil genius, or just for an initial chaotic fluctuation, then
amplified by cultural loops of positive feedback?

II

Contemporary culture presents no more powerful symbol, or palpable product, of   *14*
pervasive, coordinated commercialization than the annual release of "blockbuster" films for the summer viewing season. The movies themselves are sufficiently awesome, but when you consider the accompanying publicity machines,
and the flood of commercial tie-ins from lunch pails to coffee mugs to T-shirts,
the effort looks more like a military Blitzkrieg than an offer of entertainment.
Therefore, every American who is not mired in some Paleozoic pit surely knows
that dinomania reached its apogee with the release of Steven Spielberg's film version of Michael Crichton's fine novel *Jurassic Park*. As a paleontologist, I could
not possibly feel more ambivalent about the result—marveling and cursing,
laughing and moaning. One can hardly pay greater tribute to the importance of
an event than to proclaim the impossibility of neutrality before it.

John Hammond (an entrepreneur with more than a touch of evil in the book,   *15*
but kindly and merely overenthusiastic in the film) has built the ultimate theme
park (for greedy profits in the book, for mixed but largely honorable motives in
the film) by remaking living dinosaurs out of DNA extracted from dinosaur blood
preserved within mosquitoes and other biting insects entombed in fossil Mesozoic
amber. Kudos to Crichton for developing the most clever and realistic of all scenarios for such an impossible event, for plausibility is the essence of good science
fiction. (The idea, as Crichton acknowledges, had been kicking around paleontological labs for quite some time.)

In fact, the amber scenario has been yielding some results—tiny DNA frag-   *16*
ments of the entombed insects themselves, not of anyone else's blood within the
insects! In the September 25, 1992, issue of *Science*, a group of colleagues, headed
by R. De Salle, reported the successful extraction of several DNA fragments
(fewer than two hundred base pairs each) from a 25 to 30-million-year-old termite
encased in amber. Then, in a publishing event tied to the opening of *Jurassic
Park*, the June 10, 1993, issue of the leading British journal *Nature*—same week
as the film's premiere—reported results of another group of colleagues, led by
R. J. Cano, on the extraction of two slightly larger fragments (315 and 226 base
pairs) from a fossil weevil. The amber enclosing this insect is 120-135 million
years old[1]—not quite as ancient as Jurassic, but from the next geological period,
called Cretaceous and also featuring dinosaurs as dominant creatures of the land
(most of the *Jurassic Park* dinosaurs are Cretaceous in any case!).[2]

17   This remarkable blurring of pop and professional domains emphasizes one of the most interesting spinoffs—basically positive in my view—of the *Jurassic Park* phenomenon. When a staid and distinguished British journal uses the premiere of an American blockbuster film to set the sequencing of its own articles, then we have reached an ultimate integration. Museum shops sell the most revolting dinosaur kitsch. Blockbuster films employ the best paleontologists as advisers to heighten the realism of their creatures. Orwell's pigs° have become human surrogates walking on two legs—and "already it was impossible to say which was which" (nor do I know anymore who was the pig, and who the person, at the outset—that is if either category be appropriate).

18   If all this welcome scientific activity gives people the idea that dinosaurs might actually be re-created by Crichton's scenario, I hasten (with regret) to pour frigid water upon this greatest reverie for any aficionado of ancient life. Aristotle wisely taught us that one swallow doesn't make a summer—nor, his modern acolytes might add, does one gene (or just a fragment thereof) make an organism. Only the most prominent, easily extracted, or multiply copied bits of fossil DNA have been sequenced—and we have no reason to believe that anything approaching the complete genetic program of an organism has been preserved in such ancient rocks. The most comprehensive and rigorous study of fossil DNA—the sequencing of a complete chloroplast gene from a 20 million year old magnolia leaf—found no nuclear DNA at all, while the recovered gene occurs in numerous copies per cell, with a correspondingly better chance of preservation. More than 90 percent of all attempted extractions in the magnolia study yielded no DNA at all. The amber DNA described above is nuclear, but represents bases coding for the so-called 16S and 18S ribosomal RNA genes—among the most commonly and easily recovered segments of the genetic program.

19   DNA is not a geologically stable compound. We may recover fragments, or even a whole gene here and there, but no wizardry can make an organism from just a few percent of its codes. *Jurassic Park* acknowledged this limitation when its genetic engineers used modern frog DNA to fill in the missing spaces in their dinosaur programs. But, in so doing, the scientists of *Jurassic Park* commit their worst scientific blunder—the only one that merits censure as a deep philosophical error, rather than a studied and superficial conceit consciously indulged to bolster the drama of science fiction.

20   An amalgamated code of, say, 80 percent dinosaur DNA and 20 percent frog DNA could never direct the embryological development of a functioning organism. This form of reductionism is simply silly. An animal is an integrated entity, not the summation of its genes, one by one. Fifty percent of your genetic code can't construct a perfectly good half of you; it makes no functioning organism at all. Genetic engineers might get by with a missing dab or two, but large holes cannot be plugged with DNA from a different zoological class. (Moreover, frogs and dinosaurs are not even close evolutionary relatives, for their lines diverged

in the Carboniferous period, more than 100 million years before the origin of dinosaurs. I suppose that Crichton used frogs because they conjure up an image of primitivity, and dinosaurs are ancient too. But evolutionary "closeness" involves timing of branching on the tree of life, not external appearances. Jurassic Park's scientists should have used modern birds, the closest living kin of dinosaurs.) The embryological decoding of a DNA program into an organism represents nature's most complex orchestration. You need all the proper instruments and conductors of a unique evolutionary symphony. You cannot throw in 20 percent of a rock band playing its own tunes by its own rules, and hope for harmony.[3]

When a scientist soberly states that something cannot be done, the public has   *21* every right to express doubts based on numerous historical precedents for results proclaimed impossible, but later both achieved and far surpassed. Unfortunately, the implausibility of reconstructing dinosaurs by the amber scenario resides in the different category of stronger argument.

Most proclamations of impossibility only illustrate a scientist's lack of imagi-   *22* nation about future discovery—impossible to see the moon's backside because you can't fly there, impossible to see an atom because light microscopy cannot resolve such dimensions. The object was always there: atoms and the moon's far side. We only lacked a technology, possible in principle to attain, but unimagined in practice.

But when we say that a particular historical item—like a dinosaur species—   *23* can't be recovered, we are invoking a different and truly ineluctable brand of impossibility. If all information about a historical event has been lost, then the required data just aren't there anymore, and the event cannot be reconstructed. We are not lacking a technology to see something that truly exists; rather, we have lost all information about the thing itself, and no technology can recover an item from the void. Suppose I want to know the name of every soldier who fought in the battle of Marathon.° The records, I suspect, simply don't exist, and probably never did. No future technology, no matter how sophisticated, can recover events with crucially missing information. So too, I fear, with dinosaur DNA. We may make gene machines more powerful by orders of magnitude than anything we can now conceive. But if full programs of dinosaur DNA exist nowhere—only the scrap of a gene here and there—then we have permanently lost these particular items of history.

III

I liked the book version of *Jurassic Park*. Crichton not only used the best possible   *24* scenario for making dinosaurs, but also based the book's plot upon an interesting invocation of currently fashionable chaos theory. To allay the fears of his credi-tors, John Hammond brings a set of experts to Jurassic Park, hoping to win their endorsement. His blue-ribbon panel includes two paleontologists and a preachy iconoclast of a mathematician named Ian Malcolm— the novel's intellectual and philosophical center. Malcolm urges—often, colorfully, and at length—a single devastating critique based on his knowledge of chaos and fractals: the park's safety system must collapse because it is too precariously complex in coordinating so many, and such intricate, fail-safe devices. Moreover, the park must fail both unpredictably and spectacularly. Malcolm explains in the book:

> It's chaos theory. But I notice nobody is willing to listen to the consequences of the mathematics. Because they imply very large consequences for human life. Much larger than Heisenberg's principle° or Gödel's theorem,° which everybody rattles on about...Chaos theory concerns everyday life...I gave all this information to Hammond before he broke ground on this place. You're going to engineer a bunch of prehistoric animals and set them on an island? Fine. A lovely dream. Charming. But it won't go as planned. It is inherently unpredictable...We have soothed ourselves into imagining sudden change as something that happens outside the normal order of things. An accident like a car crash. Or beyond our control, like a fatal illness. We do not conceive of sudden, radical, irrational change as built into the very fabric of existence. Yet it is. And chaos theory teaches us.

25   Moreover, Malcolm uses this argument—not the usual and vacuous pap about "man treading where God never intended" (Hollywood's only theme in making monster movies)—to urge our self-restraint before such scientific power: "And now chaos theory proves that unpredictability is built into our daily lives. It is as mundane as the rainstorm we cannot predict. And so the grand vision of science, hundreds of years old—the dream of total control—had died, in our century."

26   This reliance on chaos as a central theme did, however, throw the book's entire story line into a theoretically fatal inconsistency—one that, to my surprise, no reviewer seemed to catch at the time. The book's second half is, basically, a grand old rip-roaring chase novel, with survivors managing to prevail (unscratched no less) through a long sequence of independent and excruciatingly dangerous encounters with dinosaurs. By the same argument that complex sequences cannot proceed as planned—in this case, toward the novelistic necessity of at least some heroes surviving—not a *Homo sapiens* in the park should have been able to move without harm through such a sequence. Malcolm even says so: "Do you have any idea how unlikely it is that you, or any of us, will get off this island alive?" But I do accept the literary convention for bending nature's laws in this case.

27   I expected to like the film even more. The boy dinosaur enthusiast still dwells within me, and I have seen them all, from *King Kong* to *One Million Years B.C.* to *Godzilla*. The combination of a better story line, with such vast improvement in monster-making technology, seemed to guarantee success at a spectacular new level of achievement.

The dinosaurs themselves certainly delivered. As a practicing paleontologist, I   *28*
confess to wry amusement at the extended roman-à-clef embedded in the reconstructions. I could recognize nearly every provocative or outré idea of any colleague, every social tie-in now exploited by dinosaurs in their commanding role
as cultural icons. The herbivores are so sweet and idyllic. The giant brachiosaurs
low to each other like cattle in the peaceable kingdom. They rear up on their
hind legs to find the juiciest leaves. Individuals in the smaller species help each
other—down to such subtle details as experienced elders keeping young
Gallimimus in the safer center of the fleeing herd.

Even the carnivores are postmodernists of another sort. The big old fearsome   *29*
standard, *Tyrannosaurus rex*, presides over Jurassic Park in all her glory (and in
the currently fashionable posture, with head down, tail up, and vertebral column
nearly parallel to the ground). But the mantle of carnivorous heroism has clearly
passed to the much smaller *Velociraptor*, Henry Fairfield Osborn's Mongolian
jewel. Downsizing and diversity are in; constrained hugeness has become a tragic
flaw. *Velociraptor* is everything that modern corporate life values in a tough
competitor—mean, lean, lithe, and intelligent. They hunt in packs, using an old
military technique of feinting by one beast in front, followed by attack from the
side by a co-conspirator.

Spielberg didn't choose to challenge pop culture's canonical dinosaurs in all   *30*
details of accuracy and professional speculation; blockbusters must, to some
extent, play upon familiarity. Ironically, he found the true size of *Velociraptor*—
some six feet in length—too small for the scary effects desired, and he enlarged
them to nearly ten feet, thus moving back toward the old stereotype, otherwise
so effectively challenged. He experimented, in early plans and models, with
bright colors favored by some of my colleagues on the argument that birdlike
behavior might imply avian styles of coloration for the smaller dinosaurs. But he
eventually opted for conventional reptilian dullness ("your same old, ordinary,
dinosaur shit-green," lamented one of my graduate students who had expected
more obeisance to modernity).

But let me not carp. The dinosaur scenes are spectacular. Intellectuals too   *31*
often either pay no attention to such technical wizardry or, even worse, actually
disdain special effects with such dismissive epithets as "merely mechanical." I
find such small-minded parochialism outrageous. Nothing can be more complex
than a living organism, so the technological reconstruction of accurate and
believable animals therefore becomes one of the greatest all-time challenges to
human ingenuity.

The field has a long and honorable history of continually improving tech-   *32*
niques—and who would dare deny this story a place in the annals of human
intellectual achievement? An old debate among historians of science asks
whether most key technological inventions arise from practical need (more often
in war than in any other activity), or from fooling around in maximal freedom

from practical pressures. My friend Cyril Smith, the wisest scientist-humanist I ever knew, strongly advocated the centrality of "play domains" as the major field for innovations with immense practical utility down the road. (He argued that the block-and-tackle was invented, or at least substantially improved, in order to lift animals from underground storage pits to the game floor of the Roman Colosseum.) Yes, *Jurassic Park* is "just" a movie—but for this very reason, the filmmakers had freedom (and funds) to develop techniques of reconstruction, particularly computer generation, to new heights of astonishing realism. And yes, these advances matter—for immediately aesthetic reasons, and for innumerable practical possibilities in the future.

33   Spielberg originally felt that computer generation had not yet progressed far enough, and that he would have to film all his dinosaur scenes with the fascinating array of modeling techniques long used, but constantly improving, in Hollywood—stop-motion with small models, people dressed in dinosaur suits, puppetry of various sorts, robotics with hydraulic apparatus moved by people sitting at consoles.

34   But computer generation improved greatly during the two-year gestation of *Jurassic Park*, and the dinosaurs of the most spectacular scenes are drawn, not modeled—meaning, of course, that performers interacted with empty space during the actual shooting. I learned, after watching the film, that my two favorite dinosaur scenes—the fleeing herd of *Gallimimus*, and the final attack of *Tyrannosaurus* upon the last two *Velociraptors*—were entirely computer generated. (The effect does not always work. The very first dinosaur scene—when paleontologist Grant hops out of his vehicle to encounter a computer-generated *Brachiosaurus*—is the film's worst flop. Grant is clearly not in the same space as the dinosaur, and I could only think of Victor Mature, similarly out of synch with his beasts in *One Million Years B.C.*)

35   The dinosaurs are wonderful, but they aren't on set enough of the time. (Yes, I know how much more they cost than human actors.) Unfortunately, the plot line for human actors has been reduced to pap and drivel of the worst kind, the very antithesis of the book's grappling with serious themes. I fear that Mammon, and false belief in a need to "dumb down" for mass audiences, has brought us to this impasse of utter inconsistency. How cruel, and how perverse, that we invest the most awesome expertise (and millions of dollars) in the dinosaurs, sparing no knowledge or expense to render every detail, every possible nuance, in the most accurate and realistic manner. I have nothing but praise for the thought and care, the months and years invested in each dinosaur model, the pushing of computer generation into a new realm of utility, the concern for rendering every detail with consummate care, even the tiny bits that few will see and the little sounds that fewer will hear. I think of medieval sculptors who lavished all their skills upon invisible statues on the parapets, for God's view must be best (internal satisfaction based on personal excellence, in modern translation). How ironic that we

permit a movie to do all this so superbly well, and then throw away the story because we think that the public will reject, or fail to comprehend, any complexity beyond a Neanderthal "duh," or a brontosaurian bellow.

I simply don't believe that films, to be popular at the box office, must be dumbed *36* down to some least common denominator of universal comprehension. Science fiction, in particular, has a long and honorable tradition for exploring philosophically complex issues about time, history, and the meaning of human life in a cosmos of such vastness. Truly challenging films, like Kubrick and Clarke's *2001*, have made money, won friends, and influenced people—and even such truly mass-marketed series as *Star Wars*, *Star Trek*, and *Planet of the Apes* base their themes on the meaty issues traditionally used by the genre as centerpieces of plot lines.

But the film of *Jurassic Park* has gutted Crichton's book and inverted his inter- *37* esting centerpiece about chaos theory to Hollywood's most conventional and universal pap. We feel this loss most keenly in the reconstruction of Ian Malcolm as the antithesis of his character in the book. He still presents himself as a devotee of chaos theory ("a chaotician"), but he no longer uses the argument to formulate his criticisms of the park. Instead he is given the oldest diatribe, the most hackneyed and predictable staple of every Hollywood monster film since *Frankenstein*, that human technology must not disturb the specific and proper course of nature; we must not tinker in God's realm. What dullness and disappointment (and Malcolm, in the film, is a frightful and tendentious bore, obviously so recognized by Spielberg, for he effectively puts Malcolm out of action with a broken leg about halfway through the film).

Not only have we heard this silly argument a hundred times before (can *38* Spielberg really believe that his public could comprehend no other reason for criticizing a dinosaur park?), but Malcolm's invocation of the old chestnut utterly negates his proclaimed persona and cardinal belief, as his cinematic argument invokes the antithesis of chaos, and thereby engenders whopping inconsistency to boot. Two related flubs make the story line entirely incoherent.

First, as Malcolm rails against genetic reconstruction of lost organisms, *39* Hammond asks him if he would really hesitate to bring the California condor back to life (from preserved DNA), should the last bird die. Malcolm answers that he would not object, and would view such an act as benevolent, because the condor's death would have been an accident caused by human malfeasance, not an expression of nature's proper course. But we must not bring back dinosaurs because they disappeared along a natural and intended route. "Dinosaurs," he says, "had their shot and nature selected them for extinction." But such an implied scenario of groups emerging, flourishing, and dying, one after another in an intended and predictable course, negates the primary phenomena of chaos theory and its crucial emphasis on the great, accumulating effect of apparently insignificant perturbations, and on the basic unpredictability of long historical sequences. How can a chaotician talk about nature's proper course at all?

40   Second, if "nature selected them for extinction," and if later mammals therefore represent such an improvement, why can the dinosaurs of Jurassic Park beat
any mammal in the place, including the most arrogant primate of them all? You
can't have it both ways. If you take dinosaur revisionism seriously, and portray
them as smart and capable creatures able to hold their own with mammals, then
you can't argue against reviving them by depicting their extinction as both predictable and appointed, as life ratcheted onward to greater complexity.

41   Since Malcolm actually preaches the opposite of chaos theory, but presents
himself as a chaotician and must therefore talk about the theory, the film's
material on chaos becomes a vestigial and irrelevant caricature in the most
embarrassing of all scenes—Malcolm's halfhearted courting of the female paleontologist. He grasps her hand, drips water on the top, and uses chaos theory to
explain why we can't tell which side the drop will run down! How are the mighty
fallen, and the weapons of war perished.

IV

42   In the film, John Hammond flies his helicopter to the excavation site of Ellie
Sattler and Alan Grant, the two paleontologists chosen to "sign off" on his park
and satisfy his investors. They say at first that they cannot come, for they are hard
at work on the crucial phase of collecting a fossil *Velociraptor*. Hammond promises to fund their research for three years if they will spend one weekend at his
site. Grant and Sattler suddenly realize that they would rather be no place else
on earth; the *Velociraptor* can wait (little do they know...).

43   This scene epitomizes the ambivalence that I feel as a professional paleontologist about the *Jurassic Park* phenomenon, and about dinomania in general.
Natural history is, and has always been, a beggar's game. Our work has never
been funded by or for itself. We have always depended upon patrons, and upon
other people's perceptions of the utility of our data. We sucked up to princes
who wanted to stock their baroque *Wunderkammern*° with the most exotic
specimens. We sailed on colonial vessels for nations that viewed the cataloguing of faunas and floras as one aspect of control (we helped Captain Bligh°
bring breadfruit from Tahiti to feed slaves in the West Indies). Many, but not
all, of these partnerships have been honorable from our point of view, but we
have never had the upper hand. Quite the contrary, our hand has always been
out.

44   Few positions are more precarious than that of the little guy in associations
based on such unequal sizes and distributions of might. The power brokers need
our expertise, but we are so small in comparison, so quickly bedazzled and often
silenced by promises (three years as a lifetime's dream for the paleontologists and
an insignificant tax write-off for Hammond), so easily swallowed up—if we do
not insist on maintaining our island of intact values and concerns in the midst of
such a different, and giant, operation. How shall we sing the Lord's song in a
strange land?

I do not blame the prince, the captain, or his modern counterparts: the government grantor, the commercial licenser, or the blockbuster filmmaker. These folks know what they want, and they are usually upfront about their needs and bargains. It is our job to stay whole, not to be swallowed in compromise, not to execute a pact of silence, or endorsement, for proffered payoff. The issue is more structural than ethical: we are small, though our ideas may be powerful. If we merge without maintaining our distinctness, we are lost.

Mass commercial culture is so engulfing, so vastly bigger than we can ever be. Mass culture forces compromises, even for the likes of Steven Spielberg. He gets the resources to prepare and film his magnificent special effects; but I cannot believe that he feels comfortable about ballyhooing all the ridiculous kitsch now for sale under the coordinated marketing program of movie tie-ins (from fries in a dinosaur's mouth at McDonald's—sold to kids too young for the movie's scary scenes—to a rush on amber rings at fancy jewelry stores); and I cannot imagine that either he or Michael Crichton is truly satisfied with their gutless and incoherent script as an enjoined substitute for an interesting book. Imagine, then, what compromises the same commercial world forces upon the tiny principality of paleontological research?

As a symbol of our dilemma, consider the plight of natural history museums in the light of commercial dinomania. In the past decade, nearly every major or minor natural history museum has succumbed (not always unwisely) to two great commercial temptations: to sell a plethora of scientifically worthless and often frivolous, or even degrading, dinosaur products by the bushel in their gift shops; and to mount, at high and separate admission charges, special exhibits of colorful robotic dinosaurs that move and growl but (so far as I have ever been able to judge) teach nothing of scientific value about these animals. (Such exhibits could be wonderful educational aids, if properly labeled and integrated with more traditional material; but I have never seen these robots presented for much more than their colors and sound effects [the two aspects of dinosaurs that must, for obvious reasons, remain most in the realm of speculation].)

If you ask my colleagues in museum administration why they have permitted such incursions into their precious and limited spaces, they will reply that these robotic displays bring large crowds into the museum, mostly of people who otherwise never come. These folks can then be led or cajoled into viewing the regular exhibits, and the museum's primary mission of science education receives a giant boost.

I cannot fault the logic of this argument, but I fear that my colleagues are expressing a wish or a hope, not an actual result, and not even an outcome actively pursued by most museums. If the glitzy displays were dispersed among teaching exhibits, if they were used as a springboard for educational programs (sometimes they are), then a proper balance of Mammon and learning might be reached. But, too often, the glitz occupies a separate wing (where the higher admission charges can be monitored), and the real result gets measured in increased body counts and profits. One major museum geared all its fancy fund-raising apparatus for years to the endowment of a new wing—and then filled the space with a massive gift shop, a fancy restaurant, and an Omnimax theater, thus relegating the regular exhibits to neglect and disrepair. Another museum intended the dinosaur robots as a come-on to guide visitors to the permanent exhibits. But they found that the robots wouldn't fit into the regular museum. Did they cancel the show? Not at all. They moved the robots to another building on the extreme opposite end of the campus—and even fewer people visited the regular museum as a result.

50   I may epitomize my argument in the following way: Institutions have essences—central purposes that define their integrity and being. Dinomania dramatizes a conflict between institutions with disparate essences—museums and theme parks. Museums exist to display authentic objects of nature and culture— yes, they must teach; and yes, they may certainly include all manner of computer graphics and other virtual displays to aid in this worthy effort; but museums must remain wedded to authenticity. Theme parks are gala places of entertainment, committed to using the best displays and devices from the increasingly sophisti-cated arsenals of virtual reality to titillate, to scare, to thrill, even to teach.

51   I happen to love theme parks, so I do not speak from a rarefied academic post in a dusty museum office. But theme parks are, in many ways, the antithesis of museums. If each institution respects the other's essence and place, this opposi-tion poses no problem. But theme parks represent the realm of commerce, muse-ums the educational world—and the first, by its power and immensity, must trump the second in any direct encounter. Commerce will swallow museums if educators try to copy the norms of business for immediate financial reward.

52   Speaking about the economics of major sporting events, George Steinbrenner,° the man we all love to hate, once opined that "it's all about get-ting the fannies into the seats." If we have no other aim than to attract more bod-ies, and to extract more dollars per fanny, then we might as well convert our museums to theme parks and fill the gift shop with coffee mugs. But then we will be truly lost—necessarily smaller and not as oomphy as Disneyland or Jurassic Park, but endowed with no defining integrity of our own.

53   Our task is hopeless if museums, in following their essences and respecting authenticity, condemn themselves to marginality, insolvency, and empty corri-dors. But, fortunately, this need not and should not be our fate. We have an absolutely wonderful product to flog—real objects of nature. We may never entice as many visitors as Jurassic Park, but we can and do attract multitudes for the right reasons. Luckily—and I do not pretend to understand why—authentic-ity stirs the human soul. The appeal is cerebral and entirely conceptual, not at all visual. Casts and replicas are now sufficiently indistinguishable from the originals that no one but the most seasoned expert can possibly tell the difference. But a

cast of the Rosetta Stone° is plaster (however intriguing and informative), while the object itself, on display in the British Museum, is magic. A fiberglass *Tyrannosaurus* merits a good look; the real bones send shivers down my spine, for I know that they supported an actual breathing and roaring animal some 70 million years ago. Even the wily John Hammond understood this principle, and awarded museums their garland of ultimate respect. He wanted to build the greatest theme park in the history of the world—but he could do so only by abandoning the virtual reality of most exemplars, and stocking his own park with real, living dinosaurs, reconstructed from authentic dinosaur DNA. (I do appreciate the conscious ironies and recursions embedded in *Jurassic Park*'s own reality—that the best dinosaurs are computer-generated within a movie based on a novel.)

For paleontologists, *Jurassic Park* is both our greatest opportunity and our most   *54* oppressive incubus—a spur for unparalleled general interest in our subject, and the source of a commercial flood that may truly extinguish dinosaurs by turning them from sources of awe into clichés and commodities. Will we have strength to stand up in this deluge?

Our success cannot be guaranteed, but we do have one powerful advantage, if   *55* we cleave to our essence as guardians of authenticity. Commercial dinosaurs may dominate the moment, but must be ephemeral, for they have no support beyond their immediate profitability. Macbeth, in the soliloquy cited at the outset of this essay, recognized a special problem facing his plans, for he could formulate no justification beyond personal advantage: "I have no spur to prick the sides of my intent, but only vaulting ambition, which o'erleaps itself." This too shall pass, and nothing of human manufacture can possibly challenge the staying power of a dinosaur bone—65 million years (at least) in the making. ◆

1995

Endnotes

1. Since I wrote this review of *Jurassic Park* in 1993, two claims for dinosaur DNA (teensy fragments, of course, not blueprints of whole organisms) have appeared in the literature—but I am highly skeptical of both claims (and my doubts are widely shared by professional colleagues). Incidentally, I will not be at all surprised (but rather overjoyed) if bits and pieces of genuine dinosaur DNA are recovered in the near future though I strongly doubt that full DNA programs for entire dinosaurs exist anywhere in the fossil record. I am even more dubious (though I root for the result and hope for its validation) about the May 1995 claim for revivified bacteria from the stomachs of 30-million-year-old bees trapped in amber.

2. Pardon some trivial professional carping, but only two of the dinosaurs featured in the film *Jurassic Park* actually lived during the Jurassic period—the giant sauropod *Brachiosaurus*, and the small *Dilophosaurus*. All the others lived during the subsequent Cretaceous period—a perfectly acceptable mixing, given the film's premise that amber of any appropriate age might be scanned for dinosaur blood. Still, the majority might

rule in matters of naming, though I suppose that Cretaceous Park just doesn't have the same ring. When I met Michael Crichton (long before the film's completion), I had to ask him this small-minded professional's question: "Why did you place a Cretaceous dinosaur on the cover of *Jurassic Park?*" (for the book's dust jacket—and now the film's logo—features a Cretaceous *Tyrannosaurus rex*). I was delighted with his genuine response: "Oh my God, I never thought of that. We were just fooling around with different cover designs, and this one looked best." Fair enough; he took the issue seriously, and I would ask no more.

3. As my colleague Adam Wilkins said to me, the situation is even more hopeless, and the reductionistic error of *Jurassic Park* more intense. Even 100 percent of dinosaur DNA won't make a functioning organism by itself. A complex newborn animal is not an automatic product of its molecular code—for the code needs to work in, and interact with, the proper environment for embryological growth. After all, the code may act as a chief directing engineer, but not as a mason, carpenter, or plasterer. In dinosaurs, the main material must be present in the maternal egg. Moreover, and most vitally, organisms are not constructed only by their own genes. Certain maternal genes must produce products and chemical signals needed by the fertilized egg nucleus for its early divisions and differentiations. If these maternal transcripts are not present in the dinosaur egg before fertilization, the embryo will not develop. Thus the genetic engineers of *Jurassic Park* must know not only the full code for the dinosaur itself, but also the number, location, and action of maternal genes needed to construct the right environment for development.

Glossary

Henry Fairfield Osborn: (1857–1935) American paleontologist and museum administrator who had a profound impact on both fields in the United States and Great Britain.

Jungian or archetypal theme: refers to the separation of the psyche into three levels in Jungian psychoanalysis (conscious ego, personal unconscious, collective unconscious). Carl Jung (1865–1961) called the components of the collective unconscious "archetypes."

Orwell's pigs: central characters in George Orwell's novel *Animal Farm* (1944). These pigs' behaviour was so human-like that at one point, the other animals could not tell which was the pig and which was the person.

battle of Marathon: military battle that took place in ancient Attica, northeast of Athens, in which the Greeks emerged victorious over the advancing Persians; according to legend, news of the Persians' defeat was conveyed to Athens by a messenger, Pheidippides, who ran the entire 26 miles and 385 yards, the distance of modern marathon races.

Heisenberg's principle: from Werner Heisenberg (1901–1976), a German physicist who, through experiments in quantum mechanics, developed what has since been labelled the "Heisenberg principle of indeterminacy"; it states that on the microcosmic level of particle physics, accurate measurements of the position of electrons, for example, cannot reliably be determined.

Gödel's theorem: from Friedrich Gödel (also spelled Jödl) (1849–1914), a German philosopher who argued that reality should be an object of scientific inquiry.

Wunderkammern: *wunder* means wonderful in German; *kammern* means chambers or rooms. *Wunderkammern* refers to a collection of wonders or curiosities.

Captain Bligh: (1754–1874) English admiral and captain of HMS *Bounty*; his extreme brutality led to a 1787 mutiny aboard the ship by his crew.

George Steinbrenner: (b. 1930) controversial and volatile American owner of the New York Yankees professional baseball club.

Rosetta Stone: fragment of a stone tablet found in 1799 in a French archeological excavation in Egypt which enabled Jean François Campolion to decipher the ancient Egyptian system of hieroglyphics.

Explorations

- Were you ever a "dinosaur nut"? Have you ever taken part in a fad or craze?

- Like Gould, do you think that commercialism is behind fads and crazes? If so, what do you think is the source of the "initial push"? That is, what do you think motivates people to want to sell dinosaurs or yo-yos at a particular point in time?

- How has commercialism affected institutions other than museums?

Stephen Lewis was born in Ottawa in 1937. He is known as a politician, a diplomat, and a humanitarian. He has held many posts in Canadian and international politics, including leader of the Ontario NDP (1970–1978); while leading the party he became Leader of the Opposition in 1975. In the 1980s, Lewis was the Canadian ambassador to the United Nations, and later he was deputy executive director of the United Nations Children's Fund (UNICEF). He is currently appointed as Special Envoy for HIV/AIDS in Africa. He holds 15 honorary degrees from Canadian universities and is a radio and television commentator and labour relations arbitrator. "AIDS in Africa" was Lewis' keynote address to the G6B (Group of Six Billion) People's Summit at the University of Calgary, June 21, 2002.

AIDS in Africa

Stephen Lewis

1   I've wrestled with this speech for two reasons.

2   First, I recognize that many people here would wish this keynote to be an omnibus exploration of the perverse and destructive nature of globalization. It will be, but only in narrow part, and only in a particular way. I am appeased, however, by the recognition that you have significant numbers of plenary and panel sessions that will bare the heartless soul of this globalization for all to see.

3   Second, what I intend to do instead, is to deal directly with NEPAD, the G8° Summit response and HIV/AIDS, especially HIV/AIDS. I've been travelling through Africa for more than a year now, and it's impossible to emerge unscathed, intellectually or emotionally, by the monumental devastation of the pandemic. But I must admit that to deal with these Summit matters head on raises, for me, some awkward considerations that I'd like to confront directly.

4   I live two lives: one is speaking within Canada to a variety of groups; the other is the role of UN Envoy on AIDS in Africa. Inevitably the two roles intermingle. But tonight, of all nights, I want to retain at least twelve degrees of separation. Tonight I'm speaking in what diplomacy elegantly calls "my personal capacity."

5   But of course there's more. Implicit and explicit in my remarks will be criticism of NEPAD, which gives me some anxiety. NEPAD, after all, has been fashioned within Africa itself; indeed, four African Presidents, the Secretary-General of the United Nations and the head of the Economic Commission for Africa are here to act as advocates for NEPAD. That doesn't compromise my determination to deal with difficult issues; it would be insulting were any of us to back away from intellectual engagement just because the document and its authors are indigenous to the continent. But it does give me pause, because far too often in the past, western criticism has been gratuitous and insufferably overbearing. I should

add, I guess, that some of the members of the auspicious African delegation are friends with whom I have worked closely, at one time or another, over the last several years. I have known the Secretary-General for seventeen years now, and I report to him today. The President of Nigeria, President Obasanjo, is a man for whom I have the greatest regard, and one of the African leaders moving heaven and earth to defeat the pandemic of AIDS—in fact we have worked together on AIDS in Nigeria—and it pains me that we should find ourselves at odds. So I confess to all of you that on various grounds, I am somewhat clutched about some of the views I intend to disgorge. That doesn't mean I won't deliver them. It means only that beneath the rhetorical broadsides, there are heavy-duty palpitations.

Let me proceed to deal with the issues. 6

NEPAD—the New Partnership for African Development—is a document 7 driven by the fashionable current tenets of liberalized trade, governance, democratization and anti-corruption. They all sound fine in themselves, but I happen to believe that that prescription is faulty; indeed it is reminiscent of many similar analyses of Africa that have gone before, and have come to naught.

I say this with some feeling and a strong sense of history. I vividly remember 8 chairing the first UN session ever held on a single region of the world ... the Special Session on Africa in May/June of 1986. After two weeks of gruelling and relentless negotiation we emerged—even though the western and eastern blocs were still locked into the Cold War—with a consensus document. That document had similarities to the document of today. African governments undertook certain commitments to change, in response to which the rich nations made certain commitments to resources, trade and the dramatic reduction of debt. That document—known by the excruciating acronym of UNPAAERD, the United Nations Programme of Action for African Economic Recovery and Development —was betrayed within months of its embrace. The western commitments took the form of structural adjustment programmes, bogus promises on trade (witness the abject travesty of the Uruguay Round°), and dismal debt relief. And that began a procession of similar programmes, within multilateralism, every five years, each and every one of which made a mockery, on both sides, of the promises so eagerly tendered. It was a culture of wilful, mutual, repetitive deceit.

And so we come to NEPAD, for the first time ever a comprehensive pro- 9 gramme fashioned by Africa alone. I intend to withhold final judgement on NEPAD overall. I know that there are numbers of people in this hall with strong reservations, but they, as I, hope against hope that it works. I should add that there are those within Africa itself who argue that NEPAD is intellectually scarred by the inadequate consultation or the absence of consultation at the grass roots. And that obviously gives further pause. It was the North-South Institute in Ottawa that recently produced an excellent monograph on NEPAD, vigorously making the same point about consultation.

10   On the broad economic and consultative dimensions of NEPAD, therefore, I'm going to leave the debate to others, although there is one matter I must raise. It seems to me that the element of manipulative deceit rears its head again on the question of liberalized trading arrangements. The mantra of the aristocratic patricians of the G8 countries is that trade will set you free. But how in God's name can you promise a liberalized trading regimen on the one hand, while promulgating $190 billion worth of domestic agricultural subsidies on the other? And that's just the United States. Add another $160 billion or more from the European Union, throw in other heavily protected industries, and you effectively deliver a message to Africa that the new round of trade talks under the WTO° are a Machiavellian illusion.

11   It was the Prime Minister himself, just ten days ago in Montreal, who called the avalanche of subsidization an exercise in hypocrisy. It was the Minister of Finance himself who three days ago took the American Secretary of the Treasury out behind the woodshed to administer a metaphysical beating, so angered was John Manley by the subsidization frenzy. Someone has to explain how the cornerstone of NEPAD, namely liberalized trade, is going to work under present circumstances. I agree with my Prime Minister: it won't work. Why then the self-congratulatory exuberance of the G8 countries? You can't have it both ways: you can't have the announcement of a stirring new partnership on the one hand, when the economic centrepiece is an illusion. You end up with orchestrated hype rather than reality.

12   A footnote, and I'll move on. In 1988, before I left the UN, I attended a lunch in honour of Michel Camdessus, the then Managing Director of the International Monetary Fund, who explained, in exquisite detail, to several developing country ambassadors, how the emerging Uruguay Round of trade talks would be their salvation. I remember vividly to this day the Ambassador of Ghana saying to Mr. Camdessus that it was all transparent poppycock (although it's possible he didn't use those exact words). Mr. Camdessus, hand on heart, promised otherwise. Michel Camdessus was wrong. The Ghanaian Ambassador was right. The Uruguay Round did nothing for Africa. In fact, as is well-known, Africa's terms of trade declined. There is an unsettling resonance between then and now.

13   But allow me to get to the main burden of my remarks.

14   It seems to me that there's a critical flaw at the heart of the NEPAD document. For all its talk of trade, and investment, and governance, and corruption, and matters relating to financial architecture, there is only a pro forma sense of the social sectors, only modest references to the human side of the ledger. And in a fashion quite startling, in fact, disturbingly startling, NEPAD hardly mentions HIV/AIDS at all. But how can you talk about the future of sub-Saharan Africa without AIDS at the heart of the analysis? The failure to do so leads to a curious and disabling contradiction.

NEPAD has a number of stunning goals. They are essentially the Millennium   *15*
Development Goals: attain an annual growth rate of 7% for fifteen years; cut
poverty in half by the year 2015; reduce infant mortality rates by two-thirds;
reduce maternal mortality rates to three-quarters of what they were before; have
every child enter school who is eligible, thereby reinforcing the principle of gender
equality. A more admirable agenda could not be imagined.

But there's a dreadful conundrum. And it lies, somewhat elusively—you might   *16*
almost say in hiding—in the middle of the document at paragraph 125. Let me
quote the two key sentences: "One of the major impediments facing African
development efforts is the widespread incidence of communicable diseases, in
particular HIV/AIDS, tuberculosis and malaria. Unless these epidemics are
brought under control, real gains in human development will remain an impossible hope." Let me repeat—and remember, this isn't the gentle ranting of a
maniacal socialist; this is straight from the NEPAD text itself—"Unless these
epidemics are brought under control, real gains in human development will
remain an impossible hope."

There's actually a faintly comic aspect to this paragraph. Until a recent revi-   *17*
sion, the original text read that real gains in human development will remain a
"pipedream." The word "pipedream" became too evocative in a text that was otherwise a model of somnambulent bureaucratese, so they dumped it in favour of
"impossible hope." The meaning, however, remains clear: unless we deal with
HIV/AIDS, all the proud declarations of NEPAD are doomed.

I cannot put the case too strongly. There will be no continuous 7% annual   *18*
growth rate in the twenty-five countries where the prevalence rate of HIV is
above 5%—considered to be the dangerous take-off point for the pandemic—
unless the pandemic is defeated. In fact, it is virtually certain that several of
those countries will experience a negative rate of growth year over year under
present circumstances. There will be no cutting poverty in half by the year 2015
unless the pandemic is defeated; poverty exacerbates the pandemic, but the
reverse is equally true. When family income is gutted as wage earners die, as
plots of land are left untended, as every penny goes to the care of the sick and
the dying, it is preposterous to pretend that poverty will be halved. There will
be no reduction in infant mortality by two-thirds, unless the pandemic is defeated.
How can there be? Two thousand infants a day are currently infected—a certain
death warrant—maintaining or elevating the already impossibly high infant
mortality rates. There will be no reduction in maternal mortality rates unless the
pandemic is defeated. How can there be? We've learned over the years that
maternal mortality is one of the most intractable health problems throughout the
developing world; in a situation where the health systems are under assault,
where hospitals and community clinics can't cope, there's no chance of reducing
maternal mortality by three-quarters. Seldom has the word "pipedream" been
more applicable.

19   And there is certainly no chance of putting every eligible child in school, especially the girls, unless the pandemic is defeated. UNESCO° has very recently
released a study showing that four out of every ten primary school age children
are now not in school in sub-Saharan Africa. Young girls are regularly pulled out
of classrooms to look after ailing parents. There are thirteen million orphans in
Africa, the numbers rising inexorably, huge cohorts of them living on the streets,
or attempting to survive in child-headed households after the extended family is
gone and the grandmothers are dead. These kids have nothing; they certainly
have no money to afford school fees, or books, or uniforms. And it's not just the
children, it's the teachers. I was in New York last month for the Children's
Summit, sharing a panel with Peter Piot, head of UNAIDS, when he used the
startling figure that last year alone, a million African children lost their teachers
to AIDS. The government of Mozambique just issued a statement that 17% of its
teachers will die of AIDS by the end of this decade. As I travel, when I speak to
Ministers of Education, they haven't the faintest idea how they're going to
replace the teachers that are gone, or how they will ever find trained or adequate
substitute teachers to fill in for the regular classroom teachers who are off sick for
extended periods of time. We're talking about an unprecedented calamity.
There's nothing more noble than the objective of putting every child in school,
but if the objective is not to be more than some kind of ephemeral mockery, then
AIDS must be defeated.

20   In other words, quite simply, taken all in all, and I emphasize again, taken from
NEPAD itself, the development goals of Africa are an "impossible hope" until we
have turned the pandemic around.

21   I remember visiting a little Catholic community centre in Windhoek, Namibia,
in February. It was a place where people living with AIDS could network, find a
support group, have a meal, try to earn some money through an income generat-
ing project. What was the project in that instance? The Sister running the centre
took me out back to show me. A group of men were making miniature paper
maché coffins for infants, and as they affixed the silver handles, they said to me
with a mixture of pride and anguish: "We can't keep up with the demand."

22   I guess that was, for me, the nadir of this last year of travelling through Africa.
This is a sophisticated and knowledgeable audience; I don't have to drive the nail
through the wall. It's simply self-evident truth, that in country after country
where the pandemic is grievously rooted, the development process has been dealt
a mortal blow. The G8 Summit next week is, in a way, the last best chance for
Africa. The G8 leaders, straitjacketed in the kind of denial that afflicted the
African leaders for twenty years, must make an Herculean effort to break free and
provide a binding commitment to the continent.

23   On Wednesday of this week, in the *Globe and Mail*, there was a brilliant piece
of journalism from Malawi by Stephanie Nolen. With a profusion of images and
examples which linger in the mind, Stephanie Nolen chronicled the devastation

to the continent, some of it irreversible, exacted by the scourge of AIDS. Towards the end of the piece, she wrote: "Next week, when the G8 looks at Africa, the rest of the world will have a chance to look at the bigger picture. There will be much talk of the continent's wars, its corrupt governments and its disastrous economic policies, which keep it mired in poverty. And there will be just as much talk about the great hope that peace, trade, investment and better management can bring to the world's poorest continent. But to assess any of these, and to decide what role the North should play in Africa's future, the leaders of the world's richest nations must grapple with the impact of AIDS as never before. First and last, it has become the dominant force in African development. The reality of AIDS means that nothing short of a new approach to Africa will work."

That argument mirrors the views of the recent remarkable study from the   24
World Health Organization, authored by Jeffrey Sachs, the noted former Harvard economist, now an advisor to Kofi Annan, entitled the "Report of the Commission on Macroeconomics and Health."

For many years now, some might say decades, the argument has always been   25
that if you generate sufficient economic growth, the health of a society will be secured. It's essentially the old trickle-down theory. Those who explain the current G8 process are making the same argument, indeed embroidering it further to say that AIDS can soak up all our money, but until Africa has investment, trade, pays taxes and grows, nothing will change for Africa.

In the first instance, no one has suggested it's all or nothing. Surely, even the   26
most elemental pragmatism indicates that a mix is possible. But far more important is the argument of Sachs, based on what seems to me to be irrefutable analysis, that the existing paradigm has to be turned on its head. He says, in part: "The linkages of health to poverty reduction and to long-term economic growth are powerful, much stronger than is generally understood. The burden of disease in some low-income regions, especially sub-Saharan Africa, stands as a stark barrier to economic growth and therefore must be addressed frontally and centrally in any comprehensive development strategy. The AIDS pandemic represents a unique challenge of unprecedented urgency and intensity. This single epidemic can undermine Africa's development over the next generation...."

In this international primer of common sense development imperatives, Sachs   27
is not about to take the developing countries off the hook. He demands of them what the African governments, in NEPAD, demand of themselves: transparency, accountability, good governance. But he requires a quid pro quo: "The high-income countries would simultaneously commit vastly increased financial assistance, in the form of grants, especially to the countries that need help most urgently, which are concentrated in sub-Saharan Africa." Then, in the only sentence in the report which is italicized, Sachs writes: *"They would resolve"*—i.e., the G8—*"They would resolve that lack of donor funds should not be the factor that limits the capacity to provide health services to the world's poorest peoples."*

28   And therein lies the rub. In fact, therein lies the rot. Sadly, inexplicably, the G8 is guilty of a profound moral default. They simply will not meet the commitments which they have previously pledged—pledged as far back as 1970, when Lester Pearson chaired the committee of the OECD countries which agreed that 7/10ths of 1 percent of Gross Domestic Product, i.e. the famous 0.7% of GDP, should be the foreign aid quota for the wealthy nations. The present Official Development Assistance equals 0.22% or $53 billion for the entire developing world. If it were at 0.7%, it would yield $175 billion today, and $200 billion by 2005. In other words, by any calculation, we would have enough money to staunch the fatal lacerations of AIDS, to provide free universal primary education and to deal with nutrition, potable water and sanitation. The result would be the virtual eradication of poverty by 2015; the Millennium Development Goals would be exceeded.

29   Over the last months, days and weeks leading up to next week in Kananaskis,° there has been such a proliferation of figures as to make the mind reel. We hear about George Bush at the Financing for Development conference in Monterrey increasing American aid by 50%; we hear about the European Union at Monterrey providing an additional $20 billion; we hear about Jean Chrétien increasing the CIDA budget by 8% ad infinitum; we see a *Toronto Star* headline announcing $60 billion for Africa over the next decade, based on the G8 contributing half of its new foreign aid (whatever that means) to Africa; we see a headline in the *Globe and Mail* indicating G8 support for a schools package which, according to the World Bank, would be another $4 billion a year; we hear a new announcement from the US President of $500 million, or $300 million, depending on the interpretation, over two years, or three years, depending on the interpretation, for the prevention of mother-to-child transmission in eight countries, or twelve countries, depending on the interpretation, and so it endlessly goes in a welter of unfathomable arithmetic configurations until the mirrors and smoke sting the eyes with incredulity.

30   Look, the calculations don't have to be that complicated. George Bush said, at Monterrey, that he would increase American foreign aid by $5 billion overall, annually, by the year 2006. The current level is $10 billion; hence the claim of a 50% increase. The truth is that the increase in American aid brings them to 0.15% of GDP, or roughly to 20% of the target. The EU said, at Monterrey, that by the year 2006, it would add, overall, annually, another $7 billion, equivalent to 0.39% of GDP, or roughly 50% of the target. But let's be clear about what's being said: the United States and the European Union, four to five years down the road from now, will be providing, together, an additional $12 billion in foreign aid annually. That's not today; that's in the future. In fact, if I may put it starkly, another ten million people will have died before we reach those levels of assistance. Nor, by the way, does it all go to Africa. Nor, by the way, does it come without conditions.

Jean Chrétien said, at Monterrey, that he would increase Official Development   *31*
Assistance by 8% a year until the level of aid had doubled by around 2008. Alas, our
CIDA budget has been so severely cut by the present administration over the last
eight or nine years, that to double it over the next eight or nine years will bring it,
as a percentage of GDP, roughly back to the level of 1985! There is, to be fair, the
promise of a one-shot additional $500 million for Africa, but when that will become
available, and over what period of time and for what purpose, no one can figure out.

The truth is that over the next several days, we're going to witness an ava-   *32*
lanche of competing figures and contributions, most of which would challenge
the beautiful minds of the best mathematicians. Somehow we have to emerge
from the G8 Summit with a true and clear accounting of what's been pledged.
And I use the word "pledged" advisedly: there has so often been a chasm between
promise and delivery that it is truly difficult to trust what is announced. Just look
at what has happened to the debt initiative of the World Bank and the
International Monetary Fund and countless G7 incarnations of debt relief; just
look at what has happened to the guarantee of the eradication of hunger made
back in 1996; just look at what has happened to the pledges on universal primary
education, dating back to 1990; just look at the gap between promise and fulfill-
ment of the goals which were set at the first Summit for Children twelve years
ago, and to bring it right up to date, just look at the striking shortfall between the
pledges for Afghanistan and the actual delivery.

It's painful to be so skeptical. But history dictates that judgement be suspended   *33*
until we see what happens 'twixt cup and lip.

Except in one instance. And for me, albeit not for others, that instance will be   *34*
the litmus test for the G8 Summit. What are they going to pledge to the Global
Fund for AIDS, Malaria and Tuberculosis—the three communicable diseases
specifically identified in NEPAD?

Let me provide the context. Last year, at the AIDS Summit in Abuja, Nigeria,   *35*
the Secretary-General of the United Nations formally proposed the Global Fund,
and asked for $7 to $10 billion per year from all sources, but particularly from
governments. After a great deal of cajoling and persuasion, the rich nations have
contributed, thus far, $2.1 billion, but over three years. I repeat: over three years.
At the higher and more realistic level of $10 billion, it then amounts to about
7% of the need over those three years. It's a shocking piece of international
financial delinquency, and it's a shocking rejection of Africa. It's so deeply disap-
pointing that words are hard to find.

The Global Fund has an excellent apparatus for the disbursement of monies.   *36*
It has a Board representing governments of South and North, and civil society,
and the private sector. It has the capacity to expertly evaluate individual country proposals. It has the administrative backup of UN agencies. It is already in the
process of distributing hundreds of millions of dollars of the $2.1 billion in the
coffers. At present rates, it will very soon run out of money.

37   If the G8 Summit takes NEPAD seriously, if it wishes to make development more than an "impossible hope," if it adds to trade and investment a pledge to rescue the human condition in Africa, if it wants to redeem the Summit process, so tainted by previous posturing and irrelevance, then it will provide a guarantee, year by year, of the monies that Kofi Annan has requested for the Global Fund. In one fell swoop, the entire Summit would then be credible. Jean Chrétien will have his legacy, a legacy of principle, compassion and honour.

38   If, however, nothing, or an infinitesimal sum, is earmarked for the Global Fund, then a number of countries in sub-Saharan Africa will be in a desperate struggle for survival. The possible neglect of the Global Fund is not conjecture. *The New York Times* has an editorial today pointing out that the most recent announcement from President Bush involves purely bilateral money, and in the process deals a serious blow to the prospects for the Global Fund. And by the way, the use of the word "survival" is not mine. It's the word used by African leaders when they addressed the United Nations General Assembly Special Session on HIV/AIDS in June of last year.

39   One of the interesting things about the Global Fund is that no one ever proposed a schedule of payments, including the amounts that might legitimately be expected from each of the contributing countries. So in the interest of fair play, I'd like to make such a proposal.

40   Some little time ago, it occurred to me that there was an obvious analogy to be employed. All of the member states of the United Nations have accepted a formula to be applied to the budget of the UN and to its peacekeeping operations. The formula is based on population, and per capita income and other relevant indices. Simply put, it provides a scale of contributions in which each country pays a given percentage of the UN budget and the UN peacekeeping budget. In the case of Canada, that's 2.579% per annum. We've accepted the calculations as valid, we've always paid the equivalent dollar amount in full and on time, as have other countries. Even the United States, although lamentably delinquent in its payments, has accepted the existing formula. It seems to me logical, therefore, to apply the formula, universally agreed upon, to the Global Fund. After all, it is a Fund suggested by the Secretary-General of the United Nations. The calculation then becomes remarkably simple … if, for Canada, it's 2.579% of $7 billion, that amounts to 180 million US dollars per annum. If it's 2.579% of $10 billion, that amounts to 250 million US dollars per annum. As it happens, the Canadian Centre for Policy Alternatives just this week issued a statement that includes the calculations, based on the same formula, for the other G8 countries. It would be an act of extraordinary statecraft, an act that would truly revive a sense of international idealism, an act that would restore hope to an entire continent were the leaders of the world to make such a commitment.

41   At the end of Jeffrey Sachs' stirring exegesis, he says: "There is no excuse in today's world for millions of people to suffer and die each year for lack of 34 dol-

lars per person needed to cover essential health services. A just and far-sighted world will not let this tragedy continue."

Alas, it is not a just and far-sighted world.

Let me be clear: while the situation feels apocalyptic, it can be addressed. AIDS has done and is doing terrible things to Africa, but we know how to defeat it. That's what drives me crazy—we know how to defeat it. We know all about voluntary counselling and testing; we simply have to train more counsellors and get rapid testing kits into the hands of those who administer the tests. We know all about the prevention of mother-to-child transmission. We know about the wonder drug Nevirapine; one tablet to the mother at the onset of labour, one tablet during the birthing process, one dose of liquid equivalent to the baby within hours of birth and transmission of the virus can be reduced by up to 53%. We know about anti-retroviral treatment, the so-called drug cocktails that keep people alive. Largely as a result of competition from generic manufacturers in India, Thailand and Brazil, the cost of "ARVs" has dropped dramatically, but no matter how dramatic, the drugs are still beyond the capacity of Africans to afford when people live on less than a dollar a day. But it could be afforded through external financing, and it is one of the gruesome iniquities of the present situation that people are dying, everywhere, in huge numbers, unnecessarily. We know about prevention, particularly in the key youth communities aged 15 to 24. Through what they call peer counselling and peer education, using music, dance, drama, drums and poetry, questions of sexuality and condoms and abstinence and behaviour change are confronted in a fashion so explicit, so real, so frontal as to take your breath away. What has to be done of course, is to generalize prevention programmes throughout any given country, that is, to take prevention to scale. And it's possible if only Africa had the resources. We know about care at community level, where the sickness and the dying take place. The women of Africa, in particular, are incredibly sophisticated at the grass roots, with networks of community-based and faith-based organizations to provide care and compassion and love where there would otherwise exist only isolation, stigma and fear. In this instance, adequate resources would serve a two-fold purpose. Voluntary "home-based care," as we now know it, is really conscripted labour for women, an extension of gender oppression, the kind of oppression which, along with the absence of sexual autonomy, and predatory male behaviour, has made AIDS a gender-based disease. Fifty-five percent of the new infections are amongst women. If we had the money, we could encourage a network where men and women together provided the care, and women could assert their sexual and reproductive rights. We know about the strength of the associations of People Living With AIDS; we know about National AIDS Councils and National AIDS Control Commissions; we know about five-year plans; we know about dealing with high-risk groups—truck drivers, commercial sex workers, mobile populations—we now know about engaging political and religious leadership ... we know, in short, enough about the pandemic to turn it around.

44   To be sure, there are vexing, sometimes overwhelming problems of infrastructure, and overwhelming problems of finding the human capacity to do the job. When funerals are more pervasive than any other form of social gathering, when hospital wards are chambers of horrors, the life force of a society is slowly being strangled. But as I stand here, I genuinely believe, to the depths of my being, that we could save and prolong millions of lives, if only we had the resources to do so.

45   Let me end on an intensely personal note. Over the last few days, people have told me—not unpleasantly—that I get very emotional about the subject of AIDS in Africa. Some of my good friends worry about my psychological equanimity. I guess, in part, men are supposed to be stoic and bravely unfeeling, or at least self-contained.

46   I make no apologies for the occasional emotional catharsis. I can't help it. All my adult life, as a democratic socialist, along with countless colleagues, sometimes in partnership with people of other ideological beliefs, I've raged against injustice. But I've never seen anything like this. I don't know how to get a grip on it. I don't know how to make sense of it. Is the behaviour of the western world just appalling insensitivity, is it unacknowledged racism, is it sheer unbridled indifference, is it the comfortable assumption of hopelessness in order to avoid contributing money; is it possible that the political leadership is completely out of touch with the vast populations—like the people of Canada—over whom it holds sway?

47   I feel so angry and so impotent simultaneously. I privately wish that the African leadership had openly confronted the G8 on the issue of AIDS, rather than muting its impact within NEPAD. I know how tough it is to ask for money—Africa is asking for $64 billion a year, most of it from outside—to finance NEPAD, so it's intensely human and political not to want to disconcert your donors. But that makes it far too easy for the donor nations.

48   I carry around with me the images of young mothers, sitting on makeshift benches, in the shade under a tree, fifteen or twenty at a time, all of them exhibiting AIDS-related symptoms, and urgently, with great dignity, asking who will care for their soon-to-be-orphaned children, asking about medicines for straightforward opportunistic infections, asking about treatment, and so help me, I can't give any answers.

49   Somehow, this G8 Summit has to be a turning point. Africa is coming to us, pledging reform, asking for help. If we raise it to the intellectual and academic level, it really does become a question of globalization. Can globalization respond to global issues? If we see it at a human level, it demands from all of us the best we have to give. I note that the Secretary-General of the United Nations has recently written to the G8 leaders saying, in part, "The peoples of the developing world [will be] bitterly disappointed if your meeting confined itself to offering them good advice and solemn exhortations, rather than firm pledges of action in areas where your own contribution can be decisive." And by contribu-

tion, he includes dollars. On another occasion, writing the preface to the Declaration of Commitment which emerged from the HIV/AIDS Special Session last year, the Secretary-General said: "In the war against HIV/AIDS, there is no us and them, no developed and developing countries, no rich and poor—only a common enemy that knows no frontiers and threatens all peoples. But we must all remember that while HIV/AIDS affects both rich and poor, the poor are much more vulnerable to infection, and much less able to cope with the disease once infected. The leadership and commitment shown in this Declaration will [allow] ... the millions of suffering [to] ... know that the world is finally summoning the will—and committing the resources ... to win this war for all humanity."

Interesting that he uses the metaphor of war. In times of war, everything is a 50 national emergency. In times of war, every apparatus of the state is conscripted into battle. In times of war, resources are somehow found that are thought not to exist—just think of the so-called war on terrorism, with scores of billions of dollars hurled into the fray overnight to avenge the horrendous deaths of three thousand people. So explain to me why we have to grovel to extract a few billion dollars to prevent the deaths of over two million people every year, year after year after year?

Why is the war against terrorism sacrosanct, and the war against AIDS 51 equivocal?

In the answer to that question lies the challenge for NEPAD and the true test 52 for the G8. ◆

2002

Glossary

G8: an informal group of eight countries: Canada, France, Germany, Italy, Japan, Russia, the United Kingdom, and the United States of America.

Uruguay Round: officially, the 1986–1994 Uruguay Round Final Act of Trade Negotiations for the World Trade Organization Agreements. The Uruguay Round, in which 125 countries took part, brought about the biggest reform of the world's trading system since the General Agreement on Tariffs and Trade (GATT) was signed in 1947.

WTO: World Trade Organization. Based in Geneva, this organization has 135 members and is responsible for monitoring national trading policies, handling trade disputes, and enforcing the GATT agreements, which are designed to reduce tariffs and other barriers to international trade and to eliminate discriminatory treatment in international commerce.

UNESCO: an agency of the United Nations charged with instituting and administering programs for cooperative, coordinated action by member states in education, science, and the arts.

Kananaskis: the region of southwest Alberta where the G8 summit was held in June 2002.

Explorations

- Before reading this speech, were you aware of the widespread incidence of HIV/AIDs in Africa? If so, where did you hear about it? If not, why might that be?

- Explain, in your own words, why Lewis agrees with the NEPAD statement that development in Africa is an "impossible hope" until the HIV/AIDS epidemic is brought under control.

- If the situation is so serious in Africa, why do you think the Western world has not responded more effectively to Africa's request for help?

Lee Maracle, born in 1950, is granddaughter to the late Chief Dan George, and a Coast Salish orator, essayist, poet, and fiction writer. Her many books include Bobbi Lee, I Am Woman, Sun Dogs, *and* Ravensong. *Maracle has taught creative writing for a number of colleges and universities, Native organizations, and women's groups, and is currently working as Distinguished Professor of Canadian Culture at Western Washington University.*

Native Myths:
Trickster Alive and Crowing

Lee Maracle

There is a controversy in the realm of fiction writing in Canada. A good many   1
Native writers across Canada have been objecting of late to the appropriation of
our stories by Canadian writers. Our objections have given rise to a number of
accusations ranging from 'censorship' to the more innocent question of 'Who are
these women of colour?' who are objecting to appropriation? As one of the
women of colour who objects, I like to respond to the dilemma 'in my own voice.'

The sounds of night join my nocturnal obsession again; odd lonely automobile   2
sounds between long pauses of steady neon hum. Urban sleep is suddenly interrupted by a Raven coddling her aching wing. From my politically correct, three-
year-old co-op townhouse fence, she nurses her wing.

'Raven, why aren't you sleeping? You are disrupting some important business   3
with your pitiful "broken wing again" dance.' Edgar Allan Poe° lies overtop a Bob
Dylan° album cover. His words emerge from Trickster laughing at this thirty-
nine-year-old girl-child clinging tenaciously to an ancient indigenous image
immortalized by desperate white men more than one hundred years distant from
each other.[1] 'It's a bad joke Raven... to remind me that these white men re-stirred
dreams of you in me when I was so young. Go to sleep, while I wrestle with truth
and conscience.'

Raven stops coddling her wing, struts cockily forth and back across my fence   4
and I have to remind myself that this typewriter, which is supposed to be a computer printer, and will probably die a typewriter before the terminals ever reach
her, is my real friend. My typewriter and I have been together for some five
years—'twas a hasty wedding entered into on the promise of the purchase of her
twin, the computer, sometime in the future. Some time wedged between the
needs of four growing children. They have already made too many sacrifices for
their nocturnal mother's childhood dream and their great grandmother's hope
that she become a writer. The offensive article on the issue of 'Indian Mythology'

and 'censorship' to the right of me, my thoughts churning in front of me, and my library to the left, I stare at Raven, unable to begin.

5   Censorship; Noah Webster° jumps off the shelf, heavy with his unabridged-ness, tattered by fifty years of life, and spills the meaning of censorship into the vortex of my confusion: 'Anyone empowered to suppress a publication.' ('Any of the officials at a British University'; a most useless but interesting secondary meaning, Noah.) Publisher: 'Anyone who arranges the publication of a work.' The work belongs to the publisher in the sense that he (to which we must now add she) organizes and distributes it to the public, subject to the conditions out-lined in a contract between himself (read herself for women's presses) and the author.

6   Raven flaps her wings at me, chuckling hysterically. I feel small in my moment of embarrassing discovery.

7   'Naturally,' she crows. 'Why do you think the publisher garners the lion's share and the writer but the leftover morsels? Why do you think the customary prac-tice of publishers is to claim the publishing rights for the life of the book?' (Because it belongs to them?)

8   'Well, that helps, Raven, but it doesn't answer my question, at least not entirely. It tells me the publishers have the right to choose what they publish. "Letters to the *Sun* are edited for brevity and good taste." ... "your work has been rejected because...." Perfectly just, given that the publisher is responsible for making the work public. My dilemma is that the publisher is *ipso facto* absolved of any accu-sations regarding censorship, given her right to choose. Censorship requires a third party official.'

9   Raven just disappears, leaving me with the nagging suspicion that it is not just intellectual confusion that tears at my nocturnal wanderings.

10   From the shelves of my library, which steal more and more of my living space, dance W. B. Yeats's 'Second Coming,'° and Sam Shepard's *Cowboy Mouth*.° An odd pair of white male writers which, I am embarrassed to admit to my feminist friends and even more ashamed to display before Native people, are a deep source of joy and inspiration to me.

11   'Ah, but *Cowboy Mouth*, William, is such a wonderfully wicked modern ren-dering of your "rough beast" slouching "towards Bethlehem." That one of the sons of Europe one hundred years after you, in a place thousands of miles away, could take your "Second Coming," and dramatize it through the cowboy mouth of a woman—that a man could do this sincerely, honestly, almost prophetically, holds me in awe, William.' The typewriter pauses to accompany my awed pause and there she be again, regal like a queen, chest puffed up, black, beautiful and still, a raven centurion taking the applause for Yeats and Shepard.

12   'Tis my turn to laugh. 'Yes, the ol' black crow is Shepard's "second coming," Raven.' Raven; she just stares obliquely at my immodest cackling, another trick tucked within her wings. With uncommon slow grace her wings rise to form a

perfect circle. Her eyes recess, harden, and take on a familiar slant. T'a'ah emerges, her steely gaze centred on my childish indiscretion.² Mirth leaves me, replaced by a mature sense of loneliness for the old granny that took one hundred years to part with her grandchildren. Her look reminds me of the origins of 'eating crow.' Only Black people were ever forced to eat our ridiculed crow ... only white humans ever reduced this crow to a pie to be eaten by Blacks. 'Four and twenty blackbirds baked in a pie ...' (that Black people were forced to eat, likening them to cannibals). Our Raven, forever tainted by this ugly metaphor for white supremacy. Trickster. Our Raven takes the human spirit to a higher place, a second becoming, a new humanity, yet I possessed enough of Europe's poison to mock Raven.

The truth faced; T'a'ah relaxed her glare and spoke: 'You don't remember 13
child, your own delight at the words of Emerson° not so long ago ... "Look here, this sounds exactly like my T'a'ah ... truth is universal ... it is human, honest, riddled with the responsibility of personal choice, social conscience and love of nature... don't read the ancients to parrot their words devoid of understanding."' Her words, my exact paraphrase of the *American Scholar.*° The soft earth colours of T'a'ah's paisley cotton gown and matching scarf faded that my own fire might burn bright.

The onion is peeling back, exposing tears of shame. I rise, move to the com- 14
fort of the twin sisters—the lions. The twins, one of which perished in the lap of the other.³ There they sit, mountainous reminders of the glory of twinning spirits.⁴ Yeats, Shepard. Poe, Dylan. Rusty and Lee.⁵ Yeats perished; in the breast of a cowboy mouth woman he found his final resting place. Poe perished in drugged madness to be reborn in the songs of Dylan. Like Poe, and Yeats, in the sparse walls of her kitchen, Rusty had found her resting place in the memory of her twin's mind—Lee—the woman who would strive unremittingly, in her brutal determination to survive, to bring Trickster/Raven to the modern world and move humanity to another place.

Raven, large and full feathered, rose above me from my bedding on the floor, 15
melded with the ceiling and left me looking at the clock. I had only slept a half hour but I owed the world another gawdamned story. Birds chirped and I dragged my aching back to my chiropractically-recommended chair and began my obsession.

Granny, wispy and ghostlike, sat next to me cajoling my reluctance into 16
enthusiasm:

'It's just another hill to climb, hee, hee, hee.'

'Sounds like unbridled bragging to me,' I respond.

'What? That you had a twinning spirit? Everyone has one.'

'No.'

'That you can write, everyone that reads can write, they just don't.'

'It's that I do.'

'You're just obsessed, that's all.'

'T'a'ah, the very definition of obsession requires that I admit I am pathological, sick.'

17   Her last 'hee, hee, hee' linked itself with the sound of my old friend going ticky-tack-type whilst my eyes stared catatonically at the street and my fingers reconstructed the craziness of my dream.

18   The truth is that you Europeans came here when we had the land and you had the Bible. You offered us the Bible and took our land, but I could never steal the soul of you. Occasionally, your sons and daughters reject the notion that Europe possesses a monopoly on truth and that other races are to be confined to being baked in pies or contained in reservation misery. They are an inspiration to me, but they are not entirely satisfying. Your perception of my Raven, even when approached honestly by your own imagination, is still European. The truth is that a statement I made at the Third International Feminist Book Fair, objecting to the appropriation of our stories, has nothing to do with censorship. 'We are not monkey grunters in need of anyone to tell our stories.'[6]

19   'We have a voice.'[7] 'Don't buy books about us, buy books by us.'[8] 'And, Move over.'[9]

20   Since then, the debate about the appropriation of our voice and our culture has focused on censorship and freedom of imagination. On June 10, 1989, *The Globe and Mail* printed an interview with a white woman, Darlene Barry Quaife, who had appropriated our mythology. She admitted that she had lied and used us as a cover; when challenged, she squirmed, squeaking censorship to unnamed persons and the Women's Press. The truth is that creeping around libraries full of nonsensical anthropocentric drivel, imbuing these findings with falsehood in the name of imagination, then peddling the nonsense as 'Indian Mythology' is literary dishonesty. (An odd thing for a writer to defend given the origins of literature: litera, truth.)

21   The laws against plagiarism were born to protect the intellectual integrity of the literary community. To cry 'censorship' when caught trafficking in such truck is at best cowardly. I am told by a host of the *fifth estate*° (who has yet to air the interview with Anne Cameron and myself) that Timothy Findley, among others, is categorizing my objection (and that of the Women's Press) to such abuse and appropriation of our cultural heritage and sacred ways 'fascist.' Ms Quaife claims it is 'not exploitation,' as her pockets jingle, full of the royal coins of copyright, gained at our expense. Our stories had original authors; we are not dead. Someone told these stories to someone else who reaped copyright, royalties, credit and the dubious privilege of bastardizing them. We have lost both revenue and dignity in the process.

22   The truth is that yesterday, my grandmother and I thought little of such things as copyright, royalties and exploitation. We were a desperate people facing extinction whose first consideration was the land, along with the laws and sacred

ways of our people that would protect the land from the fate this country had destined for us. Under duress, we parted with our stories in the hope that in the wake of our annihilation, our land would survive intact. We have survived. Not only did we survive but we speak our own language, understand our ways and write in English. To continue appropriating our stories and misusing them in the name of 'freedom of imagination' is just so much racism. My old typewriter and I sit in my bedroom where the magic of Trickster lives. We object to the theft of our stories and the distortion of our lives. Those who would hide behind the lie of censorship to justify thievery and dishonesty don't hold the same terror for us.

Raven and I will have the last laugh. The Women's Press 'Front of the Bus' *23* coalition split with its lesser half because stories about women of colour written by white women are riddled with bias, stereotype and intellectual dishonesty. What is more important is that women of colour are entitled to author their own stories. I do not hear any outcries from any corner of the writing community about the penchant that women's presses have for publishing books about (white) women, written by (white) women and not men. In the minds of some white women, and many white men, women of colour do not enjoy equal rights. My typewriter is screaming now, Raven. I too look for the day when Canada's white parents attempt to induce their children to 'tell the truth' and their children throw back the food of censorship for their parents to eat. The fact is that a white person appropriating our stories because they lack imagination or knowledge of their own is still telling a European story. Use whatever you like to ground your story, intellectual Canada, but be honest. It is your story—it is not about me. ◆

1989

Endnotes

1. Trickster is a mythic figure in the Native cultures of North America. He is known by the names Nanabuzo, Raven and Coyote.

2. T'a'ah is a Native word for Grandmother.

3. The lions are a pair of mountains behind my father's village. Story has it that centuries ago these mountains were twin sisters, one of which died in the interest of the survival of their joint lineage. The two were immortalized as mountains, a reminder to her descendants that sometimes supreme sacrifices must be made in order to secure the survival of all. This sense of self and community is the foundation of our culture.

4. Twinning spirits: two people with a common world view, like spirits, but not necessarily living within the same time frame.

5. Rusty, from my book *I Am Woman* (Vancouver: Write-On Press Publishers, 1988).

6. Jeannette Armstrong, author of *Slash* (Penticton: Theytus Books, 1988).

7. Chrystos, author of *Not Vanishing* (Vancouver: Press Gang Publishers, 1988).

8. Viola Thomas, editor/promoter of Native women's books, organizer of hapless B.C. poets and all-round loyal indigenous woman.

9. Lee Maracle, author of *I Am Woman* and *Bobby Lee*.

Glossary

Edgar Allan Poe: (1809–1849) American poet, critic, and short-story writer known for his macabre and gothic tales.

Bob Dylan: (b. 1941) American singer and songwriter who, since his emergence in the 1960s, has released more than 30 albums, and who has had a profound impact on popular music.

Noah Webster: (1758–1843) American lexicographer and author best known as the compiler of *Webster's American Dictionary of the English Language*, first published in 1828.

W.B. [William Butler] Yeats' 'The Second Coming': a poem that uses swirling imagery of chaos and terror, and a vision of history as cyclical, to prophesy the cataclysmic end of an era. Critics have read Yeats's poem, included in the collection *Michael Robartes and the Dancer* (1921), as an extended allusion to several calamitous events, including the Easter Uprising in Ireland in 1916, the Russian Revolution of 1917, and the rise of fascism throughout Europe in the early 1920s.

Sam Shepard's *Cowboy Mouth*: a play first produced in New York in 1971, with Patti Smith in the lead role of Cavale. The play makes much of various shamanistic visions induced by drugs.

Emerson: Ralph Waldo Emerson (1803–1882), American poet, essayist, and philosopher who became chief spokesperson for the Transcendental Movement in the United States.

The American Scholar: a collection of Emerson's best-known speeches and addresses, first published in 1837.

the fifth estate: CBC television program devoted to investigative reporting of current affairs.

Explorations

- Do you think that telling someone else's story is intellectual dishonesty? Why or why not?

- Do you think that not wanting someone else to tell your story is censorship? Why or why not?

- In what way do you think Native stories told by Natives differ from Native stories told by non-Natives?

Bharati Mukherjee was born in 1940 in Calcutta, India. She obtained her B.A. and M.A. at the universities of Calcutta and Baroda, respectively, before earning her M.F.A. and Ph.D. from the University of Iowa in the 1960s. Mukherjee lived with her husband, the writer Clark Blaise, and their two children in Montreal from 1966 to 1980, where she taught at McGill University. In 1980 she and her family moved to the United States; Mukherjee currently teaches in the Department of English at the University of California at Berkeley. Her books include Wife, The Tiger's Daughter, Darkness, The Middleman and Other Stories, *winner of the National Book Critics Circle Award,* Jasmine, The Holder of The World, Leave It to Me, *and with Blaise,* Days and Nights in Calcutta *and* The Sorrow and the Terror: The Haunting Legacy of the Air India Tragedy.

An Invisible Woman

Bharati Mukherjee

This story begins in Calcutta and ends in a small town in New York State called 1 Saratoga Springs. The very long, fifteen-year middle is set in Canada. In this story, no place or person fares well, but Canada comes off poorest of all.

I was born in Calcutta, that most Victorian and British of post-independence 2 Indian cities. It was not the Calcutta of documentary films—not a hell where beggars fought off dying cattle for still-warm garbage—but a gracious, green, subtropical city where Irish nuns instructed girls from better families on how to hold their heads high and how to drop their voices to a whisper and still be heard and obeyed above the screams of the city.

There was never a moment when we did not know that our city and our coun- 3 try were past their prime. We carried with us the terrible knowledge that while our lives were comfortable, they would be safer somewhere else. Ambition dictated emigration. In the 1950s everyone was waiting for the revolution. "The first thing the Communists do," my best friend told me when we were fifteen, "is feel your hands. If your hands are soft, it's *kaput* for you." In our school every girl had soft hands. But when Stalin died, the nuns prayed for his soul: this was known as "fair play," an example for us pliant, colonial girls to follow.

In a city continually blistered with revolutionary fervour, we plodded through 4 our productions of The Mikado.° At least twice I was escorted by van loads of police past striking workers outside the gates of my father's factory so that I could go to school and dance a quadrille or play a walk-on part. "Our girls can take their places with the best anywhere in the world," Mother John-Baptist, the head-mistress, had promised my father on my first day of school. (And we have, all over India and the English-speaking, even German-speaking, world.) On a sticky August night in 1961, when my younger sister, who was going to Vassar

College, and I, on my way to the University of Iowa, left by Air India for New York, I felt that I could.

5   Great privilege had been conferred upon me; my struggle was to work hard enough to deserve it. And I did. This bred confidence, but not conceit. I never doubted that if I wanted something—a job, a scholarship—I could get it. And I did. I had built-in advantages: primarily those of education, secondarily those of poise and grooming. I knew that if I decided to return to India after my writing degree at Iowa was finished, my father would find me a suitable husband. I would never work, never be without servants and comfort, and I could dabble in the arts until they bored me. My daughters would attend the same school as I had, my sons a similar school. It was unthinkable that they would not be class leaders, then national leaders, and that they would not perpetuate whatever values we wished to give them. Such is the glory, and the horror, of a traditional society, even at its tattered edges.

6   I had no trouble at Iowa, and though I learned less about those Vietnam and assassination years° than I might have, I liked the place well enough to stay on and arrange for extensions of my scholarship. I married an American, Clark Blaise, whose parents had come from Canada and then divorced, and whose mother had returned to Winnipeg. I stayed on for a PhD, thus cutting off forever the world of passive privilege I had come from. An MA in English is considered refined, but a doctorate is far too serious a business, indicative more of brains than beauty, and likely to lead to a quarrelsome nature. We had a son, and when that son was almost two we moved to Canada. Clark had dreamed restless dreams of Canada, especially of Montréal. Still unformed at twenty-five, he felt it was the place that would let him be himself.

7   It is now the summer of 1966, and the three of us cross at Windsor in a battered VW van. Our admission goes smoothly, for I have a lecturer's position at McGill. I say "smoothly," but I realize now there was one curious, even comic event that foreshadowed the difficulties faced by Indians in Canada. A middle-aged immigration officer, in filling out my application, asked me the year of my birth. I told him, in that private-school accent of which I was once so proud. Mishearing, he wrote down "1914" and remarked, "Ah, we're the same age." He happened to be exactly twice my age. He corrected his error without a fuss. Ten minutes inside Canada, and I was already invisible.

8   The oldest paradox of prejudice is that it renders its victims simultaneously invisible and over-exposed. I have not met an Indian in Canada who has not suffered the humiliations of being overlooked (in jobs, in queues, in deserved recognition) and from being singled out (in hotels, department stores, on the streets, and at customs). It happened to me so regularly in Canada that I now feel relief, just entering Macy's° in Albany, New York, knowing that I won't be followed out by a security guard. In America, I can stay in hotels and *not* be hauled out of ele-

vators or stopped as I enter my room. It's perhaps a small privilege in the life of a North American housewife—not to be taken automatically for a shoplifter or a whore—but it's one that my years in Canada, and especially my two years in Toronto, have made me grateful for. I know objections will be raised; I know Canadians all too well. Which of us has *not* been harassed at customs? On a summer's night, which of us *can* walk down Yonge Street° without carloads of stoned youths shouting out insults? We have all stood patiently in bakery lines, had people step in front of us, we've all waved our plastic numbers and wailed, "But I was next—"

If we are interested in drawing minute distinctions, we can disregard or explain away nearly anything. ("Where did it happen? Oh, *Rosedale.*° Well, no *wonder...*" Or, "Were you wearing a sari? No? Well, no wonder..." Or, "Oh, *we* wouldn't do such a thing. He must have been French or something...") And I know the pious denials of hotel clerks. In a Toronto hotel I was harassed by two house detectives who demanded to see my room key before allowing me to go upstairs to join my family—harassed me in front of an elevator-load of leering, elbow-nudging women. When I complained, I extracted only a "some of my best friends are Pakis" from the night manager, as he fervently denied that what I had just experienced was in fact a racial incident.

And I know the sanctimonious denials of customs officers, even as they delight in making people like me dance on the head of a bureaucratic pin. On a return from New York to Toronto I was told, after being forced to declare a $1 valuation on a promotional leaflet handed out by a bookstore, that even a book of matches had to be declared. ("I didn't ask if you *bought* anything. Did you hear me ask about purchases? Did you? I'll ask you again in very clear English. *Are you bringing anything into the country?*")

Do not think that I enjoy writing this of Canada. I remain a Canadian citizen. This is the testament of a woman who came, like most immigrants, confident of her ability to do good work, in answer to a stated need. After the unsophisticated, beer-swilling rednecks of Iowa, British-commonwealth Canada, and Montréal in particular, promised a kind of haven. At the road-stops in Iowa and Illinois, when I entered in a sari, silverware would drop, conversations cease; it was not the kind of attention I craved. It was never a hostile reaction (it might have been, in the Deep South, but I avoided that region). It was innocent, dumbfounded stupefaction, and I thought I would be happy enough to leave it behind. As we drove past Toronto on the 401, we picked up the strains of sitar music on the radio; Montréal had spice shops and was soon to have Indian restaurants. It should have been a decent country, and we should have been happy in it.

I have been in America, this time, for only a few months, but in that time I've been attacked by a streaker on Sixth Avenue in New York; my purse has been snatched on Fifth Avenue; our car has been rammed and our insurance defrauded

9

10

11

12

in Saratoga Springs; a wallet has been stolen and our children have complained of the drinking and dope-smoking even in their schoolrooms. Yes, it's America: violent, mindlessly macho, conformist, lawless. And certainly no dark-skinned person has the right to feel comfortable inside American history. Yet I do. If I am not exempt from victimization here, neither are Clark or my sons, and neither am I exempt from redress. I am less shocked, less outraged and shaken to my core, by a purse-snatching in New York City in which I lost all of my dowry-gold— everything I'd been given by my mother in marriage—than I was by a simple question asked of me in the summer of 1978 by three high-school boys on the Rosedale subway station platform in Toronto. Their question was, "Why don't you go back to Africa?"

13   It hurt because of its calculation, its calm, ignorant satisfaction, its bland assumption of the right to break into my privacy. In New York, I was violated because of my suspected affluence (a Gucci purse) and my obviously foreign, heedless, non-defensiveness. Calcutta equipped me to survive theft or even assault; it did not equip me to accept proof of my unworthiness. (Friends say, "Rosedale? Well..." or "Teenagers, well..." and I don't dispute them. But I owe it to my friends, and I have many friends in Canada, to dig deeper.)

14   Thanks to Canadian rhetoric on the highest level, I have learned several things about myself that I never suspected. The first is that I have no country of origin. In polite company, I am an "East Indian" (the opposite, presumably, of a "West Indian"). The East Indies, in my school days, were Dutch possessions, later to become Indonesia. In impolite company I'm a "Paki" (a British slur unknown in America, I'm happy to say). For an Indian of my generation, to be called a "Paki" is about as appealing as it is for an Israeli to be called a Syrian. In an official Green Paper on Immigration and Population° I learn that I'm something called a "visible minority" from a "non-traditional area of immigration" who calls into question the "absorptive capacity" of Canada. And that big question (to which my contribution is really not invited) is, "What kind of society do we really want?"

15   A spectre is haunting Canada: the perfidious "new" (meaning "dark" and thus, self-fulfillingly, "non-assimilatable") immigrant, coming to snatch up jobs, welfare cheques, subway space, cheap apartments, and blue-eyed women.

16   The Green Paper in 1975—which seemed an admirable exercise in demographic planning, an open invitation to join in a "debate"—was really a premeditated move on the part of the government to throw some bones (some immigrants) to the howling wolves. The "we" of that open question was understood to mean the Anglo-Saxon or Québec-French "founding races"; it opened up the sewers of resentment that polite, British-style forbearance had kept a lid on. My kind of Canadian was assumed, once again, not to exist, not to have a legitimate opinion to offer. ("Well, you could have made an official deposition through the proper multi-cultural channel whenever hearings were held in your community...")

Most Indians would date the new up-front violence, the physical assaults, the *17*
spitting, the name-calling, the bricks through the windows, the pushing and
shoving on the subways—it would be, by this time, a very isolated Indian who
has not experienced one or more of those reactions—from the implied consent
given to racism by that infamous document. I cannot describe the agony and the
betrayal one feels, hearing oneself spoken of by one's own country as being somehow exotic to its nature—a burden, a cause for serious concern. It may have been
rhetorically softened, it may have been academic in tone, but in feeling it was
Nuremberg,° and it unleashed its own mild but continuing *Kristallnacht.*° In that
ill-tempered debate, the government itself appropriated the language, the reasoning, the motivation that had belonged—until then—to disreputable fringe
groups. Suddenly it was all right, even patriotic, to blame these non-assimilatable
Asian hordes for urban crowding, unemployment, and welfare burdens. And the
uneducated, unemployed, welfare-dependent, native-born *lumpen* teenagers
leaped at the bait.

It is not pleasant to realize your own government has betrayed you so coldly. *18*

What about the "absorptive capacity" of the ambitious immigrant to take in all *19*
these new, startling descriptions of himself? It creates double-vision when self-
perception is so utterly at odds with social standing. We are split from our most
confident self-assumptions. We must be blind, stupid, or egomaniacal to maintain self-respect or dignity when society consistently undervalues our contribution. In Montréal, I was, simultaneously, a full professor at McGill, an author, a
confident lecturer, and (I like to think) a charming and competent hostess and
guest—*and* a house-bound, fearful, aggrieved, obsessive, and unforgiving queen of
bitterness. Whenever I read articles about men going berserk, or women committing suicide, and read the neighbours' dazed pronouncements ("But he was
always so friendly, so outgoing, never a problem in the world..."), I knew I was
looking into a mirror. Knowing that the culture condescended toward me, I
needed ways of bolstering my self-respect—but those ways, at least to politely
raised, tightly disciplined women of my age and origin, can only be achieved in
society, in the recognition of our contributions.

And there, of course, I am up against another Canadian dilemma. I have *20*
always been struck by an oddity, call it a gap, in the cultural consciousness of the
Canadian literary establishment. For fifteen years I was a professor of English and
of creative writing at McGill. I published novels, stories, essays, reviews. In a land
that fills its airports with itinerant poets and story-tellers, I was invited only once
to give a reading by myself (after *Days and Nights in Calcutta* appeared, Clark and
I, who had written it together, were frequently invited together). On that one
occasion, I learned, after arriving in a mining town at three in the morning, that
I'd been invited from the jacket photo and was expected to "come across." ("The
others did.") No provisions had been made for my stay, except in my host's bach-

elor house. ("Oh, you let him meet you at the airport at three a.m.? And you went back to his house thinking there was a wife?") Friends explained to me that really, since nothing happened (except a few shoves and pushes), I shouldn't mention it again. Until now, I haven't.

21   Of course, it is possible to interpret everything in a different light. While no one likes to be pawed, isn't it nice to be acknowledged, even this way? (Don't laugh, it was suggested.) My point is simply this: an Indian slips out of invisibility in this culture at considerable peril to body and soul. I've alluded briefly (in *Days and Nights*) to the fact that I was not invited to join the Writers' Union of Canada, back at its founding, even though at that particular moment I was a Canadian and Clark was not (my Indian citizenship conferred special dispensations that his American one did not). The first explanation for the oversight was that the invitation extended to Clark was "assumed" to include me. While even a low-grade feminist might react uncomfortably to such a concoction, another, and I think truthful, explanation was offered. "We didn't know how to spell your name, and we were afraid of insulting you," a well-known writer later wrote me. She's right; I would have been insulted (just as I'm mildly insulted by Canada Council letters to "Mr. Bharati Blaise"). And then, with a tinge of self-justification, she continued: "Your book was published by an American publisher and we couldn't get hold of it, so..."

22   Well, it's an apology and an explanation and it's easy to forgive as an instance of the persistent amateurism in the Canadian soul. But if you scrutinize just a little harder, and if you've dipped into the well of forgiveness far too often, you see a very different interpretation. *If you don't have a family compact name, forget about joining us*. If you don't have Canadian content, forget about publishing here. "The only Canadian thing about the novel is that it was written by a woman who now lives in Montréal," said a reviewer of my second novel, *Wife*, in *Books in Canada* (she was herself a feminist and emerging ethnicist), not even recognizing a book aimed right at her. "How can you call yourself a Canadian writer if you didn't play in snow as a child?" asked a CBC television interviewer. And more severely: "How do you justify taking grants and then not writing about Canada?"

23   The answer to all that is that I do write about Canada, perhaps not as directly as I am writing now, but that I refuse to capitulate to the rawness of Canadian literature—and, more to the point, I refuse to set my work in Canada because to do so would be to reduce its content to the very subject of this essay: politics and paranoia and bitter disappointment. The condition of the Indian in Canada is a sociological and political subject. We've not yet achieved the ease that would permit us to write of the self and of the expanding consciousness. To set my work in Canada is necessarily to adopt an urgent and strident tone; I would find irony an ill-considered option in any such situation. I advocate, instead, fighting back.

In case anyone finds a copy of *Wife*, it should be read in the following way: the *24*
nominal setting is Calcutta and New York City. But in the mind of the heroine,
it is always Toronto.

Fifteen years ago, the Indian was an exotic in America, except in university *25*
towns and maybe New York City. Now I doubt if there's a town in America without its Indian family—even Saratoga Springs has Indian dentists and pediatricians. I am no longer an exotic butterfly (people used to stagger up to me, quite
unconscious that there was a young woman inside the folds of brilliant cloth, just
to feel the material, and then walk away). Nor am I a grubby, dishonest, smelly,
ignorant, job-snatching, baby-breeding, unassimilatable malcontent. For the first
time in my adult life, I am unemployed—the price I was obliged to pay for immigration to the United States. Clark this year is teaching in the local college. Our
income is less than a third of what it has been, and dark times are coming. Next
year, I can take the job Clark is filling now; the college has made us an interesting proposal, though it leaves many questions unanswered. Will Clark then stay
here or return? He doesn't know.

America trusts confrontation; its rough sense of justice derives from slugging it *26*
out. It tolerates contradictions that seem, in retrospect, monstrous. Perhaps it
trusts to the constitution and the knowledge that somehow, someday, that document will resolve all difficulties. This is not the British style, not the Canadian
style, in which conflict is viewed as evidence of political failure. In Canada,
Parliament's sacred duty is the preservation of order; its mandate, at least in
recent years, is to anticipate disorder. I can appreciate that, and if I were a white
mainstream Canadian I'd probably endorse it wholeheartedly. Toronto really is a
marvellous, beautiful city, as I tell all my American friends. Good God, if ever
there was a city I should have been happy in, it was Toronto.

But when you are part of the Canadian and Toronto underbelly, invisible and *27*
nakedly obvious, you can't afford a white man's delusions. It's in Canada that a
columnist can write a glib and condescending book, attack the frail, ineffective
civil liberties legislation in the country, and be called a brilliant and daring intellectual. It's Canada that struggles against a constitution of its own, and its pre-
miers who downgrade the concept of a human rights charter.

While preparing to write this account, I interviewed dozens of people, mostly *28*
of Indian and Pakistani origin, in many parts of Canada. I read until I grew sick—
of the assaults, the recommendations, the testimonies. I attended meetings, I
talked to grandparents, and I talked to high-schoolers. I walked with the police
down the troubled streets of east-end Toronto; I pursued some of the more lurid
stories of the past year in Toronto. I turned down collaboration on some other
stories; I did not feel Canadian enough to appear on a TV programme celebrat-
ing the accomplishments of new Canadians; nor did I wish to take part in a TV
show that set out to ascribe suicides among Indo-Canadian women solely to community pressures to have male children. Friends who supported this research will

probably not find their observations in this piece; they will find, instead, that I turned it all inside out.

29   To a greater or lesser extent those friends and I share a common history. We came in the mid-1960s for professional reasons. We saw scope and promise, and we were slow to acknowledge the gathering clouds. Some of us have reacted positively, working with the local or provincial governments, serving as consultants, as organizers, as impresarios of understanding. Others have taken hockey sticks on vigilante patrols to protect their people. Many, including myself, have left, unable to keep our twin halves together. ◆

1981

Glossary

The Mikado: a 1885 Gilbert and Sullivan operetta.

those Vietnam and assassination years: a period of U.S. history in the 1960s which witnessed some of the bloodiest fighting in the Vietnam War (1955–1975), as well as the assassinations of John F. Kennedy (in 1963), and Malcolm X (1965).

Macy's: a department store chain whose main store occupies an entire city block at Herald Square (34th Street and Broadway) in New York City.

Yonge Street: the main north-south thoroughfare in Toronto.

Rosedale: a wealthy Anglo-Celtic enclave in Toronto.

Green Paper on Immigration and Population: a Crown-sponsored document on government policy, the Green Paper was released for public debate in 1975 only after the federal government of Canada had already drafted legislation based on its recommendations.

Nuremberg: an industrial city in the Bavarian region of southern Germany that has become inextricably identified as the site of the Allied War Crimes Tribunal set up to try top Nazi officials in the aftermath of World War II.

Kristallnacht: also known as the "Night of Broken Glass," this term refers to a night of violence and looting directed against Jewish Germans and their property on November 9–10, 1938.

Explorations

* Have you ever been made to feel "invisible" or "over-exposed" because of your racial background?

* Are you surprised by Mukherjee's view that racial prejudice is more evident in Canada than in the United States? Why or why not?

* Do you tend to "disregard" or "explain away" racial discrimination when it occurs? If so, why do you think you do this?

George Orwell, a pseudonym for Eric Hugh Blair, was born in 1903 in Motihari, Bengal. He held numerous occupations, including working for the Indian Imperial Police, teaching at a private school and writing. A journalist and satirical novelist, his most famous work includes a pair of politically allegorical and dystopic novels about the future, Animal Farm *(1944) and* Nineteen Eighty-Four *(1949), which reflect Orwell's concern for the direction in which he felt the modern world was moving. Orwell died of tuberculosis in 1950.*

Politics and the English Language

George Orwell

Most people who bother with the matter at all would admit that the English language is in a bad way, but it is generally assumed that we cannot by conscious action do anything about it. Our civilization is decadent and our language—so the argument runs—must inevitably share in the general collapse. It follows that any struggle against the abuse of language is a sentimental archaism, like preferring candles to electric light or hansom cabs to airplanes. Underneath this lies the half-conscious belief that language is a natural growth and not an instrument which we shape for our own purposes.   1

Now, it is clear that the decline of a language must ultimately have political and economic causes: it is not due simply to the bad influence of this or that individual writer. But an effect can become a cause, reinforcing the original cause and producing the same effect in an intensified form, and so on indefinitely. A man may take to drink because he feels himself to be a failure, and then fail all the more completely because he drinks. It is rather the same thing that is happening to the English language: It becomes ugly and inaccurate because our thoughts are foolish, but the slovenliness of our language makes it easier for us to have foolish thoughts. The point is that the process is reversible. Modern English, especially written English, is full of bad habits which spread by imitation and which can be avoided if one is willing to take the necessary trouble. If one gets rid of these habits one can think more clearly, and to think clearly is a necessary first step towards political regeneration: so that the fight against bad English is not frivolous and is not the exclusive concern of professional writers. I will come back to this presently, and I hope that by that time the meaning of what I have said here will have become clearer. Meanwhile, here are five specimens of the English language as it is now habitually written.   2

These five passages have not been picked out because they are especially bad—I could have quoted far worse if I had chosen—but because they illustrate various of the mental vices from which we now suffer. They are a little below the   3 average, but are fairly representative samples. I number them so that I can refer back to them when necessary:

1. I am not, indeed, sure whether it is not true to say that the Milton who once seemed not unlike a seventeenth-century Shelley had not become, out of an experience ever more bitter in each year, more alien [*sic*] to the founder of that Jesuit sect which nothing could induce him to tolerate.

   (Professor Harold Laski, Essay in *Freedom of Expression*)

2. Above all, we cannot play ducks and drakes with a native battery of idioms which prescribes such egregious collocations of vocables as the Basic *put up with* for *tolerate* or *put at a loss for bewilder*.

   (Professor Lancelot Hogben, *Interglossa*)

3. On the one side we have the free personality: by definition it is not neurotic, for it has neither conflict nor dream. Its desires, such as they are, are transparent, for they are just what institutional approval keeps in the forefront of consciousness; another institutional pattern would alter their number and intensity; there is little in them that is natural, irreducible, or culturally dangerous. But *on the other side*, the social bond itself is nothing but the mutual reflection of these self-secure integrities. Recall the definition of love. Is not this the very picture of a small academic? Where is there a place in this hall of mirrors for either personality or fraternity?

   (Essay on psychology in *Politics* [New York])

4. All the "best people" from the gentlemen's clubs, and all the frantic Fascist captains, united in common hatred of Socialism and bestial horror of the rising tide of the mass revolutionary movement, have turned to acts of provocation, to foul incendiarism, to medieval legends of poisoned wells, to legalize their own destruction of proletarian organizations, and rouse the agitated petty-bourgeoisie to chauvinistic fervour on behalf of the fight against the revolutionary way out of the crisis.

   (Communist pamphlet)

5. If a new spirit *is* to be infused into this old country, there is one thorny and contentious reform which must be tackled, and that is the human-ization and galvanization of the B.B.C. Timidity here will bespeak canker and atrophy of the soul. The heart of Britain may be sound and of strong beat, for instance, but the British lion's roar at present is like that of Bottom in Shakespeare's *Midsummer Night's Dream*—as gentle

as any sucking dove. A virile new Britain cannot continue indefinitely to be traduced in the eyes, or rather ears, of the world by the effete languors of Langham Place, brazenly masquerading as "standard English." When the Voice of Britain is heard at nine o'clock, better far and infinitely less ludicrous to hear aitches honestly dropped than the present priggish, inflated, inhibited, school-ma'amish arch braying of blameless, bashful, mewing maidens!

(Letter in *Tribune*)

Each of these passages has faults of its own, but, quite apart from avoidable 4 ugliness, two qualities are common to all of them. The first is staleness of imagery; the other is lack of precision. The writer either has a meaning and cannot express it, or he inadvertently says something else, or he is almost indifferent as to whether his words mean anything or not. This mixture of vagueness and sheer incompetence is the most marked characteristic of modern English prose, and especially of any kind of political writing. As soon as certain topics are raised, the concrete melts into the abstract and no one seems able to think in turns of speech that are not hackneyed: prose consists less and less of *words* chosen for the sake of their meaning, and more and more of *phrases* tacked together like the sections of a prefabricated henhouse. I list below, with notes and examples, various of the tricks by means of which the work of prose-construction is habitually dodged:

Dying metaphors. A newly invented metaphor assists thought by evoking a 5 visual image, while on the other hand a metaphor which is technically "dead" (e.g., *iron resolution*) has in effect reverted to being an ordinary word and can generally be used without loss of vividness. But in between these two classes there is a huge dump of worn-out metaphors which have lost all evocative power and are merely used because they save people the trouble of inventing phrases for themselves. Examples are: *Ring the changes on, take up the cudgels for, toe the line, ride roughshod over, stand shoulder to shoulder with, play into the hands of, no axe to grind, grist to the mill, fishing in troubled waters, rift within the lute, on the order of the day, Achilles' heel, swan song, hotbed.* Many of these are used without knowledge of their meaning (what is a "rift," for instance?), and incompatible metaphors are frequently mixed, a sure sign that the writer is not interested in what he is saying. Some metaphors now current have been twisted out of their original meaning without those who use them even being aware of the fact. For example, *toe the line* is sometimes written *tow the line.* Another example is *the hammer and the anvil,* now always used with the implication that the anvil gets the worst of it. In real life it is always the anvil that breaks the hammer, never the other way about: a writer who stopped to think what he was saying would be aware of this, and would avoid perverting the original phrase.

6   *Operators*, or *verbal false limbs*. These save the trouble of picking out appropriate verbs and nouns, and at the same time pad each sentence with extra syllables which give it an appearance of symmetry. Characteristic phrases are *render inoperative, militate against, prove unacceptable, make contact with, be subjected to, give rise to, give grounds for, have the effect of, play a leading part (role) in, make itself felt, take effect, exhibit a tendency to, serve the purpose of*, etc. etc. The keynote is the elimination of simple verbs. Instead of being a single word, such as *break, stop, spoil, mend, kill*, a verb becomes a *phrase*, made up of a noun or adjective tacked on to some general-purpose verb such as *prove, serve, form, play, render*. In addition, the passive voice is wherever possible used in preference to the active, and noun constructions are used instead of gerunds (*by examination of* instead of *by examining*). The range of verbs is further cut down by means of the *-ize* and *de-* formations, and the banal statements are given an appearance of profundity by means of the *not un-* formation. Simple conjunctions and prepositions are replaced by such phrases as *with respect to, having regard to, the fact that, by dint of, in view of, in the interests of, on the hypothesis that*; and the ends of sentences are saved from anticlimax by such resounding commonplaces as *greatly to be desired, cannot be left out of account, a development to be expected in the near future, deserving of serious consideration, brought to a satisfying conclusion*, and so on and so forth.

7   *Pretentious diction*. Words like *phenomenon, element, individual* (as noun), *objective, categorical, effective, virtual, basic, primary, promote, constitute, exhibit, exploit, utilize, eliminate, liquidate*, are used to dress up simple statements and give an air of scientific impartiality to biased judgments. Adjectives like *epoch-making, epic, historic, unforgettable, triumphant, age-old, inevitable, inexorable, veritable*, are used to dignify the sordid processes of international politics, while writing that aims at glorifying war usually takes on an archaic colour, its characteristic words being: *realm, throne, chariot, mailed fist, trident, sword, shield, buckler, banner, jackboot, clarion*. Foreign words and expressions such as *cul de sac, ancien régime, deus ex machina, mutatis mutandis, status quo, Gleichschaltung, Weltanschauung*, are used to give an air of culture and elegance. Except for the useful abbreviations *i.e., e.g.*, and *etc.*, there is no real need for any of the hundreds of foreign phrases now current in English. Bad writers, and especially scientific, political, and sociological writers, are nearly always haunted by the notion that Latin or Greek words are grander than Saxon ones, and unnecessary words like *expedite, ameliorate, predict, extraneous, deracinated, clandestine, subaqueous*, and hundreds of others constantly gain ground from their Anglo-Saxon opposite numbers.[1] The jargon peculiar to Marxist writing (*hyena, hangman, cannibal, petty bourgeois, these gentry, lackey, flunkey, mad dog, White Guard*, etc.) consists largely of words and phrases translated from Russian, German, or French; but the normal way of coining a new word is to use a Latin or Greek root with the appropriate affix and, where necessary, the *-ize* formation. It is often easier to make up words of this kind (*deregionalize, impermissible, extramarital, non-fragmentary*, and so forth) than to think up

the English words that will cover one's meaning. The result, in general, is an increase in slovenliness and vagueness.

Meaningless words. In certain kinds of writing, particularly in art criticism and   *8*
literary criticism, it is normal to come across long passages which are almost completely lacking in meaning.[2] Words like *romantic, plastic, values, human, dead, sentimental, natural, vitality,* as used in art criticism, are strictly meaningless, in the sense that they not only do not point to any discoverable object, but are hardly even expected to do so by the reader. When one critic writes, "The outstanding feature of Mr. X's work is its living quality," while another writes, "The immediately striking thing about Mr. X's work is its peculiar deadness," the reader accepts this as a simple difference of opinion. If words like *black* and *white* were involved, instead of the jargon words *dead* and *living,* he would see at once that language was being used in an improper way. Many political words are similarly abused. The word *Fascism* has now no meaning except in so far as it signifies "something not desirable." The words *democracy, socialism, freedom, patriotic, realistic, justice,* have each of them several different meanings which cannot be reconciled with one another. In the case of a word like *democracy,* not only is there no agreed definition, but the attempt to make one is resisted from all sides. It is almost universally felt that when we call a country democratic we are praising it: consequently the defenders of every kind of régime claim that it is a democracy, and fear that they might have to stop using the word if it were tied down to any one meaning. Words of this kind are often used in a consciously dishonest way. That is, the person who uses them has his own private definition, but allows his hearer to think he means something quite different. Statements like *Marshal Pétain was a true patriot, The Soviet press is the freest in the world, The Catholic Church is opposed to persecution,* are almost always made with intent to deceive. Other words used in variable meanings, in most cases more or less dishonestly, are: *class, totalitarian, science, progressive, reactionary, bourgeois, equality.*

Now that I have made this catalogue of swindles and perversions, let me give   *9*
another example of the kind of writing that they lead to. This time it must of its nature be an imaginary one. I am going to translate a passage of good English into modern English of the worst sort. Here is a well-known verse from Ecclesiastes°:

I returned and saw under the sun, that the race is not to the swift, nor the battle to the strong, neither yet bread to the wise, nor yet riches to men of understanding, nor yet favour to men of skill; but time and chance happeneth to them all.

Here it is in modern English: *10*

Objective consideration of contemporary phenomena compels the conclusion that success or failure in competitive activities exhibits no

tendency to be commensurate with innate capacity, but that a considerable element of the unpredictable must invariably be taken into account.

11   This is a parody, but not a very gross one. Exhibit (3), above, for instance, contains several patches of the same kind of English. It will be seen that I have not
made a full translation. The beginning and ending of the sentence follow the
original meaning fairly closely, but in the middle the concrete illustrations—race,
battle, bread—dissolve into the vague phrase "success or failure in competitive
activities." This had to be so, because no modern writer of the kind I am discussing—no one capable of using phrases like "objective consideration of contemporary phenomena"—would ever tabulate his thoughts in that precise and
detailed way. The whole tendency of modern prose is away from concreteness.
Now analyse these two sentences a little more closely. The first contains forty-
nine words but only sixty syllables, and all its words are those of everyday life.
The second contains thirty-eight words of ninety syllables: eighteen of its words
are from Latin roots, and one from Greek. The first sentence contains six vivid
images, and only one phrase ("time and chance") that could be called vague. The
second contains not a single fresh, arresting phrase, and in spite of its ninety syllables it gives only a shortened version of the meaning contained in the first. Yet
without a doubt it is the second kind of sentence that is gaining ground in modern English. I do not want to exaggerate. This kind of writing is not yet universal, and outcrops of simplicity will occur here and there in the worst-written
page. Still, if you or I were told to write a few lines on the uncertainty of human
fortunes, we should probably come much nearer to my imaginary sentence than
to the one from Ecclesiastes.

12   As I have tried to show, modern writing at its worst does not consist of picking out words for the sake of their meaning and inventing images in order to
make the meaning clearer. It consists in gumming together long strips of words
which have already been set in order by someone else, and making the results
presentable by sheer humbug. The attraction of this way of writing is that it is
easy. It is easier—even quicker, once you have the habit—to say *In my opinion it
is not an unjustifiable assumption that* than to say *I think*. If you use ready-made
phrases, you not only don't have to hunt about for words; you also don't have to
bother with the rhythms of your sentences, since these phrases are generally so
arranged as to be more or less euphonious. When you are composing in a hurry—
when you are dictating to a stenographer, for instance, or making a public
speech—it is natural to fall into a pretentious, Latinized style. Tags like *a consideration which we should do well to bear in mind* or *a conclusion to which all of us would
readily assent* will save many a sentence from coming down with a bump. By using
stale metaphors, similes, and idioms, you save much mental effort, at the cost of
leaving your meaning vague, not only for your reader but for yourself. This is the
significance of mixed metaphors. The sole aim of a metaphor is to call up a visual image. When these images clash—as in *The Fascist octopus has sung its swan*

song, the jackboot is thrown into the melting pot—it can be taken as certain that the writer is not seeing a mental image of the objects he is naming; in other words he is not really thinking. Look again at the examples I gave at the beginning of this essay. Professor Laski (1) uses five negatives in fifty-three words. One of these is superfluous, making nonsense of the whole passage, and in addition there is the slip—*alien* for akin—making further nonsense, and several avoidable pieces of clumsiness which increase the general vagueness. Professor Hogben (2) plays ducks and drakes with a battery which is able to write prescriptions, and, while disapproving of the everyday phrase *put up with*, is unwilling to look *egregious* up in the dictionary and see what it means. (3), if one takes an uncharitable attitude towards it, is simply meaningless: probably one could work out its intended meaning by reading the whole of the article in which it occurs. In (4) the writer knows more or less what he wants to say, but an accumulation of stale phrases chokes him like tea leaves blocking a sink. In (5), words and meaning have almost parted company. People who write in this manner usually have a general emotional meaning—they dislike one thing and want to express solidarity with another—but they are not interested in the detail of what they are saying. A scrupulous writer, in every sentence that he writes, will ask himself at least four questions, thus: What am I trying to say? What words will express it? What image or idiom will make it clearer? Is this image fresh enough to have an effect? And he will probably ask himself two more: Could I put it more shortly? Have I said anything that is avoidably ugly? But you are not obliged to go to all this trouble. You can shirk it by simply throwing your mind open and letting the ready-made phrases come crowding in. They will construct your sentences for you—even think your thoughts for you, to a certain extent—and at need they will perform the important service of partially concealing your meaning even from yourself. It is at this point that the special connection between politics and the debasement of language becomes clear.

In our time it is broadly true that political writing is bad writing. Where it is   *13* not true, it will generally be found that the writer is some kind of rebel, express- ing his private opinions and not a "party line." Orthodoxy, of whatever colour, seems to demand a lifeless, imitative style. The political dialects to be found in pamphlets, leading articles, manifestoes, White Papers and the speeches of undersecretaries do, of course, vary from party to party, but they are all alike in that one almost never finds in them a fresh, vivid, home-made turn of speech. When one watches some tired hack on the platform mechanically repeating the familiar phrases—*bestial atrocities, iron heel, bloodstained tyranny, free peoples of the world, stand shoulder to shoulder*—one often has a curious feeling that one is not watching a live human being but some kind of dummy: a feeling which suddenly becomes stronger at moments when the light catches the speaker's spectacles and turns them into blank discs which seem to have no eyes behind them. And this is not altogether fanciful. A speaker who uses that kind of phraseology has gone some distance towards turning himself into a machine. The appropriate noises are coming out of his larynx, but his brain is not involved as it would be if he were choosing his words for himself. If the speech he is making is one that he is accustomed to make over and over again, he may be almost unconscious of what he is saying, as one is when one utters the responses in church. And this reduced state of consciousness, if not indispensable, is at any rate favourable to political conformity.

14   In our time, political speech and writing are largely the defence of the indefensible. Things like the continuance of British rule in India, the Russian purges and deportations, the dropping of the atom bombs on Japan, can indeed be defended, but only by arguments which are too brutal for most people to face, and which do not square with the professed aims of political parties. Thus political language has to consist largely of euphemism, question-begging and sheer cloudy vagueness. Defenceless villages are bombarded from the air, the inhabitants driven out into the countryside, the cattle machine-gunned, the huts set on fire with incendiary bullets: this is called *pacification*. Millions of peasants are robbed of their farms and sent trudging along the roads with no more than they can carry: this is called *transfer of population* or *rectification of frontiers*. People are imprisoned for years without trial, or shot in the back of the neck or sent to die of scurvy in Arctic lumber camps: this is called *elimination of unreliable elements*. Such phraseology is needed if one wants to name things without calling up mental pictures of them. Consider for instance some comfortable English professor defending Russian totalitarianism. He cannot say outright, "I believe in killing off your opponents when you can get good results by doing so." Probably, therefore, he will say something like this:

> While freely conceding that the Soviet régime exhibits certain features which the humanitarian may be inclined to deplore, we must, I think, agree that a certain curtailment of the right to political opposition is an unavoidable concomitant of transitional periods, and that the rigours which the Russian people have been called upon to undergo have been amply justified in the sphere of concrete achievement.

15   The inflated style is itself a kind of euphemism. A mass of Latin words falls upon the facts like soft snow, blurring the outlines and covering up all the details. The great enemy of clear language is insincerity. When there is a gap between one's real and one's declared aims, one turns as it were instinctively to long words and exhausted idioms, like a cuttlefish squirting out ink. In our age there is no such thing as "keeping out of politics." All issues are political issues, and politics itself is a mass of lies, evasions, folly, hatred, and schizophrenia. When the general atmosphere is bad, language must suffer. I should expect to find—this is a guess which I have not sufficient knowledge to verify—that the German, Russian and Italian languages have all deteriorated in the last ten or fifteen years, as a result of dictatorship.

But if thought corrupts language, language can also corrupt thought. A bad   *16*
usage can spread by tradition and imitation, even among people who should and
do know better. The debased language that I have been discussing is in some ways
very convenient. Phrases like *a not unjustifiable assumption, leaves much to be
desired, would serve no good purpose, a consideration which we should do well to bear
in mind*, are a continuous temptation, a packet of aspirins always at one's elbow.
Look back through this essay, and for certain you will find that I have again and
again committed the very faults I am protesting against. By this morning's post I
have received a pamphlet dealing with conditions in Germany. The author tells
me that he "felt impelled" to write it. I open it at random, and here is almost the
first sentence that I see: "[The Allies] have an opportunity not only of achieving
a radical transformation of Germany's social and political structure in such a way
as to avoid a nationalistic reaction in Germany itself, but at the same time of
laying the foundations of a co-operative and unified Europe." You see, he "feels
impelled" to write—feels, presumably, that he has something new to say—and
yet his words, like cavalry horses answering the bugle, group themselves automatically into the familiar dreary pattern. This invasion of one's mind by ready-
made phrases (*lay the foundations, achieve a radical transformation*) can only be
prevented if one is constantly on guard against them, and every such phrase
anaesthetizes a portion of one's brain.

I said earlier that the decadence of our language is probably curable. Those   *17*
who deny this would argue, if they produced an argument at all, that language
merely reflects existing social conditions, and that we cannot influence its development by any direct tinkering with words and constructions. So far as the general tone or spirit of a language goes, this may be true, but it is not true in detail.
Silly words and expressions have often disappeared, not through any evolutionary process but owing to the conscious action of a minority. Two recent examples
were *explore every avenue* and *leave no stone unturned*, which were killed by the
jeers of a few journalists. There is a long list of flyblown metaphors which could
similarly be got rid of if enough people would interest themselves in the job; and
it should also be possible to laugh the *not un-* formation out of existence,[3] to
reduce the amount of Latin and Greek in the average sentence, to drive out foreign phrases and strayed scientific words, and, in general, to make pretentious-
ness unfashionable. But all these are minor points. The defence of the English
language implies more than this, and perhaps it is best to start by saying what it
does *not* imply.

To begin with it has nothing to do with archaism, with the salvaging of obso-   *18*
lete words and turns of speech, or with the setting up of a "standard English"
which must never be departed from. On the contrary, it is especially concerned
with the scrapping of every word or idiom which has outworn its usefulness. It
has nothing to do with correct grammar and syntax, which are of no importance
so long as one makes one's meaning clear, or with the avoidance of

Americanisms, or with having what is called a "good prose style." On the other hand it is not concerned with fake simplicity and the attempt to make written English colloquial. Nor does it even imply in every case preferring the Saxon word to the Latin one, though it does imply using the fewest and shortest words that will cover one's meaning. What is above all needed is to let the meaning choose the word, and not the other way about. In prose, the worst thing one can do with words is to surrender to them. When you think of a concrete object, you think wordlessly, and then, if you want to describe the thing you have been visualizing you probably hunt about till you find the exact words that seem to fit it. When you think of something abstract you are more inclined to use words from the start, and unless you make a conscious effort to prevent it, the existing dialect will come rushing in and do the job for you, at the expense of blurring or even changing your meaning. Probably it is better to put off using words as long as possible and get one's meaning as clear as one can through pictures or sensations. Afterwards one can choose—not simply *accept*—the phrases that will best cover the meaning, and then switch round and decide what impression one's words are likely to make on another person. This last effort of the mind cuts out all stale or mixed images, all prefabricated phrases, needless repetitions, and humbug and vagueness generally. But one can often be in doubt about the effect of a word or a phrase, and one needs rules that one can rely on when instinct fails. I think the following rules will cover most cases:

1. Never use a metaphor, simile, or other figure of speech which you are used to seeing in print.

2. Never use a long word where a short one will do.

3. If it is possible to cut a word out, always cut it out.

4. Never use the passive where you can use the active.

5. Never use a foreign phrase, a scientific word, or a jargon word if you can think of an everyday English equivalent.

6. Break any of these rules sooner than say anything outright barbarous.

These rules sound elementary, and so they are, but they demand a deep change of attitude in anyone who has grown used to writing in the style now fashionable. One could keep all of them and still write bad English, but one could not write the kind of stuff that I quoted in those five specimens at the beginning of this article.

19   I have not here been considering the literary use of language, but merely language as an instrument for expressing and not for concealing or preventing thought. Stuart Chase and others have come near to claiming that all abstract words are meaningless, and have used this as a pretext for advocating a kind of political quietism. Since you don't know what Fascism is, how can you struggle against Fascism? One need not swallow such absurdities as this, but one ought to

recognize that the present political chaos is connected with the decay of language, and that one can probably bring about some improvement by starting at the verbal end. If you simplify your English, you are freed from the worst follies of orthodoxy. You cannot speak any of the necessary dialects, and when you make a stupid remark its stupidity will be obvious, even to yourself. Political language—and with variations this is true of all political parties, from Conservatives to Anarchists—is designed to make lies sound truthful and murder respectable, and to give an appearance of solidity to pure wind. One cannot change this all in a moment, but one can at least change one's own habits, and from time to time one can even, if one jeers loudly enough, send some worn-out and useless phrase—some *jackboot, Achilles' heel, hotbed, melting pot, acid test, veritable inferno*, or other lump of verbal refuse—into the dustbin where it belongs. ◆

1946

Endnotes

1. An interesting illustration of this is the way in which the English flower names which were in use till very recently are being ousted by Greek ones, *snapdragon* becoming *antirrhinum*, *forget-me-not* becoming *myosotis*, etc. It is hard to see any practical reason for this change of fashion: it is probably due to an instinctive turning away from the more homely word and a vague feeling that the Greek word is scientific.

2. Example: "Comfort's catholicity of perception and image, strangely Whitmanesque in range, almost the opposite in aesthetic compulsion, continues to evoke that trembling atmospheric accumulative hinting at a cruel, an inexorably serene timelessness.... Wrey Gardiner scores by aiming at simple bull's-eyes with precision. Only they are not so simple, and through this contented sadness runs more than the surface bittersweet of resignation." (*Poetry Quarterly*)

3. One can cure oneself of the *not un-* formation by memorizing this sentence: *A not unblack dog was chasing a not unsmall rabbit across a not ungreen field.*

Glossary

Ecclesiastes: book in the Old Testament that is characterized by its despairing tone, emphasis on the inherent evil of human beings, and the universality of death.

Explorations

• Do you suffer from any of the "mental vices" that Orwell points out? Are your images stale and your words imprecise?

• Do you find that political writing is particularly corrupt?

• Do you believe that if we got rid of our bad writing habits, we could think more clearly? Does the language we use make a difference?

Amy Tan was born in 1952 in Oakland, California. She holds a graduate degree in linguistics from California State University. Tan is a best-selling novelist who writes about trying to assimilate into the mainstream American world, often humorously challenging her Chinese heritage. She has published several novels, including The Joy Luck Club, The Kitchen God's Wife, The Hundred Secret Senses, *and* The Bonesetter's Daughter, *as well as children's books, including* The Moon Lady.

Mother Tongue

Amy Tan

1   I am not a scholar of English or literature. I cannot give you much more than personal opinions on the English language and its variations in this country or others.

2   I am a writer. And by that definition, I am someone who has always loved language. I am fascinated by language in daily life. I spend a great deal of my time thinking about the power of language—the way it can evoke an emotion, a visual image, a complex idea, or a simple truth. Language is the tool of my trade. And I use them all—all the Englishes I grew up with.

3   Recently, I was made keenly aware of the different Englishes I do use. I was giving a talk to a large group of people, the same talk I had already given to half a dozen other groups. The nature of the talk was about my writing, my life, and my book, *The Joy Luck Club.* The talk was going along well enough, until I remembered one major difference that made the whole talk sound wrong. My mother was in the room. And it was perhaps the first time she had heard me give a lengthy speech, using the kind of English I have never used with her. I was saying things like, "The intersection of memory upon imagination" and "There is an aspect of my fiction that relates to thus-and-thus"—a speech filled with carefully wrought grammatical phrases, burdened, it suddenly seemed to me, with nominalized forms, past perfect tenses, conditional phrases, all the forms of standard English that I had learned in school and through books, the forms of English I did not use at home with my mother.

4   Just last week, I was walking down the street with my mother, and I again found myself conscious of the English I was using, the English I do use with her. We were talking about the price of new and used furniture and I heard myself saying this: "Not waste money that way." My husband was with us as well, and he didn't notice any switch in my English. And then I realized why. It's because over the twenty years we've been together I've often used the same kind of English with him and sometimes he even uses it with me. It has become our language of intimacy, a different sort of English that relates to family talk, the language I grew up with.

So you'll have some idea of what this family talk I heard sounds like, I'll quote   5
what my mother said during a recent conversation which I videotaped and then
transcribed. During this conversation, my mother was talking about a political
gangster in Shanghai who had the same last name as her family's, Du, and how
the gangster in his early years wanted to be adopted by her family, which was rich
by comparison. Later, the gangster became more powerful, far richer than my
mother's family, and one day showed up at my mother's wedding to pay his
respects. Here's what she said in part:

"Du Yusong having business like fruit stand. Like off the street kind. He is   6
Du like Du Zong—but not Tsung-ming Island people. The local people call
putong, the river east side, he belong to that side local people. That man want
to ask Du Zong father take him in like become own family. Du Zong father
wasn't look down on him, but didn't take seriously, until that man big like
become a mafia. Now important person, very hard to inviting him. Chinese
way, came only to show respect, don't stay for dinner. Respect for making big
celebration, he shows up. Mean gives lots of respect. Chinese custom. Chinese
social life that way. If too important won't have to stay too long. He come to
my wedding. I didn't see, I heard it. I gone to boy's side, they have YMCA
dinner. Chinese age I was nineteen."

You should know that my mother's expressive command of English belies how   7
much she actually understands. She reads the *Forbes* report,° listens to *Wall Street
Week*,° converses daily with her stockbroker, reads all of Shirley MacLaine's°
books with ease—all kinds of things I can't begin to understand. Yet some of my
friends tell me they understand 50 percent of what my mother says. Some say
they understand 80 to 90 percent. Some say they understand none of it, as if she
was speaking pure Chinese. But to me, my mother's English is perfectly clear, perfectly natural. It's my mother tongue. Her language, as I hear it, is vivid, direct,
full of observation and imagery. That was the language that helped shape the way
I saw things, expressed things, made sense of the world.

Lately, I've been giving more thought to the kind of English my mother speaks.   8
Like others, I have described it to people as "broken" or "fractured" English. But
I wince when I say that. It has always bothered me that I can think of no way to
describe it other than "broken," as if it were damaged and needed to be fixed, as
if it lacked a certain wholeness and soundness. I've heard other terms used, "limited English," for example. But they seem just as bad, as if everything is limited,
including people's perceptions of the limited English speaker.

I know this for a fact, because when I was growing up, my mother's "limited"   9
English limited *my* perception of her. I was ashamed of her English. I believed
that her English reflected the quality of what she had to say. That is, because she
expressed them imperfectly her thoughts were imperfect. And I had plenty of
empirical evidence to support me: the fact that people in department stores, at

banks, and at restaurants did not take her seriously, did not give her good service, pretended not to understand her, or even acted as if they did not hear her.

10   My mother has long realized the limitations of her English as well. When I was fifteen, she used to have me call people on the phone to pretend I was she. In this guise, I was forced to ask for information or even to complain and yell at people who had been rude to her. One time it was a call to her stockbroker in New York. She had cashed out her small portfolio and it just so happened we were going to go to New York the next week, our very first trip outside California. I had to get on the phone and say in an adolescent voice that was not very convincing, "This is Mrs. Tan."

11   And my mother was standing in the back whispering loudly, "Why he don't send me check, already two weeks late. So mad he lie to me, losing me money."

12   And then I said in perfect English, "Yes, I'm getting rather concerned. You had agreed to send the check two weeks ago, but it hasn't arrived."

13   Then she began to talk more loudly. "What he want, I come to New York tell him front of his boss, you cheating me?" And I was trying to calm her down, make her be quiet, while telling the stockbroker, "I can't tolerate any more excuses. If I don't receive the check immediately, I am going to have to speak to your manager when I'm in New York next week." And sure enough, the following week there we were in front of this astonished stockbroker, and I was sitting there red-faced and quiet, and my mother, the real Mrs. Tan, was shouting at his boss in her impeccable broken English.

14   We used a similar routine just five days ago, for a situation that was far less humorous. My mother had gone to the hospital for an appointment, to find out about a benign brain tumor a CAT scan had revealed a month ago. She said she had spoken very good English, her best English, no mistakes. Still, she said, the hospital did not apologize when they said they had lost the CAT scan and she had come for nothing. She said they did not seem to have any sympathy when she told them she was anxious to know the exact diagnosis, since her husband and son had both died of brain tumors. She said they would not give her any more information until the next time and she would have to make another appointment for that. So she said she would not leave until the doctor called her daughter. She wouldn't budge. And when the doctor finally called her daughter, me, who spoke perfect English—lo and behold—we had assurances the CAT scan would be found, promises that a conference call on Monday would be held, and apologies for any suffering my mother had gone through for a most regrettable mistake.

15   I think my mother's English almost had an effect on limiting my possibilities in life as well. Sociologists and linguists probably will tell you that a person's developing language skills are more influenced by peers. But I do think that the language spoken in the family, especially in immigrant families which are more insular, plays a large role in shaping the language of the child. And I believe that

it affected my results on achievement tests, IQ tests, and the SAT.° While my English skills were never judged as poor, compared to math, English could not be considered my strong suit. In grade school I did moderately well, getting perhaps B's, sometimes B-pluses, in English and scoring perhaps in the sixtieth or seventieth percentile on achievement tests. But those scores were not good enough to override my opinion that my true abilities lay in math and science, because in those areas I achieved A's and scored in the ninetieth percentile or higher.

This was understandable. Math is precise; there is only one correct answer. 16 Whereas, for me at least, the answers on English tests were always a judgment call, a matter of opinion and personal experience. Those tests were constructed around items like fill-in-the-blank sentence completion, such as, "Even though Tom was _____, Mary thought he was _____." And the correct answer always seemed to be the most bland combinations of thoughts, for example, "Even though Tom was shy, Mary thought he was charming," with the grammatical structure "even though" limiting the correct answer to some sort of semantic opposites, so you wouldn't get answers like, "Even though Tom was foolish, Mary thought he was ridiculous." Well, according to my mother, there were very few limitations as to what Tom could have been and what Mary might have thought of him. So I never did well on tests like that.

The same was true with word analogies, pairs of words in which you were sup- 17 posed to find some sort of logical, semantic relationship—for example, "*Sunset* is to *nightfall* as _____ is to _____." And here you would be presented with a list of four possible pairs, one of which showed the same kind of relationship: *red* is to *stoplight, bus* is to *arrival, chills* is to *fever, yawn* is to *boring.* Well, I could never think that way. I knew what the tests were asking, but I could not block out of my mind the images already created by the first pair, "*sunset* is to *nightfall*"—and I would see a burst of colors against a darkening sky, the moon rising, the lowering of a curtain of stars. And all the other pairs of words—red, bus, stoplight, boring—just threw up a mass of confusing images, making it impossible for me to sort out something as logical as saying: "A sunset precedes nightfall" is the same as "a chill precedes a fever." The only way I would have gotten that answer right would have been to imagine an associative situation, for example, my being disobedient and staying out past sunset, catching a chill at night, which turns into feverish pneumonia as punishment, which indeed did happen to me.

I have been thinking about all this lately, about my mother's English, about 18 achievement tests. Because lately I've been asked, as a writer, why there are not more Asian Americans represented in American literature. Why are there few Asian Americans enrolled in creative writing programs? Why do so many Chinese students go into engineering? Well, those are broad sociological questions I can't begin to answer. But I have noticed in surveys—in fact, just last week—that Asian students, as a whole, always do significantly better on math achievement tests than in English. And this makes me think that there are other Asian-American students whose English spoken in the home might also be described as "broken" or "limited." And perhaps they also have teachers who are steering them away from writing and into math and science, which is what happened to me.

19   Fortunately, I happen to be rebellious in nature and enjoy the challenge of disproving assumptions made about me. I became an English major my first year in college, after being enrolled as premed. I started writing nonfiction as a freelancer the week after I was told by my former boss that writing was my worst skill and I should hone my talents toward account management.

20   But it wasn't until 1985 that I finally began to write fiction. And at first I wrote using what I thought to be wittily crafted sentences, sentences that would finally prove I had mastery over the English language. Here's an example from the first draft of a story that later made its way into *The Joy Luck Club*, but without this line: "That was my mental quandary in its nascent state." A terrible line, which I can barely pronounce.

21   Fortunately, for reasons I won't get into today, I later decided I should envision a reader for the stories I would write. And the reader I decided upon was my mother, because these were stories about mothers. So with this reader in mind—and in fact she did read my early drafts—I began to write stories using all the Englishes I grew up with: the English I spoke to my mother, which for lack of a better term might be described as "simple"; the English she used with me, which for lack of a better term might be described as "broken"; my translation of her Chinese, which could certainly be described as "watered down"; and what I imagined to be her translation of her Chinese if she could speak in perfect English, her internal language, and for that I sought to preserve the essence, but neither an English nor a Chinese structure. I wanted to capture what language ability tests can never reveal: her intent, her passion, her imagery, the rhythms of her speech and the nature of her thoughts.

22   Apart from what any critic had to say about my writing, I knew I had succeeded where it counted when my mother finished reading my book and gave me her verdict: "So easy to read." ♦

1990

Glossary

Forbes report: a prestigious American financial journal.

Wall Street Week: a syndicated American television program that chronicles business and financial matters.

Shirley MacLaine: popular Hollywood actor, entertainer, and author.

SAT: Standardized Aptitude Test; administered to all high school seniors in the United States who are seeking admission to a college or university, the SAT tests mathematical, verbal, and cognitive skills through a series of multiple-choice questions.

Explorations

- How many different "Englishes" are spoken by you or members of your family?

- Why do you think it is more difficult for adults to become fluent in a second language than it is for younger people?

- What is your perception of "broken" English? Is this perception based on common stereotypes? If so, in what ways do you think such a view limits non-native speakers of English?

Deborah Tannen was born in 1945 in Brooklyn, New York. She has published numerous books, including That's Not What I Meant!, Talking Voices, *and* Talking from 9 to 5, *and is best known as the author of* You Just Don't Understand. *In addition to her linguistic research and writing, Dr. Tannen has published poetry, short stories, and personal essays. She is currently university professor and professor of linguistics in the Department of Linguistics at Georgetown University in Washington.*

Fighting for Our Lives

Deborah Tannen

1   This is not another book about civility. "Civility" suggests a superficial, pinky-in-the-air veneer of politeness spread thin over human relations like a layer of marmalade over toast. This book is about a pervasive warlike atmosphere that makes us approach public dialogue, and just about anything we need to accomplish, as if it were a fight. It is a tendency in Western culture in general, and in the United States in particular, that has a long history and a deep, thick, and far-ranging root system. It has served us well in many ways but in recent years has become so exaggerated that it is getting in the way of solving our problems. Our spirits are corroded by living in an atmosphere of unrelenting contention—an argument culture.

2   The argument culture urges us to approach the world—and the people in it—in an adversarial frame of mind. It rests on the assumption that opposition is the best way to get anything done: The best way to discuss an idea is to set up a debate; the best way to cover news is to find spokespeople who express the most extreme, polarized views and present them as "both sides"; the best way to settle disputes is litigation that pits one party against the other; the best way to begin an essay is to attack someone; and the best way to show you're really thinking is to criticize.

3   Our public interactions have become more and more like having an argument with a spouse. Conflict can't be avoided in our public lives any more than we can avoid conflict with people we love. One of the great strengths of our society is that we can express these conflicts openly. But just as spouses have to learn ways of settling their differences without inflicting real damage on each other, so we, as a society, have to find constructive ways of resolving disputes and differences. Public discourse requires *making* an argument for a point of view, not *having* an argument—as in having a fight.

4   The war on drugs, the war on cancer, the battle of the sexes, politicians' turf battles—in the argument culture, war metaphors pervade our talk and shape our thinking. Nearly everything is framed as a battle or game in which winning or losing is the main concern. These all have their uses and their place, but they are

not the only way—and often not the best way—to understand and approach our world. Conflict and opposition are as necessary as cooperation and agreement, but the scale is off balance, with conflict and opposition over-weighted. In this book, I show how deeply entrenched the argument culture is, the forms it takes, and how it affects us every day—sometimes in useful ways, but often creating more problems than it solves, causing rather than avoiding damage. As a sociolinguist, a social scientist, I am trained to observe and explain language and its role in human relations, and that is my biggest job here. But I will also point toward other ways for us to talk to each other and get things done in our public lives.

The Battle of the Sexes

My interest in the topic of opposition in public discourse intensified in the years 5
following the publication of *You Just Don't Understand*, my book about communication between women and men. In the first year I appeared on many television and radio shows and was interviewed for many print articles in newspapers and magazines. For the most part, that coverage was extremely fair, and I was— and remain—indebted to the many journalists who found my ideas interesting enough to make them known to viewers, listeners, and readers. But from time to time—more often than I expected—I encountered producers who insisted on setting up a television show as a fight (either between the host and me or between another guest and me) and print journalists who made multiple phone calls to my colleagues, trying to find someone who would criticize my work. This got me thinking about what kind of information comes across on shows and in articles that take this approach, compared to those that approach topics in other ways.

At the same time, my experience of the academic world that had long been my 6
intellectual home began to change. For the most part, other scholars, like most journalists, were welcoming and respectful in their responses to my work, even if they disagreed on specific points or had alternative views to suggest. But about a year after *You Just Don't Understand* became a best-seller—the wheels of academia grind more slowly than those of the popular press—I began reading attacks on my work that completely misrepresented it. I had been in academia for over fifteen years by then, and had valued my interaction with other researchers as one of the greatest rewards of academic life. Why, I wondered, would someone represent me as having said things I had never said or as having failed to say things I had said?

The answer crystallized when I put the question to a writer who I felt had mis- 7
represented my work: "Why do you need to make others wrong for you to be right?" Her response: "It's an argument!" Aha, I thought, that explains it. When you're having an argument with someone, your goal is not to listen and understand. Instead, you use every tactic you can think of—including distorting what your opponent just said—in order to win the argument.

8   Not only the level of attention *You Just Don't Understand* received but, even more, the subject of women and men, triggered the tendency to polarize. This tendency to stage a fight on television or in print was posited on the conviction that opposition leads to truth. Sometimes it does. But the trouble is, sometimes it doesn't. I was asked at the start of more than one talk show or print interview, "What is the most controversial thing about your book?" Opposition does not lead to truth when the most controversial thing is not the most important.

9   The conviction that opposition leads to truth can tempt not only members of the press but just about anyone seeking to attract an audience to frame discussions as a fight between irreconcilable opposites. Even the Smithsonian Institution°, to celebrate its 150th anniversary, sponsored a series of talks billed as debates. They invited me to take part in one titled "The Battle of the Sexes." The organizer preempted my objection: "I know you won't be happy with this title, but we want to get people interested." This is one of many assumptions I question in this book: Is it necessary to frame an interchange as a battle to get people interested? And even if doing so succeeds in capturing attention, does it risk dampening interest in the long run, as audiences weary of the din and begin to hunger for more substance?

Thought-Provoking or Just Provocative?

10   In the spring of 1995, Horizons Theatre in Arlington, Virginia, produced two one-act plays I had written about family relationships. The director, wanting to contribute to the reconciliation between Blacks and Jews, mounted my plays in repertory with two one-act plays by an African-American playwright, Caleen Sinnette Jennings. We had both written plays about three sisters that explored the ethnic identities of our families (Jewish for me, African-American for her) and the relationship between those identities and the American context in which we grew up. To stir interest in the plays and to explore the parallels between her work and mine, the theater planned a public dialogue between Jennings and me, to be held before the plays opened.

11   As production got under way, I attended the audition of actors for my plays. After the auditions ended, just before everyone headed home, the theater's public relations volunteer distributed copies of the flyer announcing the public dialogue that she had readied for distribution. I was horrified. The flyer announced that Caleen and I would discuss "how past traumas create understanding and conflict between Blacks and Jews today." The flyer was trying to grab by the throat the issue that we wished to address indirectly. Yes, we were concerned with conflicts between Blacks and Jews, but neither of us is an authority on that conflict, and we had no intention of expounding on it. We hoped to do our part to ameliorate the conflict by focusing on commonalities. Our plays had many resonances between them. We wanted to talk about our work and let the resonances speak for themselves.

Fortunately, we were able to stop the flyers before they were distributed and   *12*
devise new ones that promised something we could deliver: "a discussion of heritage, identity, and complex family relationships in African-American and
Jewish-American culture as represented in their plays." Jennings noticed that the
original flyer said the evening would be "provocative" and changed it to
"thought-provoking." What a world of difference is implied in that small change:
how much better to make people think, rather than simply to "provoke" them—
as often as not, to anger.

It is easy to understand why conflict is so often highlighted: Writers of head-   *13*
lines or promotional copy want to catch attention and attract an audience. They
are usually under time pressure, which lures them to established, conventional-
ized ways of expressing ideas in the absence of leisure to think up entirely new
ones. The promise of controversy seems an easy and natural way to rouse interest. But serious consequences are often unintended: Stirring up animosities to get
a rise out of people, though easy and "provocative," can open old wounds or create new ones that are hard to heal. This is one of many dangers inherent in the
argument culture.

For the Sake of Argument

In the argument culture, criticism, attack, or opposition are the predominant if   *14*
not the only ways of responding to people or ideas. I use the phrase "culture of
critique" to capture this aspect. "Critique" in this sense is not a general term for
analysis or interpretation but rather a synonym for criticism.

It is the *automatic* nature of this response that I am calling attention to—and   *15*
calling into question. Sometimes passionate opposition, strong verbal attack, are
appropriate and called for. No one knows this better than those who have lived
under repressive regimes that forbid public opposition. The Yugoslavian-born
poet Charles Simic is one. "There are moments in life," he writes, "when true
invective is called for, when it becomes an absolute necessity, out of a deep sense
of justice, to denounce, mock, vituperate, lash out, in the strongest possible language." I applaud and endorse this view. There are times when it is necessary and
right to fight—to defend your country or yourself, to argue for right against wrong
or against offensive or dangerous ideas or actions.

What I question is the ubiquity, the knee-jerk nature, of approaching almost   *16*
any issue, problem, or public person in an adversarial way. One of the dangers of
the habitual use of adversarial rhetoric is a kind of verbal inflation—a rhetorical
boy who cried wolf: The legitimate, necessary denunciation is muted, even lost,
in the general cacophony of oppositional shouting. What I question is using
opposition to accomplish *every* goal, even those that do not require fighting but
might also (or better) be accomplished by other means, such as exploring,
expanding, discussing, investigating, and the exchanging of ideas suggested by
the word "dialogue." I am questioning the assumption that *everything* is a matter

of polarized opposites, the proverbial "two sides to every question" that we think embodies open-mindedness and expansive thinking.

17   In a word, the type of opposition I am questioning is what I call "agonism." I use this term, which derives from the Greek word for "contest," *agonia*, to mean an automatic warlike stance—not the literal opposition of fighting against an attacker or the unavoidable opposition that arises organically in response to conflicting ideas or actions. An agonistic response, to me, is a kind of programmed contentiousness—a prepatterned, unthinking use of fighting to accomplish goals that do not necessarily require it.

How Useful Are Fights?

18   Noticing that public discourse so often takes the form of heated arguments—of having a fight—made me ask how useful it is in our personal lives to settle differences by arguing. Given what I know about having arguments in private life, I had to conclude that it is, in many cases, not very useful.

19   In close relationships it is possible to find ways of arguing that result in better understanding and solving problems. But with most arguments, little is resolved, worked out, or achieved when two people get angrier and less rational by the minute. When you're having an argument with someone, you're usually not trying to understand what the other person is saying, or what in their experience leads them to say it. Instead, you're readying your response: listening for weaknesses in logic to leap on, points you can distort to make the other person look bad and yourself look good. Sometimes you know, on some back burner of your mind, that you're doing this—that there's a kernel of truth in what your adversary is saying and a bit of unfair twisting in what you're saying. Sometimes you do this because you're angry, but sometimes it's just the temptation to take aim at a point made along the way because it's an easy target.

20   Here's an example of how this happened in an argument between a couple who had been married for over fifty years. The husband wanted to join an HMO° by signing over their Medicare benefits to save money. The wife objected because it would mean she could no longer see the doctor she knew and trusted. In arguing her point of view, she said, "I like Dr. B. He knows me, he's interested in me. He calls me by my first name." The husband parried the last point: "I don't like that. He's much younger than we are. He shouldn't be calling us by first name." But the form of address Dr. B. uses was irrelevant. The wife was trying to communicate that she felt comfortable with the doctor she knew, that she had a relationship with him. His calling her by first name was just one of a list of details she was marshaling to explain her comfort with him. Picking on this one detail did not change her view—and did not address her concern. It was just a way to win the argument.

21   We are all guilty, at times, of seizing on irrelevant details, distorting someone else's position the better to oppose it, when we're arguing with those we're clos-

est to. But we are rarely dependent on these fights as sources of information. The same tactics are common when public discourse is carried out on the model of personal fights. And the results are dangerous when listeners are looking to these interchanges to get needed information or practical results.

Fights have winners and losers. If you're fighting to win, the temptation is 22 great to deny facts that support your opponent's views and to filter what you know, saying only what supports your side. In the extreme form, it encourages people to misrepresent or even to lie. We accept this risk because we believe we can tell when someone is lying. The problem is, we can't.

Paul Ekman, a psychologist at the University of California, San Francisco, 23 studies lying. He set up experiments in which individuals were videotaped talking about their emotions, actions, or beliefs—some truthfully, some not. He has shown these videotapes to thousands of people, asking them to identify the liars and also to say how sure they were about their judgments. His findings are chilling: Most people performed not much better than chance, and those who did the worst had just as much confidence in their judgments as the few who were really able to detect lies. Intrigued by the implications of this research in various walks of life, Dr. Ekman repeated this experiment with groups of people whose jobs require them to sniff out lies: judges, lawyers, police, psychotherapists, and employees of the CIA, FBI, and ATF (Bureau of Alcohol, Tobacco, and Firearms). They were no better at detecting who was telling the truth than the rest of us. The only group that did significantly better were members of the U.S. Secret Service. This finding gives some comfort when it comes to the Secret Service but not much when it comes to every other facet of public life.

Two Sides to Every Question

Our determination to pursue truth by setting up a fight between two sides leads 24 us to believe that every issue has two sides—no more, no less: If both sides are given a forum to confront each other, all the relevant information will emerge, and the best case will be made for each side. But opposition does not lead to truth when an issue is not composed of two opposing sides but is a crystal of many sides. Often the truth is in the complex middle, not the oversimplified extremes.

We love using the word "debate" as a way of representing issues: the abortion 25 debate, the health care debate, the affirmative action debate—even "the great backpacking vs. car camping debate." The ubiquity of this word in itself shows our tendency to conceptualize issues in a way that predisposes public discussion to be polarized, framed as two opposing sides that give each other no ground. There are many problems with this approach. If you begin with the assumption that there *must* be an "other side," you may end up scouring the margins of science or the fringes of lunacy to find it. As a result, proven facts, such as what we know about how the earth and its inhabitants evolved, are set on a par with claims that are known to have no basis in fact, such as creationism.

26   The conviction that there are two sides to every story can prompt writers or producers to dig up an "other side," so kooks who state outright falsehoods are given a platform in public discourse. This accounts, in part, for the bizarre phenomenon of Holocaust denial. Deniers, as Emory University professor Deborah Lipstadt shows, have been successful in gaining television airtime and campus newspaper coverage by masquerading as "the other side" in a "debate."

27   Appearance in print or on television has a way of lending legitimacy, so baseless claims take on a mantle of possibility. Lipstadt shows how Holocaust deniers dispute established facts of history, and then reasonable spokespersons use their having been disputed as a basis for questioning known facts. The actor Robert Mitchum, for example, interviewed in *Esquire*, expressed doubt about the Holocaust. When the interviewer asked about the slaughter of six million Jews, Mitchum replied, "I don't know. People dispute that." Continual reference to "the other side" results in a pervasive conviction that everything has another side—with the result that people begin to doubt the existence of any facts at all.

The Expense of Time and Spirit

28   Lipstadt's book meticulously exposes the methods used by deniers to falsify the overwhelming historic evidence that the Holocaust occurred. That a scholar had to invest years of her professional life writing a book unraveling efforts to deny something that was about as well known and well documented as any historical fact has ever been—while those who personally experienced and witnessed it are still alive—is testament to another way that the argument culture limits our knowledge rather than expanding it. Talent and effort are wasted refuting outlandish claims that should never have been given a platform in the first place. Talent and effort are also wasted when individuals who have been unfairly attacked must spend years of their creative lives defending themselves rather than advancing their work. The entire society loses their creative efforts. This is what happened with scientist Robert Gallo.

29   Dr. Gallo is the American virologist who codiscovered the AIDS virus. He is also the one who developed the technique for studying T-cells, which made that discovery possible. And Gallo's work was seminal in developing the test to detect the AIDS virus in blood, the first and for a long time the only means known of stemming the tide of death from AIDS. But in 1989, Gallo became the object of a four-year investigation into allegations that he had stolen the AIDS virus from Luc Montagnier of the Pasteur Institute in Paris, who had independently identified the AIDS virus. Simultaneous investigations by the National Institutes of Health, the office of Michigan Congressman John Dingell, and the National Academy of Sciences barreled ahead long after Gallo and Montagnier settled the dispute to their mutual satisfaction. In 1993 the investigations concluded that Gallo had done nothing wrong. Nothing. But this exoneration cannot be considered a happy ending. Never mind the personal suffering of Gallo, who was

reviled when he should have been heralded as a hero. Never mind that, in his words, "These were the most painful years and horrible years of my life." The dreadful, unconscionable result of the fruitless investigations is that Gallo had to spend four years fighting the accusations instead of fighting AIDS.

The investigations, according to journalist Nicholas Wade, were sparked by an 30 article about Gallo written in the currently popular spirit of demonography: not to praise the person it features but to bury him—to show his weaknesses, his villainous side. The implication that Gallo had stolen the AIDS virus was created to fill a requirement of the discourse: In demonography, writers must find negative sides of their subjects to display for readers who enjoy seeing heroes transformed into villains. The suspicion led to investigations, and the investigations became a juggernaut that acquired a life of its own, fed by the enthusiasm for attack on public figures that is the culture of critique.

Metaphors: We Are What We Speak

Perhaps one reason suspicions of Robert Gallo were so zealously investigated is 31 that the scenario of an ambitious scientist ready to do anything to defeat a rival appeals to our sense of story; it is the kind of narrative we are ready to believe. Culture, in a sense, is an environment of narratives that we hear repeatedly until they seem to make self-evident sense in explaining human behavior. Thinking of human interactions as battles is a metaphorical frame through which we learn to regard the world and the people in it.

All language uses metaphors to express ideas; some metaphoric words and 32 expressions are novel, made up for the occasion, but more are calcified in the language. They are simply the way we think it is natural to express ideas. We don't think of them as metaphors. Someone who says, "Be careful: You aren't a cat; you don't have nine lives," is explicitly comparing you to a cat, because the cat is named in words. But what if someone says, "Don't pussyfoot around; get to the point"? There is no explicit comparison to a cat, but the comparison is there nonetheless, implied in the word "pussyfoot." This expression probably developed as a reference to the movements of a cat cautiously circling a suspicious object. I doubt that individuals using the word "pussyfoot" think consciously of cats. More often than not, we use expressions without thinking about their metaphoric implications. But that doesn't mean those implications are not influencing us.

At a meeting, a general discussion became so animated that a participant who 33 wanted to comment prefaced his remark by saying, "I'd like to leap into the fray." Another participant called out, "Or share your thoughts." Everyone laughed. By suggesting a different phrasing, she called attention to what would probably have otherwise gone unnoticed: "Leap into the fray" characterized the lively discussion as a metaphorical battle.

Americans talk about almost everything as if it were a war. A book about the 34 history of linguistics is called *The Linguistics Wars*. A magazine article about claims that science is not completely objective is titled "The Science Wars." One about breast cancer detection is "The Mammogram War"; about competition among caterers, "Party Wars"—and on and on in a potentially endless list. Politics, of course, is a prime candidate. One of innumerable possible examples, the headline of a story reporting that the Democratic National Convention nominated Bill Clinton to run for a second term declares, "DEMOCRATS SEND CLINTON INTO BATTLE FOR A 2D TERM." But medicine is as frequent a candidate, as we talk about battling and conquering disease.

35   Headlines are intentionally devised to attract attention, but we all use military or attack imagery in everyday expressions without thinking about it: "Take a shot at it," "I don't want to be shot down," "He went off half cocked," "That's half the battle." Why does it matter that our public discourse is filled with military metaphors? Aren't they just words? Why not talk about something that matters—like actions?

36   Because words matter. When we think we are using language, language is using us. As linguist Dwight Bolinger put it (employing a military metaphor), language is like a loaded gun: It can be fired intentionally, but it can wound or kill just as surely when fired accidentally. The terms in which we talk about something shape the way we think about it—and even what we see.

37   The power of words to shape perception has been proven by researchers in controlled experiments. Psychologists Elizabeth Loftus and John Palmer, for example, found that the terms in which people are asked to recall something affect what they recall. The researchers showed subjects a film of two cars colliding, then asked how fast the cars were going; one week later, they asked whether there had been any broken glass. Some subjects were asked, "About how fast were the cars going when they bumped into each other?" Others were asked, "About how fast were the cars going when they smashed into each other?" Those who read the question with the verb "smashed" estimated that the cars were going faster. They were also more likely to "remember" having seen broken glass. (There wasn't any.)

38   This is how language works. It invisibly molds our way of thinking about people, actions, and the world around us. Military metaphors train us to think about—and see—everything in terms of fighting, conflict, and war. This perspective then limits our imaginations when we consider what we can do about situations we would like to understand or change.

39   Even in science, common metaphors that are taken for granted influence how researchers think about natural phenomena. Evelyn Fox Keller describes a case in which acceptance of a metaphor led scientists to see something that was not there. A mathematical biologist, Keller outlines the fascinating behavior of cellular slime mold. This unique mold can take two completely different forms: It can exist as single-cell organisms, or the separate cells can come together to form multicellular aggregates. The puzzle facing scientists was: What triggers aggrega-

tion? In other words, what makes the single cells join together? Scientists focused their investigations by asking what entity issued the order to start aggregating. They first called this bosslike entity a "founder cell," and later a "pacemaker cell," even though no one had seen any evidence for the existence of such a cell. Proceeding nonetheless from the assumption that such a cell must exist, they ignored evidence to the contrary: For example, when the center of the aggregate is removed, other centers form.

Scientists studying slime mold did not examine the interrelationship between the cells and their environment, nor the interrelationship between the functional systems within each cell, because they were busy looking for the pacemaker cell, which, as eventually became evident, did not exist. Instead, under conditions of nutritional deprivation, each individual cell begins to feel the urge to merge with others to form the conglomerate. It is a reaction of the cells to their environment, not to the orders of a boss. Keller recounts this tale to illustrate her insight that we tend to view nature through our understanding of human relations as hierarchical. In her words, "We risk imposing on nature the very stories we like to hear." In other words, the conceptual metaphor of hierarchical governance made scientists "see" something—a pacemaker cell—that wasn't there. 40

Among the stories many Americans most like to hear are war stories. According to historian Michael Sherry, the American war movie developed during World War II and has been with us ever since. He shows that movies not explicitly about war were also war movies at heart, such as westerns with their good guy–bad guy battles settled with guns. *High Noon*, for example, which became a model for later westerns, was an allegory of the Second World War: The happy ending hinges on the pacifist taking up arms. We can also see this story line in contemporary adventure films: Think of *Star Wars*, with its stirring finale in which Han Solo, having professed no interest in or taste for battle, returns at the last moment to destroy the enemy and save the day. And precisely the same theme is found in a contemporary low-budget independent film, *Sling Blade*, in which a peace-loving retarded man becomes a hero at the end by murdering the man who has been tormenting the family he has come to love. 41

Put Up Your Dukes

If war provides the metaphors through which we view the world and each other, we come to view others—and ourselves—as warriors in battle. Almost any human encounter can be framed as a fight between two opponents. Looking at it this way brings particular aspects of the event into focus and obscures others. 42

Framing interactions as fights affects not only the participants but also the viewers. At a performance, the audience, as well as the performers, can be transformed. This effect was noted by a reviewer in *The New York Times*, commenting on a musical event: 43

Showdown at Lincoln Center. Jazz's ideological war of the last several years led to a pitched battle in August between John Lincoln Collier, the writer, and Wynton Marsalis, the trumpeter, in a debate at Lincoln Center. Mr. Marsalis demolished Mr. Collier, point after point after point, but what made the debate unpleasant was the crowd's blood lust; humiliation, not elucidation, was the desired end.

44   Military imagery pervades this account: the difference of opinions between Collier and Marsalis was an "ideological war," and the "debate" was a "pitched battle" in which Marsalis "demolished" Collier (not his arguments, but him). What the commentator regrets, however, is that the audience got swept up in the mood instigated by the way the debate was carried out: "the crowd's blood lust" for Collier's defeat.

45   This is one of the most dangerous aspects of regarding intellectual interchange as a fight. It contributes to an atmosphere of animosity that spreads like a fever. In a society that includes people who express their anger by shooting, the result of demonizing those with whom we disagree can be truly tragic.

46   But do audiences necessarily harbor within themselves a "blood lust," or is it stirred in them by the performances they are offered? Another arts event was set up as a debate, between a playwright and a theater director. In this case, the metaphor through which the debate was viewed was not war but boxing—a sport that is in itself, like a debate, a metaphorical battle that pitches one side against the other in an all-out effort to win. A headline describing the event set the frame: "AND IN THIS CORNER...," followed by the subhead "A Black Playwright and White Critic Duke It Out." The story then reports:

the face-off between August Wilson, the most successful black playwright in the American theater, and Robert Brustein, longtime drama critic for The New Republic and artistic director of the American Repertory Theatre in Cambridge, Mass. These two heavyweights had been battling in print since last June....

Entering from opposite sides of the stage, the two men shook hands and came out fighting—or at least sparring.

47   Wilson, the article explains, had given a speech in which he opposed Black performers taking "white" roles in color-blind casting; Brustein had written a column disagreeing; and both followed up with further responses to each other.

48   According to the article, "The drama of the Wilson-Brustein confrontation lies in their mutual intransigence." No one would question that audiences crave drama. But is intransigence the most appealing source of drama? I happened to hear this debate broadcast on the radio. The line that triggered the loudest cheers

from the audience was the final question put to the two men by the moderator, Anna Deavere Smith: "What did you each learn from the other in this debate?" The loud applause was evidence that the audience did not crave intransigence. They wanted to see another kind of drama: the drama of change—change that comes from genuinely listening to someone with a different point of view, not the transitory drama of two intransigent positions in stalemate.

To encourage the staging of more dramas of change and fewer of intransigence, *49* we need new metaphors to supplement and complement the pervasive war and boxing match metaphors through which we take it for granted issues and events are best talked about and viewed.

Mud Splatters

Our fondness for the fight scenario leads us to frame many complex human inter- *50* actions as a battle between two sides. This then shapes the way we understand what happened and how we regard the participants. One unfortunate result is that fights make a mess in which everyone is muddied. The person attacked is often deemed just as guilty as the attacker.

The injustice of this is clear if you think back to childhood. Many of us still *51* harbor anger as we recall a time (or many times) a sibling or playmate started a fight—but both of us got blamed. Actions occur in a stream, each a response to what came before. Where you punctuate them can change their meaning just as you can change the meaning of a sentence by punctuating it in one place or another.

Like a parent despairing of trying to sort out which child started a fight, peo- *52* ple often respond to those involved in a public dispute as if both were equally guilty. When champion figure skater Nancy Kerrigan was struck on the knee shortly before the 1994 Olympics in Norway and the then-husband of another champion skater, Tonya Harding, implicated his wife in planning the attack, the event was characterized as a fight between two skaters that obscured their differing roles. As both skaters headed for the Olympic competition, their potential meeting was described as a "long-anticipated figure-skating shootout." Two years later, the event was referred to not as "the attack on Nancy Kerrigan" but as "the rivalry surrounding Tonya Harding and Nancy Kerrigan."

By a similar process, the Senate Judiciary Committee hearings to consider the *53* nomination of Clarence Thomas for Supreme Court justice at which Anita Hill was called to testify are regularly referred to as the "Hill-Thomas hearings," obscuring the very different roles played by Hill and Thomas. Although testimony by Anita Hill was the occasion for reopening the hearings, they were still the Clarence Thomas confirmation hearings: Their purpose was to evaluate Thomas's candidacy. Framing these hearings as a two-sides dispute between Hill and Thomas allowed the senators to focus their investigation on cross-examining Hill rather than seeking other sorts of evidence, for example by con-

sulting experts on sexual harassment to ascertain whether Hill's account seemed
plausible.

Slash-and-Burn Thinking

54   Approaching situations like warriors in battle leads to the assumption that intellectual inquiry, too, is a game of attack, counterattack, and self-defense. In this
spirit, critical thinking is synonymous with criticizing. In many classrooms, students are encouraged to read someone's life work, then rip it to shreds. Though
criticism is one form of critical thinking—and an essential one—so are integrating
ideas from disparate fields and examining the context out of which ideas grew.
Opposition does not lead to the whole truth when we ask only "What's wrong
with this?" and never "What can we use from this in building a new theory, a new
understanding?"

55   There are many ways that unrelenting criticism is destructive in itself. In innumerable small dramas mirroring what happened to Robert Gallo (but on a much
more modest scale), our most creative thinkers can waste time and effort
responding to critics motivated less by a genuine concern about weaknesses in
their work than by a desire to find something to attack. All of society loses when
creative people are discouraged from their pursuits by unfair criticism. (This is
particularly likely to happen since, as Kay Redfield Jamison shows in her book
Touched with Fire, many of those who are unusually creative are also unusually
sensitive; their sensitivity often drives their creativity.)

56   If the criticism is unwarranted, many will say, you are free to argue against it,
to defend yourself. But there are problems with this, too. Not only does self-
defense take time and draw off energy that would better be spent on new creative
work, but any move to defend yourself makes you appear, well, defensive. For
example, when an author wrote a letter to the editor protesting a review he considered unfair, the reviewer (who is typically given the last word) turned the very
fact that the author defended himself into a weapon with which to attack again.
The reviewer's response began, "I haven't much time to waste on the kind of
writer who squanders his talent drafting angry letters to reviewers."

57   The argument culture limits the information we get rather than broadening it
in another way. When a certain kind of interaction is the norm, those who feel
comfortable with that type of interaction are drawn to participate, and those who
do not feel comfortable with it recoil and go elsewhere. If public discourse included
a broad range of types, we would be making room for individuals with different
temperaments to take part and contribute their perspectives and insights. But
when debate, opposition, and fights overwhelmingly predominate, those who
enjoy verbal sparring are likely to take part—by calling in to talk shows, writing
letters to the editor or articles, becoming journalists—and those who cannot
comfortably take part in oppositional discourse, or do not wish to, are likely to
opt out.

This winnowing process is easy to see in apprenticeship programs such as act- 58
ing school, law school, and graduate school. A woman who was identified in her
university drama program as showing exceptional promise was encouraged to go
to New York to study acting. Full of enthusiasm, she was accepted by a famous
acting school where the teaching method entailed the teacher screaming at students, goading and insulting them as a way to bring out the best in them. This
worked well with many of the students but not with her. Rather than rising to
the occasion when attacked, she cringed, becoming less able to draw on her talent, not more. After a year, she dropped out. It could be that she simply didn't
have what it took—but this will never be known, because the adversarial style of
teaching did not allow her to show what talent she had.

Polarizing Complexity: Nature or Nurture?

Few issues come with two neat, and neatly opposed, sides. Again, I have seen this 59
in the domain of gender. One common polarization is an opposition between two
sources of differences between women and men: "culture," or "nurture," on one
hand and "biology," or "nature," on the other.

Shortly after the publication of *You Just Don't Understand*, I was asked by a 60
journalist what question I most often encountered about women's and men's conversational styles. I told her, "Whether the differences I describe are biological or
cultural." The journalist laughed. Puzzled, I asked why this made her laugh. She
explained that she had always been so certain that any significant differences are
cultural rather than biological in origin that the question struck her as absurd. So
I should not have been surprised when I read, in the article she wrote, that the
two questions I am most frequently asked are "Why do women nag?" and "Why
won't men ask for directions?" Her ideological certainty that the question I am
most frequently asked was absurd led her to ignore my answer and get a fact
wrong in her report of my experience.

Some people are convinced that any significant differences between men and 61
women are entirely or overwhelmingly due to cultural influences—the way we
treat girls and boys, and men's dominance of women in society. Others are convinced that any significant differences are entirely or overwhelmingly due to
biology: the physical facts of female and male bodies, hormones, and reproductive
functions. Many problems are caused by framing the question as a dichotomy:
Are behaviors that pattern by sex biological or cultural? This polarization
encourages those on one side to demonize those who take the other view, which
leads in turn to misrepresenting the work of those who are assigned to the opposing camp. Finally, and most devastatingly, it prevents us from exploring the interaction of biological and cultural factors—factors that must, and can only, be
understood together. By posing the question as either/or, we reinforce a false
assumption that biological and cultural factors are separable and preclude the
investigations that would help us understand their interrelationship. When a

problem is posed in a way that polarizes, the solution is often obscured before the search is under way.

Who's Up? Who's Down?

62 Related to polarization is another aspect of the argument culture: our obsession with ratings and rankings. Magazines offer the 10, 50, or 100 best of everything: restaurants, mutual funds, hospitals, even judges. Newsmagazines tell us Who's up, Who's down, as in *Newsweek*'s "Conventional Wisdom Watch" and *Time*'s "Winners and Losers." Rankings and ratings pit restaurants, products, schools, and people against each other on a single scale, obscuring the myriad differences among them. Maybe a small Thai restaurant in one neighborhood can't really be compared to a pricey French one in another, any more than judges with a vast range of abilities and beliefs can be compared on a single scale. And timing can skew results: Ohio State University protested to *Time* magazine when its football team was ranked at the bottom of a scale because only 29 percent of the team graduated. The year before it would have ranked among the top six with 72 percent.

63 After a political debate, analysts comment not on what the candidates said but on the question "Who won?" After the president delivers an important speech, such as the State of the Union Address, expert commentators are asked to give it a grade. Like ranking, grading establishes a competition. The biggest problem with asking what grade the president's speech deserves, or who won and who lost a campaign debate, is what is not asked and is therefore not answered: What was said, and what is the significance of this for the country?

An Ethic of Aggression

64 In an argument culture aggressive tactics are valued for their own sake. For example, a woman called in to a talk show on which I was a guest to say, "When I'm in a place where a man is smoking, and there's a no-smoking sign, instead of saying to him 'You aren't allowed to smoke in here. Put that out,' I say, 'I'm awfully sorry, but I have asthma, so your smoking makes it hard for me to breathe. Would you mind terribly not smoking?' Whenever I say this, the man is extremely polite and solicitous, and he puts his cigarette out, and I say, 'Oh, thank you, thank you!' as if he's done a wonderful thing for me. Why do I do that?"

65 I think this woman expected me to say that she needs assertiveness training to learn to confront smokers in a more aggressive manner. Instead, I told her that there was nothing wrong with her style of getting the man to stop smoking. She gave him a face-saving way of doing what she asked, one that allowed him to feel chivalrous rather than chastised. This is kind to him, but it is also kind to herself, since it is more likely to lead to the result she desires. If she tried to alter his behavior by reminding him of the rules, he might well rebel: "Who made you the enforcer? Mind your own business!" Indeed, who gives any of us the authority to set others straight when we think they're breaking rules?

Another caller disagreed with me, saying the first caller's style was "self- abasing" and there was no reason for her to use it. But I persisted: There is nothing necessarily destructive about conventional self-effacement. Human relations depend on the agreement to use such verbal conventions. I believe the mistake this caller was making—a mistake many of us make—was to confuse *ritual* self-effacement with the literal kind. All human relations require us to find ways to get what we want from others without seeming to dominate them. Allowing others to feel they are doing what you want for a reason less humiliating to them fulfills this need.

Thinking of yourself as the wronged party who is victimized by a lawbreaking boor makes it harder to see the value of this method. But suppose you are the person addicted to smoking who lights up (knowingly or not) in a no-smoking zone. Would you like strangers to yell at you to stop smoking, or would you rather be allowed to save face by being asked politely to stop in order to help them out? Or imagine yourself having broken a rule inadvertently (which is not to imply rules are broken only by mistake; it is only to say that sometimes they are). Would you like some stranger to swoop down on you and begin berating you, or would you rather be asked politely to comply?

As this example shows, conflicts can sometimes be resolved without confrontational tactics, but current conventional wisdom often devalues less confrontational tactics even if they work well, favoring more aggressive strategies even if they get less favorable results. It's as if we value a fight for its own sake, not for its effectiveness in resolving disputes.

This ethic shows up in many contexts. In a review of a contentious book, for example, a reviewer wrote, "Always provocative, sometimes infuriating, this collection reminds us that the purpose of art is not to confirm and coddle but to provoke and confront." This false dichotomy encapsulates the belief that if you are not provoking and confronting, then you are confirming and coddling—as if there weren't myriad other ways to question and learn. What about exploring, exposing, delving, analyzing, understanding, moving, connecting, integrating, illuminating ... or any of innumerable verbs that capture other aspects of what art can do?

The Broader Picture

The increasingly adversarial spirit of our contemporary lives is fundamentally related to a phenomenon that has been much remarked upon in recent years: the breakdown of a sense of community. In this spirit, distinguished journalist and author Orville Schell points out that in his day journalists routinely based their writing on a sense of connection to their subjects—and that this sense of connection is missing from much that is written by journalists today. Quite the contrary, a spirit of demonography often prevails that has just the opposite effect: Far from encouraging us to feel connected to the subjects, it encourages us to feel critical, superior—and, as a result, distanced. The cumulative effect is that citizens feel more and more cut off from the people in public life they read about.

71   The argument culture dovetails with a general disconnection and breakdown of community in another way as well. Community norms and pressures exercise a restraint on the expression of hostility and destruction. Many cultures have rituals to channel and contain aggressive impulses, especially those of adolescent males. In just this spirit, at the 1996 Republican National Convention, both Colin Powell and Bob Dole talked about growing up in small communities where everyone knew who they were. This meant that many people would look out for them, but also that if they did something wrong, it would get back to their parents. Many Americans grew up in ethnic neighborhoods that worked the same way. If a young man stole something, committed vandalism, or broke a rule or law, it would be reported to his relatives, who would punish him or tell him how his actions were shaming the family. American culture today often lacks these brakes.

72   Community is a blend of connections and authority, and we are losing both. As Robert Bly shows in his book by that title, we now have a *Sibling Society*: Citizens are like squabbling siblings with no authority figures who can command enough respect to contain and channel their aggressive impulses. It is as if every day is a day with a substitute teacher who cannot control the class and maintain order.

73   The argument culture is both a product of and a contributor to this alienation, separating people, disconnecting them from each other and from those who are or might have been their leaders.

What Other Way Is There?

74   Philosopher John Dewey° said, on his ninetieth birthday, "Democracy begins in conversation." I fear that it gets derailed in polarized debate.

75   In conversation we form the interpersonal ties that bind individuals together in personal relationships; in public discourse, we form similar ties on a larger scale, binding individuals into a community. In conversation, we exchange the many types of information we need to live our lives as members of a community. In public discourse, we exchange the information that citizens in a democracy need in order to decide how to vote. If public discourse provides entertainment first and foremost—and if entertainment is first and foremost watching fights— then citizens do not get the information they need to make meaningful use of their right to vote.

76   Of course it is the responsibility of intellectuals to explore potential weaknesses in others' arguments, and of journalists to represent serious opposition when it exists. But when opposition becomes the overwhelming avenue of inquiry—a formula that *requires* another side to be found or a criticism to be voiced; when the lust for opposition privileges extreme views and obscures com-

plexity; when our eagerness to find weaknesses blinds us to strengths; when the atmosphere of animosity precludes respect and poisons our relations with one another; then the argument culture is doing more damage than good.

I offer this book not as a frontal assault on the argument culture. That would be in the spirit of attack that I am questioning. It is an attempt to examine the argument culture—our use of attack, opposition, and debate in public discourse—to ask, What are its limits as well as its strengths? How has it served us well, but also how has it failed us? How is it related to culture and gender? What other options do we have? *77*

I do not believe we should put aside the argument model of public discourse entirely, but we need to rethink whether this is the *only* way, or *always* the best way, to carry out our affairs. A step toward broadening our repertoires would be to pioneer reform by experimenting with metaphors other than sports and war, and with formats other than debate for framing the exchange of ideas. The change might be as simple as introducing a plural form. Instead of asking "What's the other side?" we might ask instead, "What are the other sides?" Instead of insisting on hearing "both sides," we might insist on hearing "all sides." *78*

Another option is to expand our notion of "debate" to include more dialogue. This does not mean there can be no negativity, criticism, or disagreement. It simply means we can be more creative in our ways of managing all of these, which are inevitable and useful. In dialogue, each statement that one person makes is qualified by a statement made by someone else, until the series of statements and qualifications moves everyone closer to a fuller truth. Dialogue does not preclude negativity. Even saying "I agree" makes sense only against the background assumption that you might disagree. In dialogue, there is opposition, yes, but no head-on collision. Smashing heads does not open minds. *79*

There are times when we need to disagree, criticize, oppose, and attack—to hold debates and view issues as polarized battles. Even co-operation, after all, is not the absence of conflict but a means of managing conflict. My goal is not a make-nice false veneer of agreement or a dangerous ignoring of true opposition. I'm questioning the *automatic* use of adversarial formats—the assumption that it's *always* best to address problems and issues by fighting over them. I'm hoping for a broader repertoire of ways to talk to each other and address issues vital to us. ◆ *80*

1998

Glossary

Smithsonian Institution: a research and education centre in Washington, D.C.; founded in 1846.

HMO: Health Maintenance Organization. A type of prepaid medical service in the United States in which members pay a monthly or yearly fee for all health care.

John Dewey: (1859–1952) an American educator and philosopher as well as a political activist who advocated women's suffrage, progressive education, and world peace.

Explorations

- Like Tannen, do you believe that North Americans live in an "argument culture"? Do you think the tendency to approach public discourse as a fight is as prevalent in Canadian culture as it is in American culture?

- Why do you think people are so interested in discussion that is promoted as a battle? Can you think of other ways to attract an audience?

CHAPTER SIX

Identifying and Writing about Rhetorical Strategies

In *Landmarks*, we have focused on the writing process, introducing several rhetorical techniques and demonstrating their uses with various essays. In this chapter, we will offer strategies for developing essays in which you identify particular rhetorical devices in non-fiction prose and discuss how the author uses these devices to help convey the essay's message to the audience.

Often, students approach the analysis of essays with the idea that they must find hidden meanings. In fact, meaning is created through the words on the surface of the page and their arrangement, not hidden inside as though the essay were a gift to be unwrapped.

Evaluating non-fiction prose is similar to the other types of evaluation we do daily. When we see a painting or movie, read a book or hear a piece of music, we evaluate it. We consider the tools and techniques available to the artist, as well as those they have developed or adapted, and consider how these choices work to convey a message. For instance, when telling a friend about the movie you saw last night, you might mention how well it incorporates an important element common to that type of film—if you'd seen a *Star Wars* or a *Star Trek* movie, you might evaluate the special effects, or how the film adapts, adheres to, or alters ongoing storylines. If you'd seen *Emma* or *Romeo and Juliet*, you'd be more likely to look at cinematography or at how the film interprets the text; in either case you might evaluate sound or costume or acting. When you tell your friends and family about the film, you usually first briefly summarize the plot to provide a context, but you don't simply repeat the entire plot—that would spoil the film for them.

Writing about non-fiction prose demands a similar process: it involves evaluating an essay's rhetorical strategies, selecting those devices that are central to the text's focus and development, and conveying your findings in a cohesive reading that focuses on a few related elements. In other words, you'll identify the techniques the author has chosen and show your audience how they contribute to the essay's purpose and effectiveness. (If you are uncertain about how a particular strategy works, please refer to the chapter of *Landmarks* in which we discuss that strategy.)

Analysis of non-fiction prose has the same purpose and shares the conventions of literary analysis: both types of essay consider the strategies an author uses to achieve a particular effect, both are written in the present tense, and both are primarily argumentative essays—essays that provide evidence and examples from the text you are analyzing to support your claims about the text. Your purpose in writing an analysis is to convince your audience, using evidence from the text, that they should consider your insights into the text in their evaluation of it.

Keep the following factors in mind as you begin planning your essay:

- The strategies you choose to analyze should support your own interpretation of the text; your essay should offer a cohesive reading, pointing out overall patterns rather than simply listing and providing examples of various strategies.

- Once you've identified the text's rhetorical devices, you must show how those devices work to underscore the author's thesis and to influence the audience.

- You will not be able to discuss, in one analysis, all of the essay's strategies. Choose three or four strategies that are central to your understanding of the piece and focus your analysis on those.

The following seven steps, "Reading the Essay," "Presenting Introductory Details," "Selecting Data and Formulating Your Thesis," "Arranging and Developing Body Paragraphs," "Concluding," "Proofreading," and "Crafting a Title," will guide you through the process of identifying and discussing rhetorical strategies. Annie Dillard's "Living like Weasels" illustrates the steps, and we have included a full-length analysis of "Living like Weasels" and one of Marni Jackson's "Gals and Dolls: The Moral Value of 'Bad' Toys" at the end of the chapter.

Step One: Reading the Essay

As you read the essay for the first time, keep the following questions in mind:

Context

- What is the essay's title? How does the title reflect the author's central idea(s)?
  Never underestimate the power of a title! "Living like Weasels" reveals several things about the essay: the tone of the title is informal, hinting that the essay will be informal, rather than a biological examination of the weasel's living habits; it also suggests an analogy at the heart of the essay, and when a title suggests a central device like metaphor or analogy, the essay will

likely support that central metaphor or analogy with other comparisons, metaphors, similes, and/or analogies.

- When was the essay first published? Is the publication date significant to fully understanding the essay's context or purpose?

    "Living like Weasels" was first published in 1982, but the nature of the essay doesn't tie it to a particular time except in defining the essay's audience. On the other hand, the publication date of Margaret Atwood's "The Female Body" is likely important in a discussion of the essay, since it positions the essay at a particular stage in cultural relations between genders.

Diction, Syntax, Audience and Tone

- Who is the essay's primary audience? How do you know?

    The diction of "Living like Weasels" is often sophisticated and/or innovative, suggesting a well-educated audience. That the images are set at the intersection of suburbia and the pond suggests a suburban, possibly young professional American audience. In addition, Dillard expects her audience to recognize the clichés she has revitalized and their significance.

- What tone(s) does the author convey? How does diction help the author achieve the tone(s)? What does the tone of the essay say about the author's attitude toward the essay's subject and its audience?

    Dillard's diction and images are evocative, the syntax often challenges the "rules," and she speaks from the first-person point of view; these strategies contribute to a sometimes passionate, sometimes dreamy, sometimes informative tone. The passion of the essay's tone echoes the author's passion for her topic. You might consider how the frequent "I" affects Dillard's relationship with her audience: does it distance the audience? Draw them in? Make the essay seem intensely personal?

Figurative Language

- Where does the author employ figurative language, and how do the figurative devices create or underscore meaning?

    Metaphors, similes, symbols, alliteration, assonance, and images all support the central analogy of "Living like Weasels." Identifying the figurative devices of a passage is just part of the process, though. You may find it more challenging to understand how the particular devices an author chooses affect the essay; if so, begin by asking yourself what image a metaphor or simile evokes and why that image is significant to the discussion at hand. For instance, "thin as a curve, a muscled ribbon, brown as fruitwood, soft-furred, alert" conveys meaning to the audience by characterizing the weasel in terms we usually associate with thin, tensile strength—appropriate for conveying to the audience a sense of the weasel's incredible will. Dillard also incorporates images of eagles, symbols of freedom, in her introduction and conclusion; these "frame" the essay, reminding the audience of the "perfect freedom of... necessity."

Purpose and Thesis

* What are the essay's purpose and thesis?

    Note: We can begin to understand an essay's purpose by identifying its "main rhetorical aim." Most essays have a main, or primary, rhetorical aim: expressive, expository, or argumentative. Be sure not to confuse an essay's rhetorical aim(s) with its thesis: an essay's thesis presents the essay's focus, the main point(s) it will develop, while an essay's rhetorical aim(s) will be to elicit an emotional response from the audience, to teach them something, or to convince them of your point of view. The main rhetorical aims are: expressive, expository, and argumentative.

    Expressive writing creates a mood, describes a setting, tells a story. It tries to make the audience feel immediately involved with the images and story, often eliciting an emotional response.

    Expository writing gives the audience information about a subject or a process; it "exposes" the audience to new information.

    Argumentative writing attempts to convince the audience of the author's point of view on an issue. Most essays combine these aims, but most often one of the aims is more prevalent than the others. The less prevalent aim(s) are called "subordinate rhetorical aims."

    "Living like Weasels" argues that we should live in "necessity"; it also has a subordinate aim in that the author expresses her feelings about the natural world, describing Hollins Pond's landscape in detail.

* Does the author appeal to *logos, ethos,* or *pathos*? What are the effects of these appeals?

    Dillard's passion about her topic and her willingness to share her insights with her audience both help her establish an appeal to ethos, as does her reference to naturalist Ernest Thompson Seton to support her claim that weasels are tenacious.

* Is the essay, in your opinion, effective in achieving its purpose?

    You have to answer this question according to your own reading, but you can begin by recording your initial reactions to the piece you're analyzing; then, as you reread and develop a short summary of the essay for your introduction, you can determine whether your opinion of the text has deepened or altered.

Organization and Development

* What methods does the author use for developing body paragraphs? How are the ideas in the essay organized?

Dillard develops her body paragraphs with description, narration, and comparison and contrast. The essay develops inductively, with the sample of a specific weasel leading to a general conclusion about how humans should live their lives.

The first step in preparing to write an analysis—invention—involves determining which of the passage's rhetorical strategies are central to your reading of the text. As you find the answers to the above questions, make notes on the page, and once you're confident you understand the essay and have identified its various strategies you can determine which of them you'd like to focus on.

Step Two: Presenting Introductory Details

Generally, the introduction to a rhetorical analysis explains the rhetorical situation of the essay you're analyzing. Your introduction should do the following:

- Begin with a sentence or two designed both to reflect the main idea of the essay and to engage the interest of your audience. An introductory sentence for an essay on "Living like Weasels" might be, "We think of weasels as sneaky, sly and untrustworthy—to call a person a 'weasel' is to imply that the person is sneaky and sly rather than a good role model for human behaviour."

- Present the title, the author, and the main rhetorical aim of the piece; you may also want to include the author's credentials and the date of publication if they are significant to your analysis. For instance, "In her essay 'Living like Weasels,' American essayist Annie Dillard argues that we should indeed emulate the weasel, in particular for its obedience to instinct."

- Indicate the essay's intended audience: be specific. This might be expressed, "Dillard writes for an audience of educated young Americans faced with a myriad of decisions and choices."

- Provide a summary of the essay in one or two sentences. Do not allow yourself to wander off into a long summary; focus on the main idea of the essay by asking yourself, "What is this essay about?" For example, "Dillard contends that humans live their lives 'in choice, hating necessity and dying at the last ignobly in its talons,' and maintains that if we were to live in necessity, as weasels do, we would, paradoxically, be freed from the chains of obligation and duty."

Step Three: Selecting Data and Formulating Your Thesis

Writers use many strategies in developing an essay, and no one analysis can realistically incorporate all of them. Remember that this is *your* analysis, and you should choose the rhetorical strategies that best support your interpretation of the essay. Your thesis will indicate to your audience which strategies you have chosen to discuss and how they are important to the essay. For instance, one possible thesis for an analysis of Dillard's essay would be, "Dillard compares weasels and humans, nature and civilization, appealing to the audience's physical senses with figurative language and renewed clichés, and framing her essay with images of soaring eagles."

Step Four: Arranging and Developing Body Paragraphs

Your thesis will determine how your essay will be arranged: the body paragraphs will present the strategies being analyzed in the same order you list them in your thesis. You may discuss several related strategies in one paragraph, or you may feel that particular strategies are significant enough to merit an entire paragraph of their own. However you decide to organize your discussion, remember that you must provide specific evidence from the text to illustrate your points. Choose those quotations that best illustrate the strategies the paragraph analyzes, keeping your evidence brief and direct: do not fall into the trap of quoting long sections of the text—just enough to illustrate your claims (see the sample analyses). Remember, too, that you must show how the strategies you focus on help to develop the piece's thesis and purpose.

The body paragraphs for the Dillard analysis will focus on comparison, figurative language, clichés, and the essay's frame.

Paragraph One:

- Strategy: comparison

- Examples: civilization imposed on nature (55 mph highway at one end, nesting ducks at the other; a "muskrat hole or a beer can," motorcycle tracks and turtle eggs).

- Effect: these examples highlight the differences between the way humans and weasels live: wild animals lay their eggs in motorcycle tracks from necessity; humans leave beer cans because they choose to. The comparisons establish and reinforce the juxtaposition of nature and civilization, necessity and choice.

Paragraph Two:

- Strategy: figurative language (metaphor, simile)

- Examples: metaphor (the weasel was socketed into the naturalist's hand; humans should "stalk their calling" as a weasel stalks prey); simile (the weasel was "thin as a curve").

- Effect: the metaphors and simile highlight the weasel's tenacity and suggest steely strength; the paradox builds on Dillard's characterization of "choice" as burden, "necessity" as freedom.

Paragraph Three:

- Strategy: revitalized clichés

- Examples: their "eyes locked, and someone threw away the key" (based on "they should lock him up and throw away the key"); "held on for a dearer life" (based on "he was driving so fast I had to hold on for dear life"); "down is out, out of your ever-loving mind" (based on "he's down and out," which suggests that he suffers extreme financial hardship).

- Effect: Dillard surprises her audience by slightly shifting the diction of clichés to illustrate that old, worn out, and meaningless phrases can be revitalized, and suggests that humans can also enjoy renewal.

Paragraph Four:

- Strategy: the essay's frame

- Examples: The eagle at the beginning of the essay is grounded, dead, shot from the sky with a weasel's skull latched onto its throat by the jaw; Dillard resurrects the eagle at the end of the essay to soar: it will "seize you up aloft...lightly, thoughtless, from any height at all...."

- Effect: the eagles symbolize the necessity that we should grasp in order to achieve freedom; the final image suggests the soaring possibilities inherent in leaving the old and embracing the new.

Step Five: Concluding

The conclusion of a rhetorical analysis should not simply restate the thesis or repeat the strategies you have discussed in the body of the essay. Keep in mind that if you have observed both strengths and weaknesses in the essay, the conclusion is the place for you to weigh them in order to make an overall determination of the essay's effectiveness. The following are some points you may want to consider when formulating your conclusion:

- How effective is the essay overall? What is the effect of specific rhetorical strategies, and how well has the author achieved his or her purpose?

- Does the essay you are analyzing point to larger issues that go beyond your discussion of specific rhetorical strategies? If so, while you do not want to introduce a new topic in your conclusion, you might gesture towards these issues in order to leave your audience with something to think about.

At the heart of Dillard's analogy between humans and weasels lies a paradox that makes the negative—the sneaky weasel and images of confinement—positive: while humans generally feel that the freedom to choose is fundamental,

Dillard assures us that choice can be crippling, that it can keep us from following our instincts, and urges us to live in "the perfect freedom of single necessity." "Living like Weasels" is compelling in its insistence that we follow our passions, according to need, rather than floundering in the confinement of choice.

Step Six: Proofreading

Proofread your essay for paragraph structure, development, transitions, and, of course, for the kinds of errors you commonly make. Read the introductory paragraph and the concluding paragraph together to ensure that your essay is cohesive and balanced in content, form, and style. Pay particular attention to the distinction between your point of view and the author's, as it is quite easy, when you are focusing on someone else's writing, to abandon your own voice and adopt that of the essay you are analyzing.

Step Seven: Crafting a Title

- Choose a title that describes your essay and distinguishes it from others. Your title will determine your audience's first impression of your essay.

- If you have difficulty creating titles, or if you feel it would be appropriate, lift a significant word or phrase from the essay you are analyzing and make that your title. Remember, however, that if your title **is** a quotation, then, and only then, do you put your title in quotation marks. If **part** of your title is a quotation, put only that part in quotation marks.

Sample Essay 1

[1] original title

Barbie Bashing[1]

[2] intriguing question to capture reader's attention and introduce topic

[3] brief summary

[4] thesis

[5] intended audience

[6] overall evaluation of essay

Can denying children the toys they desire render them "benumbed adults, lost to themselves and predisposed to violence"?[2] This question is the crux of Marni Jackson's argument in her 1991 essay, "Gals and Dolls: The Moral Value of 'Bad' Toys." Jackson bases her argument on the premise that when parents impose moral values on children, they send the message, "Your desires and feelings are not good enough," and that refusing boys access to toy guns and girls to Barbie dolls constitutes an imposition of moral values.[3] Jackson develops her points deductively through appeals,[4] directed to an audience of parents,[5] to <u>ethos</u> and <u>logos</u>; however, the lack of definition of key terms undercuts the essay's effectiveness, and the underlying assumption of the argument—that saying "no" to Barbie causes more damage than good—is not fully substantiated.[6]

1

2   Jackson's appeal to <u>ethos</u> is directed to parents.[7] She admits, in the first paragraph, that she thought she knew exactly how to raise children until she actually became a parent and had to deal with the extent to which culture influences parenting. In paragraph three she again pokes fun at herself when she accuses herself of doing what she is arguing against—moralizing—and in paragraph five she admits that she allows her son to watch too much television.[8] Each of these instances foregrounds Jackson's fallibility and, thus, her credibility: she is the voice of experience, and by voicing the fears most parents also feel, she attempts to forge a bond between the audience and the writer, insinuating that parental fears are often unfounded. In fact, Jackson goes on to compare the irrational fears of parents to the "impeccable" logic of children, who are "not pushovers," and who have a surprising amount of "savvy and shit-detection." Jackson's experience has taught her that parents' rules are too often based on a need to alleviate their fear of being inadequate parents. However, her attempt to build up credibility is weakened when she suggests that parents too easily put their own, rather than their children's, needs first; here, Jackson runs the risk of alienating instead of winning her audience.[9]

3   Jackson bases her contention that rules often serve the needs of parents on the work of psychoanalyst Alice Miller, whose expertise strengthens the appeal to <u>ethos</u>.[10] Jackson uses Miller's causal link between children whose parents have imposed moral values on them, and "benumbed adults...predisposed to violence," to propose the idea that banning "bad" toys can ultimately be debilitating to the child.[11] Again, parents are the target; unlike both "savvy" children and the expert psychoanalyst, parents do not seem to know what children need to become happy and healthy adults.

4   Miller's causal link becomes the basis of Jackson's appeal to <u>logos</u>.[12] Jackson arranges her argument deductively, beginning with a generalization which posits that imposing "<u>any</u> system of moral values on children is potentially damaging," that many parents do impose moral values on their children, and that, therefore, these parents potentially damage their children.[13] She goes on to characterize the nature of this damage by suggesting that "pedagogy... sends a hidden message" to children that they are inadequate: children who hear the message "you are inadequate" generate "a

[7] topic sentence indicates rhetorical strategy

[8] specific examples

[9] evaluation

[10] topic sentence with transition to show link to previous point

[11] analysis

[12] topic sentence indicates another rhetorical strategy

[13] analysis

core of inexplicable shame," and since many children hear this message, many children have a core of "inexplicable shame." Children who develop "a core of inexplicable shame" are "most likely to grow into benumbed adults, lost to themselves and predisposed to violence." Most of the remainder of the essay focuses on drawing specific conclusions about the importance of guns to boys and, more important, of Barbies to girls, implying that parents who deny their children these toys impose "moral values" and potentially cause their children to develop into asocial adults. Jackson does not make this connection directly, but provides the framework that leads her audience to move from the general premise about the dangers of imposing values on children to the conclusion that banning Barbie can cause psychological damage.

In leading the audience to conclude that banning "bad" toys 5 potentially leads to damage, Jackson conflates but does not define terms such as "moral values" or "pedagogy," which somewhat clouds the issues she is attempting to clarify. Pedagogy is simply the art or science of teaching, and the word does not imply, as Jackson suggests it does, the imposition of irrational rules. If objections to Barbie do not constitute an imposition of irrational rules, will denying children the toy lead to the horrors she has outlined? While Jackson's point that constantly putting rigid restrictions on children can interfere with their sense of play is valid, she does not substantiate her contention that denying Barbie dolls constitutes a rigid restriction.

Although Jackson makes an important point about the "moral 6 value of 'bad' toys," she does not give a great deal of credit to a parent's judgment or to a child's ability to find alternative playthings, nor does she fully explore the cultural message both Barbie and guns send, but maintains instead that they are culturally significant for children and therefore children should not be denied them. She does not deal with the fact that they may perpetuate the same cultural values that cause parents to object to them, nor does she substantiate the claim that parents do object to Barbie dolls; apparently, 98% of Canadian parents of daughters aged four to ten are buying Barbie dolls. Are girls attracted to Barbie because she is "bad," or are they attracted to her because she is aggressively marketed by a corporation which exploits the image of a stereotypical female body for profit?[14] "Gals and Dolls: The

14 concluding
comments

Moral Value of 'Bad' Toys" is a provocative essay, but weaknesses in the argumentative appeals and the failure to define key terms leave questions unanswered and crucial points unexamined.[15]

15 overall evaluation weighs strengths and weaknesses

Sample Essay 2

The Confinement of Choice

1   We think of weasels as sneaky, sly and untrustworthy—to call a person a "weasel" is to imply that the person is sneaky and sly rather than a good role model for human behaviour. However, in her essay "Living like Weasels," American essayist Annie Dillard argues that we should indeed emulate the weasel, in particular for its obedience to instinct. Writing for an audience of educated young Americans, Dillard contends that humans live their lives "in choice, hating necessity and dying at the last ignobly in its talons," and maintains that if we were to live in necessity, as weasels do, we would, paradoxically, be freed from the chains of obligation and duty. Dillard effectively compares weasels and humans, nature and civilization, appealing to the audience's physical senses with figurative language and renewed clichés, and framing her essay with images of soaring eagles.

2   Dillard compares humans and weasels, civilization and nature by littering images of nature with signs of human civilization. For instance, "there's a 55 mph highway at one end of [Hollins] Pond, and a nesting pair of weed ducks at the other," and around the pond, a "muskrat hole or a beer can" can be found "under every bush," and the "fields and woods" are "threaded everywhere with motorcycle tracks—in whose bare clay wild turtles lay eggs." These comparisons highlight the differences between the way humans and weasels live: wild animals lay their eggs in motorcycle tracks from necessity; humans leave beer cans because they choose to. The comparisons establish and reinforce the juxtaposition of nature and civilization, necessity and choice.

3   Dillard reinforces her comparisons between nature and civilization, freedom and choice by appealing to her audience's physical senses with images developed through metaphor and simile. For example, she illustrates the weasel's tenacity with metaphors: a weasel was "socketed" into a naturalist's hand, and humans should "stalk [their] calling" the way a weasel stalks prey, "in a

certain skilled and supple way." Similes are especially effective in conveying the determination and strength of the weasel's will with phrases like "thin as a curve, a muscled ribbon...he would have made a good arrowhead." These images highlight the weasel's tenacity and suggest a steely strength of will that humans would do well to emulate instead of clinging to their old, boring routines.

The most startling strategy Dillard employs is the rejuvenated 4 cliché. When she meets the weasel at Hollins Pond, their "eyes locked, and someone threw away the key." This cliché usually suggests imprisonment of some kind, but for Dillard it paradoxically leads to a sense of the freedom of a weasel's life. She says that she should have held on to the weasel, "held on for a dearer life." To hold on for dear life is to hold on lest letting go result in disaster, but, again, Dillard reverses the meaning so that holding on to the weasel would have led to a dearer, a better life. She inverts meaning again when she says "down is out, out of your everloving mind and back to your careless senses," so that instead of suggesting a life of misery, "down and out" suggests the joy of living by instinct. Dillard surprises her audience by slightly shifting the syntax of clichés to illustrate that old, worn out, and meaningless phrases can be revitalized, and that we, too, could feel rejuvenated.

Dillard also invokes a sense of rebirth in the essay's frame. The 5 eagle at the beginning of the essay is grounded, dead, shot from the sky, a weasel's skull latched onto its throat by the jaw. At the end of the essay, Dillard resurrects the eagle and it soars, "seiz[ing] you up aloft...lightly, thoughtless, from any height at all...." The eagles symbolize the necessity that we should grasp in order to achieve freedom, the final image suggesting the soaring possibilities inherent in leaving the old and embracing the new.

At the heart of Dillard's analogy between humans and weasels 6 lies a paradox that makes the negative—the sneaky weasel and images of confinement—positive: while humans generally feel that the freedom to choose is fundamental, Dillard assures us that choice can be crippling, that it can keep us from following our instincts, and urges us to live in "the perfect freedom of single necessity." "Living like Weasels" is compelling in its insistence that we follow our passions, according to need, rather than floundering in the confinement of choice.

CHAPTER SEVEN

Writing Research Papers

As we have emphasized throughout *Landmarks,* writing is a process of self-exploration; writing a research paper is a process which, although a more demanding task than writing a short argument or exposition, is also an exploration—of others' opinions, ideas, and findings. Academic writing often requires that writers build on the work of others in order to arrive at their own, new conclusions; in fact, research may be one of the most exciting activities in which scholars engage.

In this section, we will introduce many possible approaches to research methods, but you should keep in mind that these methods are as individual as each writer: there is no one right way to research. As you become more experienced scholars, you will discover methods and processes that work well for you, but even writing your first research paper can be a rewarding experience if you approach the research project systematically and give yourself adequate time to work through each stage of the project.

The Research Paper

A research paper (also referred to as a "documented essay" or sometimes as a "term paper") allows you to explore a concept deeply and honestly with the help of the ideas and findings of others. Thus, the research paper reflects not only the writer's views and experiences, but also those of other sources. Because documented essays incorporate a great deal of information, they tend to be longer than other types of writing you may be asked to do. Despite this difference, research papers build on the same principles of effective composition that you have learned in other writing tasks: invention, development, arrangement, and style. However, you will find that, because the research paper is a longer project, you will probably work through the process more than once. You will begin by gathering, developing, and arranging your own ideas on your topic and will repeat the process by gathering, developing, and arranging the facts and ideas you locate in your sources. Finally, you will draft and revise the paper, considering the elements of style.

This process can be broken down into five steps: inventing an idea/topic, locating relevant information, evaluating that information, drafting the paper, and revising and polishing the paper. It is normal to feel a little overwhelmed when beginning a large project, but if you keep in mind these steps, you will likely find that writing a research paper is a dynamic and rewarding process.

The Assignment

Before beginning your project, you must determine the parameters of the assignment. Have you been given a list of topics from which to choose, or will you have the opportunity to choose your own topic? Are you presenting your research primarily to persuade or to inform your audience? What will be the length of the finished paper? Are you restricted as to the types or the number of sources you can use? What style of documentation will you use? Will you be submitting a proposal? A formal outline? Ensure that you know whether your research paper must meet particular criteria.

Step One: Choosing a Topic

If you are given a topic, it will likely be broad enough for students of different backgrounds and experiences to address, so you will have to narrow and focus it. Whether you are asked to write on a specific topic or are given the opportunity to choose your own topic, you should use some of the methods of invention outlined in Chapter 1 to see what you already know about your topic and to discover the central questions you want to explore in your essay. Do this before you go to the library, so that you have a direction to follow when you begin to choose sources.

Choosing your own topic allows you to relate your own experience and background to your academic work. Often research papers will take weeks, or in some cases months, to complete. Since you will be putting a great deal of time and effort into your paper, choose a topic that has relevance for your personal or your academic life, one that genuinely interests and excites you. Your interest in your topic will come across on the page.

Once you have been given your assignment, choose your topic as soon as possible; even though you will not begin your research right away, your mind will begin working on the topic. Begin by brainstorming: list ideas that particularly interest you and those you would like to learn more about. Brainstorm on issues currently in the news, issues raised by movies you have seen or books you have read, issues on campus or those raised in any of the courses you are taking, or issues related to your own interests and hobbies. Once you have an idea of your research area, continue to brainstorm to narrow your topic so that it is as focused as possible.

You might want to freewrite on your topic in order to determine what you already know and what it is you want to learn about it; the latter will become the central question and the related peripheral questions your paper will address. Maret Rehnby, whose paper is reprinted at the end of this section, used a computer to freewrite on a topic which had personal significance for her. We have reproduced the freewrite below exactly as it was written, except to introduce, in square brackets, points that need clarification.

> When I was having so many difficulties deciding upon a sub-
> ject, nevermind a topic for my research paper, I at first was
> in the midst of a streak on the coffee make that caffeine wagon.
> I had kicked the stuff, as I had so many times in the past, gone
> through the withdrawal symptoms and was on the road to full
> recovery, away from dependency. However, the stress of the
> task at hand, and other factors, including close daily proximity
> to an espresso machine whoops—telephone interruption in
> the person of my grandmother—caused me to fall off the
> wagon on the road to recovery and into the mire of renewed
> dependence upon the drug called caffeine. When I told [my
> instructor] that the search for the research topic was not
> proving successful and described my lapse from abstinence,
> and its attendant symptoms, she raised her eyebrows and
> pointed out that I had inadvertanlty that should be inadver-
> tently no both look wrong stumbled upon a topic that could
> prove to be of adequate interest in the realm of [the course]
> while allowing me to benefit health-wise in gaining knowledge
> of this magical liquid. And so here I am. But as far as finding
> a perfect wealth of information on the subject, well, there are
> many studies out there, monographs concerning the affects of
> caffeine on gastrointestinal function which are about as witty
> as such a title suggests, and far too advanced for a layperson
> such as myself to effectively glean a thorough knowledge with-
> out a scientific background. Anything which includes diagrams
> of a chemical nature does not win my confidence as a work
> which could benefit me in a quick and insightful way. I guess
> this last thought indicates my need for easy answers at this
> late date.

Rehnby had discovered that most of the health-related information was too specialized for her purposes, and worked from that point to question why caffeine's effects on the body were not generally known or accessible.

Once you are fairly certain of your topic, it is critical that you begin to narrow your focus. If you try to address too many questions in your paper, you may only be able to deal with them on a superficial level; if you confine your questions to a few, you will be able to investigate your topic more thoroughly. Remember that while 10 or 15 pages may seem like a great deal, once you start using sources, you will quickly fill the pages. Rehnby, as we have shown, initially proposed a research paper that would answer questions about the health risks and addictive nature of coffee. She narrowed her topic so that her paper would address the historical factors that have informed the public's current ignorance about caffeine.

The Proposal

Whether or not your instructor requires you to submit a proposal, it is a good idea to write one; indeed, it can help keep you focused and ensure that you accomplish each task in time to submit your paper by the due date. A proposal should do the following:

- Present your topic
- Identify the purpose and significance of your paper
- Set out the central questions you want to address
- Suggest the types of research you expect to do
- Propose the dates by which you intend to have the various phases of your paper completed

Keep in mind that the purpose of a proposal is to indicate that you know what you want to explore, why it is important to explore it, and how you will go about exploring it. Knowing the topic, purpose, and central questions of your project will allow you to draft a working thesis—the central idea that you want to pursue. Although your working thesis will likely change as you research and write the paper, it will give you a place to start.

Notice how Rehnby's proposal provides her with a clear path of inquiry, enabling her to investigate her topic—coffee consumption—in a detailed and organized way.

Maret Rehnby
English 303, section 951
Roberta Birks
July 16, 2002

Proposal for Research Essay

Topic: Coffee consumption

Purpose: To address the cult of modern coffee drinking and the health effects of such, which seem not to be widely known. We have invented words and terms which encourage a friendly aura around this addictive beverage, including "coffee break," "coffee klatch," "coffee cake," "coffee shop," but the recent proliferation of "cafés" which cater to this addiction suggests that there is a powerful force behind the projection of the benevolent face of Juan Valdez.

Central Questions: Is coffee harmful to health? Is it psychologically addictive? Are people being warned about its effects? Are we getting the facts about coffee production?

Projected Research: I am considering conducting a poll. There is information in the Bio-Medical library about coffee's effects on the body, and in Macmillan Library to do with coffee's production; however, the exponential growth of coffee-beaneries in the city is not documented, though I could check the telephone books of the past few years. I can cite myself as an expert in the capacity of a recovering addict who, unable to master my addiction, has fallen off the wagon.

Schedule of Work to be Completed:

Complete library research: July 16th to July 25th

Conduct poll: July 18th to July 25th

Complete first draft of essay: July 20th to July 30th

Revise essay: July 31st to August 5th

Submit completed essay: August 6th

Audience and Purpose

Give some thought to your audience and purpose before you begin your research. Although your immediate audience may seem to be the instructor who assigned the project, defining the audience further will help you to make decisions about sources, tone, style, and so on. Your research will allow you to know a great deal more about your topic than the average, educated audience, so it is essential to keep their needs in mind as you write and revise your paper. You will have to provide adequate background to keep your audience fully informed, and define terms with which they may not be familiar or that have several connotative meanings so that they know exactly how you are using these terms. The following questions will be helpful in determining the needs of your audience:

- How much does my audience already know about my topic?
- Do they have specific expectations about the number and type of sources that I should use?

- Will my audience require that I use a specific voice (first person, third person, etc.)?
- What style and approach will be best suited to them?

Also give thought to the purpose of your paper. Are you being asked simply to gather and record information (e.g., to define the different kinds of financial dealers in the Canadian bond market), to use sources to support an opinion (e.g., to show that photo radar is unethical in a democracy), or to evaluate sources (e.g., to determine the biases or inaccuracies in biographies of Oscar Wilde)? In some papers, two or three of these purposes might be combined; for instance, Rehnby gathers information about the history of coffee, uses medical research to support her opinion that caffeine is potentially harmful, and evaluates the bias of sources that do not adequately investigate the effects of caffeine. If your instructor has assigned you a specific question, decide the purpose of your response. If you are choosing your own topic, decide whether you want to inform, persuade, or analyze, or whether your topic lends itself to a combination of approaches.

Keep in mind that the style of research paper that best suits your audience and purpose depends on the academic situation and discipline in which you are writing. As a university student, you may be asked to write within a particular research genre—one that requires you to position yourself within an established body of knowledge. Typically, in this situation, the audience expects you to show your understanding of a topic (for example, by introducing the topic with citations from recognized sources), and to identify a "knowledge deficit" (Giltrow 286). To identify a knowledge deficit, you can point out the limitations of existing research, or you can show that there is a gap in understanding about a topic. Your purpose for writing your paper is to present your findings to the scholarly community, and to fill in any gaps that you have exposed.

The Scratch Outline

Once you have determined your audience and purpose and the central questions your paper will address, you may find it useful to generate a "scratch outline." A scratch outline is a quick map of the direction you think the paper might take. The outline will help you to see what information you will need to discover and allow you to begin to think about the organization of your paper. Rehnby's scratch outline looked like this:

> Historical spread of coffee use:
> — began in indigenous coffee regions: Africa and Mid-East
> — origin of coffee houses; recognition of euphoric nature of coffee spread through wars and colonialism
> Conflicting opinions re coffee use:
> — scientific studies do not agree; no conclusive evidence re positive effects

— vested interests in fostering a positive public perception
— coffee lobby
— pharmaceutical companies

Coffee continues to be grown despite serious concerns re its growth and consumption

— social forces gain clout: new ideas become steadfast traditions
— "coffee" as an activity, something one can "do": changes the language
— vestiges of patriarchy from earlier in century
— cookbooks, women's magazines ostensibly aid women
— doctors' opinions re coffee's health benefits used to weight ads

Step Two: Locating Relevant Information

There are two types of sources: primary sources and secondary sources. A primary source is a first-hand observation of an event or experience, or a literary text. For instance, a novel, interview (in person or via e-mail), autobiography, lab report, electronic database and diary are all primary sources. Secondary sources comprise what others say about your topic or about your primary sources. A biography, an analysis of a literary work, a web site that comments on your topic, and an evaluation of statistical evidence are all examples of secondary sources, as they are reflections on, or analyses of, an idea, event, experience, or literary text. Many research papers will combine primary and secondary sources, but whether this is possible or not will depend on your specific topic. For example, Rehnby relied primarily on secondary sources that detail the history and the effects of coffee.

There is no right number of sources for a research paper, but in order to show that your findings are reliable, you should provide information from as wide a variety of sources as possible. You will likely discover that four or five sources are more important, and that you rely heavily on them, but if you use only one or two sources, your conclusions may not stand the test of scholarly scrutiny.

Library Resources

Once you know the parameters of your paper and have sufficiently focused your topic, you can begin to seek sources of information. You will probably begin in the library, which will offer books, journals, newspapers, and magazine articles in either print or electronic format, video and audio tapes and CDs, photographic slides, and reference works including indices, bibliographies, collections of abstracts, encyclopedias, atlases, biographical dictionaries, and more. This list is not exhaustive; our intention here is simply to make you aware of the range of materials your library will offer.

This stage is one of the more time-consuming parts of writing a research paper, and it can also be one of the most overwhelming parts, because libraries are large, complex buildings that contain a plethora of materials. However, almost all libraries offer tours of resources and schedule tutorials in using specific research tools like the CD-ROM or the Internet. Take advantage of these aids. The more familiar you are with your library, the easier using it will be. Do not overlook the possibility that the indices and "works cited" lists of the books you find initially can lead you to further sources; you may also look on the shelves around texts you have located to determine whether there are other texts nearby on the same topic. Also remember that reference librarians have a tremendous amount of knowledge and are there to help you: do not hesitate to ask them questions. If you have looked for a specific piece of information for 10 minutes and have not been able to find it, ask for assistance. Do not search aimlessly: you will become frustrated and will waste valuable time.

In addition to library sources, you may gather additional information from out-side sources, such as brochures published by organizations concerned in some way with your topic, or the Internet (see "Evaluating Information" below for guide-lines on evaluating electronic sources). You may also wish to formulate questionnaires or conduct interviews.

Interviews and Questionnaires

Often the most valuable information comes not from published material but from personal interviews with people who have expertise in your subject area. Check the yellow pages of the telephone book to determine whether there are organizations that might be able to help you (this can be a valuable resource for finding pamphlets or brochures as well). For example, if your topic is "The Role of Food Banks in Canadian Cities," the director or public relations officer of your local food bank might agree to an interview.

Here are some guidelines to keep in mind for interviews:

- Speak with your instructor to discuss whether your university or college has guidelines for primary research involving human subjects. Many post-secondary institutions require that researchers follow established ethical guidelines and ask for approval for their project before beginning the research phase. Your instructor can guide you through this process.

- Contact the person or organization you want to interview well in advance of the date you would like to see them; explain clearly who you are, what your project is, where you will meet, and what you would like them to do. Arrange a suitable time to meet with your subject, and ask how long he or she can spend with you. Thirty to forty-five minutes is a reasonable length of time for an interview.

- Do preliminary reading in advance so that you are informed and prepared for the interview.

- Prepare a list of detailed questions before you go to the interview, and, if pos-sible, send the subject the list in advance of your meeting; limit your questions to those pertaining to your subject's area of expertise.

- Arrive at the meeting a few minutes early so that you can be directed to the person you are to interview. Dress appropriately for the environment in which you will be conducting the interview. If you are interviewing a steel-worker on the floor of a factory, do not wear heels and a skirt or dress shoes and a suit; conversely, if you are going to interview the partner of a law firm, do not arrive in jeans and running shoes. The key is to dress so that your respect for your subject is evident.

- Decide whether you want to make brief notes during the interview or use a tape recorder; ensure that your subject agrees to your method before the interview begins.

- Start with an easy question to break the ice, and then proceed to more chal-lenging questions. Be prepared to ask questions that occur to you during the interview itself.

- When your interview is concluded, thank your subject and explain that he or she will be cited in your paper. Offer to send the interviewee a copy of the finished paper—either in hardcopy or by e-mail. Send a thank you note immediately after your interview, and follow up by sending a copy of your paper, if your interviewee requested one, when it is completed.

- Immediately after your interview, make notes about your reactions and thoughts, clearly indicating any direct quotations.

You might also decide to distribute a questionnaire, either randomly or to spe-cific types of people. For instance, if your research paper focuses on current prac-tices among professors for assessing students, you might want to distribute questionnaires to the professors in those faculties you will focus on, or if you are researching the degree of security students feel on campus after dark, you could distribute questionnaires among students randomly in your student union build-ing. The following are some important points to remember about gathering data in this way:

- The responses you receive will probably be from those who feel most strongly about your topic area, and you therefore must be prepared for bias in responses.

- The wording of your questions must be as clear and objective as possible; that is, you do not want to *impose* a bias on your respondents.

- Try to avoid questions for which a "yes" or "no" answer is required unless you have considered all the implications.

For instance, the question "Do you penalize students when they make gram-matical errors?" does not take into account the type of assignment (home or in-class), and the question "Do you feel secure walking back to residence after a night class?" does not account for the time of night or whether the respondent habitually leaves class alone. Phrase your questions so that they elicit the maximum amount of unbiased information without requiring your respondents to spend a great deal of time writing responses. In the above examples, better questions would be, "Under what circumstances, if ever, do you penalize students for grammatical errors?" or "Do you ever walk alone on campus at night?" followed by "If you have answered 'Yes' to the above question, are there circumstances in which you feel unsafe?" Word your questions so that the responses will be complete and accurate.

Step Three: Evaluating Information

Evaluating the Reliability of Secondary Sources

As you have seen, a mass of information will be available to you. You will have to determine not only how best to access, organize, and integrate the materials you need, but also which of the available materials will be useful to you and which are not particularly helpful or are outdated, heavily biased, or unreliable in some other way. Remember that in any writing situation, you need to evaluate the needs of your audience. When your audience is your instructor or, more generally, the scholarly community, you will be expected to be aware of any biases the sources have. Understanding the importance of evaluating sources can be difficult for junior researchers because often in non-academic writing situations, writers and speakers intentionally use biased sources—without acknowledging their biases—to great effect. In an academic writing situation, you should begin by choosing sources that present relevant and up-to-date information and that are published by credible presses (ask a librarian or your instructor if you are not sure). You should also acknowledge any biases of the source.

You will likely begin by doing an Internet search for your topic, and will likely find a great deal of relevant information. While it is easy to assume that everything available on the Internet is credible and reliable, keep in mind that anyone can create a web site with whatever information they wish. The fact that information is on the web does not alone make it reliable, just as the fact that information is published in a book does not alone make it reliable either. Be particularly careful to evaluate online sources critically by considering questions such as:

- To whom is the web site attributed ? A group? An individual? An organization?

- What biases or positions does the group, individual, or organization have? (You probably won't be able to tell this from the web site itself, but an Internet search should provide you with more context for evaluating the source of the information.)

- Does the information seem well researched and reliable? Does the web site acknowledge the sources of information it provides?

If you have questions about the reliability of the online information, you may wish to search further for other sources, and may ultimately decide not to use the questionable information. Or you may wish to include it and caution the reader about its limitations. For example, in making a pro-life argument you might choose to cite an online source written by an extremist pro-life group, but would want to put the information in context by providing some background about the group to make the reader aware that its views do not represent mainstream thought.

Providing context for your sources will help you to:

- Establish the authority/credibility of the source (for persuasion)
- Clarify why an old source is still relevant
- Clarify misconceptions the audience might have about the source
- Clarify any issues of bias/perceived bias
- Clarify where information is coming from

For instance, you might point out your source's link to a respected research institution in order to establish the source's credibility and/or authority. You might identify whether a web site you are citing is a government web site or a site sponsored by a particular special interest group to clarify issues of bias or reliability of statistics in a given case. You might add brief context to indicate why your source from 1968 is still relevant and/or compelling. Or you might add context to indicate that the statistics or the laws you are referring to are Canadian or American in origin.

Provide brief context under the following conditions:

- When your audience is likely to be unfamiliar with your source or unlikely to automatically see your source as credible or as an authority on an issue
- When your audience won't immediately see why your source from 1968 is still useful today
- When leaving out the context for a source might lead the reader to draw inaccurate conclusions about the information
- When leaving out the context for a source might lead to accusations that you misrepresented information or tried to intentionally mislead the audience
- When there are likely to be questions of bias or perceived bias about a source

Often, in using a wide variety of sources, you will find discrepancies in opinions and perhaps even facts; a good research paper will take these discrepancies into account and analyze them, rather than gloss over or ignore them. For instance, Rehnby identifies, on page 401, the International Life Sciences Institute as being employed by the soft drinks industry, and she therefore questions whether it is an appropriate body to research the safety of caffeine. In her conclusion, she examines the dismissive nature of the findings of an author who addresses the correlation between caffeine and reproductive problems. A good research paper will reflect the process of discovery that you have engaged in during your research. As Rehnby discovered, information that does not seem to fit or is puzzling at first could offer useful insights.

Evaluating the Relevance of Sources to Your Project

As soon as you begin locating sources of information—both print and electronic—you will also begin to evaluate their relevance to your project. You might approach each potential source with a list of questions that will help you to determine whether or not the material will be useful. You need not read an entire book or article in order to do a preliminary assessment; you may be able to eliminate some sources without having to do extensive reading. You can apply the following questions to the table of contents of a book or the abstract of an article:

- Does this source cover recent work in this field? (In some cases, early work may be helpful in a variety of ways; past statistics and conclusions or the positions experts have taken in the past might be of use, particularly if you are researching the history or development of an idea or a product. If, however, your topic focuses on the current thinking on your topic, you will want to ensure that your sources are up to date.)

- Does the material directly engage with any of the questions I have formulated around my topic?

- Will the material provide background information useful for establishing a context for my work or for my audience?

- Does this source provide original research on the topic, or does it evaluate the work that others have done in the field? (If the latter, the source will lead you to further sources.)

- Does this source confirm other sources I have found, or do the authors differ in their conclusions?

- Can this source lead me to other relevant sources?

While you are researching, either through an online catalogue or the CD-ROM, you will be able to eliminate some sources immediately; others you will have to locate on the shelves in order to assess their usefulness. Wherever possible, determine the experts in the field of your topic; you will probably notice two or three names popping up repeatedly in your catalogue search. Remember, too, that most experts publish their findings in journal articles before publishing them in books or anthologies.

The Working Bibliography

Being methodical and organized in the preliminary stages of a research project will save time and frustration later on. Many researchers find that having a notebook with them at all times is helpful: they record all the publication information for the useful sources they find in their initial search. List each of these sources, whether or not you are sure which ones you will ultimately use. As your paper develops, you may find that you need a source you only vaguely remember; your working bibliography will tell you exactly where to locate that source. In your notebook, or on index cards, record the author(s) or editor(s) names, the title of the source, the volume numbers of journals, the place and date of publication, the call number, and the source's location in the library.

Note-taking

You will want to record anything you read that seems valuable for your project. You may choose to quote directly from the source; in this case, put quotation marks around the material so you remember that it is a quotation. You may also decide to summarize the main idea in a long passage, or paraphrase a specific passage in your own words. Your notes will probably contain a combination of all three types of material, but whatever you do, be sure to record the full information for the source you are using each time you make a note, and to record the page numbers on which you found the material. You will need this information later to cite the source properly.

It is also a good idea to jot down any ideas or questions that occur to you as you read. Remember that a research essay must be more than just a patchwork of quotations: it must include your analysis. You might record your thoughts when you are noting textual information, but be sure to label them clearly so that you do not confuse them with material from your sources. A useful device is a reading journal, which you keep with you at all times so that you can record your reactions.

The three main places to record the information you want to retain from your sources are on index cards, on sheets of lined paper, or directly into a computer file. Each has its benefits and drawbacks, and we encourage you to try each one to see which works best for you.

The Formal Outline

You may be asked to write a formal outline for your instructor's comments before the actual draft of your research essay is due. Unlike the "scratch outline" that you write for your own reference early in a project, a formal outline has to make sense to others as well. A formal outline is like a blueprint that an architect draws up for a contractor: it shows your reader the components of your essay's structure and how they will fit together. You are ready to write a formal outline only after you have taken notes on most of your sources and have had time to think about them. You may decide to limit your topic further at this point, refining the working thesis you drafted before you began your library research.

Whether you are required to write a formal outline or not, preparing one for your own use is a good idea: it allows you to see the parts of your essay, how you can break down the writing of the paper, and where you might integrate your sources. It will also make writing the paper easier, since you will have determined the coherence and flow of your paper in your outline. However, you should not follow your outline slavishly. As you write, you will make new discoveries or find that some of your material would be more effective if shifted around. You may even find that you have to go back to the library and research an entirely new section for your paper. Keep in mind that writing is a dynamic process of exploration; you should not hesitate to follow inspiration as it strikes if it will help you to communicate your material more effectively.

There are some conventions for the format of the formal outline that you must keep in mind. The example here follows the most common format. Designate the main categories of your essay with Roman numerals and the supporting points for each main category with capital letters. Use numbers for consequent points and small letters for the supporting details for the consequent points.

Here is Rehnby's outline in its entirety:

I. Religion
    A. Islam
        1. Attendance at mosques lowers with the popularity of coffee-houses
        2. Religious leaders debate - refer to Koran
    B. Christianity
        1. Pope baptizes beverage previously know as "black brew of Satan"
        2. Mormons still do not drink coffee

II. Monarchy
    A. England
        1. Coffeehouses flourish as meeting places for literary men
        2. Charles II bans coffeehouses as seditious
    B. Sweden
        1. Coffee introduced early in 1700s
        2. King bans coffee due to citizens' ardency
    C. Prussia
        1. Frederick II highly esteems coffee
        2. Attempt to create aristocratic control of the beverage

III. Colonialism
    A. Past
        1. Exploitation of coffee growing lands
        2. Cheap native labour
    B. New World
        1. Coffee introduced as crop to South and Central America
        2. Plantations use slave labour

IV. Contemporary World

    A. "Developing" countries

        1. Farmers in "developing" countries still controlled from without

        2. Coffee displaces population's own food crops

    B. "Developed" countries

        1. Consumption of coffee increases

        2. Price to the grower drops

V. Patriarchy

    A. Advertising

        1. 20th Century advertising preys on women

        2. Coffee infiltrates home (and bloodstream) and becomes a tradition

    B. Research

        1. Issues of import to women generally ignored

        2. Findings suggesting links between caffeine and reproductive abnormalities dismissed

            a. Tone suggests lack of importance of women's concerns

            b. Implication: if link exists, it is the woman's fault for ingesting a drug

Note that each section of Rehnby's outline moves from the general to the particular. The following is a list of the other formal considerations to keep in mind when producing an outline:

- Logic should be the governing strategy of an outline. You want to inform your reader about how all the parts of your essay logically fit together. If there are problems in the way you have been thinking about the components of your topic, you should be able to spot them once you have written an outline.

- Place topics of equal weight under equal headings and keep a reasonable proportion in the parts of an outline. For instance, each of the main headings in the above outline is developed through two main points at the second level, except heading II, which has three main points at the second level.

- Ensure that your headings are grammatically parallel. If a heading at one level is a noun or a noun phrase, all entries at that level must also be nouns or noun phrases. The same applies to the letter and number levels. Notice how Rehnby uses a noun or a noun phrase for each heading at the first two levels; at the third and fourth levels, she uses independent clauses.

- You can only have sub-categories if there are more than one for each level. If you have an "A," you **must** have a "B"; if you have a "l," you **must** have a "2." If, for any section, you find that you have only one sub-category, you must either generate another or absorb the one you have into the level above it.

- Make headings meaningful. Headings are the seeds from which the topic sentences and supporting details of your paper grow. An outline will also suggest to you tentative paragraph structures.

- Have at least one transitional sentence between any two headings to ensure coherence of your paragraphs.

Step Four: Drafting the Paper

The real assimilation of information begins when you start writing the paper. Begin by reviewing your reading journal and the material you generated when using invention methods before you began your library work. Then sort your notes into groups according to the plan your outline provides. Organize any useful information from these sources and your notes (be clear about what material is your own and what is not). Redraft the writing schedule for the project, amending the schedule in your proposal as necessary. Be sure to leave yourself significant time before the paper is due to revise and polish it. The formal outline may offer you a way to manage your time, as it breaks the project down into sections. You may find it useful to write one section each day or every other day.

Many writers find that the best time to write the introduction to their paper is after they have written the body paragraphs and the conclusion rather than when they begin writing; others find that beginning with the introduction gives them a sense of direction. You might also consider combining these methods. Draft an introduction when you first begin to write the paper and modify it afterwards according to the needs of the paper.

Styles of Documentation

You must document your sources every time you quote from, paraphrase, or summarize them, or whenever a source has significantly influenced your thinking on a topic. Failure to acknowledge the ideas or words of others—whether intentionally or unintentionally—is plagiarism, a serious academic crime that can be punished by expulsion from university. Different disciplines use different styles of documentation; be sure to ask your instructor which style of documentation you will be expected to use. Following these instructions is important because you will be learning the standards of scholarship in your discipline, and your ability to document properly will add scholarly integrity to your essay.

The two most common styles of documentation are those of the Modern Language Association (MLA), used primarily in the humanities, and the American Psychological Association (APA), used primarily in the social sciences. The *Chicago Manual of Style* (CMS) and the style of the Council of Science Editors (CSE—formerly the Council of Biology Editors, CBE) are also used in other disciplines. Each style provides a system to acknowledge secondary sources in your essay so that your reader can consult your sources if they wish to verify your information or seek additional information on the topic.

Your college or university bookstore will probably sell copies or summaries of the documentation style handbook you will need to use, and your library should have several copies available. You'll also find detailed information from the style guides on the following web sites:

- Modern Language Association: **www.mla.org**
- Publication Manual of the American Psychological Association: **www.apastyle.org**
- Chicago Manual of Style and Council of Science Editors: **www.bedfordstmartins.com/online/citex.html**

The Bedford St. Martin's *Online! A Reference Guide to Using Internet Sources* is a particularly useful resource as it contains links and information about several documentation styles, including MLA, APA, the *Chicago Manual of Style*, Council of Science Editors, and others.

Citing Electronic Sources

Styles for documenting electronic sources both within the text of your paper and in your Works Cited also vary amongst academic disciplines. Because the type of material available electronically is rapidly changing, styles for documenting electronic documents are also rapidly evolving. We encourage you to consult the style guides in your academic field, and recommend the Online Writing Lab at Purdue University for a list of discipline-specific electronic guides: **http://owl.english.purdue.edu/handouts/research/r_docelectric.html**

Taking time to properly document electronic sources will add to your credibility as an academic researcher, and thus to the impact of your paper on the reader.

Integration of Secondary Sources

The most challenging facet of drafting the paper is finding a balance between your own ideas and questions and the material from your sources. Remember that a research paper is more than a series of quotations or paraphrases combined with transitional sentences. You need to show that you have assimilated the ideas from your sources and used them to address the questions you identified in the invention process before you began your research. Try using the freewriting technique to draft each section of your paper, adding in your secondary material afterwards: this way, the sources support your own ideas and do not dominate the paper. This technique will also allow you to establish your own style. Too often, when incorporating the work of others, writers allow the style of their sources to dictate the style of their entire paper.

Whatever method you use to draft, be sure that whenever you use a source, you integrate it into your own ideas. Whenever possible, use a paraphrase or summary of the source; use direct quotations only when the language of the original is vital to the point that you are making. Try to avoid filling space by writing lengthy paraphrases from a single source. Also, try to use short quotations rather than long ones, so that your sources do not take over the essay. Reserve long quotations for places where they will have impact. The following are examples of the way Rehnby integrates paraphrases, summaries, and short and longer quotations with her own ideas.

Paraphrase:

Pope Clement VIII found it so delectable, however, that around 1600 he baptized coffee and "made it Christian" (Ford and Sturmanis "Foreword").

Summary:

Al-Aydarus, known as the father of coffee, claimed to have eaten the berries of the coffee bush, which stimulated his brain, made him alert, and helped him to perform his religious tasks (Hattox 21).

Short quotation incorporated into a sentence:

From its humble beginnings as a weed, and then as a cultivated shrub in Arabia, around 575 AD the genus <u>Coffea</u> has grown to be "the world's most widely traded commodity after oil" (James 5).

Long quotation introduced with a phrase:

Jimenez points out the following:

[The coffee lobbying arm] soon financed research on the relationship between coffee and labor productivity which concluded that the natural rhythms of mid-morning and mid-afternoon lassitude could be countered by the consumption of the beverage at those times of the day...thus [coffee] effectively became a handmaiden in the making of the new industrial order which emerged in this period. (49)

Note that in this quotation, Rehnby replaces, with ellipses, words or phrases which have no bearing on her point and inserts in square brackets a clarifying word of her own.

Step Five: Revising

Revising is the final and most crucial step in producing a finished piece of writing. It involves much more than just editing or correcting errors. Revising is, according to composition theorist Don Murray, "the process of seeing what you have said to discover what you have to say." Revising a long essay requires the same skills that you have been perfecting in your other writing projects; the difference is that you will need to revise while you are producing various parts of your essay, and as well when you have completed an entire initial draft. Be prepared not just to rewrite or reword, but to relocate information and change your thesis. Also, if you have not already done so, look closely at your essay's stylistic features. Does it have an intriguing title that informs your readers of your essay's main focus, a lead that engages their interest, and a memorable final paragraph and final sentence that will remain in their minds long after they have finished reading the essay?

You may find that reading your draft aloud—or getting others to read it and respond to it—will help you identify parts of your essay that are lacking in vitality or are difficult to understand. The following five skills may assist you in revising such problematic areas:

1. Amplifying: expand sentences, paragraphs, and/or ideas
2. Eliminating: cut other material that does not work
3. Relocating: reorganize material within the piece
4. Rephrasing: clarify for readability and tone
5. Proofreading: correct grammar and punctuation, and ensure that your spacing, layout, title page, and pagination conform to the style you have been asked to follow.

Most writers, professional and student alike, will agree that the revising process could go on indefinitely. If you have a due date to consider, you will not have too much trouble deciding when to stop. However, despite the constraints you may face, keep in mind that your goal is to produce a final draft you are proud of, one that truly represents the discoveries you made during the project. You may wish to reread Murray's "The Maker's Eye: Revising Your Own Manuscript" and Zinsser's "Simplicity" and consider how their advice could apply to your paper.

Works Cited

Giltrow, Janet. *Academic Writing: Writing and Reading in the Disciplines.* 3rd ed. Peterborough: Broadview, 2002.

Sample Student Essay: MLA Style of Documentation

Here is the final draft of Rehnby's research paper. Like most writing, there are areas that could be improved. The strengths, though, are many and include Rehnby's ability to use her own voice and to capture the process of discovery she engaged in while researching and writing on her topic. The annotations point out her use of the MLA style of documentation, structural elements of the essay, and some of the essay's strengths and weaknesses.

1/2"

Rehnby 1

Maret Rehnby

Roberta J. Birks

English 303, Section 951

14 August 2002[1]

Let's Not Have Another Cup of Coffee[2]

The history of coffee illuminates the history of some past and present-day power structures. While I began my research in a coffee-induced frenzy, with an eye toward documenting the effects of coffee on a body such as my own, I soon discovered aspects of coffee consumption which I had not considered thoroughly, and was thus led on by new interest to view coffee with eyes both bleary and fresh.[3] Coffee and coffee culture surround us here in the north half of the Western Hemisphere as we begin a new millennium. Can we remember a time without it? No. Does this mean we have always cherished it and relied upon it? No.[4]

The use of coffee has elicited many strong responses from both its proponents and opponents during its short entanglement with human society. Coffee, both as a resource and a beverage, has been used by a succession of small, yet strong, groups of people to influence, or control, weaker groups in order to maintain power. Religion, monarchy, colonialism, capitalism, and patriarchy are some of the societal structures which have been maintained, in part, by using coffee as a tool to preserve the influence inherent in each construct.[5] The fact that people have embraced coffee as an accepted, and even essential, part of daily modern life without considering its history is a sad indictment of the manner in which we who live in the developed world do not always question our assumptions.[6] Though it may seem harmless at times, or fashionable in certain contexts, coffee has not innocently filtered into our lives:[7] often one group has exerted its power over another, and coffee has been a device by which oppression has been perpetuated.

From its humble beginnings as a weed,[8] and then as a cultivated shrub in Arabia around 575 AD, the genus <u>Coffea</u> has grown to be "the world's most widely traded commodity after oil" (James 5), and "the most widely consumed psychoactive substance in the world"[9] (James ii).[10] The area in which coffee first became enmeshed in society as a commodity, a social beverage, and a

1

2

3

---

1 MLA format for the first page of an essay without a title page. You may have a separate title page; if so, do not number the title page, but begin numbering on the first page of the text

2 title introduces subject and captures the reader's interest by playing on the common expression "Let's have another cup of coffee"

3 explains the evolution of her research question

4 rhetorical questions indicate the focus of the next paragraphs

5 thesis

6 writer's evaluation

7 an appropriate metaphor

8 begins by presenting coffee's early history

9 effectively integrates short quotations into syntax

10 parenthetical references show sources of quotations

matter for religious leaders to ponder,[11] was the Near East, or what today is called the Middle East. The far-flung cities of Damascus, Cairo, Istanbul, and Mecca were important Islamic centres, even then. A controversy surrounding coffee arose because some turned to the Koran and demonstrated that it was not a specifically prohibited food or drink. Others also consulted the Muslim holy book and cited the passage which declared suicide to be sinful, and since destruction at one's own hand was not allowed, "[w]hat[12] clearer indication can there be of prohibition of the source of destructive things?" (Hattox 62); and this group maintained that coffee possessed harmful qualities. Coffee had acquired the name <u>quhwa</u>, the same name given to wine, which suggests an association between the two beverages: either coffee was seen as a harmless alternative to outlawed wine, or it was viewed as being similarly "noxious and unholy" (19). Al-Aydarus, known as the father of coffee, claimed to have eaten the berries of the coffee bush, which stimulated his brain, made him alert, and helped him to perform his religious tasks (21). However, Muhammad was supposed to have spoken well of temperance and reservation in speech, which was then applied to acceptable behaviour; the "frenetic activity...and foolish banter" which appeared to be caused by consumption of the beverage was held to reveal coffee in a poor light (116).

4   Debate over the beverage in the Near East appears to have waned until the tremendously successful spread of coffeehouses in the early sixteenth century.[13] Islamic leaders tried to take action when it became apparent that men were spending more time gambling, gossiping, and coffee-drinking at the coffeehouses than they were in prayer or religious study at the mosques. The Muslim faith viewed these pastimes as illicit because they took time away from religious duties. Edicts were announced, raids were made, and whippings were carried out as punishment. Yet "formerly the lights at night burned mostly at the mosque...[but now] the lights burned far into the night at coffeehouses" (Hattox 128). The attempts to control the people by controlling their drinking habits were not wholly successful.

5   The debate over coffee in the Christian world was apparently less turbulent, but also less documented. English speakers who

[11] needs to clarify the cause and effect relationship between holy books and the controversy

[12] uses square brackets to show changes made to the original quote

[13] informative use of comparison

had visited the Near East referred to coffee as "the wine of Araby" (Ford and Sturmanis 12) because the Arabs drank so much of it. Perhaps because it was associated with Islamic people, who would be viewed as infidels, coffee was denounced by the Christian church as a "hellish black brew" and "a Satanic threat to the soul" (12). Pope Clement VIII found it so delectable, however, that around 1600 he baptized coffee, thus making it Christian (12).[14] In the New World in the late 1820s, Joseph Smith, who was the founder of the Mormon Church, declared it sinful to consume intoxicating beverages based on his interpretation of ancient texts. To this day, members of the Mormon Church do not drink coffee, tea, or cola, presenting the possibility that they could be a useful control group in studies of caffeine consumers. Whether for or against its consumption, religious leaders attempted to hold sway over their flocks by declaring rules by which others ought to live.

Monarchical power is another structure which my investigation revealed to be entwined with coffee.[15] During the era of the Protectorate and the Restoration which followed, coffeehouses flourished in England. They were frequented by literary men, and became known for the patrons they attracted. These were not as exotic as the French or Turkish houses, but rather tended to be smoke-filled and dirty; however, the conversation elevated them from loitering places such as taverns (Ford and Sturmanis 13). In 1673, King Charles issued a decree that the country's 3000 coffeehouses be closed as "seditious meeting places" (14).[16] His order proved so unpopular, though, that it was almost immediately withdrawn. In the early 1700s, following the introduction of coffee to the Swedish kingdom, citizens became so ardent for the new drink that it was banned. Like the twentieth-century American prohibition on alcohol, the ban led to clandestine brewing, raids, and havoc until the ban was lifted (17).[17] Sweden remains to the present day one of the countries with the highest per capita consumption of coffee, rivalled only by its geographical and cultural northern European neighbours.[18] Yet one more ruler who took the issue of coffee drinking to be of import was Frederick II of Prussia (known as "Frederick the Great," 1740-86). He esteemed the beverage so highly that he bade physicians scatter amongst his lowest subjects the report that it caused infertility. He issued exclusive licences for

6

14 uses a paraphrase effectively

15 uses a one-word transition to show links between paragraphs

16 provides only page number in parenthetical references because the same source is referred to throughout the paragraph

17 concise summary

18 sentence seems out of place

roasting coffee beans to the nobility, and went so far as to hire smelling spies to circulate among the people and search for the scent of illegitimate roast.

7   Colonialism is another power structure which can be found intertwined with the history and world-wide spread of coffee and coffee-drinking. European nations "discovered" and "conquered" lands which often proved to provide "exploitable sub-tropical soils" (Roseberry 10). Danish author Isak Dinesen (Karen Blixen) set her autobiographical novel Out of Africa[19] on a coffee plantation which employed cheap native labourers to produce a crop which provided an unnecessary drink for the privileged back at home. Coffee production in the New World, likewise, has a tarnished history. It was introduced as a crop to South and Central America in the eighteenth century, and the plantations were first worked by slaves stolen from Africa; in Guatemala, the plantations in thinly populated areas "depended upon state-enforced migration of highland Maya populations for extended periods of plantation labour" (5).

[19] questionable choice of a fictional rather than historical source

8   In the present day, coffee continues to be grown by poor Third World workers for the consumption of the relatively wealthy few in the First World. A 1982 survey[20] identifies the highest coffee-consuming countries as Denmark, Finland, Sweden, Norway, Austria, and Belgium at between 8.24 and 12.52 kilos of coffee per capita; France, Germany, the Netherlands, and Switzerland followed with between 6.33 and 9 kilos, and Canada, Cyprus, Italy, Spain, the United Kingdom, and the United States consumed between 3.38 and 4.86 kilos (James 8). The nations in which people labour to grow coffee are not the nations which have large coffee-drinking populations. The propagation of coffee demands the destruction of natural habitat: the two species of cultivated Coffea, arabica and robusta, are foreign to all areas of major production; their cultivation creates instances of monoculture and, therefore, the displacement of the food crops necessary for the self-reliance of the Third World farmer. Coffee farming encourages in its farmers an unhealthy dependence on the success of their crops and the strength of the world market, over neither of which they can exercise control (Roseberry 5). The farmers seem to have no choice but to sell to the organized merchants who today

[20] more recent statistics would be preferable

give them one third of the price that they received in 1986 (Bridgehead 27).[21]

21 parenthetical reference to a source without an author

Of course, these power structures at times parallel, and at times overlap, each other. Those who reside at the pinnacle of such structures are necessarily in danger of oppressing those below.[22] Capitalism is a power structure that I continually recognized in my research into coffee. Coffee is the means to the end of profit, and this goal is either in the foreground or skulking in the background, ever-present nonetheless. Brazil experienced such a coffee boom in the 1850s and 1860s that it was not hindered by the concurrent doubling of the price of slaves (Roseberry 17), upon whose backs enormous fortunes were made.

22 writer's evaluation of information from sources

9

I had initially been drawn to the subject of coffee by a personal interest in caffeine,[23] and I found that the fact of caffeine's being an addictive substance seems inextricably linked with the high-powered capitalism which peddles it to the masses. Early in the twentieth century, North American coffee firms created unique strategies in successful attempts to boost the per capita consumption of their product (Roseberry 11). At first, coffee was considered the exclusive property of well-to-do consumers; however, "it became unequivocally the premier beverage of a mass consumer society through the...evolution of greater control over the work force and ever more sophisticated marketing" (Jimenez 56).

23 integrates personal experience with research

10

The research into the benefits and risks to health associated with the daily use of caffeine, especially in coffee, appears to downplay any negative facets.[24] When coupled with the possible taint of vested interests, at least in some of the source material upon which I stumbled, the studies which downplay any injurious connection between caffeine and health take on an ominous aspect. A monograph entitled <u>Caffeine: Perspectives from Recent Research</u> attempts in the foreword to explain that some research was initiated after the U.S. Food and Drug Administration (FDA) reexamined the inclusion of caffeine on the list of additives generally recognized as safe. It states,[25]

24 transition between paragraphs is unclear

11

25 indent quotations longer than four typewritten lines

> The soft drinks industry, because of their practice of adding caffeine to colas and other soft drinks, became particularly involved. Its main response, surely appro-

priate, took the form of initiation of support for scientific research on caffeine. The research program continues under the auspices of the International Life Sciences Institute, a foundation developed primarily to permit companies to pool resources to support research programs of common interest. (v)[26]

26 parenthetical references come two spaces after final end-mark of punctuation

12   How can the ILSI, an employee of the soft drinks industry, which is made up of companies who have banded together for their common interest, say that its employer's behaviour is "surely appropriate" and retain any appearance of disinterested, objective, or scientific detachment? Why would competitive companies join forces except to benefit their "common interest," otherwise known as profit? Is it surprising that a group of scientists does not unearth new evidence of harm caused by caffeine in this book, yet discovers enough new evidence to discredit earlier studies which had produced results that established that negative health effects stemmed from caffeine consumption?[27] At first I was naively startled, but now I calmly detect a sinister pattern. The coffee and soft drink companies are not threatened by concerned consumers who turn to decaffeinated beverages, since they hedge their bets in an admirably capitalistic fashion. The caffeine that people hope to avoid in one drink, they are likely to find in another; if you avoid it in the morning by drinking Sanka, you will absorb it in the evening by drinking a Cuba Libre. This is exemplified by "the fact that the total caffeine yield of soft drinks in the [U.S.] is virtually identical to the total caffeine extracted during the manufacture of decaffeinated coffee" (James 12). If health-conscious adults manage to avoid caffeine, their children are likely to ingest much of what their parents avoid, because adolescents and children are introduced early to the addictive substance caffeine, which provides the easy transition to an adulthood of continued reliance upon the drug most often consumed in the form of coffee.

27 effective evaluation of sources

13   The strength of the capitalistic power structure assures the coffee industry of a muscular lobbying arm.[28] One of the results of its efforts is that caffeine is a ubiquitous drug, available in homes, restaurants, and markets all over the world. As long as the resistance to it being labelled as a drug and being appropriately regu-

28 stronger transition needed

lated is successful, businesses will continue to profit from the public's blissful ignorance of or nonchalance to any of its ill effects. Therefore, it remains possible to consume caffeine in medications, both prescriptive and over-the-counter, without knowing it, because lobbying efforts have been successful in keeping it on the list of harmless additives.

When North American trade unions fought for, and won, coffee   14
breaks in the second decade of this century, who benefited from the innovation? At first glance, it is the worker: he or she receives a refreshing break. Yes, ruminate on that for a moment. The truth is that the revitalization of the weary worker directly benefits the employer. Jimenez points out this working relationship:[29]

29 introduces a
long quotation
with a colon

> [The coffee lobbying arm] soon financed research on the relationship between coffee and labor productivity which concluded that the natural rhythms of mid-morning and mid-afternoon lassitude could be countered by the consumption of the beverage at those times of the day...thus [coffee] effectively became a handmaiden in the making of the new industrial order which emerged in this period. (49)

Who might have benefited directly from having such a break so named?[30]

30 rhetorical ques-
tion encourages
the reader to
think critically

Quite naturally, from a historic point of view, patriarchy is a   15
power structure which is enmeshed in all the preceding power structures. However, it played and continues to play an especial role in the history of coffee in this century. As a means "to more completely integrate this product into the private realm of the household," industry leaders targeted women, and in 1913 began an energetic campaign "to educate housewives on the subject of coffee." One advertising project related "'what June brides should know about coffee'" (Jimenez 49). Advertisers preyed upon women's self-esteem by associating their worth with their skill at preparing a good cup of coffee. Physicians and home economists gave their endorsements, which pressured women to do what was "right" for their husbands, families, guests, and peers. The Joint Coffee Publicity Committee conscripted American high school administrators, who perhaps believed that they were acting for the

students' good, to allow them to target adolescent girls in home economics class. They were "'assure[d of the] triumph of the truth about coffee and its value as an aliment,'" and encouraged to "'Get a Reputation for [their] coffee'" (qtd. in Jimenez 50);[31] thus, young women were indoctrinated with the combined ideas of preserving their virginity and being judged as a housewife for and by their husbands, which served to perpetuate the gender stereotypes of the patriarchal power structure. Coffee was not always an essential part of being a good hostess, but by including coffee in advertisements, cookbooks, and home economics classes, the coffee lobby proved enormously, and detrimentally, effective.

[31] indicates a source quoted within a source

16   Caffeine is present in analgesics, diuretics, and weight-control aids, as well as baked goods, puddings, and candy,[32] all of which have been marketed aggressively to women, all the while possessing an addictive ingredient; women have not had much opportunity to resist falling under the influence of caffeine in one shape or another.

[32] uses concrete examples

17   My research concerning coffee intake made me think that women are still not served well by science. In an essay in Caffeine, Coffee, and Health titled "Coffee, Caffeine, and Reproductive Hazards in Humans," the author briefly dismisses earlier studies which indicated a correlation between pregnancy abnormalities and coffee consumption by several times mentioning that "higher quality" studies "tend to show no relationship." Who could place confidence in this scientist's vague and dismissive manner? The author fliply comments on others' reactions to a study which hypothesized that as little as 100 mg of caffeine impedes fertility by writing that the results "warranted only a letter to the editor," and then he jumps to saying that "[i]t seems reasonable to conclude that coffee and caffeine consumption by women does not impair fertility" (Leviton 353). His tone suggests that reproductive abnormalities can be attributed to the women themselves; the fault is not with what they might be ingesting, but rather with the fact that they ingest anything at all.

18   Coffee, I have learned, is neither the simple pick-me-up nor the innocuous tropical crop that I thought it to be a few weeks ago.[33] Consideration of its short history presents a short history of humans. The power structures which seem to have given us com-

[33] reflects back on research questions posited in introduction

fort and support have also served the few at the expense of the many. While we may reject several of these structures, I think that we should consider that their vestiges remain with us even in this apparently enlightened and empowered age. Coffee may be just a fashionable, warm, brown drink to many of us, but it served to control our ancestors and our working grandparents and parents; it kept our mothers and aunts in the kitchen; and it continues to keep our faceless and remote brothers and sisters oppressed now. Is this worth a cappuccino?[34]

[34] a provocative conclusion that reflects back on the essay's title

Works Cited[35]

[35] begin Works Cited on a separate page at the end of the essay. Centre title but do not underline

Bridgehead. Toronto: Oxfam, Summer 1995.[36]

Dews, P.B. <u>Caffeine: Perspectives from Recent Research</u>. Berlin: Springer-Verlag, 1984.[37]

[36] double-space within and between entries

Ford,[38] Cathy and Dona Sturmanis. <u>The Coffee Lover's Handbook</u>. Vancouver: Intermedia, 1979.

Hattox, Ralph S. <u>Coffee and Coffeehouses: The Origins of a Social Beverage in the Medieval Near East</u>. Seattle: U of Washington P, 1985.[39]

[37] indent subsequent lines of entries five spaces

James, Jack E. <u>Caffeine and Health</u>. San Diego: Academic, 1991.

Jimenez, Michael F. "'From Plantation to Cup': Coffee and Capitalism in the United States, 1830–1930." <u>Coffee, Society and Power in Latin America</u>. Ed. William Roseberry. Baltimore: Johns Hopkins UP, 1995. 38-55.

[38] arrange sources alphabetically

Leviton, Alan. "Coffee, Caffeine, and Reproductive Hazards in Humans." <u>Caffeine, Coffee and Health</u>. Ed. Silvio Garattini. New York: Raven Press, 1993. 349-362.

[39] abbreviate names of university presses

Roseberry, William, ed. <u>Coffee, Society, and Power in Latin America</u>. Baltimore: Johns Hopkins UP, 1995.

Other Styles of Documentation

As we have said earlier in this chapter, each discipline has its own style of documenting sources, and it is important that you follow the guidelines of the field to demonstrate your scholarly integrity. These examples are intended to illustrate the differences of in-text and bibliographic styles in three different disciplines to help you to see what different styles of documentation can look like.

Social Sciences

Here is an excerpt from a political science essay written by undergraduate student Elspeth Halverson titled "Eco-Labelling and International Trade." Notice how the writer uses footnotes to indicate paraphrases and direct quotations. Information about her sources is provided in Endnotes at the end of the essay; note that since she has referred to the same source for all three references in this paragraph, she uses the Latin "Ibid." to indicate this repetition:

> The [International Organization for Standardization] has already engaged in an effort to standardize the criteria for granting eco-labels, but there are some complications and there is much room for further work. Behind the desire to standardize eco-labels internationally there are three main ideas: that of equivalency, mutual recognition, and harmonization. If these three ideas are properly applied to the criteria underlying eco-labels, the programmes will be in effect standardized. The draft of the ISO standard 14020 deals with environmental labeling and establishes the need for attributes such as accuracy, accountability, and transparency.[1] It states that "the factual and technical basis for environmental labels must be verifiable" and that "information concerning the procedure and methodology used to support environmental labels shall be available and provided upon request to all interested parties."[2] This in effect outlines the steps that need to be taken to render eco-labels non-discriminatory and outlines what can be done on the part of the WTO as a regulatory body. This ISO draft mentions that "standards applicable to eco-labels should be developed through a consensus process involving all interested parties[3] but does not address on what basis those standards should be reached.

Endnotes

1 Pedro Da Motta Veiga. "Environment-related Voluntary Market Upgrading Initiatives and International Trade: Eco-labelling and the ISO 14000 Series." In <u>The Environment and International Trade Negotiations</u>, Ed. Diana Tussie, 53-71. Ottawa, ON: International Development Research Centre. 1999, 55.

2 Ibid.

3 Ibid., 60.

Biology

This example is taken from an article published in the important biology journal *Cell*. Notice how the writers use parenthetical references that include the author(s) name and date of publication along with the page number of the specific reference. Because scientific publications are often the result of collaborative research, you will notice specific methods to document in-text sources by multiple authors. Full publication details are provided at the end of the paper in the list of References:

> Genetic and phenotypic analyses of three mutant alleles of the mipA (microtubule-interacting protein) locus of Aspergillus nidulans led Weil et al. (1986) to conclude that mipA is a non-tubulin gene involved in microtubule function in vivo. The mutant mipA alleles were isolated as extragenic suppressors of benA33, a heat-sensitive ß-tubulin mutation (Oakley and Morris, 1981; Oakley et al., 1985; Weil et al., 1986; Oakley et al., 1987a). The benA gene encodes the major ß-tubulin expressed in hyphae (Sheir-Neiss et al., 1978), and this ß-tubulin is essential for mitosis and nuclear migration (Oakley and Morris, 1980, 1981).

References

Oakley, B.R., and Morris, N.R. (1980). Nuclear movement is ß-tubulin dependent in Aspergillus nidulans. Cell 19, 255-262.

Oakley, B.R., and Morris, N.R. (1981). A ß-tubulin mutation in A. nidulans that blocks microtubule function without blocking assembly. Cell 24, 837-845.

Oakley, B.R., Oakley, C.E., Kniepkamp, K.S., and Rinehart, J.E. (1985). Isolation and characterization of cold-sensitive mutations at the benA, ß-tubulin, locus of Aspergillus nidulans. Mol. Gen. Genet. 201, 56-64.

Oakley, B.R., Oakley, C.E., and Rinehart, J.E. (1987a). Conditionally lethal tuba a-tubulin mutations in Aspergillus nidulans. Mol. Gen. Genet. 208, 135-144.

Sheir-Neiss, G., Lai, M.H., and Morris, N.R. (1978). Identification of a gene for ß-tubulin in Aspergillus nidulans. Cell 15, 639-647.

Weil, C.F., Oakley, C.E., and Oakley, B.R. (1986). Isolation of mip (microbtubule-interacting protein) mutations of <u>Aspergillus nidulans</u>. Mol. Cell. Biol. 6, 2963-2968.

Engineering

This excerpt is taken from an article published in the *Journal of Bridge Engineering*. The authors are setting up the parameters of an experiment that they document in the article by acknowledging important sources that influenced their work. This style also uses parenthetical references and provides full publication details at the end of the essay in the list of References:

> A significant effort was made to ensure that the models developed were accurate. The FEM technique used for the study represents the same combination of element types, mesh density, load, and physical geometry idealization rules that best matched independent experimental and field-test results of bridge behaviour. In general, the developed technique matched measured deflections and strains within 5% of reported values. Data from Wegmuller (1977); Beal (1982); Fang et al. (1990); and Wipf et al. (1990) were used for comparison. Full details are given by Eamon (2000).

References

Beal, D.B. (1982). "Load capacity of concrete bridge decks." <u>J. Struct. Div. ASCE</u>, 108(4), 814-832.

Eamon, C. (2000). "Reliability-based resistance model for bridge structural systems." PhD dissertation. Univ. of Michigan, Ann Arbor, Mich.

Fang, I.K., Worley, J., Burns, N.H., and Klinger, R.E. (1990). "Behavior of isotropic R/C bridge decks on steel girders." <u>J. Struct. Eng.</u>, 116(3), 659-678.

Wegmuller, A.M. (1977). "Overload behaviour of composite steel-concrete bridges." <u>J. Struct. Div. ASCE</u>, 103(9), 1799-1819.

Wipf, T.J., Klaiber, W.F., and Funke, R.W. (1990). "Longitudinal glued laminated timber bridge modeling." <u>J. Struct. Eng.</u>, 116(4), 1121-1134.

CREDITS

INDEX